101 VILLAINS from
VLAD THE IMPALER
to ADOLF HITLER

HISTORY'S
MONSTERS

101 VILLAINS from
VLAD THE IMPALER
to ADOLF HITLER

HISTORY'S MONSTERS

SIMON SEBAG
MONTEFIORE

With John Bew and Martyn Frampton

METRO BOOKS
NEW YORK

CONTENTS Biographies and boxed features

This book of so-called 'monsters' is a companion volume to my book of so-called 'heroes'. History can give us warnings from the past and lessons for the future. These stories of heroism and villainy are one way that we can learn to appreciate the values – such as responsibility, tolerance, decency, courage – that should be the foundations of society. We should aspire to the courage of the heroes while the crimes of the monsters stand as warnings from the past, lessons for the future, and monuments to the astonishing depravity and endless wickedness of human nature. Whether or not you agree with my choices, these are characters, stories and events that everyone should know.

Introduction

> 'History is little more than the register of the crimes, follies and misfortunes of mankind.'
> EDWARD GIBBON

But they are also, of course, fascinating for their own sake, however terrible. Indeed, despite all the efforts of John Milton's poetic genius to achieve the opposite, Satan remains the most compelling character in *Paradise Lost*. Many of the monsters in these pages were gifted, complex statesmen and generals. But none of that should divert us from chronicling their crimes.

This book is dedicated to their victims. The six million Jews killed in the Holocaust, the most appalling act of wickedness in human history, are certainly not forgotten though the actual details of that industrial slaughter still beggars belief – but here we also recall the murdered millions of the Congo, Rwanda, the Armenians and the Hereros of Namibia, and many others. In naming and chronicling their murderers, we defy the wishes of the killers who hoped that posterity would forget their crimes. 'Who now remembers the Armenians?' mused Hitler, ordering the Final Solution. His comment shows why history matters, because Hitler found encouragement and solace in the forgotten Armenian massacres. Past and present are closely linked: 'No-one remembers the boyars killed by Ivan the Terrible', said Stalin, ordering the Great Terror. In the colossally audacious, almost incredible scale of these crimes, the monsters found a diabolical sanctuary from comprehension and judgement. 'One death', said Stalin, 'is a tragedy, but a million is a statistic.' The most disgusting of these crimes were committed in the 20th century when the corrosive all-embracing utopianism of insane ideologies dovetailed with modern technology and pervasive state power to make killing easier, quicker and possible on a gargantuan scale. Hence the 20th century, and the Second World War, must be especially represented.

How did I choose these monsters? Totally subjectively. Some are obvious, such as Caligula, Vlad the Impaler, Ivan the Terrible, Idi Amin or Saddam Hussein. Hitler, Stalin, Mao – the totalitarian super-killers of the 20th century, when trains, machine-guns and telegraphs facilitated slaughter – are here. All these monsters were aided by hundreds of thousands of ordinary people who became murderers and torturers to take part in their schemes. Few were ever punished, but they share responsibility with their leaders. I include a few serial killers – repellent, banal and mediocre creatures whose obsessional inferiority complexes drove them to dominate and destroy individuals weaker than themselves.

The statesmen are the most difficult to categorize. Virtually all men of power make some decisions that cost innocent lives. One man's monster is another man's hero and such debates remain relevant today. Lenin benefited from one of the great whitewashes of history and is still revered by many misguided and ignorant people in Russia and the West: he remains honoured in his Mausoleum in Moscow's Red Square. Stalin was denounced in 1956 but the Kremlin recently presented an official textbook for history teachers that acclaimed Stalin as 'the most successful Russian leader of the 20th century', a state-builder and triumphant warlord who ranks with 'Bismarck and Peter the Great'. Chairman Mao Zedong remains the spiritual guide of the People's Republic of China.

There are certain leaders who must rank as somewhere between hero and monster. Napoleon, Peter the Great, Cromwell, Atatürk and Alexander the Great could rank as heroes or monsters, but they all appear in my earlier book 101 World Heroes, while Henry VIII, an English hero to many, appears as a monster. Genghis Khan and Tamerlane were both political-military geniuses, almost heroic, certainly monstrous. Perhaps these classic hero-monsters belong in a book of their own.

My choices are random and flawed: I could endlessly add, subtract and swap them. That is the fun of making lists. The important thing is knowledge, remembrance and judgement. We should all know these characters, remember these crimes and make our own judgements.

SIMON SEBAG MONTEFIORE

This work, like my book of heroes, is for my daughter LILY and my son SASHA

ACKNOWLEDGEMENTS

I would like to thank the team at Quercus: Anthony Cheetham, Richard Milbank and the heroic editor Slav Todorov; my co-authors John Bew and Martyn Frampton; Nick Fawcett and Ian Crofton for their truly outstanding writing and editing; designers Nick Clark and Neal Cobourne; picture researcher Elaine Willis; my agent Georgina Capel and, as always, my wife, Santa.

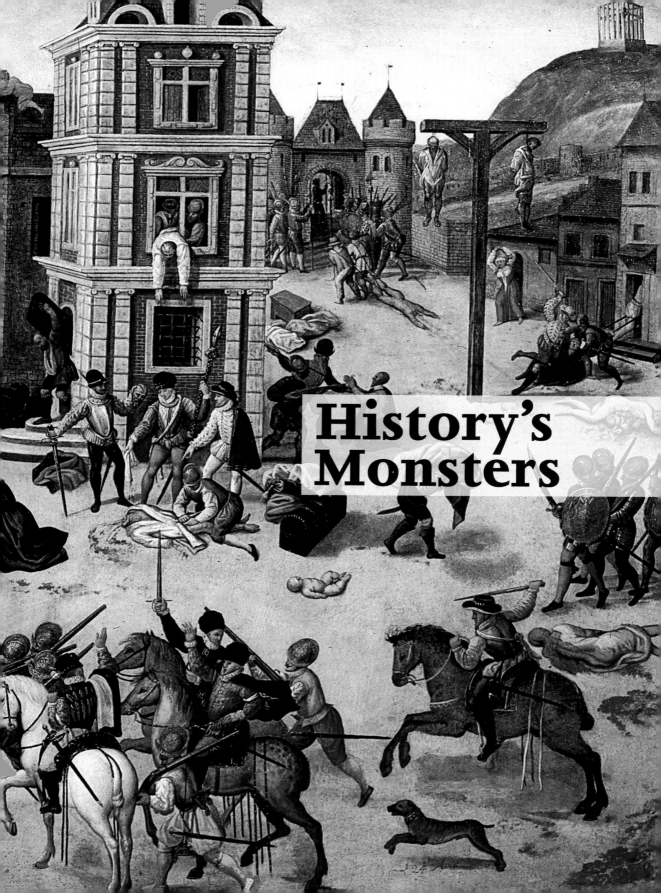

History's Monsters

The supreme villainess of the Bible, Jezebel – a Phoenician princess and wife of Ahab, king of Israel – was a bloodthirsty pagan and harlot who controlled her husband, challenged his manhood and used him as a puppet to terrorize his subjects. Her brutal end – thrown from a window and devoured by hungry dogs – is portrayed as fitting punishment for daring to challenge Yahweh, the one God of Israel.

Jezebel 9th century BC

Jezebel's story is told in the biblical books of 1 and 2 Kings. She was the daughter of Ethbaal of Tyre, king of the Phoenicians, a seafaring people who lived in city-states along the coast of modern-day Lebanon and Syria. As part of an important regional alliance she was uprooted from her home and offered in marriage to Ahab, the newly crowned king of Israel, which had separated around 920 BC from the southern kingdom of Judah. The problem, however, was that the Israelites demanded the worship of one God, Yahweh, whereas the Phoenicians worshipped a variety of deities grouped under the general name Baal, associated by many Jews with child sacrifice. Jezebel followed her religion with the same fervour that the Israelites followed theirs, making conflict inevitable.

Ahab was prepared to tolerate the religious practices of his new wife – even building a temple to Baal in the centre of the town of Samaria – but this was not enough for Jezebel. Having brought into Israel hundreds of her own Phoenician priests and prophets, she demanded that Ahab not only follow her religion but also impose it on his people. According to 1 Kings 18:4, she set about the systematic liquidation of her opponents, arresting and killing hundreds of Jewish priests and forcing many more into hiding.

Jezebel soon encountered a formidable opponent in Elijah, a fiery and uncompromising Israelite prophet and defender of the Jewish faith. Elijah challenged Jezebel's new religious hierarchy – 450 prophets of Baal and 400 prophets of Asherah, the god of the sea – to a tournament on Mount Carmel, to prove which religion would reign supreme. The priests of Baal built one altar and Elijah another, the challenge being to offer up a sacrificial bull without setting fire to it. According to the biblical account, Jezebel's prophets spent most of the day petitioning their gods to no effect, whereupon Elijah, having first soaked the altar, wood and offering with water, appealed to Yahweh, who sent fire from heaven that consumed not just the offering but also the timber and rocks on which it was placed. When King Ahab told Jezebel what had happened, she responded by issuing a death threat against Elijah, who fled to Mount Sinai, though not before ordering the murder of 400 of Jezebel's own prophets (a graphic example of biblical double standards).

Jezebel's hold on Ahab is most clearly seen in the story of Naboth, an Israelite who owned a vineyard bordering the royal palace at Jezreel. When Naboth refused to sell this to Ahab, the king returned to the palace dejected, prompting Jezebel to ask mockingly, 'Is this how you act as king over Israel?' She then took the initiative herself, using the king's seal to send letters to the townsmen of Jezreel instructing them to trump up a charge of blasphemy against Naboth. He was duly stoned to death, following which Ahab usurped his land.

After the death of Ahab and her oldest son Ahaziah, Jezebel ruled through her second son, Joram. But the Israelites had suffered enough and Elijah's successor, Elisha, defiantly crowned Jehu, Joram's military commander, as king in his stead. Any hopes Joram had of negotiating a settlement ended when the two men met. Accusing Jezebel of 'countless harlotries and sorceries' (2 Kings 9:22), Jehu shot an arrow through Joram's heart, dumped his body on Naboth's land, and rushed in his chariot to the royal palace where, seeing his approach, Jezebel began to dress her hair glamorously and apply black kohl to her eyelids, perhaps hoping to seduce her son's murderer. When Jehu arrived, however, he ordered Jezebel's eunuchs to throw their queen from the window onto the street below, her blood splattering onto the wall and horses. As Jehu celebrated his victory inside the palace, dogs devoured her body limb by limb, leaving only her skull, hands and feet.

Jezebel's name has become a byword for promiscuity – the archetypal femme fatale. The biblical writers saw her as a threat to their faith and accordingly portrayed her in the worst possible light. Jezebel remains the moral and political prototype of the wicked, seductive and greedy female manipulator behind the man of power.

Jezebel and Ahab taking possession of Naboth's vineyard, a biblical episode from 1 Kings 21, depicted by Frederic Leighton (1836–96). The imposing figure on the left is the prophet Elijah, who informs the cowering Ahab that he has sold himself 'to work evil in the sight of the LORD'. Elijah predicts that 'the dogs shall eat Jezebel by the wall of Jezreel'.

SALOME

Two women of the Bible – Herodias and her daughter Salome – are remembered above all for their seductiveness and calculating opportunism. After the death of Herod Philip – her first husband – Herodias had married his brother, Herod Antipas (c. 20 BC–c. AD 39; see page 26) – the Roman-appointed ruler of Galilee who was later to mock Jesus of Nazareth and send him to trial and crucifixion at the hands of Pontius Pilate. The marriage had been strongly condemned by the fiery Judaean prophet John the Baptist, who declared it contrary to the Law of Moses – as written in Leviticus 18:16 – for a man to see his brother's wife naked. As punishment, John had been arrested and put into prison, where, according to Matthew 14:3–12 and Mark 14:15–29, he was languishing when a great banquet was staged to celebrate Herod's birthday. Herodias, Mark tells us, bitterly resented John's temerity in presuming to judge her and wanted him dead, but Herod – who according to Matthew also wished to kill John – was afraid of the consequences, believing him to be a holy man and therefore protected by God. The devious and manipulative Herodias saw in the banquet an opportunity to force the issue and rid herself of John once and for all. She coaxed Salome to dance before the king, who was so delighted by her erotic dance of the seven veils that he offered her anything as a reward. 'What should I ask for?' Salome asked her mother, to which came the brusque reply, 'The head of John the Baptizer' (Mark 6:23–4). Giving the lie to any suggestion that she was merely an innocent victim of her mother's machinations, Salome eagerly hurried back with this gruesome request, demanding 'at once the head of John the Baptist on a platter' (Mark 6:25). Herod had no option but to honour his word and John was summarily executed in his prison cell, his severed head brought in on a plate and given to Salome, who passed it in turn to her triumphant mother.

Salome receives the head of St John the Baptist, one of the most gruesome and celebrated scenes in the Bible, here rendered by Michelangelo Merisi da Caravaggio (1571–1610).

Nebuchadnezzar was the Lion of Babylon and the Destroyer of Nations. Ruler of the great neo-Babylonian empire from 605 until 562 BC, he was the embodiment of the warrior-king. The Bible records that Nebuchadnezzar was the instrument of God's vengeance on the errant people of Judah – a destiny he appears to have embraced with relish. The same biblical account has it that God later chose to punish Nebuchadnezzar for his arrogant pride with seven years' madness.

Nebuchadnezzar II
630–562 BC

'Then was Nebuchadnezzar full of fury ... And he commanded the most mighty men that were in his army to bind Shadrach, Meshach and Abednego, and to cast them into the burning fiery furnace.'

DANIEL 3:19–20

Born some time after 630 BC, Nebuchadnezzar was the eldest son of King Nabopolassar (ruled 626–605 BC), the founder of the Chaldean dynasty in Babylon. Nabopolassar had successfully thrown off the yoke of the Assyrian empire to the north, and had even sacked the great city of Nineveh. Boasting of his triumphs, he had spoken of how he had 'slaughtered the land of Assyria' and 'turned the hostile land into heaps of ruin'.

As befitted a crown prince in antiquity, the young Nebuchadezzar was involved in his father's military conquests from an early age, and in 605 he oversaw the defeat of Egyptian forces at Carchemish, a

Nebuchadnezzar, a fascinating and hallucinatory depiction of the Babylonian ruler by the English poet, painter and visionary William Blake (1757–1827).

victory that helped make the Babylonians the masters of Syria. Nabopolassar died later that year, and Nebuchadnezzar mounted the throne.

Now in a position of absolute power, Nebuchadnezzar set about expanding his dominions westwards; a marriage alliance with the Median empire to the east had ensured there would be no trouble from that quarter. Between 604 and 601 various local states – including the Jewish kingdom of Judah – submitted to his authority, and Nebuchadnezzar declared his determination to have 'no opponent from horizon to sky'. Buoyed by his success, in 601 Nebuchadnezzar decided to take on his greatest rivals, sending his armies into Egypt. But they were repulsed, and this defeat provoked a series of rebellions amongst Nebuchadnezzar's previously quiescent vassals – most notably Judah.

Nebuchadnezzar returned to his Babylonian homeland, plotting his revenge. After a brief hiatus, he stormed westwards once again, carrying almost all before him. In 597 the kingdom of Judah submitted. Nebuchadnezzar had the king, Jehoiachin, deported to Babylon. In 588 Judah, under the king's uncle Zedekiah, revolted. In 587–586 Nebuchadnezzar marched on defiant Jerusalem, besieged it for months, and finally stormed it, wreaking total destruction. Nebuchadnezzar ordered the city levelled, the people slaughtered, the Jewish temple razed and Prince Zedekiah was made to witness his sons' executions before his own eyes were gouged out. The Jews were then deported east, where they mourned Zion 'by the rivers of Babylon'.

In 585 Nebuchadnezzar laid siege to the rebellious town of Tyre. The town's coastal location meant it could be supplied from the sea, enabling it to withstand the Babylonian blockade. After an extraordinary 13-year stand-off, a compromise settlement was negotiated: Tyre was spared, but it agreed to accept Nebuchadnezzar's authority.

Nebuchadnezzar's achievements on the battlefield were accompanied by a surge of domestic construction. Like many who wield absolute power, the Babylonian ruler was obsessed with architectural grandeur and was determined that his capital city should reflect his greatness. Drawing on the slave labour of the various peoples he had subjugated, Nebuchadnezzar had numerous temples and public buildings erected or renovated. The extravagant new royal palace, begun by his father, was completed. And, most famously, the king commissioned the Hanging Gardens of Babylon – one of the wonders of the ancient world – as a present for his wife.

Nebuchadnezzar thus moulded Babylon into a capital city fit for a superpower – which is what his empire had become by the time he died in 561. His life's work proved ephemeral, however: scarcely two decades after his death, Nebuchadnezzar's empire ceased to exist when Cyrus the Great of Persia conquered Babylon in 539.

Nebuchadnezzar is remembered as an empire-builder – the man who restored Babylonian greatness, however briefly: Saddam Hussein was especially determined to exploit Nebuchadnezzar's image for his own ends. For others, though, his name is indelibly associated with unbridled conquest and the brutal treatment of subject peoples – the Destroyer of Nations who fulfilled the vision of the Jewish prophet Jeremiah: 'He has gone out from his place, to make your land a waste. Your cities will be ruins, without inhabitant.'

SARGON OF AKKAD: MESOPOTAMIA'S FIRST GREAT CONQUEROR

Mesopotamia produced the first great conqueror known to history: Sargon I of Akkad (c. 2334– 2279 BC). The illegitimate son of a priestess, Sargon – who hailed from the city of Agade in the Akkad region of northern Mesopotamia – served as a cupbearer at the royal court of King Ur-Zababa of Kish. After the king grew jealous and attempted to have him killed, Sargon overthrew Ur-Zababa and launched his own conquest of Mesopotamia.

At this time, Mesopotamia was dominated by a string of independent city-states, but, one by one, they fell to Sargon as he exerted authority over all of southern Mesopotamia – the region known as Sumer. In the process, he destroyed the previously great city of Uruk and placed its ruler Lugalzagesi in a wooden collar, leading him through the streets of Agade in humiliation.

Further victories followed. After one triumph, Sargon totally levelled the city of Kazalla, so that, 'the birds could not find a place to perch away from the ground'. He eventually brought all of Sumer under his sway, arriving finally at the Persian Gulf where he is reputed to have bathed and cleansed his weapons in the sea to symbolize the success of his conquest.

Later, Sargon's led his forces west, conquering lands across the Fertile Crescent and reaching as far as Syria and eastern Asian Minor on the Mediterranean. Little wonder that one chronicler described him as having 'neither rival nor equal'.

After his death, much of the Akkadian empire rose in revolt, but his sons were able to re-establish control over the bulk of his territories, later descendants securing further conquests and one, Naram-Sin (who reigned c. 2254–2218 BC), even declaring himself 'King of the Four Quarters, King of the Universe'.

A bronze head of Sargon I, the Akkadian conqueror who declared himself 'King of the Universe'.

Qin Shi Huangdi created the first unified Chinese empire that emerged from the 'Warring States Period'. By 221 BC he had successfully destroyed the last remaining rival kingdoms within China and made himself supreme ruler: the First Emperor. A remarkable, ruthless statesman and conqueror, of manic gifts, haunted by madness, sadism and paranoia. Qin Shi Huangdi's reign quickly degenerated into a brutal and bloody tyranny. His reputation in China has always been that of a tyrant, but it was Chairman Mao Zedong, another monstrous dictator, who associated himself with the 'First Emperor' and promoted him as his glorious precursor.

Qin Shi Huangdi – the First Emperor
c. 259–210 BC

'If you govern the people by punishment, the people will fear. Being fearful, they will not commit villainies.'

LORD SHANG'S LEGALISM, ADOPTED BY QIN SHI HUANGDI AS THE BASIS FOR HIS RULE

Born a prince of the royal family of the Kingdom of Qin, Zheng, as the future emperor was named, was raised in honourable captivity. His father, Prince Zichu of Qin, was then serving as a hostage to the enemy state of Zhaou, under a peace agreement between the two kingdoms. Subsequently released, Zichu returned to Qin and assumed the crown, with his son Zheng as his heir.

In 245 BC, Zichu died and the 13-year-old Zheng acceded to the throne. For the next seven years he ruled with a regent, until in 238 BC he seized full control in a palace coup. From the beginning, Zheng showed a new ruthlessness: he regularly executed prisoners of war, contrary to the established etiquette of the time.

Zheng now vied for power with the other Chinese kingdoms, creating a powerful army. When he had come to the throne, Qin had been a vassal state of the Kingdom of Zhaou. In a sequence of military victories, six kingdoms fell to Zheng's forces: the Han (230), Zhaou (228), Wei (228), Chu (223), Yan (222) and Qi, the last independent Chinese kingdom, in 221 BC. A superb commander, Zheng was also a skilled diplomat, especially in exploiting divisions among his enemies. He now stood unchallenged within a unified China. To commemorate this feat he took a new name that reflected his unparalleled status: Qin Shi Huangdi, 'The First August Emperor of Qin'.

Qin Shi Huangdi now created a strong centralized state across his territories. In an extension of existing practice in the Kingdom of Qin, the old feudal laws and structures that had remained in much of China were abolished, to be replaced by centrally appointed officials and a new administrative apparatus. Standardization of the Chinese script, currency, weights and measures changed the spheres of economics, law and language, with a unified system of new roads and canals, to weld China together as a cohesive national unit.

There was, however, a price to be paid – borne by the ordinary people of China. A million men were put to work as forced labour to build some 4700 miles of roads. Qin Shi Huangdi would have his edicts carved in vast letters on mountain rock faces. As his projects of national unity became ever more ambitious, so too did the human toll they exacted. One such project was to link up the numerous independent frontier walls that barricaded northern China from the threat of hostile tribes. This effectively created a forerunner to the Great Wall of China, but it cost hundreds of thousands of lives.

At the same time, Qin Shi Huangdi was unwilling to accept any limits on his own power – in contradiction of the Confucian belief that a ruler should follow traditional rites. So he outlawed Confucianism and persecuted its adherents brutally. Confucian scholars were buried alive or beheaded; a similar fate befell the follower of any creed that might challenge the emperor's authority. All books not specifically approved by the emperor were banned and burned; intellectual curiosity of any kind was to be replaced by unswerving obedience.

As he grew older, Qin Shi Huangdi became obsessed with his own death. He regularly dispatched expeditions in search of an 'elixir of life' that might make him immortal. He grew ever more fearful of challenges to his position, and with good reason, as he was the target of several assassination plots. The emperor's efforts to counter such a fate became ever more paranoid and bizarre. At random, servants in the imperial household would be ordered to carry him in the middle of the night to an alternative room to sleep. Numerous 'doubles' were deployed to confuse any would-be assassins. A close watch was kept, and anyone suspected of disloyalty was instantly removed.

Ultimately, it was Qin's pursuit of immortality that was his downfall. It was widely believed that a man might live longer by drinking precious metals, gaining some of their durability. The emperor died in 210 BC, on tour in eastern China, having swallowed mercury tablets, created by his court physician in an effort to confer immortality.

Even in death, Qin Shi Huangdi seemed afraid that he might be vulnerable to attack. Long before he died he had ordered a gigantic three-mile-wide mausoleum to be built, guarded by a full-scale 'terracotta army' of over 6000 full-sized clay models of soldiers. Again, the epic scale of the building project exacted a monumental cost in terms of lives lost. Some 700,000 conscripts were required, a substantial proportion of whom did not survive its completion.

Qin Shi Huangdi: the founder of the Chinese nation? Or an autocratic monster? The reputation of the 'First Emperor' remains mired in controversy. His immediate legacy did not last long. Qin Shi Huangdi had declared that the empire he had built would last for a thousand years, but it collapsed only four years after his death, as China entered a fresh period of civil war. Yet he created the reality and the idea of a Chinese empire, a similar entity and territory to today's People's Republic of China.

A statue of Emperor Qin Shi Huangdi at the Museum of Terracotta Warriors, Lintong, Shaanxi Province. The immense underground tomb which the emperor built for himself remains unopened and largely unexplored, one of the world's most mysterious archaeological sites.

THE EMPEROR'S UNDERGROUND WORLD

In March 1974 a group of Chinese peasants sinking a well near the city of Xian made an extraordinary discovery. Digging down, they stumbled upon a vast chamber containing some 6000 life-size clay figures. Upon further exploration, it was discovered that this 'Terracotta Army' of individually sculpted infantrymen, cavalry, charioteers, archers and cross-bowmen were guarding the entrance to the enormous tomb of the 'First Emperor', Qin Shi Huangdi.

So far, only the soldiers that guard the path to the door of the tomb have been uncovered. Each is fashioned in precise detail, and each has unique facial characteristics. All of the figures face east, from where it was assumed the enemies of the eternally sleeping

Some of the clay soldiers who were meant to guard the emperor in the afterlife. The figures are believed to have been manufactured by a technique similar to that used for constructing drainage pipes. The individual soldiers vary in their height, uniform and hairstyle according to rank. All would have carried weapons, but these were stolen shortly after the army was completed.

emperor would come. In total, the entire funerary compound fills a whole mountain, covering a site of over 20 square miles. Work on its construction was carried out throughout the emperor's reign, and was only completed in the years after his death. Qin Shi Huangdi's aim was to ensure that in death, as in life, his every whim and desire would be catered for in his huge subterranean palace.

The scale of what remains to be uncovered is indicated by the words of ancient Chinese historian, Sima Qian (Ssu-ma Ch'ien; c. 145–c. 85 BC), who describes the tomb thus:

The labourers … built models of palaces, pavilions, and offices, and filled the tomb with fine vessels, precious stones and rarities. Artisans were ordered to install mechanically triggered crossbows set to shoot any intruder. With quicksilver the various waterways of the empire, the Yangtze and Yellow rivers, and even the great ocean itself, were created and made to flow and circulate mechanically. With shining pearls the heavenly constellations were depicted above, and with figures of birds in gold and silver and of pine trees carved of jade the earth was laid out below.

Grey-eyed with red-gold hair, Sulla was the general and dictator whose murderous rule sounded the death knell of the Roman Republic. A gifted but ruthless military commander and conservative politician, he annihilated his rivals, winning a reputation as half-fox, half-lion. Though he styled himself the 'guardian of the constitution', Sulla's reckless ambition was ultimately to prove its undoing.

Sulla 138–78 BC

> 'His unparalleled good fortune — up to his triumph in the civil war — was well matched by his energy … Of his subsequent conduct I could not speak without feelings of shame and disgust.'
>
> SALLUST, *THE JUGURTHINE WAR* (c. 41–40 BC)

Lucius Cornelius Sulla was a latecomer to the rough-and-tumble world of Roman politics. Although of noble birth, he was left all but penniless by the death of his father. In his late teens and twenties, according to the Roman historian Plutarch, 'He spent much time with actors and buffoons and shared their dissolute life.' One thing these experiences gave Sulla was the common touch — essential for any ambitious populist.

Sulla furthered his ambition by establishing himself as the lover of a wealthy widow, who bequeathed him her fortune when she died. On the back of this windfall, Sulla was able to embark on the *cursus honorum* — the process by which budding politicians rose through the ranks of public life under the Roman Republic. By this time, though, he was already 30. And with many of his rivals having started their careers in their early twenties, Sulla was, from the start, a man in a hurry.

In 107 BC Sulla became quaestor, and distinguished himself in a successful military campaign against the Numidian king, Jugurtha, serving under the consul Gaius Marius. Some twenty years Sulla's senior, Marius would go from being the younger man's mentor to his fiercest rival. Between 104 and 101 BC Sulla again served with distinction under Marius, and returned to Rome with a triumphant reputation and bright prospects.

At this point, however, Sulla's career entered something of a lull. It was not until the Social War of 91–88 BC, in which Rome faced a massive revolt from its hitherto loyal

Lucius Cornelius Sulla. This intimidating marble bust was made around AD 100.

Italian allies, that Sulla returned to frontline service and won a reputation as a brilliant general in his own right. In helping to defeat the insurgency he displayed the combination of military flair and savage brutality that was to become his hallmark.

Returning to Rome in triumph, Sulla became consul for the year 88 BC – the pinnacle of elected office under the Republic. He also secured an enormously lucrative post-consulsar military command, campaigning in the east against King Mithridates of Pontus. Marius, though ageing, remained supremely ambitious and believed that Sulla's command in the east should have been his. Thus, when Sulla was absent from Rome, Marius took the opportunity to have his political allies transfer Sulla's position to him.

But Marius had badly misjudged his rival. The possibility that Sulla might now lose everything for which he had worked so long and so hard made him fiercely determined to defeat his enemies by any means necessary. Sulla had at his command six legions – almost 30,000 men. He now took the scandalous and unprecedented step of marching against Rome – the First Civil War.

Marius was defeated and fled to Africa. Sulla had his foes branded 'enemies of the state', and had his original offices restored. Apart from this, his retribution was surprisingly moderate. He introduced various reforms, and then, in 87 BC, departed for the east, where he achieved significant victories over Mithridates and crushed a rebellion in Greece. During the siege of Athens, he ordered the destruction of the groves where Plato and Aristotle had reflected on the human condition. When the city itself finally fell, Sulla gave his troops free rein to pillage and murder as they saw fit.

But Sulla was again being challenged back in Rome. Taking advantage once more of his rival's absence, Marius had returned and become consul – for the seventh time. He declared all of Sulla's laws invalid and exiled him from Rome. In 82 BC Sulla returned to the capital – once more at the head of an army – and this time there was to be no limit to his vengeance.

Marius himself had died during his last consulship in 86 BC, but his political allies and family were hunted down mercilessly. Having destroyed his rivals, early in 81 BC Sulla was appointed dictator by a fearful Senate, and soon lists of 'proscribed' individuals began appearing in Rome's central forum. All proscribed individuals were condemned to be executed and their property plundered.

In the space of a few months, as many as 10,000 people may have been killed. On one notorious occasion Sulla addressed the timorous Senate even as the cries of prisoners being tortured and killed rang out from a neighbouring building. The banks of the Tiber were littered with bodies, and the public buildings filled with severed heads.

In the midst of the carnage, Sulla attempted to rebuild the integrity of the Roman Republic that he himself had helped shatter. Portraying himself as the 'guardian of the constitution', he introduced new laws to restore the power of the Senate and elected officials. In 79 BC, having vanquished his foes and completed his constitutional reforms, he ostentatiously retired from public life.

Far from saving the Republic, Sulla had paved the way for its eventual collapse. Power, he had made clear, lay not with the politicians, but with the generals. And ultimate power resided with whichever man could wield military force with the most merciless brutality. It was Sulla, with his unbridled savagery, who opened the door through which the emperors would march.

TYRANTS AND DICTATORS

Although today the words 'tyrant' and 'dictator' are applied interchangeably to anyone wielding an overbearing excess of power, in the classical world the terms had more specific and less pejorative meanings. In ancient Greece a *turannos* ('tyrant') was someone who seized power without the legal right to do so, but with the support of crucial factions within the polity, and who governed thereafter in absolute fashion. One such tyrant was Peisistratos, who ruled Athens from 560 to 527 BC. A successful military man, Peisistratos took control by force, but subsequently ruled (despite twice being exiled) with a significant degree of popular backing.

Under the Roman Republic, the post of *dictator* ('one who pronounces') was only filled in times of emergency, during which the holder wielded absolute power for a six-month term. At other times, supreme executive power was invested in the hands of the two consuls. A person could only be raised to the post of dictator after the passing of a *senatus consultum* by the Senate, which called on the two consuls to nominate someone for the position. The most famous of the traditional Roman dictators was Quintus Fabius Maximus – 'the Delayer' – who was appointed in 221 BC and again in 217 BC, as the Carthaginian general Hannibal, having marched an army over the Alps, threatened the city of Rome itself.

Scarcely a decade after Fabius Maximus had served in the role, Publius Sulpicius Galba Maximus became the final man to be appointed dictator in the traditional sense. The office fell into disuse until it was reinvigorated by Sulla – but now in very different form. His *de facto* self-elevation to a position of untrammelled power, rather than saving the Republic, heralded its demise. Sulla paved the way for Julius Caesar, some years later, to declare himself *dictator perpetuum*, dictator for life – a move that marked the beginning of the end of the Republican Rome and the birth of a new imperial age.

The Legend of Damocles, *by Richard Westall (1765–1836). When Damocles, an excessively flattering noble at the court of Dionysius II, tyrant of Syracuse hailed his master as a truly fortunate man, the tyrant decided to punish Damocles for his flattery by inviting Damocles to change places with him for a day. He held a lavish banquet at which the courtier was waited on like a king, but above his head a sword was suspended by a single horsehair, and Damocles quickly lost his appetite. The legend has long been used to demonstrate the precariousness of absolute power, and the phrase 'sword of Damocles' to denote an impending danger or disaster.*

Corpulent, greedy and vain, Marcus Licinius Crassus was a man driven by merciless avarice and ambition. To swell his fortune, he seized the money of men murdered in Sulla's 'proscriptions' and made his greatest 'killing' by adding a man to the death lists specifically to acquire his money. To promote himself, he crucified 10,000 slaves along 100 miles of the Appian Way. Known as Dives, 'The Rich Man', Crassus prospered as politician, soldier and millionaire, and as Julius Caesar's first patron – but he perished with ignominy.

Crassus c. 115–53 BC

> 'The many virtues of Crassus were darkened by the one vice of avarice, and indeed he seemed to have no other but that; for it being the most predominant, obscured others to which he was inclined.'
>
> PLUTARCH

Marcus Licinius Crassus grew up in a Rome split between the competing factions of Marius and Sulla (see page 19). His father had been an opponent of Marius and was executed with his brother. Crassus was forced to flee to Spain (where his father had been governor).

His father had combined politics with business and had endowed his son with a magnificent inheritance – much of which was in assets scattered across the Empire. Crassus spent his 'fugitive months' living in luxury.

He raised a private army of some 2500 men – an extraordinary feat in itself – and nailed his flag to Sulla's mast. Sulla had been outmanoeuvred and was in danger of being defeated, but was rescued by Crassus's decisive intervention. Crassus defeated Marian–Samnite forces at the Colline Gate in Rome in 82 BC. The resulting bloodbath was one that proved to be the making of Crassus' reputation, establishing him as a ruthless but loyal servant of Sulla.

Under the Sullan regime, Crassus was restored to his family's estates and now preyed on those 'enemies of the state' being proscribed by Sulla. He denounced anyone whose land and fortune he desired, fabulously enriching himself, until finally even Sulla felt things had gone too far and reprimanded his wayward lieutenant.

At the same time, Crassus first encountered his greatest future rival: Pompey. As Crassus had rallied to Sulla's side, so had Pompey. Physically handsome – 'nothing was more delicate than Pompey's cheeks', crowed one chronicler – and the playboy warrior hero of Rome, Pompey quickly became Crassus's nemesis: Pompey, the fashionable showman; Crassus, the backroom wheeler-dealer and political fixer. As Sulla retired in 79 BC, both men looked to their future ascent.

Crassus succeeded in becoming Praetor for 73 BC, and was soon faced with the Spartacus-led slave revolt that convulsed Italy in 73–71 BC. In this calamity, Crassus saw only personal opportunity. Using his connections in the Senate he persuaded the body to strip the sitting consuls of their powers and award him the military command.

When two of his legions disobeyed orders he had the men drawn up in formation and then decimated: every tenth man was beaten to death. Crassus crushed the rebel armies, but some 5000 escaped – only to be captured and destroyed by Pompey who was returning from Spain ahead of his own armies. Piqued with jealousy, Crassus ordered a gruesome demonstration of his own triumph over the slaves: 10,000 of them were executed along one hundred miles of the Appian Way. Every forty yards a slave was nailed to a cross with a placard that publicized Crassus's success.

Despite his rivalry with Pompey, Crassus recognized the potential advantage if they worked together. They united in 70 BC to serve their first joint consulship, set about destroying much of Sulla's reform programme that had aimed to safeguard the Republic, and guaranteed themselves lucrative post-consulship appointments.

During the 60s BC, while Pompey was abroad advancing Rome's Empire by military conquest, Crassus spent his time in the capital, building a vast political and financial empire. In 65 BC he served as a censor, but otherwise he tended to exercise influence behind the scenes. He still found time to be prosecuted for sleeping with a Vestal Virgin – a sacrilegious act, but one which Crassus overcame by bribing the jury and prosecution.

Crassus took various protégés under his wing, one of whom was an impoverished young nobleman by the name of Julius Caesar. And in 60 BC, Crassus joined with the much younger Caesar and the returning Pompey to create the informal 'First Triumvirate', by which the three men effectively divided the Roman Empire amongst themselves.

Tensions soon emerged among the triumvirs, and Crassus spent much of the next four years manoeuvring behind Pompey's back. In 56 BC, however, the two resolved their differences and the following year they served their second joint consulship. Crassus now departed to the east, where he was determined to establish a military reputation to rival Pompey and Caesar.

As governor of Syria in 54 BC, Crassus quickly found a pretext to declare war on Parthia, Rome's rival empire in the east. Accompanied by seven legions (some 44,000 men), he foolishly attempted to march across open desert – a mark of his meagre military judgement. He was ambushed by a force of over 1000 Parthian armoured knights and 10,000 mounted archers, at the Battle of Carrhae in modern-day Turkey in 53 BC. The Roman legionaries were surrounded and cut to pieces. Less than a quarter of them survived, and Crassus himself was felled in the mêlée.

A marble bust of Marcus Licinius Crassus. Among Crassus' many acts of greed and violence was the plundering of the Jewish Temple in 54 BC. The Temple was rebuilt and enlarged by Herod the Great over a period of 46 years, but was finally destroyed in the Jewish rebellion of AD 66.

CRUCIFIXION

One of the earliest references to crucifixion is in the work of the ancient Greek historian Herodotus, who recorded that it was practised by the Persians. Various other peoples adopted the practice, notably the Carthaginians, and it is probably from them that the Romans got the idea.

Crassus' contemporary, the great orator Cicero, described crucifixion as the *summum supplicum* – the ultimate punishment, held to be a worse fate than decapitation or burning. It was typically meted out to those found guilty of threatening the Roman state in some way, and was usually reserved for those who were not citizens of Rome. There were exceptions, however: in AD 66, after a Jewish revolt, the local Roman governor had several Jews who were also Roman citizens crucified in Jerusalem.

The horrendous spectacle provided by crucifixion was very deliberately used as a deterrent – particularly to keep slaves 'in their place'. By the 1st century BC the institution of slavery underpinned the entire Roman economy, and it was no coincidence that slaves comprised the vast majority of the victims of crucifixion.

Those condemned to be crucified were usually flogged first. They were then forced to carry the cross on which they were to die to the place of execution.

Stripped naked, they were attached – either by rope or nails – to the cross, which was either X-shaped or in the form of the classic Christian cross (it is now thought by some scholars, however, that Jesus suffered a form of crucifixion that involved bending the body into a sort of foetal position). A small ledge part way up provided some support for the prisoner's body, but only enough to hold him in position, rather than alleviate the pressure on his joints. Hoisted into position, the crucified were then simply left to die an agonizing death. This could take several days though many died faster from suffocation as fluids built up in their lungs. On occasion, the soldiers overseeing the execution would break the victims' legs in order that death might come more quickly. But such displays of mercy were rare. More typical were various gruesome variations, such as crucifying the prisoner upside down, or nailing genitals to the cross.

The practice of crucifixion continued in the Roman Empire for many centuries. It was not until AD 337 that the emperor Constantine abolished this form of punishment, after Christianity had been adopted as the state religion.

Willem Defoe as Jesus Christ in Martin Scorsese's The Last Temptation of Christ *(1988).*

Herod the Great was the half-Jewish, half-Idumean king of Judaea and Roman ally, whose 32-year reign saw colossal achievements and terrible crimes. He was a talented, energetic and intelligent self-made monarch who combined Hellenistic and Jewish culture, presiding over the rebuilding of the Jewish Temple, the embellishment and restoration of Jerusalem, and the building of great cities and impressive fortresses. In short, be created a large, rich and powerful kingdom with a special status at the heart of Rome's eastern empire. Yet in his lust for power, women and glory, he became the bloodthirsty villain of the Christian Gospels and the despot of Josephus' *The Jewish War*. Even though he did not actually order the Massacre of the Innocents, as told in the Gospels, he killed three of his own sons, as well as his wife and many of his rivals, and used terror and murder to hold on to power right up until his death.

Herod the Great

73–4 BC

Born around 73 BC, Herod was the second son of Antipater, chief minister of the Jewish king Hyrcanus II, great-grandson of Simon the Maccabee who had established Judaea in 142 BC as an independent Jewish state. The Maccabees (also known as the Hasmoneans) had ruled Judaea as both kings and high priests ever since, but to win back his throne in 63 BC, after his brother Aristobulus had wrested it from him, the ineffectual Hyrcanus was forced to ally himself with the Roman general Pompey the Great, ceding control of Judaea to Rome. Herod and his father Antipater were shrewd students of politics in Rome, always

The conquest of Jerusalem by Herod the Great in 36 BC, in a 15th-century depiction by the French painter Jean Fouquet. Herod, with assistance from the Romans, mercilessly retook the city from Antigonus, the last Hasmonean king of Judaea.

> 'Then Herod, when he saw that he was mocked of the wise men, was exceeding wroth, and sent forth, and slew all the children that were in Bethlehem, and in all the coasts thereof, from two years old and under.'
>
> MATTHEW 2:16

supporting the winner in the civil wars, from Pompey to Augustus, in order to keep power. When Julius Caesar subsequently appointed Antipater as governor of Judaea in 47 BC, Hyrcanus continued as king in name only, and though he survived a revolt in 43 BC led by his popular nephew Antigonus – a revolt in which Antipater was poisoned – he was exiled three years later when Antigonus rebelled again. Herod – whom his father had earlier made governor of Galilee – secured the help of Rome and for the next three years waged a bitter war against his own people, which ended with Antigonus executed and Herod appointed 'King of the Jews' by the Roman Senate.

Already hated by his people, Herod attempted to legitimize his position by discarding his first wife, Doris – who had borne him a son, Antipater – and marrying Mariamme, the teenage daughter of Hyrcanus (whom he later had executed in 30 BC). In all, he was to marry ten times, mostly for political reasons, and produce 14 children, three of whom eventually succeeded him in joint rule after his death.

Herod presided over impressive changes to his kingdom. He ordered a series of grandiose construction projects, which included aqueducts, amphitheatres, the stunning trading port of Caesarea (considered by many to be one of the great wonders of the world), and the fortresses of Masada, Antonia and Herodium. Most ambitious of all was the rebuilding of the Second Temple in Jerusalem – a massive project that took years to complete. Over 10,000 men spent 10 years constructing the Temple Mount alone, and work on the Temple courts and outbuildings continued long after Herod's death. The last supporting wall remains today the holiest site of Judaism: the Wailing or Western Wall.

Significant though they were, Herod's achievements were outweighed by his atrocities. He established early in his reign what amounted to a secret police force, having anyone suspected of disaffection arrested and executed. He controlled the Temple likewise, putting to death 46 key members of the Sanhedrin and having the high priest – his wife's brother Aristobulus, whom he feared as a potential rival – drowned in 36 BC. Not even his immediate family were safe. In 29 BC, he ordered the execution of Mariamme following suggestions she was having an affair. Later, in 7 BC, he ordered the murder of Aristobulus

THE HERODIAN DYNASTY

Herod founded a dynasty that lasted a century. His surviving sons were:

• Herod Archelaus (23 BC–c. AD 18), whose bloody rule as ethnarch of Judaea, Samaria and Idumea ended when the Romans exiled him in AD 6.

• Herod Antipas (c. 20 BC–c. AD 39), who as tetrarch of Galilee and Peraea from 4 BC brought peace and prosperity to the region, was exiled to Gaul following accusations by Herod Agrippa I that he was plotting against Caligula. Antipas was the Herod of the Gospels, who refused to judge Jesus and was portrayed frivolously in the Lloyd Webber/Rice rock opera *Jesus Christ Superstar*.

• Herod Philip II (c. 27 BC–AD 33), who as tetrarch of Ituraea and districts northeast of Galilee from 4 BC distinguished himself as an excellent, peace-loving and just ruler.

Herod's grandsons included:

• Herod Agrippa I (10 BC–AD 44), son of Aristobulus, brother of Herodias, who was made tetrarch of

and Alexander — his sons by Mariamme — after being persuaded by Antipater (his son by Doris) that the two were scheming against him. The Roman emperor Augustus joked that he would rather be Herod's pig than his son since Jews do not eat pigs.

Old age and debilitating health problems (Herod suffered from a horrifying condition that entailed a decay of the genitals, described by the Jewish historian Josephus as 'a putrification of his privy member, that produced worms') brought no respite from the killing. Stung by criticism from the Essenes — a rigid Jewish community — Herod had their monastery at Qumran burned down in 8 BC. Then, when a group of students tore down the imperial Roman eagle from the entrance to the Temple in 4 BC, he had them burned alive. Days before his death, he ordered the execution of his son Antipater, whom he suspected of plotting to take the throne, and his last act was to decree the execution of the foremost men of the nation upon his death so that his funeral would be marked by a national outpouring of grief. Fortunately, this final command was ignored.

Herod is most pilloried for a crime he did not commit: the so-called 'Massacre of the Innocents.' According to the Gospel of Matthew, when he learned that a new 'King of the Jews' had been born in Bethlehem, Herod ordered the execution there of all boys under two years old. No documentary evidence supports this claim.

Batanaea and Trachonitis by Caligula in AD 37 (receiving Galilee and Peraea in AD 39 after Herod Antipas was exiled) and king of Judaea in AD 41 by Claudius, at which point his domains rivalled those held previously by Herod the Great. Herod Agrippa was a charming and shrewd king, friend of Caligula and Claudius, and after his grandfather, the most powerful Jew of the century — but he died too soon to fulfil his potential.

• Herod of Chalcis (d. AD 48), son of Prince Aristobulus, brother of Herod Agrippa I and Herodias, who became tetrarch of Chalcis (ancient Syria) in AD 41 and was entrusted with overseeing the Jerusalem Temple following Herod Agrippa's death.

Finally, two great-grandsons continued the dynasty:

• Tigranes VI, son of Prince Alexander, was made king of Armenia by Nero in AD 58.

• Herod Agrippa II (AD 27–100), son of Herod Agrippa I, was ruler of Chalcis in AD 50, later receiving Abilene, Trachonitis, Acra, Galilee and Peraea. He advanced Hellenistic culture and tried to dissuade Jews from the AD 66–70 revolt against Rome that led to the destruction of the Temple.

Herod Antipas was ruler of Galilee and Peraea from 4 BC to AD 39, ordered the execution of John the Baptist and turned Jesus over to the Roman authorities. He is depicted here in a watercolour by Jacques Tissot (1836–1902).

The Empress Livia was the murderous, vindictive and power-hungry intriguer who long dominated the court of her husband, Augustus Caesar, the first Roman emperor and founder of the Julio-Claudian dynasty that lasted until the fall of Nero. Aristocratic and intelligent, she was in many ways an asset to Augustus. Her ambitions – to avenge slights, influence politics and place her own son Tiberius on the throne, killing by poison those who stood in her way – were ruthlessly accomplished. She remains notorious as the personification of political menace, cold ruthlessness and feminine conspiracy.

Empress Livia
58 BC–AD 29

'A terrible mother for the state as a mother, a terrible stepmother for the house of the Caesars.'

PLUTARCH

Livia was born in 58 BC into the family of Marcus Livius Drusus Claudianus, a magistrate from an Italian town, whose blood lines carried a proud heritage. She was betrothed to her cousin, Tiberius Claudius Nero, in 42 BC and gave birth to her first son (also named Tiberius Claudius Nero) – the future emperor.

It was a tumultuous time, however, to be starting a family. In the civil wars that followed the murder of Julius Caesar in 44 BC, both Livia's husband and her father supported the assassins of Caesar against Caesar's heir, his great-nephew, the young Octavian, then aged 19. When Octavian and his ally Mark Antony defeated Caesar's murderers at the Battle of Philippi in 42 BC, Livia's father committed suicide. Then her husband joined the new anti-Octavian forces that gathered around Mark Antony, whose alliance with Caesar's heir had proved short-lived. As a result, the family was forced to abandon Italy in 40 BC to escape Octavian's 'proscription' of his enemies.

After a brief time in Sicily and then Greece, Tiberius Claudius Nero and his wife were persuaded to return to Rome in 39 BC, when Octavian offered an amnesty to supporters of Mark Antony. Back in the capital, Livia was introduced to Octavian for the first time, and by all accounts he immediately became besotted with her. His cold ambition and political shrewdness matched hers. By this stage, she was pregnant with a second son, Drusus, but despite this, her husband was persuaded to divorce her and present her as a political gift to Octavian.

From the moment of her marriage to Octavian, Livia carried herself in public as a reserved, dutiful and loyal wife. As her husband's political strength grew, so her status gained recognition. In 35 BC she was made *sacrosanctas*, which gave her inviolability equal to that of a tribune. The division of the Roman Empire, between Octavian who ruled the west and Antony who ruled the east, was now falling apart. In 31 BC, Octavian defeated Antony at the Battle of Actium, winning the entire Empire. Octavian took the title princeps, or first citizen, and in 27 BC he became the first emperor, given the title Augustus, 'exalted', by the Senate.

Livia was treated with ever greater reverence, with even a statue built in her lifetime – an accolade held by almost no other woman at that time. But it was behind the scenes that she wielded her greatest, often malign, influence.

The emperor Augustus, who ruled for an astonishing 40 years, was one of the greatest of all Roman emperors, famously finding Rome in brick and leaving it in marble. He was a brilliant administrator and effective politician, consolidating imperial frontiers, military power and civil service, the foundations of centuries of empire. But his only child was Julia, a daughter from a previous marriage; and given the cultural unacceptability of a female heir, it was not clear who might succeed him. It was quite clear, though, to Livia: her own sons should inherit the throne.

The emperor's first choice was his nephew, Marcus Claudius Marcellus. However, in 23 BC, Marcellus died, in strange circumstances. Livia, who cultivated various experts on poison, was suspected of murder.

Next, Augustus favoured Marcus Vipsanius Agrippa, his closest friend and his chief military commander, the victor of Actium. In 17 BC Augustus adopted Agrippa's two youngest sons, Gaius and Lucius Caesar, and the line of succession seemed to be secure.

Agrippa died in 12 BC, however, and the question of who would succeed Augustus was thrown into further doubt when, in AD 2 and 4 respectively, Lucius and Gaius died. The circumstances of the young princes' deaths were mysterious, and again Livia was widely blamed. At last, Augustus was forced to embrace the option pushed by Livia: her son Tiberius, diffident but able, was adopted as the ailing emperor's son in AD 4 – thereby establishing him as the clear heir to the throne.

Even then, however, Livia was forced into one final intervention. In AD 4, during the final rearrangement of his succession plans, Augustus also adopted Agrippa Postumus – Agrippa's sole surviving son. Within two years, Postumus was exiled from Rome, possibly because of allegations that he had been involved in a coup plot against Augustus, though again Livia's hand in events should not be discounted. Nevertheless, by AD 14 there were signs that Augustus was looking to rehabilitate his last adoptive son. Unwilling to countenance a possible late challenger to Tiberius, Livia is said to have poisoned her own husband, the aged emperor.

After Augustus's death, Agrippa Postumus was quickly murdered, and Tiberius became emperor. Livia continued to be a figure of major importance – not least because her husband had bequeathed her one third of his estate (a highly unusual move). She now became known by the title 'Julia Augusta'. Tiberius had always been appalled by her intrigues, even though they were in his favour; now he resented her interference.

When she died in AD 29 he did not attend the funeral. He also forbade her deification and refused to honour the terms of her will. Livia's most fitting eulogy was delivered by Germanicus' son Caligula (see page 31), whom she had helped to bring up in her own household. Caligula, who would himself become one of the worst and most depraved emperors, described her as a 'Ulysses in a matron's dress' – his praise perhaps the surest damnation that Livia could ever have received.

The empress Livia, here portrayed by Siân Phillips in the BBC television drama I, Claudius, which was first broadcast in 1976 and is based on Robert Graves's celebrated historical novel of the same name.

TIBERIUS AND SEJANUS

Livia's exertions in relation to the imperial succession were for Tiberius Claudius Nero, the son from her first marriage. Though Tiberius was a competent administrator and talented general, he was not his adopted father's first choice – nor, indeed, his second or third preference. Instead, power only devolved to the morose Tiberius when all other possibilities had been exhausted, which perhaps explains why he never seemed comfortable as a ruler. Much of his reign was plagued by internal unrest and political intrigue. In AD 26, tiring of affairs of state, he moved to a palace on the island of Capri and spent the last decade of his rule in semi-retirement, leaving the Praetorian Prefect, Lucius Aelius Sejanus, as *de facto* day-to-day ruler.

The ambitious Sejanus viewed his new role as a stepping-stone towards absolute power. From AD 29 he unleashed a terror. His enemies among the senatorial and equestrian classes were falsely accused of treason, tried and executed, making him the most powerful man in Rome. Sejanus also contrived to sideline Tiberius' heirs. On becoming heir to Emperor Augustus in AD 4, Tiberius had adopted his nephew Germanicus, who became a popular general and later governed the eastern part of the Empire. In AD 19, however, Germanicus died in Syria in mysterious circumstances. Tiberius' own son Drusus died in AD 23 – almost certainly poisoned by Sejanus, who was looking to further his political ambitions by marrying Drusus' widow Livilla. Tiberius, however, refused him permission to marry her. When two of Germanicus' sons were re-moved from the scene in AD 30, the succession looked

as though it must fall to Germanicus' surviving son Caligula or to Drusus' son Tiberius Gemellus. In AD 31 Sejanus, determined to seize power for himself, hatched a plot to eliminate the emperor and the surviving male members of the imperial house. Tiberius had the Praetorian Prefect arrested, then strangled and torn to pieces by a mob.

Meanwhile in Capri, Tiberius had devoted himself to more sensual pleasures since moving from Rome. The sensationalist historian Suetonius offers a flavour of what this entailed in his shocking *Life of Tiberius*:

> On retiring to Capri he devised a pleasance for his secret orgies: teams of wantons of both sexes, selected as experts in deviant intercourse and dubbed analists, copulated before him in triple unions to excite his flagging passions. Some rooms were furnished with pornography and sex manuals from Egypt – which let the people there know what was expected of them. Tiberius also created lechery nooks in the woods and had girls and boys dressed as nymphs and Pans prostitute themselves in the open... He acquired a reputation for still grosser depravities that one can hardly bear to tell or be told, let alone believe. He had little boys trained as 'minnows' to chase him when he went swimming and to get between his legs and nibble him. He also had babies not weaned from their mother's breast suck at his chest and groin.

After Sejanus' death, the Senate issued a damnatio memoriae *('damnation of memory'). All depictions of and monuments to Sejanus were systematically destroyed. The attempted erasure of Sejanus' name can be seen on this coin, originally struck to mark his consulship.*

Caligula ascended the imperial throne as the young darling of the Romans – and ended his four-year reign with a reputation as an insanely cruel tyrant. Capricious, politically inept and militarily incompetent, sexually ambiguous and perversely incestuous, he went from beloved prince to butchered psychopath in a reign that quickly slid into humiliation, murder and madness.

Caligula AD 12–41

Caligula – properly Gaius Caesar – was the great-grandson of Augustus, the first emperor of Rome. His nickname Caligula – meaning 'little boots' – derives from the miniature army sandals he was dressed in as a boy when he accompanied his father Germanicus on campaign. This made Caligula the favourite mascot of the army. Germanicus died suddenly in AD 19, followed by Caligula's two elder brothers and his mother Agrippina. Many suspected that Caligula's great-uncle, the emperor Tiberius, had poisoned the much-loved Germanicus as a threat to his throne. In AD 31 Caligula went to live with Tiberius at his villa on the island of Capri, where the emperor was suspected of indulging in all kinds of unnatural practices. It was during this time that the dark side of Caligula's character began to emerge. As the Roman historian Suetonius (albeit not an objective source) later reported, 'He could not control his natural cruelty and viciousness, but he was a most eager witness of the tortures and executions of those who suffered punishment, revelling at night in gluttony and adultery, disguised in a wig and a long robe.' Rumours also began to circulate that Caligula was conducting an incestuous relationship with his sister Drusilla.

A still from Tinto Brass's gaudy 1970s epic Caligula, *with Malcolm McDowell in the title role. The film starred other notable mainstream actors such as Sir John Gielgud, Helen Mirren and Peter O'Toole, with a script written by Gore Vidal.* Caligula *was partly financed by* Penthouse *founder Bob Guccione, who interpolated numerous sexually explicit scenes into what had been intended as a serious historical epic.*

When Tiberius died in March AD 37 some said that Caligula had smothered the old man with a pillow. Tiberius had willed that after his death Caligula and his cousin, Tiberius Gemellus, should rule jointly, but within months of his accession, Caligula had Gemellus murdered. Caligula's lack of political experience, combined with his spoilt arrogance and lust for absolute power, would prove disastrous.

There are many examples of Caligula's megalomania. To repudiate a prophecy that he had as much chance of becoming emperor as he did of riding a horse across the Gulf of Naples, he had a bridge of ships built across the water, over which he rode in triumph, wearing the breastplate of Alexander the Great. It was also said that he elevated his favourite horse, Incitatus, to the consulship. On another occasion, while in Gaul, he ordered his troops to defeat Neptune by gathering seashells from the shore, as 'spoils of the sea'.

But not all his eccentricities were so harmless. Caligula became deeply paranoid, and made it an offence for anyone to even look at him, so sensitive was he about his increasing baldness and luxuriant body hair. Those suspected of disloyalty – often on the flimsiest of pretexts – were, prior to their execution, subjected to a variety of ingenious torments devised by the emperor, such as being covered in honey and then exposed to a swarm of angry bees.

Anyone was a potential victim. As Suetonius records, 'Many men of honourable rank were first disfigured with the marks of branding irons and then condemned to the mines, to work at building roads, or to be thrown to the wild beasts; or else he shut them up in cages on all fours, like animals, or had them sawn asunder. Not all these punishments were for serious offences, but merely for criticizing one of his shows, or for never having sworn by his Genius.'

Caligula began to believe himself to be divine. He had the heads of statues of the Olympian gods replaced with likenesses of himself, and almost provoked a Jewish revolt by ordering his godhead to be worshipped in the Temple in Jerusalem. Suetonius reports that he regularly talked to the other deities as if they stood beside him. On one occasion he asked an actor who was greater, himself or Jupiter. When the man failed to respond with sufficient alacrity, the emperor had him mercilessly flogged. His cries, Caligula claimed, were music to his ears. On another occasion, when dining with the two consuls, he started laughing manically. When asked why, he retorted, 'What do you expect, when with a single nod of my head both of you could have your throats cut on the spot?' Similarly, he used to kiss his wife's neck whilst whispering, 'Off comes this beautiful head whenever I give the word. If only Rome had one neck.' The most repugnant story of the emperor's depravity tells how, after he had made his sister Drusilla pregnant, he was so impatient to see his child that he ripped it from her womb. Whether this story is true or not, Drusilla is known to have died in AD 38, probably of a fever, whereupon Caligula declared her to be a goddess.

Caligula's unbridled narcissism and ever greater appetite for brutality alienated every section of society. The Praetorian Guard resolved that his rule must be brought to an end, and in January AD 41 two of its number killed the emperor by stabbing him in the genitals. They went on to kill his wife and baby daughter, smashing the latter's head against the wall.

The life of Caligula demonstrated how much the imperial system created by Augustus, whilst preserving the trappings of the Republic, had actually concentrated absolute power in the hands of one man. Caligula stripped away the veneer of constitutional restraint and flaunted his total authority over his subjects in the most capriciously horrific manner. Caligula personifies the immorality, bloodlust and insanity of absolute power.

Elagabalus

Caligula was just one of a number of crazed Roman emperors who fancied themselves at least semi-divine. One of the most notorious of these was Marcus Aurelius Antoninus, who, when he became emperor in AD 218, adopted the name Elagabalus, the sun god worshipped in the Syrian city of Emesa. The new emperor offended traditionally minded Romans by instituting the worship of this foreign god as the new state religion, and by taking as his wife one of Rome's Vestal Virgins.

His homosexual escapades with numerous court 'favourites' – such as the charioteer Hierocles – scandalized the Romans. Elagabalus liked to pretend that he was a female prostitute and dreamed of having a vagina surgically transplanted into his body. The Romans were appalled at an emperor who wished to become a woman by having his male genitalia mutilated. Certainly the only ruler in history to publicly contemplate such a meta-morphosis, Elagabalus was probably the first recorded transsexual. A more fanciful tale tells how he smothered the guests at a banquet by pouring masses of rose petals over them from the ceiling.

Challenged increasingly by family rivals, in 222 Elagabalus attempted to eliminate his cousin and heir, Alexander (whom he had been forced to adopt by his grandmother), in an effort to secure his position. The attempt failed and he and his mother were murdered in the imperial privy, and their bodies dumped in the River Tiber. Alexander was proclaimed as the new emperor.

Like Caligula two centuries earlier, Elagabalus stands as a testament to the inadequacies of the system of succession in imperial Rome. It could result in pampered, ill-suited youths attaining a position of absolute power by mere dint of family circumstance, with little in the way of preparation or experience. The emperor would then decline into ever more bizarre behaviour, leading to his physical annihilation.

The Roses of Heliogabalus by Sir Lawrence Alma-Tadema (1888), a lush Victorian depiction of Elagabalus's banquet, in which guests were crushed under rose petals. This extraordinary method of assassination was first mentioned in the Augustan History *(2nd–3rd century), but is now widely regarded as a propagandistic myth.*

The emperor who 'fiddled while Rome burned', Nero was the last of the Julio-Claudian dynasty that took Rome from Republic to one-man rule. Raised amidst violence and tyranny, he ruled with ludicrous vanity, demented whimsy and inept despotism. Few mourned his abdication and death amidst the chaos that he himself had created.

Nero AD 37–68

Lucius Domitius Ahenobarbus was born in AD 37 in the town of Antium, not far from Rome, while the emperor Caligula – Nero's uncle – was on the throne. Like so many, he was to suffer at Caligula's hands – forced with his mother Agrippina into exile when she lost favour with the emperor. They were allowed to return by Caligula's successor, Claudius, who had recently executed his nymphomaniacal empress, Messalina. In AD 49 Agrippina became the emperor's fourth wife. Claudius not only adopted Nero as his son but made him heir to the throne over his own son by Messalina, Britannicus.

Charles Laughton as the Roman emperor Nero in The Sign of the Cross *(1932), a film produced and directed by Cecil B. DeMille in his typically lavish and flamboyant style.*

Agrippina, however, was unwilling to allow nature to take its course and in AD 54 she poisoned Claudius (her husband), thereby casting a dark cloud over her son's reign from the outset. Relations between mother and son were also flawed, and when, in the following year, Agrippina realized her hold over Nero was slipping, she conspired in a plot to replace him with Britannicus. On discovering the conspiracy, Nero promptly had his rival poisoned and banished Agrippina from the imperial palace on the pretext of having insulted his young wife, Octavia.

Despite such intrigues, the early years of Nero's reign were marked by wise governance, largely because much state business was handled by shrewd advisers such as the philosopher Seneca and the Praetorian Prefect Burrus. This relative calm was not destined to last. Increasingly assured, Nero sought to free himself from the control of others and exercise power in his own right.

The first to feel the consequences of his new assertiveness was his mother, who had continued plotting behind his back. Tired of her machinations, Nero resolved to do away with her in AD 59. When an initial attempt to drown her in the Bay of Naples proved unsuccessful, the emperor sent an assassin to complete the job. Legend has it that, realizing what was about to happen as the killer approached, Agrippina drew back her clothes and cried, in one final act of scorn for her matricidal son, 'Here, smite my womb!'

With his mother out of the way, Nero's reign quickly sank into petty despotism. Burrus and Seneca were both brought to trial on trumped-up charges, and though eventually acquitted lost much of their influence. Yet, even as he gained greater control over the levers of power, so the emperor appeared increasingly to lose touch with reality. He became infatuated with Poppaea Sabina, wife of one of his friends, and resolved to marry her. According to the historian Suetonius, Poppaea's husband was 'persuaded' to grant her a divorce, while Nero's wife Octavia was first exiled and then murdered on the emperor's orders – paving the way for the Nero–Poppaea union.

In AD 64, a huge fire swept through Rome which the emperor observed with indifference. Indeed, according to the Roman chronicler Tacitus, Nero himself was behind the inferno. In an effort to divert attention, Nero sought a scapegoat, thus beginning his persecution of the Christians. Tacitus recounts the atrocities committed: 'Mockery of every sort was added to their deaths. Covered with the skins of beasts, they were torn by dogs and perished, or were nailed to crosses, or were doomed to the flames and burnt, to serve as a nightly illumination, when daylight had expired.'

Increasingly convinced that rivals were plotting against him, Nero had anyone he considered a threat executed, including, between AD 62–3, Marcus Antonius Pallas, Rubellius Plautus and Faustus Sulla. Then, in AD 65, a conspiracy led by Gaius Calpurnius Piso to oust the emperor and restore the Republic was uncovered. Nearly half of the 41 accused were either executed or forced to commit suicide, Seneca among them. In the same year that Rome burned, Nero began to sing and act on the public stage, spending more time in the theatre than running the Empire. He also fancied himself as a sportsman, even taking part in the Olympic Games of AD 67 – ostensibly to improve relations with Greece, but more likely to milk the obsequious praise that invariably greeted his efforts. He won various awards – mostly secured in advance by hefty bribes from the imperial exchequer.

By AD 68, elements within the army – which the dilettante emperor had largely ignored – decided that things could not continue. The governor of one of the provinces in Gaul rebelled and persuaded a fellow governor, Galba, to join him. Galba emerged as a popular focus for opposition to Nero and, crucially, the Praetorian Guard now declared their support for him. Faced with the desertion of the army, Nero was forced to flee Rome and went into hiding; a short time later, he committed suicide. His legacy was one of unrest across the Empire, as Rome suffered the Year of the Four Emperors, during which civil war broke out between competing claimants to the throne. Hostilities ended only with the emergence of Vespasian and the founding of the Flavian dynasty.

AGRIPPINA

Legend has it that when Agrippina consulted astrologers about the future of her son Nero, they predicted he would rule the Empire but kill his mother. Her response? 'Let him kill me, provided he becomes emperor.' However apocryphal the tale, it captures the burning intensity of Agrippina's all-encompassing ambition: to see her son placed on Rome's imperial throne.

Born in AD 15, Agrippina was raised, after the death of her father Germanicus (the intended heir of Tiberius), by her mother, Agrippina the Elder, in concert with her great-grandmother, the domineering matriarch Livia (see page 28). Her first marriage was to Gnaeus Domitius Ahenobarbus, who fathered Nero in AD 37 but died three years later. Following the death of Emperor

Tiberius, Agrippina rose to prominence during the reign of her brother, Caligula (see page 31), whose rumoured incestuous relationship with his sisters was one of the scandals of the age. After Caligula's feelings towards her cooled, she joined her lover, Marcus Aemilius Lepidus, in a plot to murder him, spending the next two years in exile after the scheme was uncovered. However, Caligula's murder in AD 41 prompted her uncle, the new emperor Claudius, to bring her back to Rome , whereupon she married the wealthy Gaius Sallustius Passienus Crispus, only for him also to die in AD 47 amid rumours that Agrippina had murdered him for his money. His death cleared the way for her to marry Claudius, which she duly did in AD 49. Five years later, having successfully persuaded Claudius to adopt Nero as his heir, she had him poisoned at a banquet.

Nero dissecting his mother, in an illumination from De Casibus Virorum Illustrium ('On the Fates of Famous Men') by Giovanni Boccaccio (1313–75).
Nero was reputed to have had his mother killed and her body opened, so that he could see the womb that bore him.

'*Dominus et Deus*' ('Master and God'): such was the manner in which Domitian – the last emperor of the Flavian dynasty – styled himself. Extravagant showman, avid patron of the arts, paranoid tyrant, sadistic killer and persecutor of Christians, Domitian earned the damnation of history.

Domitian AD 51–96

> '*His savage cruelty was not only excessive, but also cunning and sudden . . . In this way he became an object of terror and hatred to all.*'
>
> SUETONIUS

Domitian endured a solitary childhood. His mother and sister died when he was still young, and his father and elder brother were frequently away on active military service. During the turbulent events of the 'Year of the Four Emperors' – the mini-civil war that followed the suicide of the emperor Nero in AD 68 – Domitian's father, Vespasian, a prominent legionary commander, made his bid for the imperial throne. After six months battling with rival generals – during which time the young Domitian was placed under house arrest by another claimant and even forced to flee Rome in disguise – Vespasian eventually emerged triumphant as emperor.

In the early 70s, following his marriage to Domitia Longina, Domitian was given the title of Caesar, made a praetor with consular power and became Vespasian's representative to the Senate. Throughout this period, however, Domitian was overshadowed by his father's most trusted lieutenant, Mucianus, to whom Vespasian entrusted real authority in Rome while away campaigning. Besides his elder brother, Titus, who had proved himself a brilliant general in putting down the Judaean rebellion of AD 71, was viewed as his father's heir.

A fragment from a colossal marble statue taken from the Temple of Domitian in modern-day Izmir, Turkey, and thought to be a depiction of Domitian himself.

THE PERSECUTION OF THE CHRISTIANS

Castigated by the historian Tacitus as a 'pernicious superstition', Christianity was seen as a challenge to the gods upon whom it was widely believed the success of Rome was founded. Christian practices were commonly misunderstood: the eating of the Lord's Supper, for example, was mistaken for cannibalism, and the conferring of a kiss on fellow believers taken as evidence of immorality and licentiousness. Christian belief in life after death was considered not only heretical, but as implying a thirst for martyrdom – with many Roman rulers only too happy to oblige.

From the outset, according to the New Testament, Christians were a persecuted minority, and though the governor of Judaea, Pontius Pilate, may famously have

'washed his hands' of Christianity's founder, subsequent Roman authorities took a more proactive role in suppressing its supposedly dangerous and subversive tide. Thus, of the 11 apostles who survived Jesus (Judas Iscariot having hanged himself), only John, brother of James, managed to avoid a violent death.

The first organized persecution of the sect began when Nero decided to pin the blame for Rome's great fire of AD 64 on the Christians, with horrific consequences (see page 35). Thereafter, discrimination continued under Domitian and regularly resurfaced in the centuries that followed. Repression was often localized – as when Marcus Aurelius clamped down on the Christians of Lyons in AD 177 – but it inexorably increased. In AD 250, the Emperor Decius (r. AD 249–51), fearing that Rome's fortunes were in decline because it had abandoned its traditional religious customs, issued an edict ordering the restoration of the pagan pantheon and empire-wide suppression of Christianity. In the savage wave of repression that followed, tens of thousands lost their lives, and though

The Christian Martyrs' Last Prayer by Jean-Léon Gérôme (1824–1904). The Roman historian Tacitus wrote: 'in their deaths [Christians] were made the subjects of sport; for they were wrapped in the hides of wild beasts and torn to pieces by dogs, or nailed to crosses, or set on fire, and when day declined, were burned to serve for nocturnal lights'.

Decius' death brought a brief respite, Christians faced a renewed assault under the emperor Valerian between AD 257 and 259.

A final onslaught came at the hands of Diocletian and Galerius in the early 4th century. Between AD 303 and 311, the two rulers attempted to rid the empire of Christian influence altogether, thousands being killed or driven into exile, until, in AD 313, the emperor Constantine legalized the faith and became the first Christian emperor. Thereafter, its fortunes changed dramatically, and in AD 391 it became the official state religion of the Empire with all other faiths now banned.

With limited opportunities to exert genuine power, Domitian increasingly devoted himself to the arts and literature, paying little attention to affairs of state. However, in AD 81, the premature death of Titus – just two years after succeeding his father as emperor – brought Domitian to the imperial throne. Whether Domitian was involved in his brother's death is unclear, but he was certainly swift to ensure his succession, hurrying to the Praetorian camp, where he was declared emperor even while Titus lay dying. Desperate to escape the shadow of his brother, he staged several triumphs through Rome, though the hollow victories they celebrated only emphasized his shortcomings in comparison with Titus.

The early years of Domitian's reign coincided with a severe economic downturn, forcing him to devalue the denarius and raise taxes – both highly unpopular measures. Yet, though the recession was beyond the emperor's control, he did little to alleviate things. On the contrary, as his people laboured under material hardships, he continued to indulge his love of the arts – no matter what the cost. In AD 86 he oversaw the inaugural 'Capitoline Games' – a mass sporting event (based on the Olympic Games) that was to be held every four years, featuring such pursuits as athletics and chariot-racing, as well as oratory and music.

On a darker note, Domitian unleashed waves of repression on the Roman populace. Having unexpectedly acquired the highest office, he was perpetually fearful that opponents might try to remove him. He therefore carried out ever more frequent purges of those whom he believed to be plotting within the Roman upper classes – levelling the charge of *majestas* (treason) against suspected opponents. One of the effects of this strategy, of course, was to inspire opposition where none had previously existed.

In AD 89, a revolt by Antonius Saturninus, the governor of Upper Germany, was only put down by the intervention of loyal legions from Lower Germany, to whom Domitian had judiciously awarded a pay increase. The shock of this challenge generated an even greater surge of repression, particularly against wealthy and privileged families. The confiscated property of his victims helped pay for the increasingly extravagant public expenditure of Domitian's reign, with the emperor helping himself to a new palace and villa – as well as indulging in further games and public spectacles for the people.

From AD 93, Domitian's reign descended into terror. Thereafter, senators lived in dread of denunciation by one of Domitian's paid informers or spies that frequently resulted in spuriously sanctioned executions. Meanwhile, the increasingly autocratic and unpredictable emperor downgraded the status of the Senate itself, stripping it of decision-making power. All authority was to emanate from the emperor's person, with death the price of dissent.

The execution of the emperor's cousin, Flavius Clemens, in AD 96 gave confirmation (were any still needed) that in Domitian's Rome no one was safe. A new conspiracy was hatched, this time including his own wife among the plotters, and the emperor was stabbed eight times by a member of the Praetorian Guard in a coup organized by members of the Senate and the royal family.

In the aftermath of his death, an edict of *damnatio memoriae* was issued against Domitian – the only emperor to be subject to such a measure (see also page 30). Under this decree he was to be erased from all historical records; a just end for a man who had himself cast so many of his subjects into oblivion.

Malevolent, scheming, cruel, depraved, murderous, megalomaniacal and corrupt, Commodus has recently re-entered popular consciousness in the Hollywood film *Gladiator*. Whatever its historical accuracy, that movie captured the essence of the power-crazed Commodus, whose reign, in the judgement of the English historian Edward Gibbon, marked the early decline of the Roman Empire.

Commodus AD 161–92

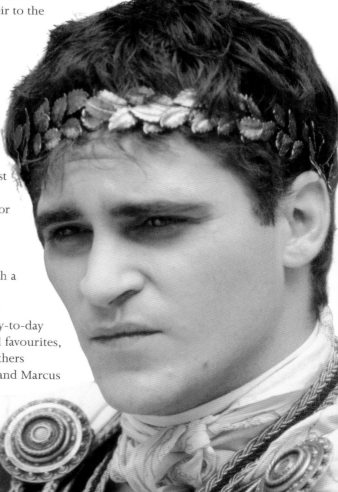

Born in Lanuvium near Rome, son of the great Marcus Aurelius, Commodus was groomed from an early age to succeed to the throne, being declared *Caesar* (effectively 'junior emperor') when he was just five years old. By AD 169, the death of his two brothers had left him as sole son and heir to the emperor, and he subsequently travelled with his father across the Empire, seeing firsthand how the business of government was conducted.

In AD 176, Commodus (still only 14) was awarded the title of *Imperator*, and a year later, that of *Augustus* as he became *de jure* co-ruler and the emperor's anointed heir. Other offices followed, including those of tribune and consul. The latter position, granted in AD 177, made him the youngest consul thus far in Rome's history. Three years later, his father died and Commodus became sole emperor in AD 180.

On attaining exclusive power, Commodus immediately signed a peace deal to end his father's military campaigns on the Danube, celebrating with a major triumph through the streets of Rome to commemorate his 'achievements'. He showed little interest, however, for affairs of state, leaving the day-to-day business of government to a succession of personal favourites, the first of whom was Saoterus – a former slave. Others included the Praetorian Prefects, Tigidius Perennis and Marcus Aurelius Cleander.

The Emperor Commodus, as portrayed by American actor Joaquin Phoenix in Ridley Scott's hugely successful epic Gladiator *(2000).*

Commodus preferred to spend time at the gladiatorial amphitheatre, both as a spectator and, more extraordinarily, as a participant. Convinced that he was the reincarnation of the mythical god-hero Hercules, he entered the arena dressed in a lion skin and carrying a club or sword. In front of startled senators and plebeians alike, the most powerful man in the Empire would comport himself like a ferocious slave (which is what most gladiators were), butchering wild beasts and slaying human opponents who had been carefully handicapped in advance. Some were reportedly wounded soldiers or amputees, brought in from the streets.

When not fighting mock battles, the emperor earned a reputation for debauchery. Rumours had it that a harem of 300 women and girls and 300 boys allowed him to play out his every sexual fantasy. Roman high society was scandalized by stories of orgies and moral decadence. Unhappiness with the drift and apparent licentiousness of Commodus' rule soon provoked unrest, and his reign became marked by a series of conspiracies and revolts. As early as 182, his eldest sister Lucilla led a plot to overthrow him; but the plans were exposed and Commodus had the conspirators executed (including Lucilla herself).

Commodus now directed a bloodspattered reign of terror. Ministers he considered insubordinate or simply insufficiently deferential were killed; so too were those who even hinted at opposition to his rule. The emperor became increasingly obsessed with personal aggrandizement, so much so that even the name 'Rome' was deemed an inadequate reflection of his majesty. The city was thus renamed *Colonia Commodiana* – the Colony of Commodus – and 're-founded' in AD 190, with Commodus portraying himself as a latter-day Romulus. He renamed the months of the year after the twelve names that he had now given himself. The legions were renamed *Commodianae*, part of the African fleet was given the title *Alexandria Commodiana Togata*, the Senate was called the Commodian Fortunate Senate, and his palace and the Roman people were all given the name *Commodianus*. Truly, this was megalomania on an enormous scale.

Unsurprisingly, conspiracies against Commodus continued, and finally, in early AD 193, a plot involving his mistress, Marcia, succeeded where others had failed. Commodus was strangled in his bath by an wrestler named Narcissus.

After his death, Rome's citizens – especially the upper classes – breathed a collective sigh of relief and the Senate proclaimed the city prefect, Publius Helivius Pertinax, as the new emperor. However, he too soon faced a challenge and the Empire slipped once more into civil war – a sad dénouement to the Antonine dynasty that had sought to end such internecine strife.

Commodus was the first emperor since Domitian – almost 80 years earlier – to take power on the basis of birth, rather than merit or force. Tragically for the future of Rome, the consequences were remarkably similar to that previous occasion. As the celebrated Roman historian Cassius Dio, observed, Commodus' rule marked the shift from 'a kingdom of gold to one of rust and iron'. *The Historia Augusta*, a collection of biographies of Roman emperors produced in the 4th century AD, records that the Senate acclaimed the following after Commodus's passing:

> Let the memory of the murderer and the gladiator be utterly wiped away . . . More savage than Domitian, more foul than Nero. As he did unto others, let it be done unto him . . . The guiltless are yet unburied; let the body of the murderer bedragged in the dust. The murderer dug up the buried; let the body of the murderer be dragged in the dust.

GLADIATORS

In the 3rd century AD the Roman satirist Juvenal complained that his fellow-citizens lived for only two things: bread and circuses. He was referring to the free food handouts and the chariot racing at the Circus Maximus, both of which the emperors subsidized in the hope of keeping the restless citizens of Rome content. But the thing that really thrilled the Romans was gladiatorial combat, in which the participants played for the highest stakes: life and death.

In Rome, these blood sports were held at the Colosseum, a circular arena where between 50,000 and 70,000 people could watch not only gladiators fighting to the death, but also shows in which convicts or Christians were torn apart by hungry lions. On one occasion at least, the ground was flooded in order to stage a mock sea battle – although there was nothing 'pretend' about the bloodshed involved.

The gladiators themselves adopted different styles of combat, from the swordsman with the *gladius* (short sword) – after which the gladiators were named – to the *retiarii* (net-fighters), so-called because they were armed with a net and trident. A typical contest ended when one gladiator had overpowered the other; he would then ask for the judgement of the sponsor – the emperor. The latter would respond with a single gesture to reflect the will of the crowd: thumbs up if the vanquished fighter was to be spared; thumbs down if he was to be slain.

Although the gladiators were drawn from the ranks of the slave class, with a few criminals thrown in, the most successful fighters attracted similar levels of adulation to modern-day celebrities, and some even found their way into the beds of respectable Roman matrons. It was this glamour that tempted a number of high-born Romans, both male and female, to try their hand in the arena – generally to the disgust of their contemporaries. However, the life of a gladiator was brutal and short, and it was resentment against such conditions that led to the great slave revolt of 73–71 BC, led by the most famous gladiator of them all – Spartacus.

Under the Republic, gladiatorial shows were put on by those who aspired to high political office; after the fall of the Republic, the emperors were the chief sponsors. The 'games' provided their patron with the opportunity to win the support and approval of the crowd: the more lavish the spectacle, the greater the kudos. The scale of some shows could be quite breathtaking: to celebrate his conquest of Dacia in AD 108–9, the emperor Trajan put on games that lasted for 123 days, and involved the slaughter of 11,000 animals and fights between 10,000 gladiators. It was only gradually, after the Roman emperors had converted to Christianity, that the most violent entertainments in the arena began to be abolished.

An early example of gladiatorial combat, as portrayed in this 4th century BC Roman mosaic. According to the Roman historian Livy, the earliest known gladiatorial games were held by the Campanians in 310 BC in commemoration of their victory over the Samnites.

Caracalla inherited an empire that was united and peaceful, but his reign as Roman emperor was to end in an abortive military expedition, slaughter, assassination and renewed civil war. In a little over six years Caracalla committed fratricide, uxoricide and indiscriminate mass murder.

Caracalla AD 186–217

'His mode of life was evil.'
SPARTIANUS

Lucius Septimius Bassianus was born in Lugdunum in Gaul in AD 186. His father was the successful general, Septimius Severus, who established himself as sole emperor in AD 197 and renamed his son Marcus Aurelius Antoninus Caesar in an effort to establish a connection with the well-respected Antonine emperors of a previous generation. However, the future emperor was widely known simply as 'Caracalla', after the hooded tunic he wore and popularized.

Educated by the finest scholars available, Caracalla in his early years was a learned, quiet and thoughtful young man, far removed from the autocratic ogre he would become in later life. Yet other less wholesome personality traits were already evolving. Forced by his father to marry Fulvia Plautilla, daughter of one of the Praetorian Guards, when he was just 14, in AD 205, he had her exiled to Sicily and her father executed for allegedly conspiring against the royal family.

Severus ruled until his death in AD 211 and seemed to have brought calm back to the Empire after the immediate post-Commodus chaos. As on previous occasions though, the prudent rule of the father was to be followed by the erratic tyranny of the son. For a few months, Caracalla ruled jointly with his brother Publius Septimius Antoninius Geta, the two of them having been elevated by their father to virtual joint rulers shortly before his death. However, personal animosity between the two men, combined with rampant ambition, ensured that the uneasy period of cooperation between them would be short-lived.

Before the end of the year, Caracalla made his move. First, Geta himself was murdered – by one account in the arms of his and Caracalla's mother. This was swiftly followed by the assassination of his wife-in-exile, Fulvia – strangled on Caracalla's orders – and her immediate family. There followed a sustained persecution of Geta's actual or suspected supporters, with Caracalla even decreeing a *damnatio memoriae* against his brother: the very memory of Geta's existence was to be expunged from Rome's historical record.

A horrific coda came in Alexandria, where Caracalla's attempts to justify the murder of Geta were greeted with derision. A satire on the episode – and on the emperor more generally – proved a step too far for Caracalla, and in AD 215, having ordered the citizens of the town to gather for his arrival, he unleashed his troops on them in an orgy of slaughter and pillage. By the time the bloodletting was over, according to one contemporary estimate, some 20,000 people had been killed. This massacre followed another in

AD 212–13 when, on a military expedition in the Rhine valley, Caracalla had ordered the wholesale slaughter of a hitherto allied Germanic tribe.

Back in Rome, Caracalla was determined to leave his mark on the Empire. Like many emperors before him, he embarked on a lavish building programme, which included construction of the splendid Baths of Caracalla. All this placed a severe strain on the Empire's finances; a strain exacerbated by the huge pay rises the emperor secured for the military (to guarantee its loyalty), as well as by his other more exotic foibles.

Throughout his reign, Caracalla was determined to emulate the feats of his great hero, Alexander the Great. It was this impulse that led him to pursue campaigns in, first, Germany and then against the Parthians in the east, whom he dreamt of conquering. Such was his idolization of Alexander that Caracalla increasingly imitated the Macedonian's style of dress and mannerisms. He even insisted that people attach the designation 'Magnus' (the Great) to his own name, just as they had to Alexander's.

Caracalla also became convinced of his own divinity. Obsessed with Serapis, the Egyptian god of the sun, to whom he believed himself related, he ordered the minting of coins that pro-claimed his heavenly status, and even had statues constructed depicting him as an Egyptian pharaoh.

Caracalla's increasingly unpredictable behaviour paved the way for his eventual assassination, which came about when he was travelling east for a campaign against the Parthians in AD 217. The circumstances of his death – which was to usher in an era of renewed upheaval across the Empire – were less than dignified: he was stabbed by one of his own guards while urinating at a road-side; perhaps a fitting end for a man who brought such humiliation upon his office. As the later Roman historian Spartianus concluded, 'this emperor [was] the most cruel of men'.

A contemporary marble head of the emperor Caracalla. The porphyry bust was a later addition.

The Barbarians

Like many Roman emperors before and after him, Caracalla campaigned against the so-called barbarians beyond the Rhine and Danube rivers. But rather than pursuing a sound strategic goal, Caracalla craved only military glory – and to this end senselessly massacred a Germanic tribe who were actually allied to Rome.

The word 'barbarian' had originally been coined by the Greeks, who called any non-Greek person *barbaros* – in imitation of their incomprehensible speech. The term encouraged a Manichean view of the world: on the one hand, the 'civilized' (i.e. the Greeks and Romans), and on the other, the 'uncivilized' (everyone else). Up to the 1st century BC the Romans had identified the Gauls as the principal group of barbarians, but once Gaul had been conquered and had grown wealthy under the *Pax Romana*, it became a prey to the new 'barbarians' – the Germanic tribes to the east. To put an end to this security threat, the emperor Augustus determined to conquer all of Germany – but his ambition was ended in AD 9 when three of his legions crossed the Rhine and were never seen alive again. A German tribal leader known to the Romans as Arminius (and by later German nationalists as Hermann) had offered to guide the Roman commander Publius Quintilius Varus and his men through the dark and difficult terrain of the Teutoburger Forest. Varus accepted, not realizing that Arminius had laid a trap. The Germans ambushed the Roman column all along its length, and in the constricted conditions of the forest the legionaries found it impossible to deploy their normal battle formations. Rome was shocked when it heard that its elite fighting force had been annihilated by the undisciplined barbarians. Henceforth Rome sought to maintain peaceable relations, only striking across the Rhine to mount punitive raids against troublesome tribes.

By the 3rd century AD the barbarian tribes fringing the Empire's borders – Franks and Alemanni along the Rhine, Goths along the lower Danube – were coming under pressure themselves from warlike nomadic peoples from the steppes to the east, above all the

The sack of Rome by the Vandal king Geiseric in 455, as portrayed by the Russian painter Karl Briullov (1799–1852).

Huns, and in turn began to push against the frontiers of the Empire. The emperors relied more and more upon the support of the legions, leading to political instability and frequent civil war: between AD 235 and 286 there were 26 different emperors, all but one of whom died a violent death.

Although the 4th century saw something of a recovery under Diocletian and Constantine, by the end of the century the Empire was divided into two. The Western Empire came under renewed pressure, and in 410 Rome itself was sacked by the Visigoths. The last Roman emperor in the west was deposed in 476 and replaced by Odoacer, king of the Goths. The Eastern Empire, based in Constantinople, was to prosper gloriously for another thousand years, until it fell in 1453 to the Ottoman Turks.

Attila, king of the Huns from 434 to 453, was an outstanding general and formidable warrior with a voracious appetite for gold, land and power. Defeated only once, he was the most powerful of the barbarian rulers who fed off the last vestiges of the crumbling Roman Empire. According to legend, he carried the 'Sword of Mars', bestowed on him by the gods as a sign he would rule the world.

Attila the Hun 406–53

'He was a man born into the world to shake the nations, the scourge of all lands, who in some way terrified all mankind by the dreadful rumours noised abroad concerning him.'

JORDANES, THE ORIGIN AND DEEDS OF THE GOTHS, 6TH-CENTURY GOTH HISTORIAN

The Huns were a collection of tribes from the Eurasian steppe, with a fearsome reputation (the Great Wall of China was built to keep them at bay). Basing themselves in what is now Hungary, they took advantage of the decline of the Roman Empire during the 4th and 5th centuries to expand their territories, until, at its peak under Attila, their empire stretched from the River Danube to the Baltic Sea, encompassing large swathes of Germany, Austria and the Balkans.

Attila was said to be as ugly as he was successful: short, squat and swarthy with a large head, deep-set eyes, squashed nose and sparse beard. Aggressive and short-tempered, he was every inch a soldier, eating meat served on wooden dishes while his lieutenants ate assorted delicacies off silver plates. In the Hunnic tradition, he would often eat and negotiate on horseback, while at camp he was entertained by a fool, dwarf or one of his many young wives.

In 434, Attila's uncle, King Ruglia, died, leaving Attila and his older brother Bleda in joint charge of the kingdom. The Roman Empire had long since been divided into two, the Eastern (also known as the Byzantine) Empire being ruled in Attila's time by

A 19th-century lithograph of Attila the Hun by Raymond Delamarre. Dubbed 'the scourge of God', Attila's insatiable passion for conquest has earned him a unique place of notoriety in human history.

Theodosius II. To avoid attack from the Huns, Theodosius had agreed to pay an annual tribute, but when he defaulted on payments, Attila invaded Byzantine territory, capturing and destroying several important cities, including Singidunum (Belgrade).

Following an uneasy truce negotiated in 442, Attila attacked again the following year, destroying numerous towns and cities along the Danube and massacring their inhabitants. The slaughter in the city of Naissus (in what is present-day Serbia) was so great that, several years later, when Roman ambassadors arrived there for negotiations with Attila, they had to camp outside the city to escape the stench of rotting flesh. Countless other cities endured a similar fate. According to one contemporary account: 'There was so much killing and bloodletting that no one could number the dead. The Huns pillaged the churches and monasteries, and slew the monks and virgins . . . They so devastated Thrace that it will never rise again and be as it was before.' Constantinople was only spared because Attila's forces were unable to penetrate the capital's walls, so he turned instead on the Byzantine army, inflicting a crushing and bloody defeat. Peace came at the cost of repaying the tribute owed and tripling future payments. Then, around 445, Bleda was murdered, leaving Attila in sole command of the kingdom. Another assault on the Eastern Empire followed in 447, as the Huns struck further east, burning down churches and monasteries as they, and using battering rams and siege towers to smash their way into cities, which they again razed to the ground, butchering the inhabitants.

Attila's only defeat came when he invaded Gaul in 451. His initial intention had been to attack the Visigothic kingdom of Toulouse rather than to overtly challenge Roman interests in the area. In 450, however, Honoria – the sister of Valentinian III, the western emperor – appealed to Attila to rescue her from an arranged marriage to a Roman senator. Having received her engagement ring, Attila took this as a proposal of marriage and demanded half of Rome's Western Empire as a dowry. When the Romans refused, Attila invaded Gaul with a massive army. In response, the Roman general Flavius Aetius combined his forces with the Visigoths to resist the Hun invasion. The rival armies clashed at Orléans, and in the ensuing Battle of Châlons (in modern Champagne), in which thousands of men from both sides were killed, the Huns were forced to retreat. It was one of the last great victories for the Western Empire but a pyrrhic one, for their forces were spent.

When the Huns invaded Italy in 452, Aetius was powerless to stop them. Mobile and rapacious, Attila's armies sacked and burned yet more towns and cities, including Aquileia, Patavium (Padua), Verona, Brixia (Brescia), Bergomum (Bergamo) and Mediolanum (Milan). Only an outbreak of illness among Attila's troops slowed his campaign, but by the spring, he was on the verge of taking Rome itself, in which the western roman emperor, Valentinian III, had taken refuge. It took a direct appeal from Pope Leo I to dissuade him from sacking the city, Attila agreeing to go no further south.

Attila's death came in 453 after a night of heavy drinking following his marriage to another young bride. He suffocated in a pool of blood after suffering a heavy nosebleed while asleep. The soldiers who buried him were killed afterwards, so that none of his enemies would ever be able to find and desecrate his grave.

To his people, Attila was an idol, helping to consolidate a mighty and prosperous empire. The sixth century Gothic historian Jordanes later described him as a 'lover of war, yet restrained in action, mighty in counsel, gracious to suppliants and lenient to those who were once received into his protection'. Yet to the Romans he was the 'Scourge of God', 'the ravager of the provinces of Europe', personally responsible for wanton cruelty and violence, and in Dante's *Divine Comedy*, he appeared in the seventh circle of Hell.

HUNS, GOTHS AND VANDALS

The names of three 'barbarian' peoples have taken on very different modern meanings.

During the First World War the Germans were colloquially described as 'Huns'. This usage is generally believed to have its origins in British press reports of a speech by Kaiser Wilhelm II in 1900, in which he urged his troops in China to fight 'like the Huns'. More far-fetched explanations include: (1) spiked German helmets of the period resembled those worn by the Huns; (2) the word *uns* in the phrase *Gott mit uns* ('God with us') emblazoned on German soldiers' buckles was mistakenly rendered as 'Huns'.

'Goths' originally denoted 3rd–6th-century Germanic tribes, while 'Gothic' refers to a late-medieval style of architecture and genre of late 18th – and early 19th – century, Romantic horror literature. But after Tony Wilson described the music of the group Joy Division as 'Gothic' on a 1978 TV programme, 'Goths' came to denote a post-punk subculture, which began in the London nightclub the Batcave in the 1980s and spread rapidly. Spurning punk violence in favour of art, literature and mystical religion, Goths adopted black clothing, often accentuated by whitened faces and blackened eyes, in stark contrast to the colour and effervescent of the contemporary disco scene.

The term 'Vandals', originally meaning wanderers, was the name of a Germanic tribe who, having created a kingdom in North Africa in the early 5th century, sacked Rome in 455, wantonly destroying priceless cultural treasures, and subsequently left a trail of mayhem through Gaul, Spain and Italy. Their name lies behind the words 'vandalize' and 'vandalism', denoting acts of gratuitous destruction.

The Course of Empire by the American artist Thomas Cole (1801–48), a spectacularly imagined depiction of the fall of Rome. The sack of Rome by Alaric's Visigoths in 410 revealed to the world the declining power of the Roman Empire.

Theodora – murderous, amoral and power-hungry – was born in the gutter, prospered as an actress, prostitute and sexual performer, and reached her apotheosis as the hated wife of Justinian, one of Byzantium's greatest emperors. The most astonishing contradiction in the otherwise shrewd and capable Justinian was his love for this extraordinary, intelligent, vain, greedy, corrupt and ruthless woman.

Empress Theodora
c. 497–548

'No other tyrant since mankind began ever inspired such fear, since not a word could be spoken against her without her hearing of it: her multitude of spies brought her the news of whatever was said and done in public or in private.'

PROCOPIUS, THE SECRET HISTORY

(6TH CENTURY AD)

What little we know of Theodora's early life mostly comes from Procopius' *Secret History*. Daughter of a bear trainer in the Hippodrome, her first career was in the theatre, as an actress working on the seamier side of her profession. She quickly gained a reputation both for her beauty and for her readiness to appear in the lewd burlesque shows that were then all the rage in Constantinople. As Procopius noted, 'No role was too scandalous for her to accept without a blush.' In one particularly striking sketch, she would lie on her back, all but naked, while grain was scattered across her entire body. Geese (representing the god-king Zeus) would then peck up the food with their bills – to the gratification of the prostrate Theodora.

Her insatiable sexual appetite became the stuff of legend. 'Often she would go picnicking with ten young men or more, in the flower of their strength and virility, and dallied with them all, the whole night through,' writes Procopius, adding that she preferred to leave none of her three orifices unfilled. It was later rumoured that she had slipped into a life of high-class prostitution. Certainly, she appears to have served as a courtesan to the wealthy and powerful of Byzantium, and it was at this time that she fell pregnant and gave birth to her only child, a son.

After struggling for several years to get by, Theodora struck gold. The elderly emperor Justin had adopted his able nephew, Justinian. The younger man fell madly in love with Theodora and brought her into the imperial household as his mistress. Such was his influence with Justin that the law was changed to allow marriage to an actress, and when he succeeded to the throne in 527 he officially made her his Augusta. Within five years she had shown her mettle by taking control during the Nika riots, which threatened Justinian's very position as emperor (see page 52).

Justinian treated Theodora as his partner in power, and many regarded her as dangerously over-mighty in her malice and intrigues. But the partnership worked. Justinian achieved great glory during his highly successful reign: he embellished his capital and also Jerusalem, codified the laws, delivered stability, administered superbly, and, using his brilliant general, Belisarius, reconquered swathes of the old Roman Empire in Spain, Italy and North Africa. Belisarius also defeated the Persians. It was a remarkable performance – and Theodora must get some of the credit.

On the debit side, the empress was utterly ruthless in maintaining her own position. She built up a secret police force and sent her spies to infiltrate any group that might serve as a potential base for opposition to the regime. Political opponents were seized by unknown assailants, flogged and – at least in the case of a man called Basanius – castrated and left to die. Others who earned her displeasure found themselves confined in the warren of private dungeons beneath her palace; among those she kept here, it was said, was her own son, whom she feared would cause her embarrassment. Those who might emerge as rivals for her husband's affections – such as the Gothic queen Amalasontha – were murdered.

All official appointments had to be approved by Theodora, as did all the marriages amongst imperial courtiers. Meanwhile, any sense of moral propriety was abandoned at court, which became notorious for its licentious, overindulgent ways.

The imperial couple were lucky to have in Belisarius one of the greatest generals of all time. Belisarius' career was undoubtedly aided by his marriage to Theodora's friend Antonina. Justinian, however, fearing Belisarius' prestige might threaten his own throne, treated him appallingly. He twice recalled the general in disgrace from Italy and later from Mesopotamia. It was only Theodora's interventions that saved him.

Theodora died, probably of cancer, aged about 50, after two decades of untrammelled authority. As for Justinian, he lived too long: the last ten years of his reign were a disaster. Perhaps the feared empress brought him luck; perhaps she was also a sharp politician. While alive, no one had dared to oppose the empress's commands, for all knew the penalties if they did. As Procopius wrote: 'When this female was enraged, no church offered sanctuary, no law gave protection, no intercession of the people brought mercy to her victim; nor could anything else in the world stop her.'

The empress Theodora depicted in a sixth-century Byzantine mosaic located in Ravenna, Italy. Many of the most scandalous stories about the empress come from Procopius's Anekdota *or* Secret History, *which included details that Procopius claimed he could not publish in his official history of the reign of Theodora's husband, Justinian I.*

THE NIKA RIOTS

During the Byzantine era the only place to be on a public holiday was the Hippodrome. There, thousands of supporters would cram in to watch their sporting icons – the charioteers – compete for honours. There were four main teams – each with their own set of fans and each defined by the colours they wore: whites, reds, greens and blues, later consolidated into two teams, the Blues and Greens. The emperor Justinian himself was a known supporter of the Blues.

In the absence of any other avenue for popular political expression, the factions served as an outlet for all grievances. Often spectators would harangue the emperor with political demands between races. When Justinian arrived at the Hippodrome in January 532, after months of popular discontent, the stage was set for a week-long rebellion that nearly brought about his downfall. By the end of the first day's competition, the Blues and Greens had united to chant 'Nika' ('win') in expression of their unhappiness with the emperor's policies.

As the baying mob at the Hippodrome declared their allegiance to an alternative emperor, riots broke out, and as Constantinople slipped out of his control, Justinian lost his nerve and prepared to flee. But Theodora stiffened his resolve, saying she would prefer to die in the imperial purple than live without it. She then devised the plan to crush the opposition forces. She and Justinian sent an emissary to the Hippodrome to buy off half the assembled crowd – a tactic that duly succeeded. Then troops under General Belisarius, a protégé of the empress, were sent in to deal with the remainder. The sand on the floor of the stadium was stained dark red as some 30,000 were slaughtered.

Extraordinary as it may seem that a sporting event could carry such political ramifications in sixth-century Byzantium, a comparable episode occurred in late-20th-century Europe. In May 1990, as Yugoslavia began to come apart under the strain of various competing nationalisms – particularly the virulent Serb nationalism promoted by Slobodan Milošević – the country was rocked by a major football riot between Croatian and Serb football fans. During a game between Dinamo Zagreb (of Croatia) and Red Star Belgrade (of Serbia) in the former's Maksimir stadium, Red Star's Delije ('Heroes') attacked the opposing team's fans – aided by Serb-dominated police. In response, Zagreb's 'Bad Blue Boys' gang broke through the police lines and many Red Star fans were assaulted. By the riot's end over 60 people had been hurt on both sides. The incident confirmed the ascendancy of Croat and Serb nationalisms and intensified the violent breakup of Yugoslavia.

The citizens of Pompeii and Neceria fight it out in the amphitheatre, AD 59, in a wall painting from Pompeii: a fascinating example of ancient sporting hooliganism, a full 400 years before the Nika riots.

The only woman in Chinese history to rule in her own right, the empress Wu was both depraved, mass-murdering megalomaniac and intelligent puppeteer. Beginning life as the emperor's concubine, she dominated the imperial court for over half a century, eventually achieving absolute power as the self-styled 'Heavenly Empress'.

Empress Wu 625–705

> '*Wu is a treacherous monster! May it be that I be reincarnated as a cat and she be reincarnated as a mouse, so that I can, for ever and ever, grab her throat.*'
>
> CONSORT XIAO, ONE OF EMPRESS WU'S MANY VICTIMS

Wu Zhao, as she was then known, was only 13 when in 638 she entered the imperial palace as a concubine of the emperor Taizong. From an early age she was aware of the power that flowed from her good looks and intelligence, and by the time Taizong died a decade or so later, she had already ingratiated herself with his son and heir, Gaozong.

As was customary for concubines following the death of their master, Wu Zhao spent a brief period in retreat at a Buddhist convent. But within a couple of years she was back at the centre of imperial court life, her return being partly driven by the empress Wang, Gaozong's wife: jealous of one of her husband's other concubines, Consort Xiao, Wang had hoped that Wu might divert his attention. It was to be a fatal move.

As Wang had anticipated, Wu quickly displaced Xiao as the new emperor's favourite concubine, and went on to bear him four sons. But Wu now wanted power for herself, and sought ways of eliminating the influence of the empress Wang. When in 654 Wu gave birth to a daughter who died shortly afterwards, Wu ensured that Wang emerged as prime suspect in the baby's death. Gaozong believed his concubine over his wife and duly had both Wang and Consort Xiao removed from their positions. In their place, Wu became empress.

The empress Wu Zetian, who usurped power during the Tang dynasty in China in the late 7th century. The empress was famed for her beauty and intelligence as well as her ruthlessness. This image is taken from an 18th-century album of portraits depicting Chinese rulers.

Increasingly, Gaozong suffered from debilitating bouts of ill-health, giving the empress Wu greater opportunities to exert her power. She used her agents to spy on and eliminate potential rivals and officials whose loyalty she doubted – including members of her own family. Some were demoted, some exiled – and many put to death. Among the hundreds who were strangled, poisoned or butchered were the former empress Wang and Consort Xiao, whose murders Wu ordered after it emerged that Gaozong might consider pardoning them. An atmosphere of general terror spread through the imperial court, with servile obedience the only guarantor of survival.

In 675, with Gaozong's health deteriorating still further, the empress Wu manoeuvred for the succession. The emperor's aunt, Princess Zhao, whom he had appeared increasingly to favour, was placed under house arrest and starved to death. Then Wu's son, Crown Prince Li Hong, died suddenly – poisoned by an 'unknown' hand. He was replaced by his brother – Wu's second son – Li Xian. Wu's relationship with him also quickly broke down, and in 680 Wu had him charged with treason and exiled. He was later forced to 'commit suicide'. The line of succession now passed to a third son, Li Zhe.

When Gaozong finally died in 684, it was Li Zhe who became emperor, taking the new name Zhongzong. Needless to say, real authority still lay with Wu, now empress dowager. When Zhongzong looked as if he was about to challenge her power, she had him deposed and replaced him with another of her sons, who became Emperor Ruizong.

Wu now exercised even greater control, preventing Ruizong from meeting any officials or conducting any government business. Anyone who questioned this state of affairs was summarily removed and, frequently, executed. In 686 she offered to return imperial powers to Ruizong, but he had the good sense to decline.

Ever on the lookout for possible threats to her position, Wu encouraged her secret police to infiltrate official circles and identify would-be conspirators. In 688 a putative plot against the empress dowager was smashed, and this sparked a particularly ferocious round of political killings. False accusations, torture and forced 'suicides' became almost routine. Then, in 690, following a series of 'spontaneous' petitions demanding that the empress dowager take the throne herself, she acceded to the request. Ruizong was demoted to crown prince and Wu became emperor.

For the next 15 years Wu ruled using the same ruthless methods that had guaranteed her elevation, and politically motivated denunciations and state-sanctioned killings remained commonplace. In 693 the wife of her son Ruizong (the former emperor and now heir again) was accused of witchcraft and executed. Ruizong was too afraid of his mother to object.

Eventually, in 705, with her own health now failing, Wu was prevailed upon by Ruizong to surrender the throne. Unlike so many of her own victims, she died peacefully in her bed that same year, at the age of 80. Whilst she was in power, imperial politics had been reduced to little more than a deadly game, in which many ended up losers. An old Chinese proverb has it that the rule of a woman is like having a 'hen crow like a rooster at daybreak'. Given the country's experience with Empress Wu, it is scarcely surprising that she has been the only person to put that maxim to the test.

MADAME MAO

The 20th century produced a communist equivalent of the figure of Empress Wu, in the form of Jiang Qing, a.k.a. 'Madame Mao', ambitious, ruthless and dogmatic.

An only child and the daughter of a concubine, Jiang became an actress after leaving university, acquiring an enduring belief in the importance of the arts. In the late 1930s, however, she met Mao Zedong, future founder of the People's Republic of China, after joining the Communist side in China's civil war, becoming his fourth and final wife in 1939 (see page 228). Since Mao was still married at the time, she had to keep a low profile for many years.

In 1966, however, Mao appointed her deputy director of the Cultural Revolution, a vast revolutionary terror, in partnership with Zhang Chunqiao (a one-time journalist), Yao Wenyuan (a literary critic) and Wang Hongwen (a former security guard) – the so-called Gang of Four. She zealously directed the repression, manipulated by Mao. Her call for radical forms of expression, instilled with 'ideologically correct' subject matter, escalated into an all-out assault on the existing artistic and intellectual elites. Renowned for her inflammatory rhetoric, she manipulated mass-communication techniques to whip young Revolutionary Guards into a frenzy before sending them out to attack – verbally and physically – anything 'bourgeois' or 'reactionary'. In an orgy of denunciation, terror and murder, the Communist Party, including moderates like President Liu Shaoqi and General Secretary Deng Xiaoping, was purged. The real victims were ordinary citizens – around three million of whom were killed while countless others were imprisoned or brutalized.

Though Mao hated her, Jiang remained powerful. On his death in 1976, his successor Deng ended her ascendancy and arrested Madame Mao in a palace coup. In 1981 Jiang was found guilty of 'counter-revolutionary' crimes. Her death sentence was commuted to life imprisonment but she committed suicide in 1991. A hated figure, she was described by one biographer as a 'vicious woman who helped dispose of many people'; the 'white-boned demon' who, in her own words (when on trial), was 'Chairman Mao's dog. Whomever he asked me to bite, I bit.'

向江青同志学习 向江青同志致敬

《工农兵画报》编辑部1967.6 定价每份0.15元

A propaganda lithograph of Jiang Qing, last wife of Chairman Mao. Jiang was the notorious leader of the 'Gang of Four', found guilty in 1981 of masterminding the excesses of the Cultural Revolution.

Justinian *Rhinotmetus* (the *Slit-Nose*) was the twice-reigning Byzantine emperor whose unsuccessful military campaigns, bloody massacres, relentless vindictiveness, religious intolerance, capricious tyranny, personal sadism and mutilated golden nose made him a grotesque monster even by the standards of the Eastern Empire.

Justinian II 669–711

'His passions were strong; his understanding was feeble; and he was intoxicated with a foolish pride that his birth had given him the command of millions, of whom the smallest community would not have chosen him for their local magistrate.'

EDWARD GIBBON, *THE HISTORY OF THE DECLINE AND FALL OF THE ROMAN EMPIRE*

Justinian, the eldest son of Constantine IV, was made joint emperor by his father in 681 when he was just 11, becoming sole ruler four years later, when Constantine died. He proved a capable ruler at first, manoeuvring successfully – both militarily and diplomatically – to restore previously lost territories. After a bold assault on Armenia, he reached a new agreement with the Muslim Umayyad caliphs to the east that regularized and increased the tribute they paid to his empire, which regained control over part of Cyprus.

With the eastern border thus secured, he turned his attention to the Balkans – where former Byzantine lands had fallen to Slavic rule. A major military campaign in 688–9 saw Justinian overpower the Bulgars of Macedonia and seize the major city of Thessalonica. Emboldened by his successes, in 691–2 he renewed hostilities against the Arabs in Armenia. Much of the manpower for this new assault was provided by the conquered Slavs, some 30,000 of whom had been drafted into Justinian's armies. Almost inevitably, this conscript force proved unreliable and many were bribed to change sides. Outnumbered and outfought, Justinian's forces were driven out of Armenia altogether by 695.

These foreign reverses were matched by brutal repression domestically – much of it religiously based. The Manichaean sect was singled out as dangerously subversive. So too were other manifestations of non-Orthodox Christianity. In 692, Justinian had established the 'Quinisext Council' to codify a more rigid interpretation of the Orthodox faith. The 102 disciplinary canons issued by the Council were henceforth to be imposed throughout the Empire – regardless of how far they clashed with other Christian practices, especially in the West. Unsurprisingly, Pope Sergius I refused to endorse the Council's conclusions.

Outraged by this papal defiance, Justinian immediately dispatched an army to compel Pope Sergius to accept the new rules, but he was undone again by troop disloyalty when his forces switched sides at Ravenna and backed the spiritual, rather than temporal, leader. It was an ominous portent for Justinian. Yet the emperor merely increased the scale of his religious and financial exactions – using the latter for a self-aggrandizing building spree across Constantinople.

Inevitably, discontent eventually erupted into popular revolt in 695 – led by one of the empire's most prominent generals, Leontius. Deposed from his throne, Justinian had his tongue cut out and nose slit, being exiled to Cherson in the Crimea. There he remained brooding for the best part of a decade, while successor emperors came and went. Leontius, who raised himself to the role of emperor after Justinian's removal, was deposed by Tiberios III in 698.

Then, in 702–3, Justinian escaped confinement and made his way to the khanate of the Khazars (who ruled the south of modern European Russia). There, the Khan of the Khazars received the former emperor warmly and even gave him his sister, Theodora, as a bride. Friendship soon turned to betrayal when the emperor Tiberios bribed the Khan to assassinate Justinian. But, forewarned by his wife of the attack, Justinian fled to the Bulgars and entered a new alliance with the Bulgar Khan, Tervel, who agreed to help Justinian (in return for lands and title) and supplied 15,000 horsemen for a march on Constantinople. The emperor regained his throne in 705, sporting a solid gold nose to conceal his mutilation and speaking in tongueless grunts through an interpreter..

The emperor now rashly attempted to reverse the concessions he had made to Tervel – but was defeated in 708. This setback was followed by further disasters against the Arab Umayyad caliphate in the east, with losses in Asia Minor, Cilicia and Cappadocia.

These foreign calamities were matched by the despotism of Justinian's domestic rule, which again bore theological undertones. Still determined to enforce the authority of the Quinisext Council, he dispatched another military expedition towards Ravenna – and this time it succeeded in forcing the new pope, Constantine, to accept the Council's religious directives.

Meanwhile, the restored emperor exhibited a relentless vindictiveness. The former emperors Leontius and Tiberios III were both mutilated and executed, along with many of their supporters, while the Patriarch of Constantinople, Kallinikos I, was deposed and blinded. Justinian ordered a frenzy of mass executions across the Empire. Eventually, this terror alienated even those who had supported Justinian's return. In 711, a fresh revolt broke out, centred on Cherson, and another general, Bardanes, proclaimed himself Emperor Philippicus and sailed for Constantinople. In the face of this challenge, few were willing to defend Justinian's crown. After offering the briefest resistance, Justinian was defeated and beheaded.

The maiming of the deposed Byzantine emperor Justinian II, as depicted by the 17th-century Swiss engraver Matthäus Merian. Justinian has his nose slit (left), while his servants are dragged off to be burnt at the stake (right).

THE SACK OF CONSTANTINOPLE

The sacking of Constantinople in 1204 was one of the greatest crimes of vandalism ever committed. The Greek city of Constantinople, the capital of the Byzantine Empire, was the bastion of Christianity. So it was ironic that those who plundered it in 1204 were fellow Christians of the Fourth Crusade.

The original destination of these Latin Crusaders – from France, Italy, Flanders and Germany – was to be Cairo, the capital of the Muslim caliphate, from where they planned to retake Muslim-held Jerusalem. They assembled in Venice, to be conveyed in Venetian ships. But Venice had signed a trade agreement with the Sultan of Egypt. The ruler of Venice – the Doge, Enrico Dandolo – was 85 years old and blind but a ruthless merchant prince. When the Crusaders could not pay the full price, the Doge suggested that, rather than sailing for Cairo, the expedition should head for Constantinople, Venice's rival in the eastern Mediterranean, topple the emperor, and establish a Latin empire. The Crusaders readily agreed, believing the Greek Orthodox Christians of Constantinople to be abhorrent schismatics, 'worse than Jews'.

Once moored in the Bosphoros, Dandolo engineered a series of political coups that led to a year of four emperors. A fire destroyed half the city. Finally, the Doge ordered the storming of Constantinople, which fell on 12 April 1204. It was said that the octogenarian Dandolo actually fought; he certainly commanded. For three days the Crusaders ransacked the burning city. Thousands of defenceless citizens were massacred, and nuns were raped on the altars. The Great Library of Constantinople was destroyed, sanctuaries were looted, priceless works of art smashed to pieces. In Hagia Sophia – the greatest church in Christendom and, later, burial place of Doge Dandolo – a whore was placed upon the throne of the patriarch to sing lewd songs. Dandolo placed Baldwin of Flanders on the imperial throne and other Latin grandees founded Latin lordships; the Doge demanded and got a Venetian empire of 'one half and one quarter of the Roman Empire', seizing Crete and other islands as well as a vast swag of loot. The Latin empire of Constantinople lasted until 1261 when Michael VIII Palaeologus retook the city for the Byzantines. But the city never recovered its former greatness, and was captured by the Turks in 1453.

The capture of Constantinople by forces of the Fourth Crusade in 1204, in a painting by the 16th-century Italian artist Palma il Giovane. Founded by Constantine I in 330, the much-besieged city was at various times the capital of the Roman, Byzantine and Ottoman empires.

Pope John XII was the most shameful pontiff to lead the Christian Church, the antithesis of Christian virtues. He lived a private life of brazen immorality, turning the Vatican into a brothel. His behaviour was duplicitous, cruel and foolish – he personified the papal 'pornocracy' of the first half of the tenth century. Fittingly, he finally brought about his own downfall through his insatiable depravity.

Pope John XII c. 937–64

'. . . this monster without once single virtue to atone for his many vices.'

THE VERDICT OF THE BISHOPS CONVENED BY OTTO TO TRY POPE JOHN XII, 963

Originally called Octavius, the future Pope John XII was the only son of Duke Alberic II of Spoleto, the Patrician of Rome, who decreed to the nobles of Rome shortly before his death that his son should be elected pope. On 16 December 955, after the death of the previous pope, Agapetus II, Octavius became the highest authority in the Christian Church, both the spiritual and temporal ruler of Rome at only 18 years old, renaming himself John XII.

Through his mother Alda of Vienne he was a descendant of Charlemagne, but he showed none of the virtues expected of a pope. His private life was a litany of sin. Disdaining the celibacy his position required, he was a rampant adulterer, fornicating with literally hundreds of women, including his father's concubine Stephna. The sacred Lateran Palace, once the abode of saints, became a whorehouse, in which lounged hundreds of prostitutes, ready to serve his sexual whims. John even had incestuous relations with two of his sisters.

Throughout his reign, John's fortunes were interwoven with those of the German King Otto I the Great, a friend of the church to whom John appealed for help after suffering defeat in a war against the Duke Pandulf of Capua, and then losing the Papal States to King Berengarius of Italy. Otto arrived in Italy with his powerful army, forcing Berengarius to back down. On reaching Rome in late January 962, Otto took an oath of allegiance to recognize John's authority, and, on 2 February 962, John crowned Otto as the Holy Roman Emperor, along with his wife, the queen Adelaide, whom he made empress.

This powerful alliance was of benefit to both John and Otto but each immediately set about struggling to dominate the other. Shortly after Otto was crowned emperor, he issued his 'Ottonian Privilege', a treaty that promised to recognize the Pope's claim to the bulk of central Italy in exchange for a pledge that all future popes would only be consecrated after they had sworn allegiance to the Holy Roman Emperor. However, when Otto left Rome in 14 February 962 to continue his war against King Berengarius, John – fearful of Otto's strength – began secret negotiations with Berengarius's son Adalbert to rise up against him, and sent letters to other European rulers, encouraging them to do the same. When German troops intercepted these letters, the plot was laid bare, and if John had any hopes of placating the furious Otto, these soon ended. After John received Adalbert in Rome with great ceremony, bishops and nobles sympathetic to the German king rebelled. On 2 November 963, John was forced to flee Rome as Otto re-entered the city.

As John hid in the mountains of Campania, Otto convened a panel of 50 bishops in St Peter's Basilica, who compiled a list of political and personal charges against him. These ranged from sacrilege (swearing oaths and toasting the devil with wine) to adultery, perjury and even murder (he was accused of blinding his confessor, Benedict, leading to his death, and of castrating and murdering his cardinal

Otto I being crowned Holy Roman Emperor by Pope John XII on 2 February 962.

subdeacon). The excesses of his private life had also led him into flagrant abuses of his office, including simony – bestowing bishoprics and other ecclesiastical titles in return for payments – in order to pay for his extensive gambling debts.

On 4 December 963, the synod found John guilty and deposed him, replacing him with Pope Leo VIII. However, the new appointment was made without following proper canonical procedure and few regarded Leo as a legitimate replacement. As Otto and Adalbert clashed on the battlefield again, a new revolt broke out in Rome, restoring John to the papacy, while Leo fled. Those who had betrayed John now suffered horrible vengeance. Cardinal Deacon John had his right hand cut off by the merciless pope while Bishop Otgar of Speyer was scourged; another official lost his nose and ears, many more were excommunicated. On 26 February 964, John repealed Otto's decrees in a special synod and re-established his own authority as Pope.

John's position was still precarious and when Otto finally defeated Berengarius on the battlefield and started back for Rome, it seemed highly likely he would be deposed again. However, on 16 May 964, lustful to the last, John collapsed and died eight days after being caught in the act of adultery. Some say he was beaten up by the jealous husband; others that he was murdered; others again that the devil had claimed him as his own. Most believed he had been struck down by divine intervention or carnal exhaustion.

Pope John XII was a stain on the name of the Christian Church. It is said that monks prayed day and night for his death. 'You are charged with such obscenities as would make us blush if you were a stage player,' was Emperor Otto's verdict, writing to him after convening a council of bishops to depose him. 'It would require a whole day to enumerate them all.'

MAROZIA, JEZEBEL OF THE PAPACY

Marozia was a political harlot and powerful noblewoman who became senatrix and patricia of Rome, queen of Italy and the mistress, murderess, mother, grandmother and great-mother of popes. Hers was an astonishing career of depravity, greed, murder and ruthlessness that dominated the papacy for decades.

Beautiful, clever, and a mistress of power and intrigue, Marozia was born in 890, the daughter of Count Theophylact and his courtesan, Theodora, known as a 'shameless whore'. Indeed both mother and daughter were infamous. As the English historian Edward Gibbon wrote:

> The influence of two prostitutes Marozia and Theodora was founded on their wealth and beauty, their political and amorous intrigues: the most strenuous of their lovers were rewarded with the Roman mitre and their reign may have suggested to darker ages the fable of a female pope. The bastard son, the grand-son and great-grandson of Marozia, a rare genealogy, were seated in the Chair of St Peter.

At 15 Marozia became Pope Sergius III's mistress, producing a son, later Pope John XI. In 909 she married Alberic, duke of Spoleto, producing another son, Alberic II. After Alberic I was killed she become mistress of the reigning Pope John X. But Marozia turned against him, marrying his enemy Guy of Tuscany. Together they conquered Rome, imprisoning the pope. Marozia had John X strangled in the Castel Sant'Angelo and then seized power for herself, ruling through her puppet popes Leo VI and Stephen VIII before raising her own papal bastard to the throne of St Peter as John XI, aged 21. Widowed again, Marozia married Hugh of Arles, king of Italy, with whom she ruled. The couple were overthrown by her son Duke Alberic II, who imprisoned his mother until her death.

Marozia (890–937), the beautiful and powerful mistress of Pope Sergius III, depicted in a 19th-century woodcut. During the so-called 'Rule of the Harlots' of the early tenth century, the papacy was influenced by a number of female members of the aristocratic Theophylact family, including Marozia and her mother Theodora.

Basil II was one of the most powerful, effective and brilliant – if merciless – rulers of the Byzantine Empire, the ultimate hero-monster. A remarkably successful statesman and soldier, perennially engaged in warfare, Basil – who never married or fathered children – reigned for 50 years, expanding his empire to its greatest extent. He converted the Russians to Christianity, defeated the Bulgars, conquered the Caucasus and patronized the arts.

Basil the Bulgar Slayer
957/8–1025

'The emperor did not relent, but every year marched into Bulgaria and laid waste and ravaged all before him ... The emperor blinded the Bulgarian captives — around 15,000 they say — and he ordered every hundred to be led back ... by a one-eyed man.'

JOHN SKYLITZES, LATE 11TH-CENTURY BYZANTINE HISTORIAN

Accounts of Basil's appearance tally well with his brutal persona. Athletic in build, with a round face, bushy moustache and piercing blue eyes, he had a habit of twirling his whiskers between his fingers whenever he was angry or agitated – a frequent occurrence given his explosive temper. Reportedly he chose his words sparingly, barking rather than speaking them, in accordance with his generally abrupt manner. Never one to relax, he was always on guard for enemies, his right hand invariably poised to reach for his sword. He scorned jewellery, dressing in armour and eating the same rations as his troops, promising to look after their children if they died in battle for him.

Basil was the grandson of Constantine VII and the son of Romanos II. But Byzantine power politics was treacherous and the early years of Basil's life were marked by intrigue and rebellion. Romanos II had died in 963, leaving five-year-old Basil and his younger brother Constantine as the joint emperors; although Constantine later succeeded Basil in 1025 and ruled for three years, he did not play an active part in Basil's reign, accepting his brother's supremacy and preferring to watch the chariot racing at the Constantinople Hippodrome (see page 52).

In 963, however, Basil was too young to rule the Empire himself so his mother Theophano married a general in the army, who became Emperor Nikephoros II in 963. In 969, Theophano had Nikephoros murdered by her next lover, John Tzimisces, who also became emperor until his death in 976. Basil, now 18, finally acceded to the throne, but he soon faced open rebellion led by two ambitious landowners: first, Bardas Skleros, whose armies were swiftly destroyed in 979, and second, Bardas Phakos, whose forces were defeated in battle in April 989 after two years of fighting. Legend has it that Basil sat patiently on his horse, with his sword in one hand and a picture of the Virgin Mary in the other, preparing to face Phakos in one-to-one combat, before the latter suddenly died of a stroke.

Still a young man, Basil – who had demanded Phakos's severed head as a trophy – had shown himself to be a brave and ruthless combatant, not afraid to lead his armies into battle. Nonetheless, government of the Empire remained largely in the hands of his uncle, the eunuch Basil Lekanpenos, the grand chamberlain of the imperial palace, so Basil accused him of secretly sympathizing with the rebel cause, and exiled him from Byzantium in 985. Distrustful of the established elite, Basil preferred to offer patronage and protection to small farmers in return for providing military service and regular taxes. He systematically toppled any other potential rivals, confiscating their lands and money to help fund his relentless military campaigns.

In 995, angered by Arab incursions into Byzantine territory, he gathered 40,000 men and attacked Syria – securing it for the Empire for the next 75 years. In the process, he sacked Tripoli and nearly reached Palestine and Jerusalem. His mortal enemy, however, was the equally ambitious and self-styled 'Tsar' Samuel of Bulgaria, who had used the distractions of the Byzantine civil wars to extend his own empire from the Adriatic to the Black Sea, swallowing up swathes of Byzantine territory. Basil's early forays against the Bulgarians, such as the siege of Sofia in 986, had been costly and unsuccessful, leading to the disastrous ambush at the Gates of Trajan, in which thousands of his soldiers were lost and he barely escaped alive. From 1001, however, having eradicated his domestic enemies, Basil

began to eat back into the territory conquered by Samuel, soon regaining Macedonia. Success was steady rather than spectacular until a massive victory at the Battle of Kleidon, on 29 July 1014, Basil's forces taking Samuel's capital.

As a brutal denouement to the campaign, Basil lined up the defeated prisoners and had them blinded. In a macabre gesture, he left one eye for every hundred men so that the hapless troops could find their way back to their homes. A reported 15,000 shuffled away in pathetic columns, wounded, blinded and utterly terrorized. According to the 11th-century historian John Skylitzes, the Tsar fainted after seeing his soldiers return and died of a stroke. In this single horrifying moment, Basil earned his epithet 'Bulgar Slayer'. He also extended Byzantine territory to include the Balkans, Mesopotamia, Georgia, Armenia and southern Italy: monstrously merciless but an admirably successful emperor.

The Byzantine emperor Basil II triumphant over the Bulgar tribes, in an image based on an 11th-century miniature from St Mark's Basilica in Venice.

BLINDERS AND STRANGLERS IN BYZANTIUM

Blinding and mutilation were designed to disqualify a claimant to the throne, while strangling was the method for killing princes without shedding royal blood.

Constantine VI (771–97), Byzantine emperor from 778 to 797, was both blinder and blinded. After succeeding his father, Emperor Leo IV, he was regarded as a weak and ineffective ruler for failing to show leadership and bravery against Kardam the Bulgarian, who defeated him in 791 and 792. When opposition to his rule formed around his uncle, Caesar Nikephoros, Constantine had his uncle arrested and both his eyes put out, also removing the tongues of each of his father's four other brothers, lest they should think to follow suit. He also blinded the Armenian general Alexios Mosele, causing the Armenians to revolt. But Constantine's mother had never been happy with her son's rule and her followers captured and blinded him, causing him to die of his wounds, while she was crowned Empress Irene.

This pattern of inter-family cruelty was a recurrent feature in the Byzantine Empire over the centuries.

Isaac II Angelos (1156–1204) was emperor from 1185 to 1195, but while he was preparing for a campaign against Bulgaria, his older brother Alexius Angelos declared himself Emperor Alexius III, captured Isaac, blinded him and imprisoned him in Constantinople. In 1203, however, Alexius III fled the Byzantine capital as a crusading army prepared to invade. Isaac was released and restored to the throne, but his health was so undermined by eight years of captivity that he handed over control to his son, Alexius IV. The new king proved equally incapable of protecting the city from the Crusaders, and in 1204 he was deposed and imprisoned by Alexios Doukas – a court official and Byzantine aristocrat nicknamed 'Mourtzouphlos' for his bushy eyebrows and sullen manner – who declared himself Alexios V. Alexius IV was subsequently strangled in prison and his father died shortly afterwards.

Mourtzouphlos's reign began in February 1204 but only lasted a few months. In November, he was captured by Crusading forces, and thrown from the top of a column in Constantinople.

The Bulgar army stumbles home following its heavy defeat in 1014 at the hands of Basil the Bulgar Slayer, 15,000 of its soldiers having been blinded on the Byzantine emperor's orders. This dramatic woodcut was inspired by a painting by the Czech artist Emil Holarek (1867–1919).

'The Old Man of the Mountain', Hassan-i-Sabbah, was arguably the forerunner of modern Jihadist terrorism, but he was also a figure of learning and mystique, a charismatic military and religious leader who achieved power for his sect far beyond its resources. His fiefdom of Alamut, high in the Elburz Mountains of northern Iran, was the base of the mysterious but deadly sect known as the Assassins. Marco Polo, who visited the area on his way back from China, told of a beautiful garden in which a powerful sheikh trained fanatical killers to become his loyal followers with hashish-fuelled promises of Paradise. These same men would then do all that the Old Man asked – even kill themselves, if that was what he desired.

Hassan–i–Sabbah, Sheikh of Alamut
1056–1124

'No man ever escaped when the Sheikh of the Mountain desired his death.'

MARCO POLO

Hassan-i-Sabbah was born in the Persian city of Qom, becoming an admired scholar of Shia Islam. Whilst still a youth, his family moved to the town of Rayy, and it was there that he resolved to devote his life to the Shia Ismaili sect.

Hassan carved an early career at the court of the Seljuq Turks, a Sunni dynasty whose empire controlled much of Iran, Mesopotamia, Syria and Palestine between the 11th and 14th centuries. In the service of the Seljuq sultan, Hassan rose to become head of intelligence, but ended up causing offence and was banished, an insult he never forgot.

Hassan roamed around the Middle East until he arrived in Egypt in about 1078. Cairo was then the capital of the North African Fatimid empire whose caliphs were Shia Ismailis. He remained there for some three years, continuing his studies and establishing himself as a religious leader of the Nizariya faction. But when he and his faction lost out in a political struggle and were driven out of Cairo, he led his sect on a new path. He and his followers established or fortified a series of remote strongholds across the Middle East, from Lebanon to Iraq, and from Syria to Iran. He returned to his native Iran, taking over Alamut Castle in the Elburz Mountains. It would remain his eyrie and capital until his death.

There Hassan set about building a militia of armed followers who could both defend his 'kingdom', proselytize on his behalf and destroy the enemies of true Islam. Through the combination of a profligate use of the psychoactive drug hashish and his own charismatic appeal, Hassan created his 'Hashishim' – hence the word 'Assassins' – to kill 'impious usurpers' and Sunni leaders. (He remained nominally loyal to the Fatimid caliphs in Cairo, but in reality he became a remarkable independent political force, feared and loathed by all the great powers of the Middle East.) His adepts called themselves the New Doctrine, while his feared fighters were the Fedayeen – or the Holy

Killers, admired by some, feared by all. Their favourite weapon was the dagger, sometimes poisoned.

Hassan ruled over his adherents with strict austerity. On discovering one of his followers playing the flute, he had the man banished. He even had his own son executed for drinking wine. Those who came to serve Hassan were indoctrinated, trained and equipped before being sent forth to carry out their master's orders. Integral to this process was the beautiful garden he had built, described by Marco Polo as the 'largest and finest' the world had ever seen. Within its walls conduits had been cut through which ran wine, milk, honey and water, while groups of beautiful women cavorted. The effect was such as to make people believe that this was indeed Paradise. Marco Polo described how Hassan manipulated young men into being his blindly obedient followers:

> The Old Man … had a potion given them, as a result of which they straightway fell asleep; then he had them taken up and put into the garden, and then awaked. When they awoke, they … saw all the things that I have told you, and so believed that they were really in Paradise. And the ladies and damsels remained with them all day, playing music and singing and making excellent cheer; and the young men had their pleasure of them. So these youths had all they could desire, and would never have left the place of their own free will.

At that point, however, they were re-drugged, removed from the garden and returned to Hassan's castle. The covenant he then offered them was simple: they could return to Paradise, of which he was the guardian, provided they did everything that he asked.

With the unswerving loyalty of his men assured, Hassan worked to foment uprisings against the Seljuq sultans and Abbasid caliphs, both Sunnis, as well as the infidel Crusaders. The Assassins murdered Seljuq and Abbasid officials and sometimes Fatimids too. They assassinated the Crusader princes Raymond II, count of Tripoli, and Conrad of Montferrat, whose murder may have been ordered by Richard I of England (Hassan was known sometimes to cooperate with Crusaders). An Assassin almost succeeded in killing Prince Edward of England, who later became Edward I, with a poisoned dagger, but he survived. It was said that the Knights Hospitallers hired Assassins to murder various of their

Hassan-i-Sabbah initiates adherents into his Hashshashin sect by giving them drugged wine, in an illumination from a 15th-century manuscript. It is thought that Hassan recruited his cohorts by inducing them to experience ecstatic visions.

A BRIEF HISTORY OF HASHISH

The earliest recorded use of 'hashish' – the dried leaves and flowers of the hemp plant, *Cannabis indica* or *C. sativa* – dates from the 3rd millennium BC, when it was employed medicinally in China. In ancient India, *ganja* (from Sanskrit *gangika*) was considered sacred, and its ritual use spread across the west Asian steppes and towards Eastern Europe. By the first millennium BC, the shamans of the Scythians, Thracians and Dacians – known as 'those who walk on clouds' – were burning the herb and inhaling the smoke to achieve ecstatic trances.

The first Western account of the drug comes from the 17th-century English explorer Thomas Bowrey, who encountered *bhang* – an infusion of cannabis seed and leaf – along the coast of Bengal. He recorded that it worked 'merrily' on his shipmates, 'each man fancying himself no less than an emperor'.

By the early 20th century, Western governments had criminalized cannabis, one 1930s US poster warning against 'the Killer Drug "Marihuana" – a powerful narcotic in which lurks *Murder! Insanity! Death!*' It has nonetheless become the fourth most popular drug in the world after caffeine, nicotine and alcohol. In Britain it was declassified to a class-C drug in 2004, despite high-strength modern varieties, including 'skunk', being linked to psychosis.

Hashish Smokers by Gaetano Previati (1852–1920). Hashish enjoyed something of a vogue in 19th-century Paris, where the 'Club des Hashischins', dedicated to the exploration of drug-induced experience and attended by such literary and artistic luminaries as Charles Baudelaire, Théophile Gautier, Gérard de Nerval and Eugène Delacroix, flourished during the 1840s.

opponents. Other Muslim leaders were outraged by the power of the Old Man of the Mountain and often tried to crush him – but he was a dangerous opponent. When the sultan Saladin resolved to destroy the Assassins, he found a dagger under his pillow, and took the warning. The great Middle Eastern princes attacked the Assassins, but each time they survived as an idiosyncratic outlaw state.

The sheikh died of natural causes in 1124. He was replaced by his henchman Kya Bozorg-Ummid who created an Assassin dynasty when he was succeeded by his son. But the Assassins were finally destroyed by the Mongol Khan and empire-builder Hulugu, Genghis Khan's grandson, who stormed Alamut in 1256. The new ruler of Egypt, Sultan Baybars, a Mameluk, wiped out the last Assassin strongholds in Syria in 1273.

The history of the Assassins stands as testament to the power of humanity's desire for the heavenly afterlife: some see the sheikh as an early bin Laden, yet the latter is a Sunni terrorist, while the former remains a respected Shia Ismaili religious leader.

The crusader warrior Godfrey of Bouillon was a brutal religious fundamentalist who led the siege of Jerusalem in July 1099. Daring and zealous, he stood for a version of Christianity that glorified the spilling of infidel blood. He became the first Christian ruler of the kingdom of Jerusalem, after indiscriminately slaughtering thousands of Jews and Muslims, 'purifying' the city in the name of God. His storming of the Holy City was one of the greatest crimes in history.

Godfrey of Bouillon
and the storming of Jerusalem
1060–1100

'. . . if you had been there you would have seen
our feet coloured to our ankles with the blood
of the slain. But what more shall I relate?
None of them were left alive; neither women
nor children were spared.'

FULCHER OF CHARTRES, MEDIEVAL CHRONICLER AND CHAPLAIN TO

THE ARMIES OF GODFREY OF BOUILLON AND HIS BROTHERS,

DESCRIBING THE SIEGE OF JERUSALEM IN 1099

Godfrey was born in 1060, probably in Boulogne-sur-Mer, to Eustace II, count of Boulogne (who had fought on the side of the Normans at the Battle of Hastings in 1066), and Ida 'the Blessed' of Boulogne (a pious and saintly figure who founded a number of monasteries). Godfrey was an athletic and fair-haired boy of 'pleasing' features, who, in the words of William of Tyre, was 'tall of stature . . . strong beyond compare, with solidly built limbs and a stalwart chest'.

As the second son of the family, Godfrey did not stand to inherit much from his father, but in 1076 his childless hunchback uncle, also called Godfrey, bequeathed him the duchy of Lower Lorraine, an area

Godfrey of Bouillon, Duke of Lower Lorraine, leader of the First Crusade and first ruler of the Kingdom of Jerusalem, as portrayed by an anonymous 16th-century German artist.

of strategic importance between France and the German states of the Holy Roman Empire. So significant was the region that, for a time, Henry IV, the German king and future emperor, took the land for himself, though he returned it in 1089 in recognition of Godfrey's continuing loyalty.

In 1095, Pope Urban II called on the nobility of Flanders to embark on the First Crusade, to give assistance to the Byzantine emperor Alexius I against Turkish forces attacking the Christian empire of Byzantium, and to liberate the Holy City of Jerusalem for Christianity. Selling or mortgaging his estates to raise the necessary funds, Godfrey gathered an army of crusaders, as did a number of other leading European nobles, including Raymond of St Gilles, the fiery Norman knight Bohemond I, and Godfrey's two brothers, Eustace and Baldwin. Godfrey declared that he was determined to avenge the blood of Jesus on the Jewish people.

In August 1096, Godfrey's army – estimated at 40,000 – began the long march through Hungary towards Constantinople. When they arrived in November, it soon became apparent that the crusaders and Alexius I had very different priorities. Alexius wanted to concentrate on winning back the lands he had lost to the Turks, whereas the crusaders were eager to conquer Jerusalem and capture the Holy Land. After a period of political tension throughout 1097 – in which Godfrey's troops pillaged the neighbourhood of Salabria – Godfrey tentatively agreed that his army would submit to Alexius's orders for a time before marching southwards towards Jerusalem.

From the summer of 1098, Godfrey – and other crusading armies – began to make inroads into Muslim lands, his reputation growing as he did so. In October, he reportedly killed 150 Turks with only 12 knights in a battle outside Antioch and the following month he cut a Turk in half with a single, downward swipe of his sword. Eventually, in February 1099, the various crusading armies united and began their advance on Jerusalem, fighting through Tripoli and Beirut before arriving to besiege the city in June. On the morning of Friday 15 July, Godfrey was among the first crusaders to breach the city's defences, after his men had built and scaled a moveable tower, which they had placed against the walls. Ferocious fighting took place at the top of the wall, as Godfrey bravely held his position and directed his men into the city so that they could open the gates.

Thousands of crusaders flooded into the streets, as the Muslim citizens fled to the al-Aqsa Mosque. Iftikhar ad-Dawla, the Fatimid governor of the city, made his last stand in the Tower of David. On condition of surrender, Iftikhar and some of his soldiers were allowed to escape, but over the next 48 hours, those left in the city – combatant and civilian, Muslim and Jew – were put to the sword and murdered in the streets. The crusaders pillaged Muslim holy sites such as the Dome of the Rock and either burned their victims to death or cut open their stomachs, believing that Muslims swallowed their gold. The city's Jews had fled to a synagogue, which the crusaders simply burned to the ground. Raymond of Aguilers reported that he saw 'piles of heads, hands and feet' scattered across the city, while Fulcher of Chartres, a chaplain to Baldwin's army, wrote approvingly that 'this place, so long contaminated by the superstition of the pagan inhabitants' had been 'cleansed from their contagion'.

At the height of the systematic massacre, Godfrey stripped to his undergarments and walked solemnly, barefoot through the blood, to pray at the Holy Sepulchre, a church at the site where Christians believe Jesus was crucified. On 22 July, his fellow crusaders chose him to be the first Christian ruler of Jerusalem, although he refused to take the name of king in the city in which Christ had died, preferring instead the title Duke and Advocate of the Holy Sepulchre. It was there that he was buried after dying of plague on 18 July 1100, his mission complete.

Godfrey was idealized by later Christian writers, and became the subject of many legends. For Robert of Rheims, writing in the 12th century, he was more monk than knight, a man who scorned the vanities of the world. Today, however, Godfrey of Bouillon appears more a sanctimoniously fanatical butcher than a hero, let alone a Christian.

BRUTISH CRUSADERS

For the Christian chroniclers of medieval Europe, the leaders of the Crusades were the ultimate heroes, pious and brave, sacrificing themselves for a divine mission. For those on the receiving end of the crusading armies, however, the crusaders were colonizers and usurpers, chasing new fiefdoms and treasures, and glorying in indiscriminate slaughter.

Pope Urban II's message for the participants in the First Crusade was very clear; they were to liberate the Holy Land and the Christians of Byzantium from Muslim rule. Many of those inspired by his message, however, used it as an excuse for sectarian attacks on the Jews of Europe, influenced by Peter the Hermit, a rabble-rousing preacher from Amiens, who made apocalyptic predictions about the Second Coming of Christ.

One such was Count Emicho, a German nobleman from the Rhineland, who in 1096, claiming that Christ had appeared to him in a dream, declared he would conquer Jerusalem. He started by terrorizing the Jewish communities of Germany and France, demanding they not only finance his adventure but also convert to Christianity in readiness for the Second Coming. His troops attacked Jewish communities in Worms, Mainz, Cologne, Trier and Metz, frequently slaughtering those who refused to convert. In Worms, his soldiers burst into the cathedral and murdered 800 defenceless people given refuge there by the city's archbishop. In Speyer, they terrorized and looted the Jewish quarter of the city. Defeat finally came in Hungary, where the army of King Coloman forced Emicho back to the Rhineland before he could even see Constantinople, let alone Jerusalem.

Another crusader thug was Bohemond I, born around 1058 in Calabria to Robert Guiscard, duke of Apulia and Calabria, and his first wife Alberada of Buonalbergo. Seeing the First Crusade as an opportunity to carve out land for himself in the east, he took the Cross in 1096, assembled a huge army and, the following year, advanced to Constantinople. From there, joined by the equally ambitious and merciless Robert II of Flanders, he moved on to Antioch, where after a long and testing siege, the city was betrayed by one of its own guards. At sunset on 2 June 1098, 60 knights, led by Bohemond and Robert, scaled the walls of the Tower of the Two Sisters – deliberately left unguarded – and opened the Gate of St George. Crusaders streamed into the city, massacring every non-Christian they found, and by evening the next day, blood soaked the streets.

The Crusader citadel of Kerak, located in the Jordan Valley. Built by the Crusader Paganus in the 1140s, Kerak was repeatedly besieged by the sultan Saladin, who finally captured it in 1189.

Andronikus schemed and murdered his way to the Byzantine throne, before overseeing a reign of terror that sounded the death-knell for his Komnenos dynasty. He was described by one chronicler as having been 'endowed by nature with the most remarkable gifts both of mind and body: he was handsome and eloquent, but licentious'. Sadly, his sexual incontinence was the least of his crimes.

Andronikus I Komnenos c. 1118–85

> 'The overripe suitor embracing the unripe maiden, the dotard and the damsel with pointed breasts, the shrivelled and languid old man with the rosy-fingered girl ...'
>
> NICETAS CHONIATES, DESCRIBING ANDRONIKUS AND HIS CHILD-BRIDE, AGNES OF FRANCE

As a successful general and able politician, Andronikus won the favour of his cousin, Emperor Manuel I Komnenos. But his passion for women proved his undoing. One of his conquests at the imperial court of Manuel I was his own niece, the beautiful princess Eudocia. According to the Byzantine historian Nicetas Choniates, the affair infuriated the emperor, and Eudocia's family devised a plot to murder him. Andronikus, forewarned of their plans, escaped.

In 1153, he joined a plot to murder Manuel I. When the conspiracy was uncovered, Andronikus was lucky to escape death, being imprisoned instead – an act of leniency that was to prove fateful for Manuel's offspring.

After absconding from prison in 1164, Andronikus effected a reconciliation with Emperor Manuel I, and the two campaigned together in Hungary. Once more, Andronikus distinguished himself with his military gifts. It was to be a short-lived reunion. The two soon fell out again when Andronikus seduced Philippa, the daughter of the prince of Antioch, who was also the sister of the emperor Manuel's wife, Mariah. Unsurprisingly, Andronikus had to flee again.

His next stop was Jerusalem, where King Amalric I received him warmly and even made him Lord of Beirut. But Andronikus once more succumbed to a forbidden temptation – this time in the shape of Theodora Komnene, the niece of Emperor Manuel. In the face of Manuel's renewed

A manuscript illumination showing the execution and dismemberment of Andronikus I Komnenos, from a 15th-century edition of William of Tyre's Histories.

anger, Andronikus now took flight yet again, taking Theodora with him. The couple spent the next years in search of refuge, but Theodora was captured by forces loyal to the emperor and sent back to Constantinople.

Unwilling to accept the loss of his mistress, Andronikus threw himself on Manuel's mercy, appearing before the Emperor with a chain around his neck, pleading for forgiveness. This was granted and the couple were allowed to retire into exile at Oeneaeum by the Black Sea. Had the story of Andronikus ended there, it would be hard to feel anything other than a certain affection for him as an incorrigible lothario.

In 1180, Manuel I died, leaving his ten-year-old son Alexius as his successor. Real power passed to his mother Mariah, who became regent. But her Frankish birth was resented by many Greeks. In the absence of his long-time antagonist Manuel, Andronikus could not resist returning to Constantinople to assert his right to be regent. Opponents of the regency organized major street riots, to coincide with Andronikus' arrival in the city in 1182 at the head of a small force of men.

On entering Constantinople, Andronikus acquiesced in the massacre of some 80,000 'Latins'. Initially, this monumental pogrom had been targeted at the predominantly Venetian merchants who controlled much of the city's economy, but it soon expanded to include anyone deemed western. His tolerance (if not active encouragement) of the slaughter secured Andronikus popular support and facilitated his ascent to power, as he outflanked Mariah and her allies. Andronikus oversaw the crowning of the prince as Emperor Alexius II Komnenos, but used him as little more than a façade for his own personal rule. He arranged for the execution of most members of Alexius' family, including his mother and half-sister. Cruelly, the young emperor was himself forced to sign Mariah's death-warrant.

Next, Andronikus elevated himself to the position of co-emperor. In 1183, he arranged for Alexius to be strangled with a bowstring, then married his widow, Agnes of France. Although Agnes was only eleven and Andronikus in his mid-sixties, the marriage was consummated.

Despite securing his status as emperor, Andronikus became more paranoid. In 1184, he faced a series of revolts from the towns of Lopadium, Nicaea and Prusa. Each met with vicious retribution. The chroniclers report wanton acts of pillage and murder – with bodies left to decay in the sun as a warning to others. In 1185, after a series of major military defeats by the Normans, the Hungarians and the Venetians, losing significant swathes of Byzantine territory, Andronikus ordered all those who had been incarcerated for sedition to be executed. In a major crack-down on any possible signs of dissent, the aristocracy were vigorously targeted, with anyone whose loyalty might be in doubt arrested and murdered.

Inevitably, such unwarranted, draconian measures stirred resentment, and in 1185 Andronikus was deposed by Isaac Angelos who was declared emperor. Andronikus attempted to flee Constantinople by sea, with his wife Agnes and his favourite concubine, Maraptike. But he was captured, brought back and handed over to a baying mob. For several days, he was tied to a post and beaten senseless by the vengeful crowds. In the process, his beard was torn out, his head shaved, his right hand cut off, his teeth pulled out and one of his eyes gouged. He was then paraded on a camel through the streets to the Hippodrome. There, he was hung upside down from his feet and repeatedly run through with swords. After his body was taken down, it was torn apart in one final act of ignominy.

Andronikus was the last of the Komnenos family to rule Constantinople. By the end of his life, the archetypal 'lovable old rogue' had become a homicidal usurper and sadistic tyrant. His bloody death mirrored the tumult and slaughter that marked his short reign as emperor.

PHOCAS AND IRENE

The crown of Byzantium was sometimes hereditary, sometimes elective and often simply the prize in palace revolutions and military coups. Designed to confer glory without rules, it often brought monsters to supreme power. In 602, Phocas, a violent soldier-turned-populist, deposed the emperor Maurice. During his eight-year reign, Phocas cruelly suppressed any hint of opposition, and thousands were put to death – including the ex-emperor Maurice who was forced to watch his own son being executed before his turn came.

Eventually Phocas was himself overthrown by Heraclius, who personally beheaded his rival before having his body mutilated and dragged through the streets of Constantinople.

Similar cruelties were meted out by many other Byzantine rulers, but perhaps none was more infamous than the empress Irene, who in 797, having dealt with her son in a most unmaternal fashion, became the first woman to rule the Empire in her own right. Today Irene is remembered fondly by many in the Eastern Church for her spiritual legacy, for it was through her patronage of the Second Council of Nicaea in 787 that the practice of icon veneration was restored after a period of prohibition – indeed, it was this that led to her subsequent canonization by the Greek Orthodox Church. However, her exploits in temporal matters were far less saintly.

After the death of her husband, Emperor Leo IV, in 780, Irene had become regent to her young son, Constantine VI. When Constantine came of age ten years later, Irene refused to relinquish the reins of power. Instead, she had Constantine placed under house arrest and demanded that the military swear an oath of allegiance directly to her. These efforts triggered a rebellion that ended with her being banished from the city. However, in 792 Constantine pardoned his mother and allowed her to return – a fatal mistake. By 797 Irene was conspiring once more against her son, and after forces loyal to her captured him, she had him thrown into prison and blinded in the same Purple Chamber where he was born, before taking sole power for herself.

Detail of a mosaic showing the empress Irene, from the Hagia Sofia in Istanbul.

Simon de Montfort IV was a French grandee who won praise for his opposition to the needless violence of the Fourth Crusade, only subsequently to lead a bitter and brutal campaign of religious-inspired slaughter in the so-called Albigensian Crusade – a 20-year campaign of annihilation against the Cathar heretics. De Montfort's troops laid waste to the Cathar heartland of southern France, sacking cities, besieging castles, usurping land and mercilessly burning heretics, before Simon finally met a bloody death, his head smashed by a rock as he prepared to suppress an uprising in Toulouse.

Simon de Montfort
and the Albigensian Crusade
1160-1218

'If by killing men and spilling blood,
By wasting souls, and preaching murder,
By following evil counsels, and raising fires,
By ruining noblemen and besmirching paratge,
By pillaging the country, and by exalting Pride,
By stoking up wickedness and stifling good,
By massacring women and their infants,
A man can win Jesus in this world, then
Simon surely wears a crown, resplendent in heaven.'

SONG OF THE CATHAR WARS

Born near Paris in 1160, Simon de Montfort IV was the second son of Simon de Montfort III (descended from the lords of de Montfort L'Amauray of France) and Amicia, daughter of Robert de Beaumont, third earl of Leicester. In 1181, he became Baron de Montfort after the death of his father, and in 1190 he married into another noble family, taking as his wife Alice de Montmorency, the daughter of Bouchard de Montmorency III. Although he had substantial land in England, he showed little interest in his estates there, instead spending most of his life in France.

In 1199, with a number of other French knights, he took part in a sporting tournament at Ecry-sur-Aisne in the province of Champagne, where he heard Fulk de Neuilly, an eloquent and popular preacher, preaching the Fourth Crusade. Along with Count Theobald of Champagne, he took the Cross, but by 1204 he had become disillusioned after some of the crusaders, flouting the orders of Pope Innocent III, plundered the Christian cities of Zara (on the Adriatic) and Constantinople (see page 58). He joined the Pope in denouncing such shameful events.

Shortly after abandoning the Fourth Crusade, de Montfort succeeded to the earldom of Leicester in England, only for King John to seize his lands in February 1207 on the pretext of unpaid debts. Again though, Simon's concerns lay elsewhere. The papal legate, Arnold the Abbot of Cîteaux, had asked him to lead a crusade against the Cathars of Languedoc. Also known as Albigensians (after the city of Albi), the adherents of the dualist Cathar sect held that the material world is evil but that the human soul is good and can allow people to be reunited with God. The papacy regarded such beliefs as dangerously heretical.

After initially refusing the request, de Montfort changed his mind and became captain-general of the army of northern French barons that marched south against the Cathars. The campaign became notorious for the crusaders' extreme cruelty, as they burned, pillaged and sacked a succession of cities and towns in the region, murdering thousands, including civilians and non-combatants. On 22 July 1210, at the town of Minerve, Simon ordered the burning of more than 150 Cathars, simply because they refused to abandon their faith. According to a contemporary poem recalling the events, 'Frantic men and crazed women . . . shrieked among the flames . . . Afterwards the bodies were thrown out and mud shovelled over them so that no stench from these foul things should bother our foreign forces.' Between June and November 1210, de Montfort also laid siege the castle of Termes, using advanced siege machinery to launch rocks and missiles onto the heads of the inhabitants. Such was his success that in the same year a plot was hatched among English barons to remove King John from the throne and replace him with Simon. De Montfort, however, was more concerned to continue the Albigensian Crusade than to take power in England.

In March 1211, he took the city of Lavaur: the head of the garrison, Aimeric-de-Montréal, was hanged along with his knights, Aimeric's sister, Lady Girauda, was thrown down a well where heavy rocks were heaped upon her, and more than 400 heretics were burned alive. Then, on 12 September 1213, came his most significant victory, with the defeat of Peter II of Aragon – who had come to the aid of his brother-in-law Raymond of Toulouse – at the Battle of Muret. Simon had now effectively crushed the Cathars, but he refused to stop there. Appointed by the Council of Montpellier in 1215 as count of Toulouse and duke of Narbonne, he used his dominance of the region – with the Pope's blessing – to continue to suppress the Cathar heresy. In 1217, however, a rebellion broke out in Provence, when the son of the defeated Count Raymond re-entered Toulouse, forcing Simon to return and lay siege to the city. The siege dragged on until 25 June 1218, when he received news during a Mass that his enemies were attempting to break out. Pious to the last, he refused to leave before the service had finished, and when he finally arrived at the battle scene, he was killed by a stone catapulted from the city walls by a woman of Toulouse – his skull was shattered and his forehead and jaw splintered under the impact.

De Montfort was as ferocious an ideologue as he was a warrior, a man marked by an extreme commitment to religious orthodoxy. Even by medieval standards of warfare, his systematic slaughter of civilians was excessive. Failing to see the hypocrisy of his twisted logic, he was disgusted by the attacks on fellow Christians that scarred the Fourth Crusade, yet treated the Cathars of his own country as subhuman, preferring to burn them alive than allow them to exist as heretics.

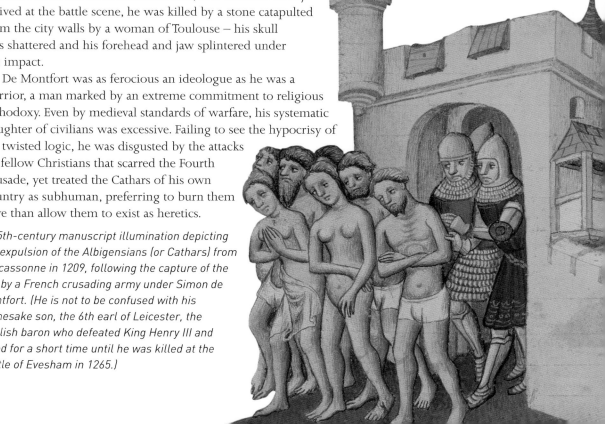

A 15th-century manuscript illumination depicting the expulsion of the Albigensians (or Cathars) from Carcassonne in 1209, following the capture of the city by a French crusading army under Simon de Montfort. (He is not to be confused with his namesake son, the 6th earl of Leicester, the English baron who defeated King Henry III and ruled for a short time until he was killed at the Battle of Evesham in 1265.)

MASSACRE AT MONTSÉGUR

At the end of the twelfth century, the Languedoc region of southern France was independent of the kingdom of France. From 1208, when Pope Innocent III called for a crusade against the Cathars, it was subjected to a sustained and brutal campaign of invasion, tyranny and coercion that lasted two decades and scarred the Languedoc for many more.

Even after the death of Simon de Montfort in 1218, the Albigensian campaign continued for another 11 years, as the Catholic Church and crusaders attempted to suppress every last sign of the Cathar faith. Pope Gregory IX pursued the Cathars with even more relish than his predecessors. In 1229 an Inquisition was established at Toulouse, which condemned and burned anyone identified as a heretic. By 1243, nearly all the major strongholds of the Cathars had been conquered by the crusaders, except for the mountain fortress of Montségur – believed by some to have housed the Holy Grail – perched 3000 feet up on a rock formation in the foothills of the Pyrenees, southwest of Carcassonne. It was here that the tragic dénouement of the Albigensian Crusade took place.

Ten thousand Catholic French troops had besieged the city for nearly ten months until, at the beginning of March 1244, a fortnight's truce was agreed to discuss terms of surrender. When this expired, on 15 March, however, they stormed the castle, dragging more than 200 Cathars down the mountain and forcing them into a specially constructed wooden pen, where they were burned alive.

The fortress of Montségur, last stronghold of the Cathars, where more than 200 members of the heretical sect were besieged and massacred by forces of the French crown in 1244.

Charismatic, dynamic, ferocious, violent and ambitious, Genghis Khan was a military genius and brilliant statesman and world conqueror who united the nomadic tribes of the Asian steppes to create the Mongol empire, the largest land empire in history. But the triumphs of this heroic monster had a terrible price – a reign of terror and mass killing across Eurasia on a scale never before seen.

Genghis Khan
c. 1163–1227

> 'The greatest happiness is to scatter your enemy, to drive him before you, to see his cities reduced to ashes, to see those who love him shrouded in tears, and to gather into your bosom his wives and daughters.'
>
> GENGHIS KHAN

Genghis Khan was born between 1163 and 1167 in the mountainous terrain of Khentii province in Mongolia, reportedly clutching a blood clot – a supposed portent of his future greatness as a warrior. He was named Temujin, after a tribesman recently captured by his father. The third son of Yesukhei – a local chieftain – and Hoelun, Temujin was soon to experience at first hand the dangerous world of Mongolian tribal politics. When Temujin was aged just 9, his father arranged for him to marry Börte, a girl from a neighbouring tribe. He was sent to live with Börte's family, but, shortly afterwards, Yesukhei was poisoned by vengeful tribesmen, and Temujin was obliged to return home. Deprived of their protector, Temujin's family were forced out into the wilderness, where they survived by eating berries, nuts, mice and other small animals. At 13, Temujin murdered his own half-brother.

Several years of nomadic wandering followed, marked by intertribal kidnapping and feuds, during which time Temujin – who soon became known and feared for his leadership, intelligence and military ability – built up a sizeable following. A tall, strong and hardened young man, with piercing green eyes and a long reddish beard, he finally married Börte at the age of 16 and was taken under the wing of Toghril Ong-Khan, ruler of the Kerait tribe

Genghis Khan, warrior leader and founder of the Mongol empire, as depicted in an 18th-century Chinese portrait. In 1206, having united the tribes of Mongolia in 20 years of unremitting warfare, he embarked on a campaign of conquest that would incorporate vast areas of northern China, most of Afghanistan and all of Iran into the Mongol khanate.

(and his father's 'blood brother'). When Börte was later kidnapped by the Merkit tribe, Temujin and Toghril joined forces with Jamuka, a childhood friend of Temujin and now a Mongol chieftan, sending a large army to rescue her. (Börte turned out to be pregnant, and Temujin brought up the child, Jochi, as his own son). The three-way alliance enabled the Mongols and Keraits to force other tribes into submission.

Following this success, in 1200 Toghril declared Temujin his adoptive son and heir – a fateful decision that enraged both Toghril's natural son, Senggum, and the ambitious Jamuka, leading ultimately to war in which Temujin defeated first Jamuka and then Toghril to establish his dominance over the Mongol tribes. In 1206, a council of leading Mongolian tribesmen – called the Kurultai – met and recognized Temujin's authority, giving him the name Genghis Khan, meaning Oceanic Khan or Ruler of the Universe.

Before 1200, the Mongols had been a scattered people, but Genghis – claiming a mandate from heaven – was swiftly to transform them into a powerful and unified nation. 'My strength', he declared, 'was fortified by Heaven and Earth. Foreordained by Mighty Heaven, I was brought here by Mother Earth.' His soldiers were mainly nomadic warriors, including deadly archers who travelled on small but sturdy Mongolian-bred ponies capable of covering great distances. Genghis turned them into a disciplined and brilliantly coordinated war machine that swept all before them.

In 1207 – having secured an alliance with the Uighurs and subjugated the Mongols' old rivals, the Merkit tribe – Genghis immediately began expansionist operations, eating into the Xi Xia territory in northwest China, as well as parts of Tibet. His target was the Silk Road – a key trade route between East and West and the gateway to wealth. In 1211, after refusing to pay the tribute to the Jin dynasty in northern China, he went to war again, besieging and destroying the Jin capital, Yanjing, now Beijing, and securing instead tribute for himself. He returned to Mongolia in triumph, taking with him booty, artisans and, above all, guaranteed trade with China.

In 1219, Genghis turned his attentions north after an attack on a caravan of traders he had sent to establish trading links with the Khwarazm empire – a realm including most of Uzbekistan, Iran and Afghanistan under the rule of the sultan Muhammed Khwarazmshah. Genghis showed restraint, but when members of a second Mongolian delegation were beheaded, he raised 200,000 troops and marched into Central Asia, with his four sons, Jochi, Ogodei, Chaghatai and Touli serving as commanders. Over the next three years, he subjected the Khwarazm people to a terrifying campaign of shock and awe, taking the cities of Bokhara, Samarkand, Herat, Nishapar and Merv – his troops lining up the civilians of the latter and, in a cold-blooded killing spree, slitting their throats.

A peerless strategist, Genghis recognized the value of fear in building an empire, often sending out envoys to cow enemies into submission through tales of his exploits: civilians slaughtered, money and booty stolen, women raped, molten silver poured into people's ears. For all this brutality, however, Genghis did not indulge in killing for the sake of it. He was loyal to his friends and generous to supporters, a shrewd manager of men, who promoted an elite of top generals giving them enormous powers. He spared those who surrendered, reserving wholesale slaughter to make an example of those who resisted. Nor did the Mongols wantonly maim, mutilate or torture – their chief interest was in booty rather than barbarism. Indeed, in some ways Genghis showed himself to be an enlightened ruler, combining political acumen with economic shrewdness. He used divide-and-rule tactics to weaken enemies and promote loyalty. He recognized the importance of good administration, fostering the spread of a unified official language across his empire and a written legal system, called Jasagti. He was also tolerant of religions and gave priests an exemption from taxation. Believing in the importance of providing a safe passage of trade between the East and the West, he forbade troops and officials to abuse merchants or citizens, his reign becoming a period of cultural interaction and advancement for the Mongolian people. He was also a patron of artists, craftsmen and literature.

After his early triumphs over the Khwarazm empire, Genghis pressed on, eager to consolidate his gains. He pushed into Russia, Georgia and the Crimea, defeating the forces of Prince Mstitslav of Kiev at the Battle of Kalka River in 1223 in which, after a feigned retreat, his forces turned on their pursuers and routed them. He now ruled a vast empire stretching from the Black Sea to the Pacific, his people enjoying ever-increasing wealth. In 1226, however, he died after he fell from his horse hurrying back to Xi Xia, where a rebellion had erupted in his absence.

The Great Khan left his empire to his son Ogodei, though it was soon divided amongst the descendants of his sons who founded their own khanates that ruled the Near East, Russia and China (where his grandson Kublai Khan founded his own dynasty). The Mongol empire thus expanded even further, until it stretched from the Pacific coast of Asia in the east to Hungary and the Balkans in the west. The Crimean khanate, longest-lasting of the successor states of the Mongol empire, would survive up until 1783.

A 'Y' chromosomal lineage in an astounding 8 per cent of men in Asia is descended from one source. Most likely this was Genghis himself.

THE COMPOSITE BOW
THE WEAPON THAT CONQUERED A CONTINENT

The key implement in the Mongolian war machine was the composite, or recurved, bow. It was made from a combination of wood, sinew and horn taken from goats or sheep on the Mongolian plains. Each layer – which was glued on to the wood base – made the bowstring tauter, allowing it to shoot arrows further and faster than previous designs like the longbow. An arrow fired from a composite bow was capable of puncturing enemy armour at nearly 190 miles per hour if fired correctly. The Mongols attacked in huge columns but preferred to inflict maximum damage on their enemies from a distance – unleashing a hail of deadly arrows from as far as 300 yards away – rather than become embroiled in close fighting. Archers could fire at enemies from horseback and even fire arrows when in retreat, turning backwards towards their pursuers to let loose another fatal strike.

A Mongol cavalry re-enactment in 2006, marking the 800th anniversary of the founding of the Mongol empire by Genghis Khan.

King John lost most of his empire, broke every promise he ever made, dropped his royal seal in the sea, impoverished England, murdered his nephew, seduced the wives of his friends, betrayed his father, brothers and country, foamed at the mouth when angry, starved and tortured his enemies to death, lost virtually every battle he fought, fled any responsibility whenever possible and died of eating too many peaches. Treacherous, lecherous, malicious, avaricious, cruel and murderous, he earned his nicknames 'Softsword' for military cowardice and incompetence, and 'Lackland' for losing most of his inheritance. He was one of the worst and most hated kings England has ever known.

King John 1167–1216

'John was a tyrant. He was a wicked ruler who did not behave like a king. He was greedy and took as much money as he could from his people. Hell is too good for a horrible person like him.'

MATTHEW PARIS, 13TH-CENTURY CHRONICLER

Born in Oxford on Christmas Eve in 1167, John was the youngest son of Henry II – the first Plantagenet king of England, who ruled from 1154 to 1189 – and his French wife Eleanor of Aquitaine. She was the heiress in her own right of Poitou, Gascony and Aquitaine, which, together with lands inherited or acquired by Henry, created the Angevin empire covering England, Ireland, Brittany, Normandy, Aquitaine, Gascony, Maine, Poitou, Anjou (the name 'Angevin' derives from the French province of Anjou) and other disputed territories such as Toulouse – indeed more of France than was ruled by its own king. Henry was to spend much of his reign repelling attacks by the ambitious Philip II of France, who was determined to extend his own borders.

Henry had four legitimate sons. The first was the so-called 'young King Henry', who died in his twenties. The second was Richard, a superb military commander and ruthless administrator who ultimately succeeded to the throne as Richard I – the Lionheart. Geoffrey, who became duke of Brittany and earl of Richmond, was the third, and John the fourth. The brutish rivalry between the old king and his greedy, jealous and violent sons was so vicious that they were known as the 'Devil's Brood'. However, the overbearing and dominating Henry II, a swashbuckling royal titan, often favoured John, perhaps because he was the weakest and least able – and therefore the lesser threat to his own power.

Richard, made duke of Aquitaine in 1172, repeatedly used his position to revolt against his father, at times even backing the French king, Philip II, against his own family. In 1188, Henry finally lost patience and declared he no longer saw Richard as his heir, at which the future Lionheart once more came out in open rebellion. Initially, John fought alongside Henry, but, in what was to become a familiar pattern, he switched sides when it was clear Richard was set to triumph. King Henry died shortly afterwards, heartbroken at the betrayal of his son, and Richard succeeded as king of England and ruler of the Angevin empire.

The dashing charisma and military brilliance of Richard the Lionheart was in stark contrast to the slipperiness, weakness and mendacity of John, who was stout and stocky and regularly binged on food and drink, whereas Richard was tall, handsome and athletic. John loved women and pleasure; Richard was ascetic and possibly homosexual. Their rivalry dominated John's life. When Richard became king in 1189, he attempted to sate his brother's irrepressible thirst for land by granting him the duchy of Normandy. In return, John agreed to stay away from English soil when Richard left the kingdom to fight in the Third Crusade in 1191. As Richard fought his campaigns against Saladin, the sultan of Damascus and Egypt, he failed to retake Jerusalem but strengthened the crusader kingdom and won a fabulous reputation before returning to his fiefdoms. But on the way back, his enemies the Emperor Henry VI and Duke Leopold of Austria captured him and held him ransom, giving John the opportunity, in January 1193, to take the crown for himself. John, however, failed in an attempt to invade England with the assistance of Philip II, and then unsuccessfully attempted to bribe Richard's captors to hand him over to his custody. As Richard once put it, 'my brother John is not the man to win lands by force if there is anyone at all to oppose him'.

On his return, Richard showed incredible leniency to his wayward brother and officially declared him his successor. So when Richard was killed in 1199 by an arrow at a siege in France, John became king of England and duke of Normandy and Aquitaine. On his succession, his nephew, Arthur, duke of Brittany, the son of Geoffrey II and Constance, was a serious rival to the throne, considered by many as the rightful king, so John quickly arrested the boy, aged 15, and – in a crime not unlike that of Richard III and the Princes in the Tower – had him murdered the following year. Arthur's murder provoked a rebellion in Brittany and a humiliating retreat for John's armies, who were forced to withdraw from the region in 1204. By 1206, Softsword had lost nearly all of England's territorial possessions in France, putting up only limp resistance. In fact, when Normandy – England's last possession on the continent – was seized by the French, John reportedly stayed in bed with his wife, as his soldiers fell in the rout.

Richard, for all his faults, had been noted for his chivalry, unlike the highly sexed John, who had countless mistresses and illegitimate children, often trying to force himself on the wives and daughters of important noblemen. His treatment of prisoners was particularly odious; he even starved to death the wife and son of one of his enemies.

A marble effigy on the tomb of King John in Worcester Cathedral. John schemed against his brother Richard, imposed oppressive taxes on his subjects, fathered at least 12 illegitimate children, and lost most of the Plantagenet empire in western and northern France through his political incompetence.

Stranded on English soil and short of funds, John implemented a ruthless process of fiscal reform, which included large increases in taxation and the merciless exploitation of his feudal prerogatives, giving rise to the popular legend of Robin Hood holding out in Sherwood Forest against royal extortion. Between 1209 and 1213, when John was excommunicated by Pope Innocent III, he shamelessly plundered the revenues of the Church.

From 1212, John faced increasing opposition from the nobility, who began to plot against him. After another thoroughly disastrous military campaign in France in 1214, rebellion finally broke out in England. At a famous meeting in a meadow by the Thames at Runnymede on 15 June 1215, the barons forced John to seal Magna Carta, the foundation of modern English liberties, guaranteeing them rights against the arbitrary rule of the king. John had no intention of keeping his word, and quickly betrayed his promise to abide by the charter, prompting a return to civil war. As he tried his rally his forces, his entourage – with his treasure and bags – was almost lost as he crossed the Wash. The tides rose unexpectedly, and in his frantic efforts to save his possessions he lost the Great Seal of England, giving rise to the legend that sums up his disastrous, murderous and absurd reign. His death too became him, the king succumbing to dysentery after an excessively voracious meal of peaches and ale.

Strange Royal Deaths

- **Herod the Great** of Judaea (4 BC): his putrefied, worm-infested genitals burst open (see page 25)
- **Herod Agrippa** of Judaea (AD 44): also 'consumed by worms'
- **Eliogabalus** Roman emperor: murdered in his privy with his mother (AD 222)
- **Valerian** Roman emperor (260): captured by Persians, made to drink molten gold, skinned alive, then stuffed
- **Edmund II** of England (1016): sword thrust up his rectum
- **Henry I** of England (1135): food poisoning following a 'surfeit of lampreys' (a type of fish, see below right)
- **Al-Musta'sim** last of the Abbasid caliphs (1258): wrapped in a rug and trampled to death by horses
- **Alexander III** of Scotland (1286): rode off a cliff while rushing home one night
- **Edward II** of England (1327): 'hot spit put through the secret place posterial'
- **Martin I** of Aragon (1410): indigestion compounded by a laughing fit
- **Humayun** Mughal emperor (1556): fell to his death trying to kneel on a library staircase after hearing the call to prayer

- **Henry II** of France (1559): brain pierced by a lance while jousting
- **Nanda Bayin** of Burma (1599): laughed to death
- **Adolf Frederick** of Sweden (1771): ate himself to death with a meal of lobster, caviar, sauerkraut, kippers, champagne and 14 helpings of his favourite pudding
- **Prince Frederick,** son of George II of Britain (1751): hit by a cricket ball
- **George II** of Britain (1760): collapsed in the privy with a ruptured aorta
- **Catherine the Great** of Russia (1796): suffered a stroke in the privy
- **Paul I** of Russia (1801): hit on the head with an inkwell, then strangled
- **Alexander** of Greece (1920): bitten by a pair of diseased monkeys

Roger Mortimer became the dictator of England through swordplay, sex and murder. A fine military commander, he was also a master of medieval politics, amassing great wealth, arranging the killing of King Edward II, and seducing his wife, Queen Isabella. Hated for his arrogance, resented for his avarice, and above all feared for his brutality, he dominated through force of arms and personality, only to meet his match in the young king, Edward III, whose father he had destroyed.

Roger Mortimer, 1st Earl of March

1287–1330

'The tongue devises mischiefs, like a sharp razor, working deceitfully. You love evil more than good, and lies more than honesty.'

PSALM 52, READ TO ROGER MORTIMER BY HIS EXECUTIONER

Mortimer was the first son of Edmund Mortimer, 2nd Baron Wigmore, and his wife, Margaret de Fiennes, second cousin to Eleanor of Castile, the wife of Edward I. His grandfather had been a close ally and friend of King Edward I, and in return for their service to the crown the family had enjoyed royal patronage ever since. Roger married Joan de Geneville, the daughter of a neighbouring lord, in 1301, when he was just 14, her eventual inheritance, coupled with his own, helping to swell the already vast family estates in the so-called Marcher lands on the border of England and Wales. When Roger's father was killed in battle in 1304, Roger – then 17 – was made a ward of the royal favourite Piers Gaveston until he came of age, after which he carved out a reputation as a soldier, defending and adding to his family's properties in Ireland and Wales.

In 1307, King Edward I died and his son became Edward II. Cowed by his father as a boy, young Edward, though outwardly imposing, was timid and easily led – a weakness that others eagerly exploited. First to do so was Mortimer's former guardian, Piers Gaveston, a one-time companion to the prince who now became his lover. The king showered him with privileges, even making him regent in 1308 when Edward travelled to France to marry Isabella, sister of the king of France. Furious and resentful, the country's barons eventually rebelled in 1312, and Gaveston was executed by order of the earl of Lancaster. To their dismay, a new favourite took his place – his name, Hugh Despenser. In 1306, Hugh had married Eleanor de Clare, a granddaughter of Edward I, and through the king's patronage, he secured ever more wealth, land and influence, becoming royal chamberlain in 1318 and one of the richest nobles in the kingdom.

The Despensers' lands bordered the Mortimers', and the families hated each other. When Hugh tried to expand his territories into South Wales, threatening Mortimer's own interests in the region, loathing for the Despensers finally outweighed his loyalty to the king and he joined the earls of Hereford, Lancaster and Pembroke – equally disenchanted with the king's behaviour – in open rebellion. In August 1321, the Contrariants, as they were known, marched to London, where they forced Edward to banish

their hated rivals. The king, however, swiftly mobilized support and a royal army, Hugh and his father among them, marched west to confront the rebels. In January 1322, abandoned by his allies, Roger surrendered in Shrewsbury.

Mortimer was imprisoned for the next two years in the Tower of London, but after drugging his jailers, he escaped from his cell, climbed out of the Tower through a chimney, crossed the Thames in an awaiting boat, and rode to Dover, from where he crossed to France. He was warmly welcomed in Paris by Edward's enemy, the French king, Charles IV. The following year, in a dispute over Edward's French territories, Edward sent Queen Isabella, accompanied by their son Edward, to negotiate a settlement. Isabella despised Hugh Despenser as much as Roger did, and Mortimer and Isabella soon became lovers.

In 1326, having moved to Flanders, Isabella and Mortimer gathered an army of 700 men and returned to England, intent on revenge. The Despensers, caught by surprise, were routed, and, within the month, King Edward, deserted by his nobles, was captured by Mortimer's forces in South Wales. Brutal reprisals followed. Hugh's father was hanged and beheaded in Bristol in October 1326. The following month, at Hereford, Hugh himself was dragged behind four horses, hanged to the point of suffocation, cut down just before he died, then tied to a ladder where his penis and testicles were sliced off and burned before his eyes. While he was still conscious, his abdomen was cut open and his entrails and heart removed. Afterwards, his head was hacked off and mounted on the gates of London, while the four quarters of his body were sent to Bristol, Dover, York and Newcastle.

Edward, meanwhile, had been forced to abdicate in favour of his son, Edward III, who was 'crowned' at a ceremony in January 1327. Though monarch in name, the new king was treated as a puppet by Mortimer, who, though taking no official position, controlled the country with Isabella for the next three years, handing out titles and lands to his family and granting himself the ostentatious title 'the earl of March'. Edward II was taken in April to Berkeley Castle, home of Mortimer's son-in-law Thomas Berkeley, and never seen again. According to a later history by Sir Thomas More, he was killed at Mortimer's instigation by means of a red-hot poker inserted into his anus (thus leaving no marks).

Mortimer's actions provoked fury among the country's barons, prompting him to keep a body of armed men at court at all times, but he finally overreached himself when, in 1330, he ordered the execution of Edward's popular uncle, Edmund, earl of Kent. Fearing that Mortimer planned to usurp the throne, prominent barons, led by his former ally the earl of Lancaster, urged Edward III to strike against Roger before it was too late, and the young king, almost come of age and determined to throw off Mortimer's hated yoke, eagerly took his chance. While the royal household was at Nottingham Castle in October, he and his supporters, guided by two members of the royal household – Richard Bury and William Montagu – bypassed Mortimer's guards via a subterranean passage (still known as 'Mortimer's Hole') and took Mortimer and Isabella by surprise in the queen's bedroom. Despite Isabella's plea, 'Fair son, have pity on the gentle Mortimer', Roger was arrested and taken to the Tower of London where, without trial, he was condemned for treason and sentenced to death. On 29 November 1330, he was taken to Tyburn, stripped naked, and hanged – the fate usually reserved for a commoner – his body being left on the scaffold for two days before being cut down.

Mortimer's rise to power was remarkable, and his fall equally spectacular. Instead of learning from the greed and arrogance of those he toppled, he repeated their mistakes, alienating his fellow barons and foolishly under-estimating the young king he attempted to control – a king who went on to become one of the greatest monarchs of the Middle Ages. The risks Mortimer took were huge – even his own son, Geoffrey, called him the 'king of folly' – and he eventually paid the price.

An idealized representation of Roger Mortimer: lover of Edward II's wife Isabella of France, instigator of Edward's brutal assassination, and for three years de facto ruler of England.

ISABELLA, THE SHE-WOLF OF FRANCE

Isabella, queen consort to Edward II, was a stunning creature, described by one contemporary as 'the beauty of beauties'. But her life was fraught with humiliations and triumphs, and in the end Edward's neglect led her to betray him.

Isabella was the only surviving daughter of Philip IV of France. When she was no more than an infant, Philip proposed her as the future wife of the heir to the English throne, with the aim of easing tensions between the two countries. The marriage duly took place in Boulogne in 1308. Isabella was only 12 years old; the lacklustre Edward II, who had succeeded his formidable father, Edward I, the year before, was twice her age.

The young king was tall, fair-haired, handsome – and almost certainly homosexual, favouring as he did a succession of young, good-looking male courtiers. Before he even returned to England after his marriage he had passed on Philip's wedding gifts to his current favourite, Piers Gaveston. Although Isabella bore him four children, Edward rarely showed her any affection, leading her to describe herself as 'the most wretched of wives'. She found Edward's fondness for Hugh Despenser, who had succeeded Gaveston in the king's affections, particularly odious; one contemporary chronicler suggested that, such was

The French actress Sophie Marceau plays Isabella in Mel Gibson's violent and fanciful medieval epic Braveheart *(1995).*

her revulsion for the man, Despenser may even have raped her. In 1321, pregnant with her fourth and final child, she begged Edward to exile Despenser and his powerful father, also called Hugh. This he did, only to recall them the following year – to Isabella's despair.

The king was oblivious to his wife's feelings. In 1325 he sent her to France as his envoy to her brother, Charles IV. Once in Paris, Isabella found excuses not to return; it seems she feared the Despensers wanted her dead. In her self-imposed exile she began to associate with some of Edward's disaffected nobles, among them Roger Mortimer, with whom she was soon sharing her bed. Crucially, they were in control of the king's heir, also called Edward, who had been sent to France to join his mother.

After their 1326 coup, the lovers ruled England in the name of Edward III, until in 1330 the young king arrested and executed Mortimer.

Isabella herself was allowed by her son, despite her betrayal of his father, to retire into rural obscurity for her remaining three decades, with all the wealth and dignities of a queen dowager. This wronged woman, capable of great love as well as great betrayal, is now remembered as an adultress, a traitor and a regicide.

Peter I, ruler of the medieval Spanish kingdom of Castile, earned the soubriquet 'Pedro the Cruel'. Unfaithful in love, as in war, Pedro presided over a vicious reign that only ended with his own brutal murder at the hands of his equally despicable bastard half-brother.

Pedro the Cruel 1334–69

'In the matter of deception, false dealing, cunning, and remorseless treachery, Pedro was no whit worse than any of his relatives or vassals. It was only in his cold-blooded ferocity, his fierce, unrestrained passions, and his intense, almost inhuman selfishness that he surpasses them...'

PETER THE CRUEL, EDWARD STORER

Pedro was the son of Alfonso XI of Castile and his Portuguese wife Maria, and his childhood was a miserable one. Alfonso abandoned Pedro's mother for Leonor de Guzman, and made it clear that he preferred the sons of his mistress to his legitimate son. The eldest of Pedro's illegitimate half-brothers, Enrique de Trastámara, would later emerge as the greatest single challenge to Pedro's birthright.

When Alfonso died in 1350, Pedro acceded to the throne. He was only 16, and during the early years of his reign he was overshadowed by his mother and her circle of favourites. The French king, John II, saw in Pedro's minority an opportunity to force Castile into a military alliance against England. At the queen

mother's behest, this alliance was concluded in 1352, and a year later Pedro was forced to marry Blanche, daughter of the duke of Bourbon. Already, however, the young king had become obsessed with his beautiful mistress, Maria de Padilla, and he soon abandoned Blanche for her. In so doing, he committed a major act of lèse-majesté against his bride, and broke the Franco-Castilian agreement that the marriage had helped cement.

Unsurprisingly, given his demolition of her careful international diplomacy, a period of conflict between Pedro and his mother followed – and, for a time, the king found himself imprisoned. But, with the aid of a loyal minister, Pedro escaped, and resolved to end his mother's influence.

Pedro the Cruel, king of Castile, depicted in a 17th-century copper engraving.

Now established as his own man, Pedro soon embarked on a decade-long clash with the neighbouring Spanish kingdom of Aragon. In the 'War of the Two Peters' (1356–66), Pedro attempted to force the submission of his namesake, Pedro IV of Aragon. It proved to be an unattainable goal.

Whilst the war was being fought (and lost) abroad, Pedro ratcheted up the level of repression at home. The king's tyrannical rule provoked a series of uprisings, and his bastard half-brother, Enrique de Trastámara, established himself as a focus for those discontented with the regime. But Pedro saw off all such challenges, ruthlessly crushing any hint of opposition. His own sense of insecurity only served to intensify the tyranny of his rule.

In 1366 an international coalition – including Charles V of France, Pope Urban V and the king of Aragon – was persuaded to support the claim of Enrique de Trastámara to the throne. When Enrique himself arrived in Castile at the head of a mercenary army, Pedro fled his kingdom – though not before one final act of brutality. Even as he prepared to abandon his throne, Pedro arranged for the murder of Archbishop Suero of Santiago, along with his dean, Peralvarez.

After departing Castile, Pedro threw himself on the mercy of the brilliant English general, Edward the Black Prince – with whose country Pedro had concluded an alliance in 1362. After achieving victory at the Battle of Nájera in 1367, Edward helped to restore Pedro to his throne. It was, however, to be a brief homecoming. In 1369 the Black Prince – already appalled at his ally's behaviour – fell ill and then left Castile. In the absence of his military guarantor and protector, Pedro's vulnerability once more became obvious, and Enrique and his French allies mounted another assault against him.

This time Pedro did not flee, and in March 1369 the opposing armies faced each other at Montiel.

ROYAL EPITHETS

Several royals are called 'the Great', but one nation's 'great' is another's monster. Alexander the Great does not enjoy this nickname in Persia for example. Herod the Great was so named simply because he was the older of a line of Herods – yet his name was based on the Greek word hērōs (hero) and despite his monstrosity he was also a great king, builder of the Temple (see page 25). Only one English king bears the epithet – Alfred the Great – yet if any earned it, it should be Edward III, Henry V and Elizabeth I. Russia has two (Peter I and Catherine II, the latter flatteringly thus named by Voltaire); Germany one (Frederick II of Prussia): all three deserve it.

Some names are self-explanatory: from Caliph Omar the Just, conqueror of Jerusalem (c. 582–644), to Alexander the Fierce of Scotland (c. 1078–1124); from Alfonso the Chaste, king of Asturias (759–842) to Ethelred the Unready of England (968–1016); and from Charles the Simple of France (879–929) to Charles the Rash of Burgundy (1433–77). Hammers denote military prowess, as in Charles Martel, who saved Europe from Muslim conquest at the Battle of Tours (732), Edward I, Hammer of the Scots (1239–1307) and Judah the Hammer or Maccabee (190–160 BC), founder of the Hasmonean Jewish dynasty. The Spanish kingdom of Aragon had two rulers called Alfonso the Magnanimous – a preferable nickname to that of the 12th-century king of León, Alfonso the Slobberer (1171–1230), or indeed his earlier counterpart, Bermudo the Gouty (956–9). Poland has Boleslaw the Brave (967–1025), Boleslaw the Wry-Mouthed (1085–1138) and Boleslaw the Curly (1120–73). Augustus the Strong, king of Poland and elector of Saxony (1670–1733), earned his name not through victory on the battlefield but prolific virility in fathering 300 children. The Holy Roman Empire boasted Charles the Bald (823–77) and Charles the Fat (839–88), the latter soubriquet shared by Alfonso II of Portugal (1185–1223) and Louis VI of France (1081–1137).

Henry the Fowler of Germany (876–936) was so called because he learned of his accession to the throne while setting up birding nets. In the early 16th century, after the death of her beloved husband Philip the Handsome of Castile (1478–1506), Queen Joanna took his coffin wherever she went, sometimes showering his corpse with kisses and becoming known as Joanna the Mad. This was probably preferable, however, to Abdul the Damned, a derogatory Western European nickname referring to the role of the Ottoman sultan Abdul

In an attempt to avert battle, Pedro agreed to a parley under the auspices of one of Enrique's allies, Bertrand du Guesclin. But no sooner had he arrived in du Guesclin's tent than he was handed over to Enrique. Face to face at last with his rival, Enrique immediately plunged his sword through Pedro's heart and declared himself Enrique II, king of Castile.

Much of Pedro's dark reputation comes from the writings of Lopez de Ayala, who became court chronicler to Enrique, the man who usurped him. Those who looked upon Pedro more favourably posthumously awarded him the epithet 'El Justiciero', the executor of justice, seeing Pedro as the king who brought the rule of law to Castile. Meanwhile, the English poet Geoffrey Chaucer remembered Pedro thus:

> O noble, O worthy Pedro, glory of Spain,
> Whem Fortune held so high in majesty,
> Well oughte men thy piteous death complain.

But such favourable appraisals were by no means disinterested. Pedro's alleged 'law-giving' was extolled by groups such as the merchants – but only because Pedro's attacks on the nobility benefited them. Similarly, Chaucer's praise must be seen in the context of England's support for Pedro after 1362. Taking the long view, the sobriquet 'Pedro the Cruel' appears more fitting for a man whose violent death was mourned by few.

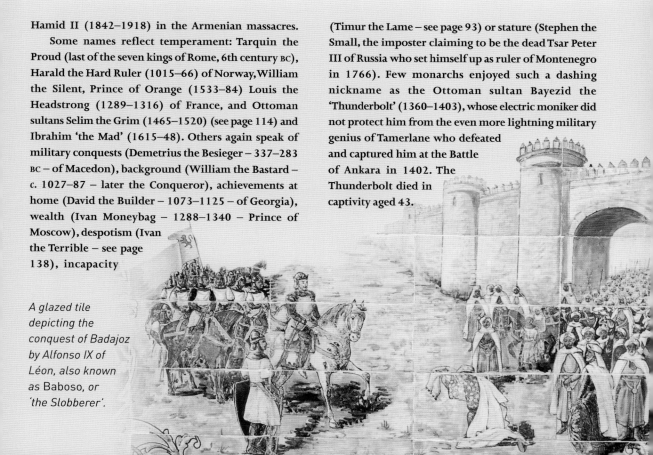

Hamid II (1842–1918) in the Armenian massacres.

Some names reflect temperament: Tarquin the Proud (last of the seven kings of Rome, 6th century BC), Harald the Hard Ruler (1015–66) of Norway, William the Silent, Prince of Orange (1533–84) Louis the Headstrong (1289–1316) of France, and Ottoman sultans Selim the Grim (1465–1520) (see page 114) and Ibrahim 'the Mad' (1615–48). Others again speak of military conquests (Demetrius the Besieger – 337–283 BC – of Macedon), background (William the Bastard – c. 1027–87 – later the Conqueror), achievements at home (David the Builder – 1073–1125 – of Georgia), wealth (Ivan Moneybag – 1288–1340 – Prince of Moscow), despotism (Ivan the Terrible – see page 138), incapacity (Timur the Lame – see page 93) or stature (Stephen the Small, the imposter claiming to be the dead Tsar Peter III of Russia who set himself up as ruler of Montenegro in 1766). Few monarchs enjoyed such a dashing nickname as the Ottoman sultan Bayezid the 'Thunderbolt' (1360–1403), whose electric moniker did not protect him from the even more lightning military genius of Tamerlane who defeated and captured him at the Battle of Ankara in 1402. The Thunderbolt died in captivity aged 43.

A glazed tile depicting the conquest of Badajoz by Alfonso IX of Léon, also known as Baboso, or 'the Slobberer'.

Tamerlane was a world conqueror, statesman and military commander of astonishing brilliance and brutal ferocity who built an empire stretching from India to Russia and the Mediterranean Sea. Never defeated in battle, the ultimate hero-monster, he ranks alongside Genghis Khan and Alexander the Great as one of the great conquerors of all time yet he left in his wake both pyramids of human skulls and the aesthetic beauty of his capital Samarkand.

Tamerlane 1336–1405

'He loved bold and valiant soldiers, by whose aid he opened the locks of terror, tore men to pieces like lions, and overturned mountains.'

ARAB WRITER AHMAD IBN ARABSHAH, DESCRIBING TAMERLANE

Timur – meaning 'Iron' in Turkic – was born in Kesh, south of Samarkand, in 1336. His father was a minor chief of the Barlas tribe, settled in Transoxiana (roughly present-day Uzbekistan), at the heart of the crumbling Mongol empire, which was breaking apart into warring factions ruled by descendants of Genghis Khan: chief among them the Jagatai, the il-Khanid dynasty and the so-called Golden Horde. The situation within the Jagatai khanate – of which the Barlas were a part – was further complicated by tensions between predominantly nomadic tribes and those wanting a settled life of peace and trade. Tribal infighting was consequently common, and participating in a raid as a young man, Timur – described by contemporaries as strong, with a large head and long beard of a reddish hue – sustained wounds that left him partially paralyzed down one side and with a distinctive limp, hence the nickname 'Timur the lame', later abbreviated to 'Tamerlane'. He nonetheless became a skilled horseman and superior soldier, quickly building up a substantial following. According to the Arab writer Arabshah, he was 'steadfast in mind and robust in body, brave and fearless, firm as rock . . . faultless in strategy'. Intellectually he was equally adept, speaking at least two languages, Persian and Turkic, and having a keen interest in history, philosophy, religion, and architecture, as well as being an enthusiastic chess player.

In 1361, Timur was put in charge of the area round Samarkand, having sworn allegiance to Tughluq, who had taken over the Jagatai khanate. When Tughluq died soon afterwards, Timur cemented his position by forming a coalition with Hussein, another tribal chief, whose power base was in Balkh. The two carved up much of the surrounding area as their armies swept aside rival tribes, but simmering tensions in their relationship – previously kept in check by family ties – erupted after the death of Timur's first wife, Hussein's sister. Timur – who had won popular support by generously rewarding loyalty – turned on and defeated his former ally, only to release him shortly afterwards, overwhelmed at the sight of his old friend in shackles. Such leniency, however, was short-lived. Timur subsequently had two of Hussein's sons executed, taking four of his wives for his own, and hunting down his prominent supporters throughout the region, beheading them and sharing their wives and children among his men like gifts.

By 1370, as the undisputed leader of an ever-expanding domain centred on Samarkand – where he had opulent temples and beautiful gardens constructed behind new defensive walls and a moat – Tamerlane began to dream of greatness. Claiming descent from Genghis Khan (though he was probably Turkic), he announced his goal of re-establishing the Mongol empire. First, though, he had to bring stability to his new regime, so he married Hussein's widow, Sarai Khanum, and used only the title Emir

– the Commander, nominally ruling through Genghizid puppets. He re-established and monopolized the Silk Road, by which trade had once passed from China to Europe. Through this strategy of war abroad and peace at home, he could satisfy those who longed for new conquests as well as those who wanted prosperous stability.

Tamerlane presided over a highly efficient war machine, divided into 'tumen', units of 10,000 men, a skilled cavalry – including, eventually, an elephant corps from India – equipped with supplies for lengthy campaigns and heavily armed with bows and swords, as well as catapults and battering rams for siege warfare. His soldiers – whose livelihoods depended on conquest – were composed of an eclectic ethnic mix, including Turks, Georgians, Arabs and Indians. Between 1380 and 1389 Timur embarked on a series of campaigns in which he conquered a colossal empire, embracing Persia, Iraq, Armenia, Georgia and Azerbaijan, Anatolia, Syria, all of Central Asia, northern India, the approaches to China and much of southern Russia: his longest struggle was against Tokhtamysh, Khan of the Golden Horde, whom he finally defeated and destroyed in 1391.

Terror was a key weapon in Tamerlane's armoury. He sent secret agents ahead of his troops to spread rumours about the atrocities he had committed – such as the vast pyramids of decapitated heads constructed by his soldiers to celebrate victories in battle or the mass killing of around 70,000 citizens in Ifshahan, 20,000 at Aleppo, the beheading of 70,000 in Tikrit and 90,000 in Baghdad, the incineration of a mosque full of people in Damascus and wholesale destruction of cities in Persia following a revolt there in 1392. Fear alone was often sufficient to ensure compliance – but many millions were killed in his campaigns. Yet he beautified Samarkand, created the game of Tamerlane chess, practised religious tolerance and engaged scholars in learned debates on philosophy and faith. He was altogether an extraordinary man, contradictory, a force of nature. In 1398 – extending his empire further than either Alexander the Great or Genghis Khan had achieved – Tamerlane invaded India and captured Delhi. A hundred thousand civilians were massacred there, and a similar number of Indian soldiers murdered in cold blood after their surrender following the Battle of Panipat. Still Tamerlane pressed on. In 1401, his men conquered Syria, rampaging through Damascus; in July 1402, after a huge and bloody battle near Ankara, Tamerlane defeated the Ottoman sultan Bayezid I, looting, among other treasures, the famous gates from the Ottoman palace of Brusa; and later the same year he annihilated the Christian city of Smyrna, floating the severed heads of his victims out to sea on candlelit dishes. By 1404, even the Byzantine emperor John I was paying him tribute in return for a guarantee of safety.

A bronze bust of Tamerlane the Great. Ruthless, determined and cruel, Tamerlane was a conqueror on a scale that rivalled Genghis Khan, from whom he claimed to be descended.

In his late sixties, Tamerlane embarked on his final adventure – an attempted invasion of China – but he became ill on the march and died in January 1405. His body was returned to Samarkand where a mausoleum was erected to him. After his death, his sons and grandsons fought for control of the empire, before his younger son, Shahrukh, finally assumed power in 1420 as the sole survivor of the family. His most illustrious descendant was Babur, founder of the Timurid dynasty that ruled India as the Mughals until 1857. A ruthless killer, whose armies were responsible for unrivalled pillage and brutality, Tamerlane was equally a shrewd statesman, brilliant general and sophisticated patron of the arts. Revered in Uzbekistan to this day – his monument in Tashkent standing where Marx's statue once presided – Tamerlane was buried in a beautiful simple tomb in Samarkand. Legend said that the disturber of his tomb would be cursed: in June 1941, a Soviet historian opened the tomb. Days later, Hitler attacked Soviet Russia.

MARLOWE'S TAMBURLAINE THE GREAT

Through the sheer scale of his barbarity, Tamerlane continued to enthral and horrify future generations in equal measure. Christopher Marlowe – the English Renaissance poet and contemporary of Shakespeare – attempted to capture the ferocity of his reign of terror in the two-part play, *Tamburlaine the Great*, first performed in 1590. Centred on Tamerlane's relationship with the Egyptian king's daughter, the play presents him as an articulate and passionate man, both temperamental and terrifying, 'a sturdy Felon and base-bred Thief'. In one scene, a messenger describes the sabre-rattling approach of Tamerlane's armies:

> Three hundred thousand men in armour clad,
> Upon their pransing Steeds, disdainfully
> With wanton paces trampling on the ground.
> Five hundred thousand footmen threatning shot,
> Shaking their swords, their speares and yron bils,
> Environing their Standard round, that stood
> As bristle-pointed as a thorny wood.
> Their warlike Engins and munition
> Exceed the forces of their martial men.

Christopher Marlowe (1564–93), one of Elizabethan England's greatest poets and playwrights, was stabbed to death in mysterious circumstances in May 1593.

Over the course of the play, Tamerlane defeats Mycetes, the Persian emperor, rests his feet on the vanquished Turkish king, Bajazeth (Bayezid), kills his own son for cowardice, burns the Qur'an and declares himself to be greater than God. 'I am Tamburlaine,' says Marlowe's hero, 'scourge of God.'

Divisive, murderous and vindictive, Robert of Geneva – later the so-called 'Anti-Pope' Clement VII – ordered the massacre of thousands of innocent men, women and children in Cesena, Italy, in the name of the Roman Catholic Church, only to undermine that same Church by setting up a rival papacy in Avignon, France, where he sullied the office with his corruption and greed.

(Anti-) Pope Clement VII

1342–94

'Both popes declared a crusade against each other. Each . . . claimed the right to create cardinals and to confirm archbishops, bishops and abbots, so that there were two Colleges of Cardinals and in many places two claimants for the high positions in the Church. Each . . . attempted to collect all the ecclesiastical revenues, and each excommunicated the other with all his adherents.'

APPRAISAL BY FR JOHN LAUX, IN HIS CHURCH HISTORY, P. 405

Robert of Geneva was born in the opulent castle of Annecy, about 20 miles south of Geneva. He was the youngest son of Amadeus III, Count of Geneva, and, through his mother, the nephew of Cardinal Guy of Boulogne, scion of a wealthy noble family with close connections to the Church.

Robert was a distinguished scholar, with a brilliant intellect, but he was to prove equally adept in the bitter power struggles that characterized the Church in the 14th century. Appointed 'protonotary apostolic' in 1359, he became bishop of Thérouanne two years later, and was made archbishop of Cambrai in 1368, aged just 26. Pope Gregory IX recognized his talents, promoting him to cardinal on 30 May 1371.

Robert achieved the reputation for viciousness that would remain with him for the rest of his life while serving as Gregory IX's legate in Italy from 1376 to 1378. During this period, the Papal States – the civil territory over which the pope claimed temporal authority – were in

The stone head of the Antipope Clement VII in the Church of St Peter, Avignon. The Great Western Schism (1378–1417) was a split in the Catholic Church, which led to the appointment of a pope in Avignon as a rival to the 'official' pope in Rome.

revolt against the authority of Rome. Charged with suppressing the rebellion, Robert enlisted the help of Sylvester Budes, leader of a band of Breton mercenaries, and Sir John Hawkwood, a notorious English soldier of fortune.

In February 1377, Hawkwood and the Bretons arrived at Cesena, an ancient city in the province of Forli, and the centre of the revolt. Situated on a hill near the River Savio, it was a heavily fortified town – but it was no match for the mercenaries, whose army, financed by the papacy, soon destroyed its defensive walls and entered the town.

Hawkwood was prepared to offer the townspeople clemency in return for surrender, but his paymaster, Robert, overruled him, ordering they be put to the sword. Gangs of drunken mercenaries were let loose upon the town, rampaging through the streets in an orgy of slaughter. Some broke into the convent and raped the nuns, while others vandalized the Church of St Stephen, killing those who had sheltered inside. Around 4000 bodies were buried over the following weeks, Robert becoming known thereafter as 'the Butcher of Cesena'.

The following year, in April 1378, Robert participated in the election of Bartolomeo Prignano as Pope Urban VI. Almost immediately, however, offended by Urban's lofty and insulting behaviour, the cardinals formed a conclave to reconsider, and in August they nullified Urban's election, opting instead on 20 September to elect Robert as Pope Clement VII.

Acting with the support of King Charles V of France, Clement VII established his papal residence at Avignon, a wealthy city on the River Rhône. France was joined by Scotland and some German states in recognizing Clement, while Urban VI continued to govern from Rome, supported by Spain and the Italian states. So began 'the Great Schism', a period of division and bitterness in the Church that only ended in 1417.

Clement's Avignon pontificate was not without its achievements, and many of the appointments he made to bishoprics in dominions accepting his authority were considered a success. Removed however from the traditional seat of religious authority, he was dragged into the murky labyrinth of French court politics, in which money and power triumphed over piety. To meet expenses, he was forced to resort to simony (the sale of ecclesiastical offices) and extortion, mainly by levying extremely heavy taxation on the French clergy. He also donated large portions of the Papal States to the powerful Louis II of Anjou, as a reward for his continued support.

Ultimately, the Catholic Church wrote Clement VII out of its official history: as far as it was concerned, the 'real' Clement VII was Giulio di Giulano de Medici, who reigned as pope from 1523 to 1534. Without his pontificate, Robert remains just the Butcher of Cesena.

ANTI-POPES AND THE FEMALE POPE

In the history of the Roman Catholic Church there have been between 30 and 40 anti-popes who in dangerous and chaotic times have claimed the allegiance of at least some of the ecclesiastical hierarchy.

The earliest anti-pope was Hippolytus of Rome, who fought the papal authorities in the third century and established a rival congregation. For his heresy, he was arrested in 235 and transported to the mines of Sardinia, where he died. However, he was posthumously reconciled with the Church and subsequently canonized as Saint Hippolytus of Rome.

Another third-century anti-pope was Novatia, who claimed the authority of the Holy See in opposition to Pope Cornelius but was hounded out of Rome in 258.

The 11th and 12th centuries were the golden age of the anti-pope, as successive Holy Roman emperors — rulers of the German states — responded to clashes with the authorities in Rome by appointing their own Supreme Pontiffs. The most famous of these was Anacletus II, dubbed 'the Jewish Pope' by Voltaire. Anacletus was a member of the hugely rich Pierleoni family — meaning 'sons of Peter Leo' — who were descended from Leo de Benedicto, an 11th-century Jewish convert. Anacletus established himself in opposition to

Pope Joan, the fictitious female pope who supposedly gave birth to a son on her way to the Lateran Palace, is shown hanging in Hell. According to a version of the legend recounted by Jean de Mailly in the 13th century, Joan was tied to the tail of a horse, dragged around Rome, stoned to death and buried at the place where she died.

the legally elected holder of the office, Pope Innocent II, whom he forced out of Rome, ruling in his place from 1131–8. Anacletus was attacked by Innocent's supporters because of his Jewish origin and appearance, and was unfairly accused of the robbery of churches, as well as incest.

For much of the medieval period, a popular rumour circulated concerning a female pope, Pope Joan, who had supposedly reigned for two and a half years during the 850s. Despite the fact that Joan probably never existed, she continued to appear in Christian iconography for centuries to come, either as an angel or as the Whore of Babylon. According to one story, she gave birth while processing from St Peter's to the Lateran — and it was said that subsequent popes always averted their eyes from the supposed place of her shame while passing that way.

Richard II's reign was a personal and political tragedy. As a ruler, he was rigid, inept, inconsistent, paranoid, untrustworthy and vindictive – yet he was also a refined patron of the arts and the boy king who bravely faced the terrifying rebellious mobs of the Peasants' Revolt. Richard's tragedy was to succeed to the throne as an unprepared, callow and foolish child in the shadow of his grandfather Edward III, one of the most heroic of English kings, and his father, the Black Prince, paragon of knighthood.

Richard II 1367–1400

'He threw down all who violated the royal prerogative; he destroyed heretics and scattered their friends.'

RICHARD II'S CHOSEN EPITAPH FOR HIS TOMB IN WESTMINSTER ABBEY

Born in Bordeaux to Edward, Prince of Wales, and the beautiful Joan the Fair Maiden of Kent, Richard became next in line to the throne after his father following the death of his elder brother in infancy. When his father died in 1376 and then his grandfather shortly afterwards, Richard became the new king in 1377, at just ten years old, assisted by his tutor, a loyal family friend, Sir Simon Burley. For the first four years of his reign, power was unofficially devolved to three royal councils but much of the government of the country fell to John of Gaunt, Richard's uncle, a controversial but capable statesman.

Richard was tall, fair and handsome but regarded as effeminate, more interested in elaborate forms of etiquette – he demanded that spoons were used at court and was said to have invented the handkerchief – than

cont p. 98

A portrait of Richard II from the 1390s. A weak, stammering character whose personality never matched the demands of kingship, Richard alienated England's powerful magnates and ushered in a century of national strife and discord.

THE PEASANTS' REVOLT

The Peasants' Revolt of 1381 was the first great popular rebellion in English history. It started in the village of Fobbing in Essex in May 1381, and another outbreak followed shortly afterwards in Kent. Before long, much of southeast England and East Anglia was affected.

The spark for the revolt was the poll tax, the third such tax in four years, intended to pay for the long drawn-out war with France – the Hundred Years' War. The tax, which demanded the same amount from every individual regardless of wealth, had been introduced largely on the advice of John of Gaunt, uncle to the young Richard II. The country was also suffering from the long-term impact of the Black Death of 1348–9, during which as much as one-third of the population may have died of plague. With fewer people to work the land, the peasantry had come to expect more money for their labour. However, the nobility had begun to work together in Parliament to keep peasant wages down.

On 12 June the Essex rebels set up camp at Mile End, on the edge of London, demanding a charter of rights. On 13 June a band of rebels from Kent arrived at Blackheath, led by the charismatic Wat Tyler. Over the next two days the poor of London rallied behind the rebels, opening the gates of the city to them. Full of anger and alcohol, the rebels burnt down the Savoy Palace, the home of John of Gaunt, as well as several villages on the fringes of the city.

On 14 June the 14-year-old Richard, surrounded by his knights and a number of lords, met the Essex rebels at Mile End, where he agreed to honour their demands. Later the same day, however, it emerged that another faction of the rebels had stormed the Tower of London, where they had seized the Archbishop of Canterbury, the Lord Chancellor and the Lord Treasurer – all associated with the poll tax – and beheaded them on Tower Hill.

On 15 June Richard met the Kentish rebels at Smithfield. They gave him a list of demands, including the abolition of the nobility and of serfdom, and the distribution of the wealth of the Church among the people. According to some chroniclers, Wat Tyler addressed the king in a rude manner, prompting the Mayor of London to attack him with his dagger. Tyler fell from his horse, and was killed by one of the king's squires. At this moment Richard rode into the centre of the crowd, demanding their loyalty and promising them concessions. Meanwhile the Lord Mayor and his men surrounded the rest of the rebel leaders and put them to the slaughter.

Outside London, vengeance against the rebels was swift and brutal. Hundreds were hanged, and on 15 June one of the rebel leaders from Kent, John Ball, known as the 'mad priest', was hanged, drawn and quartered in front of the triumphant young king.

An illumination (c. 1460/80) from Jean Froissart's Chronicles *depicting the encounter between the 14-year-old Richard II and the rebels in Smithfield, London, on 15 June 1381. The rebel leader Wat Tyler is struck by Sir William Walworth, Lord Mayor of London (left), while Richard tries to soothe the rebels.*

success on the battlefield, a betrayal of the 'warrior' tradition of English kings. In January 1382, the king married the docile and popular Anne of Bohemia and, two years after Anne's death in 1394, the seven-year-old princess Isabella, daughter of Charles VI of France. But Richard never fathered a legitimate heir and his reign was characterized by his controversial relationship with a series of male favourites – men such as Michael de la Pole and Robert de Vere, with whom Richard was alleged to have had a homosexual affair.

Following a series of costly wars with France, Richard's advisers raised levels of taxation, leading to the Peasants' Revolt of June 1381, led by Wat Tyler, in which bands of peasants and artisans from Essex and Kent marched to London, sacking the city and demanding a charter of rights (see page 97). On 16 June 1381, at just 14, Richard negotiated directly with the rebels at Smithfield. When a violent altercation broke out and Wat Tyler was murdered by the king's men, Richard took control of the crowd, declaring 'you shall have no captain but me'. As hundreds followed him away from the scene, his men rounded up and murdered the remaining rebel leaders. Richard had shown bravery and initiative but he had also participated in what was almost certainly a pre-planned and violent betrayal of his suffering subjects, in which hundreds were executed on the streets and many more were hanged over the following weeks.

Having dealt successfully with the Peasants' Revolt, Richard faced a more serious problem: opposition from some of the most powerful barons of the realm. In 1386, after Richard had made a botched attempt to invade Scotland, a group of these nobles in parliament – calling themselves 'the Lords Appellant', because of their calls for good governance – demanded that Richard remove his unpopular councillors. Led by the king's uncle, Thomas of Woodstock, duke of Gloucester, the other Lords Appellant were Thomas Beauchamp, earl of Warwick; Richard FitzAlan, earl of Arundel; Thomas Mowbray, earl of Nottingham; and his cousin, Henry Bolingbroke, earl of Derby, son of John of Gaunt and a potential rival for the throne.

When Richard accused them of treason, the Lords Appellant revolted, eventually defeating Richard's armies at Radcot Bridge, outside Oxford, and briefly imprisoning him in the Tower of London. In February 1388, eight of the king's councillors were executed by the so-called 'Merciless Parliament'. De la Pole and de Vere fled England as the Lords Appellant took control, arguing that Richard was still too young to govern the country.

The Lords Appellant failed in military campaigns against the Scots and the French – and in 1389, when John of Gaunt returned to England from Spain, Richard rebuilt his authority; Mowbray and Bolingbroke defected back to the king who, now 22, sidelined the Appellants and seized control. Increasingly arrogant and authoritarian, he believed that he had a God-given right to rule. In 1397, Richard invited Warwick to a banquet and arrested him, gave assurances to Arundel that he was not at risk, only to arrest him too, and also had Gloucester arrested in France. Arundel was executed, Warwick exiled and his uncle, the earl of Gloucester, smothered to death in Calais.

Increasingly paranoid, Richard kept an armed guard of Cheshire bowmen. In 1399 he unwisely exiled his cousin, Henry Bolingbroke, subsequently seizing his lands. When Richard departed for a military campaign in Ireland, the popular Bolingbroke, who claimed that 'the realm was on the point of being undone for default of governance and undoing of the good laws', landed with a small force in Yorkshire, triggering a widespread rebellion. By the time Richard had arrived back on the Welsh coast, most of the influential nobles of the realm had turned against him. Following his capture, Richard was taken to London and paraded through the streets, where large crowds mocked him and pelted him with rotten fruit. Deposed and humiliated, he was starved to death by his captors in Pontefract Castle in February 1400.

Sadistic, depraved and mentally unhinged, Gilles de Rais was one of the first known serial killers, accused of the torture, rape and murder of scores of boys and young men in pursuit of extreme sexual gratification. His bouts of killing were interspersed with periods in which he would be racked with guilt, only to murder again as soon as the urge gripped him.

Gilles de Rais 1404–40

'Gilles de Rais ... did cut the throats of, kill and heinously massacre many young and innocent boys ... he did practise with these children unnatural lust and the vice of sodomy ...'

REPORT OF THE BISHOP OF NANTES ON GILLES DE RAIS, 1440

Gilles de Rais was born to a wealthy French aristocratic family during the long conflict with England known as the Hundred Years' War. In 1415, when Gilles was just over ten years old, his mother became ill and died, and his father was killed by a wild boar while hunting. That same year, his uncle was killed fighting the English at the Battle of Agincourt, leaving Rais as the heir to the family fortune, which was still, for the moment, controlled by his grandfather, Jean de Craon.

Jean de Craon took custody of Gilles, but showed little interest in the boy's welfare, using him as a political pawn while giving him a free rein to pursue his every desire. After two failed attempts to marry his grandson into wealthy families, he finally succeeded in finding a bride for him – a rich heiress who was kidnapped until she agreed to the marriage. From the age of 23

Rais fought against the English with distinction, serving alongside Joan of Arc on a number of campaigns, although it is not known how close he was to her. Like Joan, he was believed to be deeply pious, and he certainly contributed to the building of a number of churches and one cathedral.

In 1432, the year after Joan had been burnt at the stake, Rais retired from military service and returned to his family's great castle at Machecoul, near the border with Brittany. With his grandfather now also dead, he began to spend his large inheritance on lavish entertainment and a luxurious lifestyle, provoking the irritation of his brother René, who was terrified that Gilles was whittling away the family fortune.

A more sordid truth lurked under the surface. From his base in Machecoul and using a number of accomplices, Gilles de Rais embarked upon a spree of carefully planned, sadistic sex murders, and may have been responsible for the killing of anything between 60 and 200 children – mainly boys – between the ages of 6 and 18.

The victims, who were usually blue-eyed and blond-haired, were either lured to the castle on a variety of pretexts or forcibly taken from the village of Machecoul or the surrounding area. The first victim was said to have been a 12-year-old messenger boy, who was hanged by his neck on a metal hook, raped by Rais, and then murdered. As more and more children disappeared, the finger of suspicion soon pointed at Rais. However, the locals were terrified and ill-equipped to challenge one of the most powerful and wealthy men in France.

The majority of the victims were tortured in a specially built chamber, where they were strung up or tied down and then raped, before being killed by a variety of methods, including dismemberment, decapitation and disembowelment. At his trial Rais confessed to admiring the severed heads of the more beautiful victims, and taking pleasure from seeing their entrails ripped out. It was also alleged that Rais indulged in black magic and devil worship.

Meanwhile, René de Rais had determined to take control of the family fortune before Gilles spent it all, and threatened to march on Machecoul. The duke of Brittany also had designs on Gilles' lands, and captured one of his castles. In response, in May 1440, Gilles seized the brother of one of his foes, a priest who had been in the middle of conducting Mass, provoking the bishop of Nantes – who also had a vested interest in Rais' downfall – to instigate an inquiry into his behaviour.

The bishop went on to interview the families of children abducted by Rais, and built up a shocking case against him. Rais was arrested in September 1440, and indicted on 34 counts of murder. Within a month he had confessed to his crimes – under the threat of torture – and been found guilty of murder, sodomy and heresy. On 16 October 1440, after expressing his remorse and being granted the right of confession, he was hanged and then burned, along with two of his servants.

To the last, Gilles de Rais professed the strength of his faith. The one charge that he refused to admit to was devil worship, and he broke down in a fit of sobbing when he was told that he would be excommunicated and denied the right of confession. Yet such flashes of conscience had done nothing to stop his campaign of sadism, murder and what he called 'carnal delight'.

Two Modern Serial Killers

Serial killers are usually bland, pathetic nonentities seeking empowerment through the destruction of those weaker than themselves. They are scarcely interesting except in the scale of their wickedness, the fascination of their crimes and the allure of their detection: because of the lack of connection with their victims, they are hard to catch, sometimes allowing them to indulge in prolific murderous rampages over many years. Here are two examples: Jeffrey Dahmer – necrophiliac, cannibal and serial killer – was born on 21 May 1960 in Milwaukee, Wisconsin, to a loving and respectable middle-class family. Unbeknownst to his parents, from his teenage years he began to develop homosexual necrophiliac fantasies.

In 1978, just after he left high school, he committed his first murder. His victim was a hitchhiker whom he had picked up. Dahmer then killed him with a barbell and buried his corpse in the woods.

Dahmer waited until 1987 before he murdered his second victim, whom he had met at a gay bar. Until his detection in 1991, he killed at least 15 young men and boys, aged between 14 and 31. He usually picked his victims up in gay bars, sometimes offering them money and drink. He would then slip them a drug, kill them, indulge in necrophilia, then dismember them. He preserved their body parts in jars, boiled their heads so he could keep their skulls as trophies, and ate strips of their flesh. In 1992 he was sentenced to 15 consecutive life terms; two years later he was murdered by a fellow inmate.

Dahmer was by no means the most prolific sex killer of the modern era. This dubious distinction goes to the 'Red Ripper' of Russia, an articulate and well-read family man and former teacher called Andrei Chikatilo, who, it seems, could only achieve sexual gratification during the act of killing. Subsequently he would bite chunks of flesh from his victims. The police eventually caught up with Chikalito in 1990, after they put him under 24-hour surveillance. At his trial he was sentenced to death for the murder of 52 people, including at least 10 young boys and more then 40 females, both young children and prostitutes. He was shot on 14 February 1994.

Andrei Chikatilo (first right), seen in a file photo from April 1992; and Jeffrey Dahmer (second right), photographed by the Milwaukee County Sheriff's office.

The very name of Tomás de Torquemada, the first inquisitor general in Spain, was enough to induce a tremor of fear among even the most hardened of his contemporaries. Since then, Torquemada – the persecutor of Jews, Moors and other supposed 'heretics' under the intolerant and repressive rule of Ferdinand and Isabella – has become a byword for religious fanaticism and persecuting zeal.

Tomás de Torquemada
1420—98

'If anyone possesses a certain amount of learning, he is found to be full of heresies, errors, traces of Judaism. Thus they have imposed silence on men of letters; those who have pursued learning have come to feel, as you say, a great terror.'

DON RODRIGO MANRIQUE, SON OF THE INQUISITOR GENERAL, LETTER TO LUIS VIVES, 1533

Little is known of the early life of Tomás de Torquemada, other than the fact that the man who would become the bane of Spain's Jews was himself of Jewish descent: his grandmother was a *converso* – a Jewish convert to Catholicism. During his youth Torquemada joined the Dominican religious order, and in 1452 he was appointed prior of a monastery in Santa Cruz. Though he continued to occupy that post for the next two decades, he also became a confessor and adviser to King Ferdinand II of Aragon and Queen Isabella I of Castile, whose marriage in 1479 effectively united the two principal Spanish kingdoms. Under their dual monarchy, a renewed effort was made to complete the Reconquista (the re-conquest of Spain from Muslim rule) that had stalled some two centuries earlier. This endeavour ended in success in 1492 with the fall of Granada, the last Muslim outpost in Spain.

In the meantime, Torquemada had convinced the government that the continued presence in Spain of Jews, Muslims and even recent converts to Christianity from those faiths represented a dangerous corruption of the true Catholic faith. As a result of Torquemada's urging, repressive laws had been passed aimed at forcing the expulsion of Spain's non-Christian minorities.

Torquemada found welcome encouragement from the papacy. In 1478 a papal bull from Sixtus IV ordered the setting up of an 'Inquisition', under the authority of the Spanish monarchy, to investigate heresy and guard against religious deviation in Spain. Four years later Torquemada was appointed as one of the 'inquisitors', and shortly afterwards he became inquisitor general, the most senior position in the entire organization.

Torquemada was now almost as powerful as Ferdinand and Isabella themselves; certainly, he was more feared than the temporal authorities. Under his guiding hand the Inquisition hit new heights of activity. In 1484 he oversaw the proclamation of '28 articles', listing the sins that the Inquisition was attempting to expose and purge. They ranged from apostasy and blasphemy to sodomy and sorcery – though many were focused on identifying and exposing Jews. During the course of their investigations, inquisitors were empowered to use all means necessary to discover the truth – a ruling that *de facto* legitimized torture in pursuit of a forced confession.

The result was a policy of violent persecution. In the month of February 1484 alone, 30 people in the city of Ciudad Real were found guilty of an assortment of 'crimes' and burnt alive. Between 1485

and 1501, 250 were burnt in Toledo; and on one occasion in 1492, in Torquemada's home town of Valladolid, 32 people were burnt in one inferno.

Arguing that the soul of Spain was in jeopardy, Torquemada declared that the Jews, in particular, were a mortal threat, and in 1492 Ferdinand and Isabella decreed that all Jews who had not accepted the truth of the Christian revelation were to be expelled from Spain. Some 40,000 left the country – many of them rescued and given sanctuary by the tolerant Islamic Ottomans in Istanbul, Izmir and Selanik (modern Thessaloniki in Greece).

The Virgin of the Catholic Monarchs Ferdinand and Isabella (1490). This allegorical painting shows the Virgin Mary, with the Christ Child on her lap, being worshipped by the Spanish 'Reyes Católicos' Isabella (1451–1504) and Ferdinand (1452–1516), two of their children, and others. Tomás de Torquemada is the friar on the left, kneeling next to the king.

Torquemada still did not deem his work done, and even refused the bishopric of Seville to continue in his role. In so doing, he found that the rewards of his exertions were not solely spiritual; indeed, he amassed a large personal fortune from the confiscated wealth of those whom the Inquisition had found guilty of heresy. Wherever he travelled, he was accompanied by 50 mounted men and 250 foot soldiers, a force that reflected his growing unpopularity, but which also added to the terror and awe inspired when he arrived in a new town to root out its heretics.

Ultimately, only death removed Torquemada from office. Over the previous two decades his relentless zeal had led to as many as two thousand people meeting a hideous end in the flames. Torquemada will forever be remembered as religious bigotry personified – the living incarnation of Fyodor Dostoyevsky's 'Grand Inquisitor' who seeks to burn Jesus Christ himself for the sake of his beloved Catholic Church, but who ends up in a spiritual abyss.

THE SPANISH INQUISITION

The Spanish Inquisition was established on 1 November 1478 by Pope Sixtus IV. Its job was to root out deviance and heresy from within the Church, and every girl over the age of 12 and every boy over the age of 14 was subject to its power. It was not the first time such an entity had been created – an Inquisition had temporarily existed in 13th-century France, to deal with the remnants of the Cathar heretics in the aftermath of the Albigensian Crusade (see page 74). This new Inquisition, however, was to be far more enduring and methodical in its operation.

The first two inquisitors were appointed in 1480, and the first burnings followed a few months later, in February 1481, when six people were executed as heretics. Thereafter the pace of killing picked up, and in February 1482, to cope with the increasing workload, a further seven inquisitors – including Torquemada – were appointed by the pope. Within a decade, the hearings of the Inquisition were operating in eight major cities across Spain.

Inquisitors would arrive in a town and convene a special Mass, which all were obliged to attend. There they would preach a sermon before calling on those guilty of heresy to come forward and confess. Suspected transgressors were given a period of 30 to 40 days to turn themselves in. Those who complied were liable to be 'rewarded' with a less severe penalty than those who proved recalcitrant. Nevertheless, all who did confess were also required to identify other heretics who had not complied. Denunciation was thus as integral to the working of the Inquisition as confession. In consequence, the Inquisition quickly became an opportunity to settle old scores.

The accused were arrested and thrown into prison, and their property, and that of their family, was confiscated. Interrogation then followed, the inquisitors being instructed to apply torture according to their 'conscience and will'. A suspect could have water forced down his throat, be stretched on the rack, or hung with his hands tied behind his back – whatever was deemed necessary to extract a confession. Many were maimed in the process; many others died. And for those who broke under the pressure, there was only one outcome: death by burning. Before being burnt alive at the euphemistically named *auto de fé* ('act of faith'), the victim had two choices. They could repent and kiss the cross, or remain defiant. In the former case they were granted the mercy of being garrotted prior to the flames being lit; otherwise, a protracted and hideously painful death was sure to follow.

Heretics being burned. A still from Stanislav Barabas's 1989 film Torquemada.

Vlad III, *hospodar* (prince) of Wallachia, claimed he was saving his Christian people from the Muslim Ottomans, but he was more interested in wielding his personal power in the treacherous intrigues of local dynastic and imperial politics. He was a degenerate, murderous sadist who displayed a cruelty so savage that he inspired the legend of Dracula. Yet the story of Dracula is tame compared with the reality. Murdering tens of thousands of people – from crippled peasants and vagrants to nobles and foreign ambassadors – he became known as the 'Impaler Prince': his favourite method of execution was to impale his victims on sharpened wooden stakes, oiled at the tip and inserted into their intestines.

Vlad the Impaler 1431–76

Vlad was most likely born in a military fortress, the citadel of Sighisoara, Transylvania, in 1431. His family name was Dracul, meaning dragon, handed down through his father who had been a member of the Order of the Dragon – which Vlad also joined at the age of five – a secret organization created by the Holy Roman Emperor to uphold Christianity and resist Muslim Ottoman incursions into Europe. His mother was a Moldovian princess and his father, Vlad II, a former prince of Wallachia, exiled in Transylvania.

When Vlad was a child, his father, under threat of attack from the Ottoman sultan, had been forced to reassure the Turks of his obedience by sending two of his sons, including Vlad, into Ottoman custody in 1444. The experience, lasting four years, in which he was beaten and whipped for his insolence and fiery character, left Vlad with a hatred of the Turks.

Wallachia (modern-day Romania) was not a traditional hereditary monarchy and although Vlad had a claim to the throne, his father's exile put him in a weak position. His elder brother, Mircea II, briefly ruled in 1442, but was forced into hiding the following year and eventually captured by his enemies in 1447, who burned out his eyes and buried him alive. Wallachian politics were duplicitous and brutal: Vlad's young brother, Radu the Handsome, later enlisted the help of the Ottoman sultan Mehmet II to oust his brother.

In 1447, the same year Mircea was killed, boyars (regional noble families) loyal to John Hunyadi, the White Knight of Hungary, also captured and

Vlad Dracul, prince of Wallachia and prototype for Bram Stoker's classic vampire novel, Dracula.

murdered Vlad's father, claiming he was too dependent on the Ottomans. The Ottomans invaded shortly afterwards to assert their control in the region and briefly installed the 17-year-old Vlad as a puppet prince in 1448, only for Hunyadi to intervene again and force him to flee to Moldovia. Vlad subsequently took the bold step of travelling to Hungary – with which Wallachia had repeatedly been at war. Impressing Hunyadi with his anti-Ottoman credentials, he eventually became Hungary's preferred candidate for the Wallachian throne.

In 1456, as the Hungarians attacked the Ottomans in Serbia, Vlad used the opportunity to invade and take control of Wallachia, killing his rival Vladislav II from the Danesti clan, and taking the throne back for the Draculs. On Easter Sunday, he invited the leading boyars to a banquet, killing the oldest and enslaving those who were still young enough to work. Many died working on new fortifications for Vlad's castles in conditions so severe that their noble finery disintegrated, leaving them naked.

Establishing Tirgoviste as his capital, Vlad was determined to make Wallachia a great kingdom, with a prosperous and healthy people. To him, however, that meant eradicating the nobility, as well as anyone else perceived as a drain on the country's resources. Among his targets were the poorest and most vulnerable – vagrants, the disabled and the mentally ill – thousands of whom he invited to a feast in Tirgoviste, only to lock them in the hall and burn them alive as soon as they had finished eating. (It was dangerous to accept an invitation from Vlad, but even more dangerous to refuse.) Vlad also persecuted women accused of immoral acts such as adultery – their breasts were cut off, and they were then skinned or boiled alive, and their bodies put on public display. German merchants living in Transylvania, whom he regarded as foreign parasites, were also the object of the wrath of Vlad. On St Bartholomew's Day, 1459, he ordered the execution of 30,000 merchants and boyars from the city of Brasov – 10,000 more followed in Sibiu the following year.

Usually his victims were impaled. Death was excruciating and could take hours, as the stake eventually made its way through the guts and out of the mouth. Executing thousands at the same time, he would organize the stakes in concentric circles round his castles, and forbid anyone to remove the victim, often dining in the presence of rotting flesh – the higher the rank, the longer the stake reserved for them. Other methods of execution included skinning and boiling, and he once hammered nails into the heads of foreign ambassadors who refused to remove their hats at his court. Such was his bloodthirstiness that it was also rumoured he drank the blood of his victims and feasted on their flesh.

In the winter of 1461–2, he crossed the Danube and pillaged the Ottoman-controlled area between Serbia and the Black Sea, killing 20,000 people. As Sultan Mehmet II gathered tens of thousands of troops for a revenge mission, they arrived on the banks of the Danube to see 20,000 Turkish prisoners whom Vlad's armies had impaled, creating a forest of bodies on stakes.

Despite a daring attempt to infiltrate the enemy camp in disguise and kill the sultan, Vlad was overwhelmed by the scale of the Ottoman onslaught. As the Turks surrounded his castle in 1462, his wife jumped from the window, while Vlad fled, and the Ottomans installed his younger brother Radu on the throne. Captured by the Hungarians, Vlad spent the next ten years in custody, dreaming of regaining his throne while impaling mice and birds on miniature stakes. Somehow, he secured the backing of the Hungarians again, remarrying into the Hungarian royal family and winning support for his invasion of Wallachia in 1476, when he briefly deposed the new ruler, Basarab the Elder of the Danesti. Once again, however, he was no match for the invading Ottomans, and he was killed near Bucharest, perhaps even by his own men, his head removed and sent back to Constantinople, where it was displayed on a stick.

Some Romanians have portrayed Vlad as a freedom fighter against foreign invaders and parasitic merchants, who aimed to regenerate Wallachia and restore its morality and pride. But his real programme was keeping his throne. Above all he was also a psychopathic predator, sadist and mass-murderer whose atrocities were diabolic even by the standards of his time and place.

Who was Dracula?

The story of Dracula, as we know it today through films and fiction, was first popularized in the 1897 novel of the same name by the Irish writer Bram Stoker. Many presumed it to be based on the figure of Vlad the Impaler, but not all scholars agree. The name 'dracul' could also translate as 'devil', and in the Balkan region it was frequently used in this wider sense rather than simply to denote members of the Dracul clan from which Vlad emerged.

Unquestionably, however, Stoker derived much of the material for the story from his extensive reading of European folklore and historical myths that had emerged from the region of Transylvania. He may also have been influenced by the story of Countess Elizabeth Báthory (see page 147), a Hungarian noblewoman who, a century after Vlad, enticed hundreds of beautiful young women into her castle – drinking their blood in order to preserve her own youth.

Stoker's novel features Jonathan Harker, a solicitor from England – who travels to a remote region on the fringes of Transylvania and makes his way to the sinister-looking castle of his client, one Count Dracula. This scenario has been repeated in many different representations of the Dracula story over the last hundred years, both in literary and cinematic forms, most famously in F.W. Murnau's 1920s German Expressionist classic *Nosferatu*.

Max Schreck as Graf Orlok in F.W. Murnau's film Nosferatu, eine Symphonie des Grauens *('Nosferatu, A Symphony of Horror'; 1921). The story of Graf Orlok is essentially the same as that of* Dracula, *but with names and other details changed because the studio that made the film could not obtain the film rights to Bram Stoker's novel.*

Richard III was the hunchbacked usurper whose infamous murder of two innocent children, one of them the rightful king of England, tainted the very throne he so craved and brought about his own destruction. In 1483, in perhaps the most cold-blooded *coup d'état* in English history, he kidnapped and slaughtered his own nephews, ensuring that he was remembered by generations of Englishmen for his grotesque and pitiless ambition.

Richard III   1452–85

> *'And thus I clothe my naked villainy With old odd ends stolen out of holy writ, And seem a saint when most I play the devil.'*
>
> RICHARD III IN WILLIAM SHAKESPEARE, RICHARD III, ACT 1, SCENE 3

Richard was the second son of Richard, 3rd duke of York, and Cecily Neville, daughter of Ralph Neville, 1st earl of Westmorland and granddaughter of John of Gaunt. An ugly child, deformed and with protruding teeth, he grew up during the War of the Roses, fought between the rival dynastic houses of Lancaster and York. After the triumph of the Yorkists in March 1461, in a struggle that saw his father killed in battle, Richard's eldest brother became King Edward IV.

From 1465 Richard was raised in the house of his cousin Richard Neville, later known as 'the Kingmaker', although there is no reason to believe that young Richard set his personal sights on the throne at this stage. He gave every sign of loyalty to his brother Edward, for which he was duly rewarded, gaining land and positions of influence. After the Lancastrians had briefly reinstated Henry VI as king in 1470, forcing the York brothers into exile in The Hague, Richard joined Edward on his campaign of 1471, in which Henry VI was deposed for a second time.

An able general and skilled administrator, Richard was entrusted with control of the north of England during Edward's reign, and earned a reputation for fairness and justice. He acquired a string of castles in Yorkshire, Durham and Cumbria during the Yorkist campaigns, but his loyalty – shown for example in a successful campaign that Richard waged on Edward's behalf against the Scots in 1481 – meant that the king tolerated his brother's growing influence.

In 1478, Richard may have first allowed himself to dream of the crown when George, the middle York brother, was executed for treason, possibly at Richard's behest, thus removing another potential obstacle to the throne. But it was when Edward IV died unexpectedly on 9 April 1483 that his ambitions were truly laid bare. Next in line to the throne was the 12-year-old Edward V, followed by his 9-year-old brother, Richard of Shrewsbury, the two sons of the king's beautiful wife, Elizabeth Woodville. As the lord protector of the late king's will, Richard initially swore allegiance to his young nephew, but less than a month later he seized first Edward, then his younger brother, and imprisoned them both in the Tower of London.

Richard initially claimed he had seized the two boys for their own protection, and, on specious charges of treason, ordered the execution of those previously entrusted with their care. Just two months later, however, he had an announcement made outside St Paul's Cathedral declaring Edward IV's marriage to Elizabeth Woodville illegitimate since, according to the testimony of an unnamed bishop, Edward was already secretly married at the time to his 'mistress', Lady Eleanor Butler. Richard forced an act through parliament to annul the marriage posthumously, simultaneously bastardizing his nephews and clearing his own way to the throne. After quashing a brief uprising against him, he was crowned Richard III at Westminster Abbey on 6 July 1483.

To secure his position, Richard seized and brutally murdered several barons who might oppose his accession. He was acutely aware, however, that, as long as they lived, his two nephews would pose a serious threat to his rule, so it must have surprised no one when, in the summer of 1483, both boys were declared missing. By autumn, it was widely assumed they were dead and nobody doubted their uncle was responsible. According to Sir Thomas More, writing some years afterwards, the two boys were smothered on the king's orders as they slept. It was not until 1647, when the skeletons of two children were discovered under a staircase in the Tower, that they were finally buried in Westminster Abbey.

That Richard had murdered the princes was accepted as true during his reign and regarded with horror even in those brutal times. His chief Lancastrian rival, Henry Tudor – who later launched an organized campaign to blacken Richard's name and present him as monster – collected an army on the continent and invaded England in a campaign that reached a climax at the Battle of Bosworth Field on 22 August 1485. The turning point of the encounter came when Henry Percy, the earl of Northumberland, refused to throw his reserves into the battle, while Richard's ostensible allies, Thomas Stanley, afterwards the earl of Derby, and his brother, Sir William – who had been waiting to see which way the battle turned – intervened on the side of Henry. Though Richard continued to fight on bravely, hacking his way through the opposing army and very nearly reaching Henry himself, he was eventually encircled and killed by the poleaxe of a Welshman. The last Plantagenet king of England, Richard had reigned for just two years.

For contemporary chroniclers, deformity was sign of an evil character and Richard's actions in 1483 evoked the image of the startlingly ugly creature they described: buck teeth, excessive body hair from birth, a crooked back, withered arm and haggard face. According to one chronicler, he was tight-lipped and fidgety, 'ever with his right hand pulling out of the sheath to the middle, and putting in again, the dagger which he did always wear'. Some historians believe that the chroniclers may have exaggerated Richard's deformities, but it says much about his reputation that it is the nervy and sinister hunchback portrayed in William Shakespeare's *Richard III* that subsequent generations have come to know, 'so lamely and unfashionable/That dogs bark at me as I halt by them'.

King Richard III, portrayed by an unknown 15th-century English artist.

KINGS WHO DIED IN BATTLE

Kings were expected to lead their armies in battle, but they took a special risk. If they were killed, the battle – and their kingdom too – might be lost:

• SAUL (first king of Israel), following defeat at the Battle of Mount Gilboa (1007 BC), unsuccessfully fell on his sword after his armour-bearer refused to kill him, subsequently begging a passing Amalekite warrior to finish the job.

• CYRUS THE GREAT won an initial victory after tricking Massagetae soldiers into getting drunk, but was killed near the Tigris (c.530 BC) after their enraged leader, Tomryis, led a second wave into battle.

• VALENS, Roman emperor, was killed at the Battle of Adrianople (378) against the Goths: his body was never found.

• KING HAROLD of England was famously killed at the Battle of Hastings in 1066 (see picture caption below).

• RICHARD THE LIONHEART died from gangrene while laying siege to a small castle in Aquitaine in 1199, after an operation to remove a crossbow bolt was bungled.

• MURAD I died (Ottoman sultan) in 1389 at the Battle of Kosovo, either during the fighting itself or at the hand of a Serbian soldier who, playing dead, leapt up and stabbed him. The Ottomans won the battle, which is now celebrated in Serbian nationalist folklore.

• CONSTANTINE XI PALAEOLOGOS (last emperor of Byzantium) died defending the gates of Constantinople in 1453, leading a final charge and being cut to pieces. His remains have never been found.

• SEBASTIAN I of Portugal was killed fighting a Moroccan army at the Battle of Alcazarquizir (1578). His Moorish ally King Mohammad II Saadi died in the same battle, which is also known as the Battle of the Three Kings.

• GUSTAVUS ADOLPHUS of Sweden, died in 1632 at the Battle of Lützen. Declaring 'The Lord God is my armour,' he disdained to put on his cuirass and was killed leading a cavalry charge.

• CHARLES XII of Sweden, an ascetic warrior king, was killed or assassinated fighting Norwegian rebels in 1718.

The death of King Harold II, last Saxon king of England, as depicted in the Bayeux Tapestry. This famous image suggests that Harold was killed when he was hit in the eye by a Norman arrow. However, it is more likely that he was cut down in the thick of battle, still in command of his men.

The Italian Dominican friar Girolamo Savonarola was a reactionary zealot and bigoted theocrat who vehemently opposed the humanism of the Florentine Renaissance. His 'Bonfire of the Vanities' burned books and art he deemed 'immoral'. Savonarola's 'Christian and religious republic' was an intolerant, sanctimonius and murderous reign of terror. His very name is a synonym for mad monks, and the crimes of theocracy and misguided virtue.

Girolamo Savonarola
1452–98

> 'The first city to be renewed will be Florence ... as God elected the people of Israel to be led by Moses through tribulation to felicity ... so now the people of Florence have been called to a similar role led by a prophetic man, their new Moses [Savonarola himself] ... In the Sabbath Age men will rejoice in the New Church and there will be one flock and one shepherd.'
>
> GIROLAMO SAVONAROLA'S 'SERMON ON THE NEW AGE', 1490S

Born and raised in the city of Ferrara (then the capital of an independent duchy), Savonarola received his first education from his paternal grandfather, Michele Savonarola, before moving on to university. His earliest writings already exhibited the mixture of pessimism and moralizing for which he would become notorious; the poems 'De Ruina Mundi' ('On the Downfall of the World') and 'De Ruina Ecclesiae' ('On the Downfall of the Church') are exemplary in this regard.

In 1475 Savonarola entered the Dominican Order at the convent of San Domenico in Bologna. Four years later he transferred back to the convent of Santa Maria degli Angeli in his native Ferrara, before finally becoming the prior of the convent at San Marco in Florence. It was here that he would earn his place in history.

From the outset, Savonarola denounced the political and religious corruption he believed to have permeated society. His Lent sermons of 1485–6 were especially vehement, and it was during those addresses that he began to call for the cleansing of the Church as a prelude to its reform.

Girolamo Savonarola, Italian sermonizer and moralizer, in a 16th-century painting by Alessandro Bonvicino.

In 1487 Savonarola left Florence for a time to return to Bologna as 'master of studies', but in 1490 he returned on the encouragement of the humanist philosopher Count Pico della Mirandola and with the patronage of Lorenzo de Medici, the ruler of Florence. Once back in Florence, Savonarola soon set about excoriating the very government that had made his return possible. In florid language, Savonarola heralded the approaching 'end of days' and claimed to be in direct contact with God and the saints. He condemned the alleged tyranny of the Medicis, and prophesied the impending doom of Florence, unless the city changed its ways.

Such predictions seemed altogether vindicated when the French king, Charles VIII, invaded Florence in 1494. Lorenzo de Medici's son and successor, Piero, was driven out of a city which was by then in the grip of Savonarola's demagoguery. With French support, a democratic republic was now established in Florence, with Savonarola as its leading figure. In his new role, combining political and religious power, he was determined to create a 'Christian and religious republic'. One of the first acts of this new, wholesome republic was to make homosexuality punishable by death.

Savonarola intensified his criticism of the Roman curia – even going so far as to attack the pope's disreputable private life. At the same time, he urged the people of Florence to live ever more ascetic lives. The result of the latter exhortations was the act for which the priest became most famous – the 'Bonfire of the Vanities', in which personal effects, books and works of art, including some by Botticelli and Michelangelo, were destroyed in a conflagration in Florence's Piazza della Signoria.

Even as Savonarola reached the height of his power and influence, domestic opposition to his rule was beginning to form. Pointing to his pronouncements against the papacy, these domestic opponents were able to secure the excommunication of Savonarola in May 1497. Beyond Florence, Savonarola was

RASPUTIN: THE MAD MONK

Grigory Yefimovich Novykh (c.1872–1916) was known as 'Rasputin', 'the debauched one' and the 'Mad Monk'.

An illiterate itinerant peasant, Rasputin was able to wield considerable influence over Russia's autocratic rulers. He rose to prominence as an enigmatic mystic, finding a ready audience for his peculiar brand of religious devotion at a time when many Russian aristocrats were fixated by mysticism and the occult. He appears to have embraced a distorted version of the 'Khlysty' creed, reworking its emphasis on flagellation to advocate sexual exhaustion as the surest path to God.

Introduced to the royal family in 1905, Rasputin eased the suffering of Tsarevich Alexei – the heir to Tsar Nicholas II of Russia and a sufferer from haemophilia. He swiftly became the confidant and personal adviser of Tsarina Alexandra (a German by birth), and when, in September 1915, Tsar Nicholas made himself commander-in-chief of the Russian armies following the outbreak of the First World War – spending much

of his time at the front – fears grew that Rasputin was effectively running the country. Alexandra heeded Rasputin's advice in sacking several ministers and appointing new ones – but ultimately authority lay with her and the tsar, who ratified all decisions and, indeed, had rebuffed Rasputin's advice to stay out of the war.

Nicholas and Alexandra were actually inept, cruel, rigid and obtuse reactionaries. Nicholas, in a speech made in 1895, had deplored the 'senseless dreams' of those seeking democracy, and had helped fund the murderous anti-Semitic Black Hundreds movement after crushing the 1905 Revolution. The country's problems, then, were firmly down to the incompetence of the tsar and tsarina, but Rasputin provided a scapegoat.

Rasputin's close relationship with the tsarina provoked rumours of sexual deviance at the Russian court led by the 'Mad Monk', and before long his position had become a national scandal. He came to

opposed not only by the corrupt Borgia pope, Alexander VI, but also by the duke of Milan – both of whom sought to overturn the king of France's regional ambitions.

When French forces withdrew from the Italian peninsula in 1497, Savonarola suddenly found himself isolated. His final undoing came in 1498, in a bizarre episode that reflected the zealous atmosphere he had done so much to create. A Franciscan monk had challenged anyone who refused to accept the pope's excommunication of Savonarola to an 'ordeal by fire'. One of Savonarola's most committed followers had duly accepted the contest, the outcome of which would be decided by he who withdrew first (that person being the loser). In the event, the Franciscan failed to appear for the trial – formally handing Savonarola the victory. Yet many felt that Savonarola had somehow 'dodged' the test. A riot ensued, in the course of which Savonarola was dragged from his convent and placed in front of a commission of inquiry, packed with his opponents.

Effectively placed on trial by papal commissioners, Savonarola was tortured into making an admission of guilt. He was then handed over to the secular authorities to be crucified and burnt at the stake. The sentence was carried out on 23 May 1498, at the very spot on which the Bonfire of the Vanities had been lit, and where Savonarola had himself overseen the execution of various 'criminals'. As his own pyre was lit, the executioner was reputed to have declared, 'The one who wanted to burn me is now himself put to the flames.'

symbolize the perceived corruption of the tsar's rule – with stories widespread about Alexandra's supposed lesbianism and Nicholas's impotence. Finally, in December 1916, a high-level plot involving senior politicians, noblemen and members of the imperial family – desperate to safeguard the regime – succeeded in eliminating the cleric. Rasputin was poisoned, shot (twice), beaten and eventually dumped into the River Neva, where he finally drowned. His astonishing resistance to poison and bullets suggested to some the mysterious potency of his powers.

Rasputin photographed in 1910. The 'Mad Monk' was renowned for his mesmerizing physical presence, and was rumoured to have seduced a number of Russian society ladies.

Sultan Selim I conquered the entire Middle East, including Mecca, Medina and Jerusalem for his Ottoman empire in a reign that was short, grim and extremely successful. Having bloodily eliminated all internal challengers, he established the Ottomans as the pre-eminent power in the Islamic world. One of the cruellest sultans, he was also one of the greatest.

Selim the Grim

1470–1520

> 'A carpet is large enough to accommodate two sufis, but the world is not large enough for two Kings.'
>
> SELIM THE GRIM

Selim was born in 1470, the son and heir apparent of Sultan Bayezid II, whose reign had been undermined by royal infighting as the sultan found himself challenged by his brother, Cem. The latter had sought assistance from various European allies – notably the military order of the Knights of St John and the papacy – but ultimately wound up dead in a Neapolitan jail. This family feud, however, was nothing compared with what was to follow.

Tall and strong, the young Selim stood out for his bravery and his keen intelligence. Many looked to him as a model ruler in waiting. One who was not so convinced, however, was his brother Ahmed, who desired the throne for himself. The rivalry between the two became increasingly bitter. In 1511, after Ahmed had pacified a rebellious Ottoman province in Asia Minor, he made as if to march on the capital, Istanbul. Selim fled.

In semi-exile as governor of Trabizon (a region of northern Anatolia, next to the Black Sea), Selim honed his military skills, leading a succession of military campaigns against Georgia and succeeding in bringing the towns of Kars, Erzurum and Artvin under Ottoman control. Selim returned from his provincial assignment in 1512, and, with the support of the Janissary militias, defeated and killed Ahmed in battle. He then forced his father to abdicate.

Bayezid died soon afterwards, and there ensued an extraordinary bout of intra-familial blood-letting. Selim understood the problems that could flow from sibling rivalry, having witnessed the clash between his father and uncle, not to mention his own experiences with his brother Ahmed. He came up with a simple but ferocious solution: the elimination of all possible rivals to the throne. He not only had his two surviving brothers and his nephews murdered, but even his own sons – with the sole exception of Suleiman, the son he had designated as his one true heir.

Selim then set about adding to his dominions. Hitherto, the focus for Ottoman expansion had been westwards into Europe – particularly the Balkans. Selim adopted a different policy. Signing a peace treaty with the European powers, he turned his attention east, to the Safavids of Persia (now Iran), whose Shi'ite empire posed a direct ideological challenge to the Ottoman sultans, upholders of the Sunni tradition. In addition, the Safavids had been stirring up unrest among the Kizilbash (Turkmen tribes in eastern Anatolia). In 1514 Selim moved decisively against his Safavid neighbours, and defeated them at the Battle of Chaldiran on the River Euphrates.

With his immediate rivals thus neutralized, Selim then prepared to take on the empire of the

Mamelukes to the south, whose rule extended from Egypt through Palestine to Syria, and who had provoked Selim's anger by their apparent interference in Ottoman affairs. Marching his army south, Selim destroyed successive Mameluke armies at Marj Dabiq (north of Aleppo) in 1516 and at al-Raydaniyyah (near Cairo) in 1517. In so doing, he brought Syria, Palestine and Egypt under Ottoman sway. Selim now proclaimed himself caliph, and was declared guardian of the Islamic holy cities of Mecca and Medina. His triumph was to be short-lived. In September 1520 he died after a short illness, probably a form of cancer.

During his brief yet extraordinary reign, Selim had consolidated his power at home and across the Middle East with a relentless, malign energy. He had let no man stand in his way, or live to threaten his position. At the time of his death, the Ottoman empire reached from the Nile in the south and the Indian Ocean in the east to the Danube in the north and the Adriatic in the west. Under his son Suleiman further expansion would take the Ottomans to the zenith of their power. Yet, while the son is known to history as 'the Magnificent', Selim – the father who would even kill his own children to further his ends – will forever be remembered as 'the Grim'.

The Ottoman sultan Selim I, known as 'the Grim', executed or murdered almost anyone who could oppose him. This anonymous painting hangs in the Topkapi Museum, Istanbul.

BOWSTRINGS AND GOLDEN CAGES

The Ottoman padishahs (emperors), also known as sultans, were initially a dynasty of extraordinarily dynamic conquerors. The succession demanded a large number of heirs, who were produced by a numerous harem of potential mothers of future sultans. However, once a padishah had succeeded, this multitude of princes was a constant threat to his throne, a problem new sultans increasingly solved by murdering all their brothers. Troublesome harem girls or princesses who interfered too much in politics were killed also. In the East, it was forbidden to shed royal blood and thus from Mongolia to the Bosphorus, princes were killed by being suffocated, crushed in carpets by horses or elephants, or strangled with a bowstring. The girls were sown up in sacks and dropped into the Bosphorus.

When Suleiman the Magnificent was informed by his favourite wife, the blonde Slavic Roxelana, that his own son Mustafa had been plotting against him, he summoned the prince and watched as he was asphyxiated before him. A similar fate befell one of Roxelana's sons, Bayezid, after he betrayed the sultan and briefly took up with the Persian shah; Bayezid's four sons were despatched in the same way.

The killing of all Ottoman princes on a new sultan's succession reached its climax when Mehmed III (1566–1603) killed 27 of his brothers, almost bringing to an end the imperial House of Osman. A more humane solution was found in the 'golden cage' whereby princes were kept in luxurious but total isolation – but ultimately this weakened the Ottoman dynasty because its unworldly, effeminate monarchs had less and less military

or political experience and were increasingly inept rulers.

Ibraham the Mad (1615–48) demonstrated the dynastic sclerosis caused by fratricide. Youngest son of Sultan Ahmed I (1590– 1617), he had spent much of his life in *de facto* imprisonment in the 'golden cage' while his uncle, Mustafa I (1591–1639), followed by his two elder brothers, Osman II (1604–22) and Murad IV (1612–40), became sultans in succession. Each murdered relatives, but they spared Ibrahim, considering him harmless. However, when Murad died, aged 27, there was no one left but Ibrahim to take the throne.

When informed of his brother's demise, Ibrahim ran through the palace screaming manically, 'the butcher is dead!' – subsequently devoting himself to an orgy of sexual wantonness. As one chronicler noted, 'In the palace gardens he frequently assembled all the virgins, made them strip themselves naked, and neighing like a stallion ran amongst them and as it were ravished one or the other, kicking or struggling by his order.' Later, having fallen entirely under the spell of a mistress named 'Sugar Cube', Ibrahim ordered the murder of his entire harem, numbering 280 women, in order to assuage her jealousy. Each concubine was trussed, placed within a sack and thrown into the river, where they drowned – all save one, who miraculously escaped. Ibrahim was deposed and murdered soon afterwards – strangled with the inevitable bowstring.

An execution by strangling during the reign of Selim I, from Sebastian Münster's Cosmographia.

Francisco Pizarro personifies the greed and callous inhumanity of the Spanish conquistadors who, in their quest for fame, money and empire, wantonly destroyed entire civilizations in the newly discovered lands of the Americas. Some went on to help rule this gold-rich empire, but many others lived the itinerant lifestyle of the military adventurer – ruthlessly exploiting native populations and extorting the wealth of the land to build vast private fortunes. Pizarro's place in history is that of the man who destroyed the empire of the Incas and delivered much of the New World into Spanish hands.

Francisco Pizarro
c. 1475–1541

'Friends and comrades! On that side [south] are toil, hunger, nakedness, the drenching storm, desertion, and death; on this side ease and pleasure. There lies Peru with its riches; here, Panama and its poverty. Choose, each man, what best becomes a brave Castilian. For my part, I go to the south.'

PIZARRO

Pizarro is still regarded as a hero in his home town of Trujillo in Spain. Like many other young Europeans of the time, he was lured by the promise of the New World, which offered opportunities of rapid advancement to those ruthless enough to seize them. By 1502 Pizarro had arrived in the Caribbean island of Hispaniola (modern Haiti and the Dominican Republic), and it was there that his career as a conquistador began. By 1513 he was fighting alongside Vasco Núñez de Balboa, but the following year Balboa was removed from his position as governor of Veragua – the territory he had helped establish for the Spanish crown. His replacement was a man named Pedrarias Dávila and, rather than stand by his comrade, Pizarro immediately professed his loyalty to Dávila. Five years later, on the orders of Dávila, Pizarro arrested Balboa, who was subsequently executed. As a reward for his allegiance to Dávila, Pizarro was made mayor of the recently founded Panama City.

Although Pizarro used his new role to accumulate significant riches, these did not satisfy his ambitions. Rumours of a fabulously wealthy country to the south – 'Piru' – had reached Panama by this time. Inspired by such stories, Pizarro formed a partnership with a soldier-adventurer, Diego de Almagro, and a priest, Hernando de Luque. The trio agreed to lead an expedition in search of 'Piru', with all the lands they conquered to be divided equally between them.

An unsuccessful attempt in 1524 was followed by a far more promising expedition in 1526, in which the existence of a wealthy empire to the south was confirmed. With their appetites whetted, the conquistadors resolved on a third trip. However, the governor of Panama had grown impatient with Pizarro's failure to deliver immediate results and ordered the venture to be abandoned.

When news reached Pizarro of the governor's decision, he drew a line in the sand with his sword and declared, 'There lies Peru with its riches; here, Panama and its poverty. Choose, each man, what best becomes a brave Castilian.' Of those present, just thirteen men committed to stay with him. Accompanied by Almagro and Luque, Pizarro now continued on his journey, and in 1528 he first entered the territories of the Inca empire. Anxious to build on this success, but short on resources,

Conquistador Francisco Pizarro meeting Atahualpa, the last independent Incan emperor, in Cajamarca, 1532. A mosaic from Cajamarca, Peru.

Pizarro now returned briefly to Europe to appeal in person to Charles V, king of Spain and Holy Roman Emperor, who now agreed to assist him.

Returning to the New World, Pizarro sent emissaries to meet the representatives of the Inca emperor, Atahualpa. It was agreed that Pizarro would meet the emperor at the town of Cajamarca in November 1532. Advancing with his army of 80,000 men, Atahualpa believed he had little to fear from Pizarro's force of 106 infantry soldiers and 62 cavalry. On arrival at Cajamarca, Atahualpa decided to leave most of his troops outside the city and entered with a far smaller retinue – not realizing he was walking into a carefully laid trap. In a brief exchange, the emperor contemptuously rejected the suggestion that he should become a Spanish supplicant. Pizarro immediately ordered his men to open fire on the astonished Incas. Almost all of Atahualpa's escort party – perhaps 3000 or 4000 men – were slaughtered, and the massacre continued outside the city. In total some 7000 Incas perished in a hail of gunfire; the Spanish took fewer than ten casualties in reply. The emperor himself was taken hostage.

Pizarro demanded a vast ransom be paid for Atahualpa's release: the room where the emperor was being held was to be filled from floor to ceiling with gold and silver. Amazingly, Atahualpa's people delivered as requested. But rather than release his enemy, Pizarro now went back on his word and had the emperor executed.

Pizarro sealed the conquest of 'Peru' by taking Cuzco in 1533, and in 1535 he founded the city of Lima as its capital. He then set about accumulating an astonishing fortune. Power and wealth breed jealousy, however, and Pizarro soon fell out with his partner, Almagro, over the spoils. In 1538 the dispute between them came to war. Pizarro defeated Almagro at the Battle of Las Salinas, and had his former comrade executed. The dead man's son vowed revenge, and in 1541 his supporters attacked Pizarro's palace and murdered him within its walls.

Pizarro died as he had lived. His readiness to kill in pursuit of wealth and power was the defining feature of his career. In the process he destroyed an ancient culture and opened up the South American continent to centuries of European exploitation: indeed, the crimes of the Spaniards who came in his wake arguably outweigh those of the man himself. Small wonder then that many Peruvians today regard him not as a hero, but as a criminal guilty of genocide.

LOPE DE AGUIRRE

Among the conquistadors, another name stands out for ruthless ferocity – that of Lope de Aguirre, the man who styled himself 'the Wrath of God'. Little is known of Aguirre prior to his arrival in Peru in 1544, and it was not until 1560 that he really made his mark. That year, he joined an expedition of several hundred men led by Pedro de Ursúa, determined to find El Dorado, the legendary lost city of gold. After pledging allegiance to de Ursúa, Aguirre turned against his cautious style of leadership and organized his overthrow. He subsequently had him executed. The man who took over from de Ursúa – Fernando de Guzman – proved no more to Aguirre's liking, and he too was put to death. Aguirre now took personal control of the mission, supposedly declaring: 'I am the Wrath of God, the Prince of Freedom, Lord of Tierra Firma and the Provinces of Chile.' ('Tierra Firma' denoted the Isthmus of Panama.)

As far as Aguirre was concerned, those who remained on the expedition were either with him or against him – his opponents being rewarded with death. On such an uncompromising basis, he pursued his quest, sailing down the Amazon – or possibly the Orinoco – to the Atlantic, slaughtering those he encountered along the way. In 1561 he seized Isla Margarita, off the coast of what is now Venezuela, from the Spanish settlers already in situ, and thereby showed himself in open rebellion against the Spanish crown. Having crossed to the mainland, he was surrounded and captured at Barquisimeto. In a gruesome final twist, with his execution approaching Aguirre is reputed to have murdered his own daughter – to ensure that no one but him could love her.

The brutal conquistador Lope de Aguirre and his daughter Florés, as played by Klaus Kinski and Cecilia Rivera in Werner Herzog's film Aguirre, the Wrath of God *(1972).*

Regarded as a heroic warrior by Turks but as a cruel pirate by his enemies, Barbarossa – a brilliant, flamboyant, victorious Ottoman admiral, shrewd politician and founder of his own dynastic kingdom – was one of the four freebooting Muslim corsair brothers who dominated the Mediterranean and slaughtered and enslaved innocent Christians with audacious enthusiasm in the early 16th century.

Barbarossa c. 1478–1546 and Silver Arm c. 1474–1518

'They came upon a ship from Genoa laden with grain and seized it on the spot. Then they saw a fortress-like galleon, a merchant ship laden with cloth, and took that without any difficulty. Returning to Tunis, they handed over the fifth of booty [due to the ruler], divided the rest, and set out again with three ships for the infidel coasts.'

KATIB CHELEBI, IN HIS HISTORY OF THE MARITIME WARS OF THE TURKS (c. 1650), DESCRIBING AN EARLY EPISODE IN THE LIFE OF BARBAROSSA AND HIS OLDER BROTHER ORUC

Barbarossa Hayreddin Pasha was born on the Aegean island of Lesbos around 1478 as Yakupoglu Hizir – one of four sons and two daughters – to a Turkish Muslim father, Yakup Aga, and his Christian Greek wife, Katerina. Hizir was an intelligent youngster, blessed with charisma and leadership. Dark in complexion, he later boasted a luxuriant beard with a reddish hue – hence his European nickname 'Barbarossa', meaning 'red beard' (in fact, a corruption of Baba Oruc, an honorific title later inherited from his gifted brother Oruc, who earned it in 1510 after helping large numbers of Spanish Muslims flee persecution).

As young men, the four brothers – Ishak, Oruc, Hizir and Ilyas – bought a boat to transport their father's pottery products, but with Ottoman vessels subject at the time to repeated raids at the hands of the hated Knights of St John, based on the Island of Rhodes, Oruc, Ilyas and Hizir soon turned to privateering, while Ishak helped oversee the family business at home. Hizir worked the Aegean Sea, and Oruc and Ilyas the coast of the Levant until their boat was intercepted by the Knights. Ilyas was killed and Oruc imprisoned for three years at the castle of Bodrum before Hizir launched a daring raid to rescue him.

Determined to avenge his brother, Oruc secured the support of the Ottoman governor of Antalya, who supplied him with a fleet of galleys to combat the Knights' marauding. In a series of attacks, he captured several enemy galleons, subsequently raiding Italy. Joining forces, from 1509 Oruc, Hizir and Ishak defeated a host of Spanish ships across the Mediterranean. In one such battle, in 1512, Oruc lost his left arm, earning the nickname 'Silver Arm' after replacing it with a silver prosthetic limb.

Undeterred, the three brothers raided yet further off the Italian and Spanish coasts, in one month alone capturing a further 23 ships. They began producing their own gunpowder, and over the next four years raided, destroyed or captured a succession of ships, fortresses and cities. In 1516, they liberated Algiers from the Spaniards, Oruc declaring himself a sultan, though he relinquished the title the following year to the Ottoman sultan, who in return appointed him governor of Algiers and chief naval governor of the western Mediterranean – positions he held until 1518, when he and Ishak were killed by the troops of Charles I of Spain (later Emperor Charles V).

Hizir, the sole surviving brother and the man remembered today as Barbarossa, took on his brother's mantle. In 1519, he defended Algiers against a joint Spanish–Italian attack, striking back the same year by raiding Provence. Then, following numerous raids along the French and Spanish coasts, he contributed in 1522 to the Ottoman conquest of Rhodes that finally vanquished the Knights of St John. In 1525, he raided Sardinia, going on to recapture Algiers and take Tunis in 1529, launching further attacks from both.

In 1530, Emperor Charles V sought the help of Andrea Doria, the talented Genoese admiral, to challenge Barbarossa's dominance, but the following year Barbarossa trounced Doria, winning the personal gratitude of Sultan Suleiman the Magnificent, who made him Capudan Pasha – fleet admiral and chief governor of North Africa, giving him the honorary name Barbarossa Hayreddin Pasha.

In 1538 – already a living legend among the Muslims for freeing African Muslim slaves from Spanish galleys and bringing glory to the Ottoman empire – Barbarossa scattered a combined Spanish, Maltese, Venetian and German fleet at the Battle of Preveza, thereby securing Turkish dominance of the eastern Mediterranean for nearly 40 years. In September 1540, Charles offered him a huge bribe to switch sides, but Barbarossa refused outright, and in 1543, as his fleet lurked in the mouth of the River Tiber, he even threatened to advance on Rome, but was dissuaded by the French, with whom he had entered into a temporary alliance. By now the cities of the Italian coast, including the proud Genoese, had given up trying to defeat him, choosing instead to send huge payments in return for being spared from attack. Barbarossa was master of the Italian and Mediterranean coasts.

In 1545, undefeated and having ensured Ottoman dominance of the Mediterranean and North Africa, Barbarossa retired to a magnificent villa on the northern shore of the Bosphorus. Here he wrote his memoirs until he died from natural causes in 1546. He left his son, Hasan Pasha, as his successor as ruler of Algiers.

He had seized and enslaved as many as 50,000 from Italian and Spanish coasts, and was famous for his savage cruelty. For the Ottomans, Barbarossa was a remarkable admiral. Christians saw him as a merciless pirate, perhaps the most terrifying that ever lived.

Barbarossa, the notorious 16th-century Barbary corsair who founded his own hereditary kingdom, here depicted in a Florentine portrait.

PRIVATEERS, PIRATES AND WOMEN CORSAIRS

The distinction between privateer and pirate depended largely on who was on the receiving end of the attack. Privateers were sanctioned by their government to attack ships of other nations, whereas pirates acted on their own authority.

One of the most celebrated privateers was Captain Henry Morgan, immortalized in the rum that bears his name. Born in Wales in 1635, he raided Spanish galleons and colonies off the coast of the New World, disrupting Spanish trade and enhancing that of England with the full blessing of King Charles II, who honoured Morgan with a knighthood in 1674 and the governorship of Jamaica in 1680.

Not all pirates/privateers conformed to the stereotypical macho image – in fact, some were women. One such was the Irishwoman Grace O'Malley (also known as the Pirate Queen Granuaile). Born in 1530, she raided merchant ships in the Irish Sea and in 1593 famously discarded a royal handkerchief after sneezing into it during an audience with Queen Elizabeth I. She was pardoned for both offences after promising to turn her skills to fighting England's enemies.

Another female buccaneer was the one-time prostitute Cheng I Sao – otherwise known as Ching Shih – who in the early 19th century terrorized the South China Sea. She took over command of the notorious Red Flag Fleet – a huge band of pirates – from her husband, the infamous Zheng Yi, following his death in 1807. Imposing ruthless discipline on her men – beheadings were frequent – she was equally merciless in combat, her 1500 shallow-hulled junks laden with cannons wreaking havoc along the Chinese and Malayan coasts. The Chinese government finally offered her an amnesty that saw her retire with all her booty, living in luxury until her death in 1844.

Two 18th-century women corsairs share a remarkable story. Anne Cormac – born in Ireland but raised in South Carolina – married and eloped with a young seaman, James Bonny, to the Bahamas, only to ditch him there for the infamous pirate 'Calico' Jack Rackham. Disguising herself as a man, she joined Jack's crew on board *The Revenge*, and embarked on a life of piracy. By an astonishing coincidence, however, the only other woman pirate in the Caribbean, Mary Read, was also on board, also disguised as a man. Raised as a boy to secure an inheritance, English-born Mary had continued the charade for much of her life, and when 'Calico' Jack's pirates waylaid her ship en route to the West Indies, they mistook her for a man and forced her into piracy. Reputed to 'Swear and Shoot as well as any Mann', she caught the eye of Anne Bonny. The two became lovers, though clearly also indulged in heterosexual relationships for when, in 1721, *The Revenge* was captured by the British and the crew sentenced to be hanged, Mary and Ann (still dressed as men) declared 'Sir, We plead our bellies', well aware that a pregnant woman could not be hanged under English law. Both were duly reprieved, and though Mary died of fever a few months later, Bonny apparently escaped justice, possibly bailed out by her wealthy father.

Anne Bonny, a female pirate who sailed the Caribbean with 'Calico' Jack Rackham and had a lesbian affair with fellow pirate Mary Read.

Lucrezia Borgia was infamous throughout Renaissance Italy for her corruption, carnality and viciousness. For Lucrezia, loyalty to her vindictive father and brothers outweighed any other bonds, and she willingly entered into several marriages to further their interests. Her monstrosity was probably exaggerated, but contemporaries regarded her as the embodiment of evil, and whispered that she wore a hollow ring from which she would discreetly pour poison into the wine of all those who stood in her way.

Lucrezia Borgia
1480–1519

> '*Lucrezia was wanton in imagination, godless by nature, ambitious and designing … she carried the head of a Raphael Madonna and concealed the heart of a Messalina.*'
>
> ALEXANDRE DUMAS, CELEBRATED CRIMES (1843)

Born in the small Italian city of Subiaco on 18 April 1480, Lucrezia was the third child and first daughter of the Spanish cardinal Rodrigo Borgia and his mistress, Vannozza Cattanei. Lucrezia's two older brothers – both of whom became embroiled in a succession of murderous political struggles – were Giovanni and Cesare.

Cesare was the oldest and the crueller of the two, a syphilis-scarred beast admired by Machiavelli. He was said to lust after Lucrezia and was allegedly responsible for the death of his brother, whose body was found in the River Tiber in 1497.

Lucrezia, a pretty, captivating child, grew into a great beauty. She was described by a contemporary as 'of middle height and graceful of form … her hair is golden, her eyes grey, her mouth rather large, the teeth brilliantly white, her bosom smooth and white and admirably proportioned'. By the age of 11

Portrait of a Woman *(thought to be Lucrezia Borgia)* by the early 15th-century artist Bartolomeo da Venezia. Lucrezia, the epitome of the *femme fatale, is thought to have murdered her second husband, Alfonso of Aragon.*

she had already been betrothed to two Spanish nobles, but the political priorities of the Borgia family changed when her father Rodrigo was elected pope as Alexander VI in 1492. Lucrezia moved into the newly built palace of Maria del Portico, which had its own private door through to St Peter's. This gave rise to rumours that Pope Alexander kept his concubines in the palace – and that among these concubines was his own daughter.

In February 1439 Alexander arranged for the 18-year-old Lucrezia to marry Giovanni Sforza, lord of Pesaro, in order to build an alliance with the Sforzas – a powerful Milanese family – against the Aragonese of Naples. The wedding, which took place at the Vatican, was a lavish affair, at which a scandalous play about pimps and mistresses was performed. Lucrezia spent two years in Pesaro, but was unhappy and returned to Rome. The Borgias, who already had a formidable reputation, suspected Giovanni of spying for Milan; when he visited his wife in Rome he became terrified when Lucrezia suddenly began to smile and show him signs of affection. Fearing for his life, he fled Rome in disguise. The alliance between Rome and Milan was no longer of use to the Borgias, who were now attempting to court Naples. Pope Alexander demanded that the Sforzas agree to a divorce, but the only legal way to do this was to force Giovanni to make a false confession that he was impotent and had therefore never consummated the marriage. Humiliated, he hit back with the allegation that Alexander had undermined the marriage in order that he could pursue a sexual interest in his own daughter.

In the midst of the divorce proceedings, Lucrezia – still claiming to be a virgin – retired to the Roman convent of San Sisto, where she was visited by a messenger from her father, the handsome courtier Pedro Calderon, with whom she soon began an affair. Within a year, a mysterious baby boy appeared among the Borgia clan, and shortly afterwards Calderon was found floating in the River Tiber, apparently murdered on the orders of a jealous Cesare. The historian Potigliotto speculated that either Cesare or Alexander had sired the boy.

In 1498, having had her claim to virginity upheld by the divorce court, Lucrezia was offered to the 17-year-old Alfonso, duke of Bisceglie, an illegitimate son of Alfonso II of Naples. However, it wasn't long before the Borgias fell out with Naples and moved closer to the French king, Louis XII. Lucrezia's young husband fled Rome in fear of his life, and when his bride convinced him to return, he was savagely attacked on the steps of St Peter's in Rome. It is possible that Lucrezia was complicit in the assault, although contemporaries believed that she genuinely loved her second husband, pointing out that she tended to his wounds and nursed him back to health. But the court of the Borgias was not a safe place to convalesce, and, on Cesare's orders, a month after the original attack Alfonso was strangled while he lay in bed.

Lucrezia was said to be distraught at her young husband's death. Nonetheless, she soon resumed her part in Borgia power politics. In 1501, the year after Alfonso's murder, she married Alfonso d'Este, son of Ercole I, duke of Ferrara. Although Lucrezia's reputation went before her, her charm rapidly won over her new in-laws, and in 1505 she became duchess of Ferrara. After Alexander VI died in 1503, Lucrezia became a respected patron of the arts and literature in Ferrara, while still finding time to have an affair with her bisexual brother-in-law and the humanist poet Pietro Bembo. She died in childbirth on 24 June 1514, aged 39.

Much mystery surrounds the life of Lucrezia Borgia. Was she, as she has traditionally been viewed, a willing actor in the ruthless political manoeuvrings of her family? Or does her grief at the murder of her second husband suggest that she was a helpless pawn in their games as they clawed their way to power and influence? To survive in the brutal atmosphere of Renaissance Rome, cunning and intrigue were indispensable, and Lucrezia was capable of assuming many guises to suit her ends. She saw the wickedness of her father and brother at first hand, yet her first loyalty was always to her family.

POISON

THE BLACK WIDOW. Of the many poisoners in Victorian England, by far the most prolific was Mary Ann Cotton. Born in October 1832 into a poor but strictly Methodist family in Low Moorsley, County Durham, she managed to kill up to 21 people with arsenic, including four husbands and many more lovers, and even her own children. Eventually she was detected, and went to the gallows on 24 March 1873.

HÉLÈNE THE HOUSEMAID. Another notorious female poisoner, who also favoured arsenic, was the French housemaid Hélène Jegado. Born in Brittany in 1803, Jegado is believed to have killed as many as 36 people over a period of 18 years. Her murderous career began in 1833, while she was working in the home of a priest; within three months, seven members of the household were dead, including the priest and her own sister, who was visiting her. She was finally arrested in July 1851 after killing two fellow maids in the household of Théophile Bidard, a law professor at the University of Rennes. She was executed by guillotine on 26 February 1852.

THE UMBRELLA MURDER. On 7 September 1978 the Bulgarian writer and anti-Soviet dissident Georgi Markov was jabbed in the leg by the tip of an umbrella on his way home from his work at the BBC in London. Within four days he had died from ricin poison, allegedly administered through the umbrella by an agent of the KGB.

DEATH BY RADIOACTIVITY. On 1 November 2006 Alexander Litvinenko – a former Russian intelligence officer who had become an opponent of President Vladimir Putin – was hospitalized shortly after a meal at a sushi bar in London. He died three weeks later from lethal poisoning by radioactive polonium-210. The British government has requested the extradition of a suspect, Andrei Lugovoi, from Russia, but this request has been refused.

Mary Ann Cotton was perhaps the most prolific female serial killer in British history. She died slowly on the noose, the hangman having miscalculated the length of the rope.

Hernán Cortés was a conquistador, one of the murderous and avaricious conquerors who brought so much of the New World under the harsh rule of Spain. Arriving in Mexico at the head of a mercenary army, he slaughtered the innocent and pillaged the land, destroying the civilization of the Aztecs and enriching himself beyond his wildest dreams.

Hernán Cortés
1485–1547

'He came dancing across the water
With his galleons and guns
Looking for the new world
In that palace in the sun …
He came dancing across the water
Cortéz, Cortéz What a killer.'

NEIL YOUNG

Cortés was born of a noble Castilian family in Medellín, Spain, in 1485. After a sickly childhood, his parents sent him to the prestigious University of Salamanca in the hope that the rarefied intellectual environment might be the making of their son. It was not to be, however, and Cortés soon returned home. Small-town provincial life proved no more satisfactory to young Cortés (except where women were concerned), and in 1502 he decided to move to the New World. Arriving in Hispaniola (modern-day Haiti and the Dominican Republic) in 1503, he soon established himself as a capable man with an eye for an opportunity. cont p. 128

Conquistador Hernán Cortés takes the surrender in 1521 of Cuauhtémoc, the last Aztec emperor, in a 19th-century painting by Carlos Maria Esquivel.

AZTECS AND INCAS

In the wake of the *conquistador* invasion of South America, empires that had stood unchallenged for decades perished. One of these was the Aztec empire, which emerged in the 14th and 15th centuries from an alliance of three rapidly growing cities – Tenochtitlán, Texcoco and Tlacopan. It was fashioned by Moctezuma I (c. 1398–1469) into a cohesive political and cultural unit, with Tenochtitlán at its capital, and reached its zenith under Ahuitzotl (c. 1486–1502), who more than doubled the territory under Aztec control. He was succeeded on his death by his nephew, Moctezuma II – the man on the throne when Cortés and his mercenaries arrived 17 years later.

Cortés' rampage through what is modern-day Mexico and Guatemala brought him face to face with the Aztecs. These native Indians had a rich and diverse culture, but perhaps most startling to the European outsider were the religious rituals of human sacrifice designed to satiate the presumed needs of the gods. Common throughout Mesoamerican societies, such practices characterized the Aztecs in particular, on one occasion in the 1480s over 84,000 prisoners reportedly being sacrificed at the Great Pyramid of Tenochtitlán.

Francisco Pizarro would likewise have encountered human sacrifice among the Inca people. They practised it less than their Aztec counterparts, but would respond to momentous events (such as a natural disaster, or the death of an emperor – who was worshipped as a God) by engaging in the tradition of *capacocha* – the sacrifice of children – in an attempt to ensure the gods' continued blessing.

Originating in the Peruvian highlands in the twelfth century, the Incas by the mid-1500s had grown into a mighty empire encompassing much of the west coast of South America. Under three particularly successful rulers (Pachacuti, r. c. 1438–c. 1471; Topa Inca, r. c. 1471–c. 1493; and Huayna Capac, r. c. 1493–1525) they came to dominate much of what is modern-day Ecudador, Peru, parts of Argentina, and Chile. Shortly before the Spaniards arrived in 1532, however, the empire was fractured by civil war that broke out during the rule of Huayna Capac's son, Atahualpa, leaving the empire a 'sitting target', especially given the technical superiority of the Incas' European assailants. The brutal reality for Aztec and Inca rulers alike was that their 'New World' societies were no match for those of 'old Europe', and they were able to offer little in the way of resistance to the onslaught of the *conquistadors*.

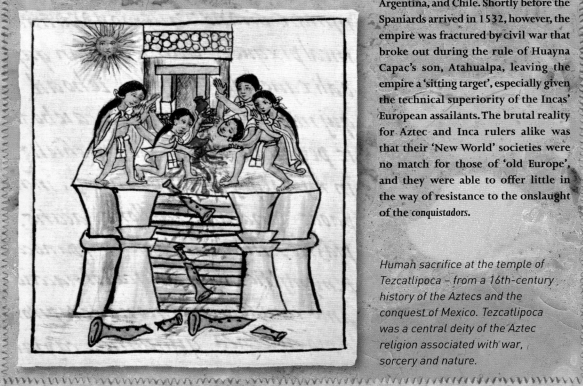

Human sacrifice at the temple of Tezcatlipoca – from a 16th-century history of the Aztecs and the conquest of Mexico. Tezcatlipoca was a central deity of the Aztec religion associated with war, sorcery and nature.

In 1510, at the age of 26, Cortés managed to obtain a place on an expedition to conquer Cuba. The expedition was led by Diego Velázquez de Cuéllar, who went on to become the governor of the newly seized territory; having impressed Velázquez, Cortés was appointed as his secretary. The cordial relationship between the two men did not last, however – in part because of Cortés' continual philandering, even as he secured the hand in marriage of Velázquez's sister-in-law, Catalina.

Cortés grew increasingly restless with his life in Cuba, and in 1518 he persuaded Velázquez to give him command over an expedition that was to explore and colonize the mainland (modern-day Mexico). At the last minute the governor changed his mind and attempted to have Cortés removed from his command. But it was too late: Cortés ignored the countermand and proceeded as originally planned.

In March 1519 Cortés and a force of some 600 men landed on the Yucatán Peninsula, and a month later he formally claimed the land for the Spanish crown. To create a reality to match the rhetoric, Cortés marched first north and then west, achieving a series of victories over hostile native tribes and proving himself a skilled exponent of 'divide and conquer'.

In October 1519 Cortés and his troops arrived at Cholula, then the second largest city in the region. Many of the city's nobility had gathered in the town's central square in the hope of parleying with the approaching Spaniard, but he was in no mood to listen to them. In an act of merciless savagery, he ordered his troops to raze the city. Thousands of unarmed citizens were butchered in the process.

In the wake of this massacre, Cortés and his men were received peacefully by the Aztec emperor, Moctezuma II, in the city of Tenochtitlán. Moctezuma believed Cortés to be the incarnation of the Aztec god Quetzalcoatl ('the Feathered Serpent'), and, having heard of the military superiority of the intruders, was anxious to avoid direct confrontation. For his part, Cortés was determined to receive the submission of the Aztec emperor to the Spanish king, and to this end he took Moctezuma prisoner.

Back in Cuba, meanwhile, Velázquez had grown jealous of Cortés' success, and in 1520 he sent a force under Pánfilo de Narváez to retrieve the insubordinate conquistador. Despite the numerical inferiority of his troops compared to those of Narváez, Cortés defeated the challenge. However, during his absence from Tenochtitlán, the man he had left in charge had slaughtered many of the city's leading figures and provoked an uprising, during which Moctezuma was killed. After attempting to re-enter Tenochtitlán, Cortés was forced to abandon it and only just avoided defeat at the hands of pursuing Aztec forces.

But Cortés was not to be denied. Having regrouped in the lands of his allies, the Tlaxcala, he returned in late 1520, intent on recapturing the city. In the war that followed, the Spaniard sought to break the Aztec resistance through a strategy of attrition. Tenochtitlán was isolated, and resistance eventually crushed. The fall of the city effectively marked the end of the Aztec empire. Cortés was now the undisputed master of the territory, which he renamed the 'New Spain of the Ocean Sea'.

As governor of the new colony from 1521 to 1524, Cortés oversaw the destruction of many artefacts of Aztec culture. The indigenous people were forced into a system of forced labour, under which they were ruthlessly exploited for centuries to come. All the while, the principal concern of the Spanish conqueror was personal aggrandisement. Those who suffered under Cortés's yoke were finally relieved of their burden when he was dismissed from his post by the Spanish king, who had received various reports of his viceroy's misrule. In 1528 Cortés returned to Spain to plead his case, but despite being made Marques del Valle de Oaxaca, Cortés was not convinced he had won the king's support.

The final two decades of Cortés' life saw the increasingly embittered conquistador journeying back and forth between Spain and his estates in the New World, and attempting to counter what he felt were the lies of his 'various and powerful rivals and enemies'. He died in 1547, en route to South America.

Henry VIII was a golden and gifted boy who grew up to become a forceful, energetic and ambitious ruler – he was a majestic and ruthless monarch who created an 'imperial' monarchy by asserting English independence, defying Rome, breaking up the monasteries, promoting his realm's military and naval power and his own autocracy, all ultimately enabling the triumph of Protestantism. Yet he became a bloated, thin-skinned tyrant who ordered the killing – on faked evidence – of many, including two of his wives, because of his own wounded pride. Both hero and monster, he was, in his paranoid cruelty, the English Stalin.

Henry VIII 1491–1547

'He never spared a man in his anger, nor a woman in his lust.'

SIR ROBERT NAUNTON,
FRAGMENTA REGALIA, 1641

Henry was second son of the shrewd, mean and pragmatic Henry VII who, as Henry Tudor, had seized the throne in 1485, reconciling the York and Lancaster factions after the Wars of the Roses, and established a new dynasty. The early death of his heir, Prince Arthur, in 1502, shortly after marrying Catherine of Aragon, highlighted the fragility of the parvenu Tudors, which explains much of Henry VIII's ruthlessness over the succession. Henry succeeded to the throne in 1509 and married his late brother's Spanish widow. He was handsome, strapping and vigorous but also highly educated: courtiers hailed the dawning of a golden age. He promoted his glory with the macho sporting entertainments of a Renaissance prince – hunting, jousting, dancing, feasting – and won popularity by executing his father's hated tax collectors, Empson and Dudley, on spurious charges. It set the pattern for how Henry would dispose of his ministers when expedient.

Henry longed to test his vigour in the lists of Europe, where Francis I of France and the Habsburg emperor, Charles V, were vying for dominance. He started to build a navy, including his huge battleship the *Mary Rose* (which later sank). At first, he backed the emperor against the French, leading an army to France and winning the Battle of Spurs in 1513, while defeating a Scottish invasion at Flodden. He made peace with France, meeting Francis at a magnificent summit, The Field of the Cloth of Gold, stage-managed by his able and hugely rich minister Cardinal Thomas Wolsey –

A portrait of Henry VIII aged 49 by Hans Holbein the Younger (c.1497–1543). Grim, corpulent and paranoid, the figure in this painting is far removed from Henry's vigorous and hearty youth.

a butcher's son who had risen to the scarlet – but after Francis was captured at Pavia in 1525, Henry again changed sides, aspiring to hold the balance of power in Europe.

Henry's queen, Catherine of Aragon, emperor Charles V's aunt, had provided him with a girl, the future Queen Mary, rather than a male heir – an affront to Henry's pride and dynastic sensitivity, so he sought, via Wolsey, to have the marriage to his brother's widow annulled. The pope, under the influence of Emperor Charles, would not permit Catherine to be cast aside. 'The king's great matter' was not just a matter of personality but of Henry's insistence that his crown was 'imperial' – not subordinate to the pope or any other power. This became even more important when he fell in love with Anne Boleyn, one of Catherine's ladies-in-waiting, who – flirtatious, intelligent and ambitious – withheld her favours before marriage. The pope remained intransigent, so Henry turned on Wolsey. The cardinal would have faced the axe but died on his way to face charges of treason.

Henry now decided on a radical course, and in his Act of Supremacy and Treason Act of 1534 declared himself head of the Church in England, independent of the pope, on pain of death. At last Henry's marriage to Catherine could be annulled, and in 1533 he married Anne Boleyn.

Henry, backed by his rising minister Thomas Cromwell, repressed anyone who questioned his religious policies: his former chancellor, Thomas More, was executed. A rebellion in the north, the Pilgrimage of Grace (1536), was defeated, then dispersed on Henry's word of honour, which he then broke, executing the rebels ruthlessly. Throughout his reign, Henry was pitiless in killing anyone who opposed him: after Dudley and Empson he went on to execute Edmund de la Pole, earl of Suffolk, in 1513, Edward Stafford, duke of Buckingham, in 1521, all the way to the young poet Henry Howard, earl of Surrey, in the last days of his life. His number of victims is hard to calculate – the historian Holinshed absurdly claimed 72,000 – but there were many.

Although Henry is sometimes credited with England's Protestant Reformation, doctrinally he remained a Catholic conservative. Nonetheless, his political revolution made a Protestant England possible. His lucrative dissolution of the monasteries – an act of vandalism on a massive scale – funded his reign and marked his new absolutism. Anne Boleyn delivered a child to Henry in 1533, but it was a girl, the future Elizabeth I. Henry turned against her, ordering Cromwell to concoct charges of adultery, incest and witchcraft, evidenced by her 'third nipple' used for suckling the Devil – actually a mole on her neck. Five men, including Boleyn's brother, were framed and executed. Anne was beheaded on 19 May 1536. Ten days later Henry married Jane Seymour, who delivered a son, the future Edward VI, but died in childbirth – the only wife Henry ever grieved for.

Cromwell, pushing a Protestant foreign policy and promoted to earl of Essex, persuaded Henry to marry Anne of Cleves. But Henry, himself now fat and prone to suppurating sores, was repelled by this 'Flanders Mare'. Cromwell was framed and executed in 1540, the very day Henry married the pretty Catherine Howard, aged just 16. Henry ordered that Cromwell's beheading should be carried out by an inexperienced youth. The head was severed on the third attempt.

Each of the English wives was backed by an ambitious political-religious family faction. The Howards were pro-Catholic, but their teenage queen was a reckless and naïve flirt whose past mischief and present adulterous adventures allowed the Protestant faction to exploit the king's fragile sexual pride. In 1542, aged 18, she was beheaded. His sensible last wife, Catherine Parr, outlived him.

Henry determined to marry his young son Edward to the infant Mary Queen of Scots, Scottish intractability resulting in the 'Rough Wooing', in which Henry sent his armies over the Border to put 'man, woman and child to fire and sword without exception'. In 1544, he laid out the succession: the Protestant Edward, then Catholic Mary, followed by Protestant Elizabeth.

Henry was both hero and monster, brutal egotist and effective politician. As the duke of Norfolk understood: 'The consequence of royal anger is death.'

ROYAL WIFE- & CHILD-KILLERS

The ambition, greed and jealousy of absolute personal power place a special tension on the families – wives and children – of autocrats. Henry VIII executed two of his wives but at least spared his children. His tally of six wives ranks with Ivan the Terrible (eight), Philip II of Spain (four) and Herod the Great (an astonishing ten) among the most married monarchs, but while Philip's wives died naturally, the others killed at least one of their own wives.

Herod the Great of Judaea killed the love of his life, the Hasmonean princess Mariamme, after her enemies turned him against her. Constantine the Great, who converted the Roman Empire to Christianity, had his wife Fausta scalded to death and eldest son Crispus poisoned when he uncovered their conspiracy against him. In 1425 Niccolò III d'Este, marquess of Ferrara, accused his wife, Parisina, of an incestuous relationship with his illegitimate son, Ugo, and had them both executed. Nearly 150 years later, in 1561, his great-great-grandson Alfonso II d'Este, duke of Ferrara, would be suspected of poisoning his wife Lucrezia de Medici. Tsar Ivan boasted of having deflowered hundreds of virgins during his life, but when he discovered his seventh wife, Maria Dolgurukaya, was not a virgin he had her drowned the day after their marriage.

Royal marital murder works both ways, however. The Roman empresses Livia and Agrippina reportedly poisoned their husbands Augustus (see page 29) and Claudius, while Catherine the Great was complicit in the murder of her husband Peter III when she seized power in 1762.

Tensions scar royal father–son relationships: sons can only become truly great when their fathers are dead, while ageing fathers are threatened by their rising sons. The ailing Herod the Great killed a record three of his own sons. Sultan Suleiman the Magnificent killed two, Constantine the Great, Ivan the Terrible and Peter the Great each killed one – Ivan and Peter doing so with their own hands.

Finally, there are the royal children who murder their parents. Alexander the Great may have played a role in the assassination of his father Philip of Macedon and Tsar Alexander I was at least complicit in the 1801 murder of his father, mad Paul I. The killing of royal mothers is less common, Emperor Nero's assassination of his mother Agrippina (see page 35) being a rare example.

So many monarchs killed their brothers and sisters, they are too numerous to mention (but some examples of Ottoman fratricide can be found on page 116).

Bluebeard, wife-killing anti-hero of the eponymous fairy tale by Charles Perrault (1628–1703), as portrayed by Gustave Doré (1832–83). Perrault is believed to have based the character of Bluebeard on the serial killer Gilles de Rais (see page 99).

Fernando Álvarez de Toledo, 3rd duke of Alba, was governor of the Habsburg-ruled Spanish Netherlands from 1567 to 1573. In this role the so-called 'Iron Duke' became the scourge of the Dutch Protestants, and earned a fearsome reputation for his callous indifference to human suffering.

The Duke of Alba and the Council of Blood 1507–82

'All I know is that when he came to this post he found the disturbances in them settled and no territory lost, and everything so quiet and secure that he could wield the knife as he wished. And by the time he left all Holland and Zealand was in the power of the enemy, as well as a good part of Guelderland and Brabant, and all the opinion of these provinces, with the finances wholly ruined.'

LUIS DE REQUESENS, THE DUKE OF ALBA'S SUCCESSOR AS GOVERNOR OF THE SPANISH NETHERLANDS, SUMMARIZES HIS PREDECESSOR'S PERFORMANCE

Fernando Álvarez de Toledo, duke of Alba, was born into a noble family with a long record of service to the Spanish crown. From an early age he was raised to be a soldier, and became well versed in the arts of war. In 1524 he joined the army, which was at that time locked in combat with French forces at Fuenterrabía. There, he so distinguished himself that he was appointed governor of the town after it had fallen.

In subsequent campaigns on behalf of Charles V, king of Spain and Holy Roman Emperor, Alba built on his reputation as one of the foremost professional soldiers of his day, known for his emphasis on discipline, training and logistics. By 1552 he had risen to the post of commander-in-chief of Charles's forces in Italy, in which role he defeated the French and established Spanish hegemony in the peninsula. But his success bred suspicion. Charles abdicated in 1556 in favour of his son, Philip II, whom he warned against Alba's burgeoning ambition, overweening sense of self-importance and megalomaniac tendencies. The new king, whilst continuing to rely on Alba's military abilities, sought to curb his freedom of manoeuvre – in a way that Charles V had not.

Despite this, in public at least, the Spanish crown's trust in the duke remained undiminished. In 1565 he was sent as Philip's emissary to France to hold negotiations with the regent Catherine de' Medici over a possible marriage alliance and a joint anti-Protestant policy. The presence of the latter on the agenda has fuelled speculation that Alba helped lay the groundwork for the massacre of French Protestants on St Bartholomew's Day, 1572 – particularly in the light of his own stridently expressed anti-Protestant views.

In 1567, following the outbreak of popular unrest in the Spanish Netherlands (comprising what is now Belgium and the Netherlands), Philip dispatched Alba as governor. Immediately upon his arrival at the head of 12,000 armed men, the duke set about restoring order – in a fierce fashion. Determined to root out and destroy heresy and subversion, he created a new 'Council of Troubles', composed of local dignitaries who were to serve as the instrument of Spanish vengeance. Setting aside existing local laws, the Council – soon dubbed the 'Council of Blood' – declared several thousand people to be guilty of rebellion and condemned them to exile, imprisonment or death. All sections of society suffered – noble birth proved to be no protection from the 'iron fist' of Alba. Thus, in August 1568, having entered Brussels, the duke oversaw the summary beheading of 22 of the town's leading citizens. Numerous massacres followed elsewhere.

Yet such brutal repression served only to fuel an insurrection against Spanish rule where none had previously existed. When the princes of Orange invaded the Low Countries from Germany and France simultaneously, they were joined by a force of exiles – the *Guezen* ('beggars') – and for a period they managed to seize control of Holland, Zeeland and several other provinces. Though the duke was subsequently able to recapture much of this territory, the further punishments he meted out simply generated additional unrest – as did his punitive and bitterly resented taxation policy.

In 1573, amidst a rising sense that Alba himself had become a central part of the problem in the Spanish Netherlands, the duke was recalled to Spain. Although he was initially feted by Phillip II, in 1579 he was placed under house arrest after his son had earned the displeasure of the king.

But the following year Philip recalled Alba to take command of an expedition against the Portuguese. For one final time, he displayed his extraordinary military gifts, winning a stunning victory over the Portuguese at the Battle of Alcântara. As in the Spanish Netherlands, however, his battlefield derring-do was matched only by his lack of restraint in the aftermath. On entering Lisbon he allowed his troops to pillage and loot the city, bringing his unique brand of terror to the Iberian Peninsula.

In December 1582, whilst still in Lisbon, the old duke suddenly died. During the course of his life he had proved himself a dedicated servant to his royal masters – and his skills as a general were unsurpassed. Yet his reputation will forever be indelibly stained with the blood of the civilians who perished on his orders. His behaviour in the Low Countries provoked a resentment against Spanish rule that led to a decades-long revolt, a revolt that culminated in independence for the Dutch – and which marked the beginning of the end of Spanish power in Europe.

Fernando Álvarez de Toledo, 3rd duke of Alba, in an intimidating likeness by the Dutch portrait painter Antonis Mor, dating from 1549.

CATHERINE DE' MEDICI AND THE ST BARTHOLOMEW'S DAY MASSACRE

Alba's interlocutor in France was Queen Catherine de' Medici – regent during the minority of her son, Charles IX, renowned for her hatred of the French Protestants (Huguenots). France was racked by internecine strife in the Wars of Religion (1562–98) fought between powerful Catholic and Protestant rivals – the House of Guise and the Catholic League versus the House of Bourbon.

When young King Charles – swayed by his trusted adviser Admiral Gaspard de Coligny – openly allied himself in 1572 with the Huguenots, the Catholic Catherine and her supporters feared that France would be dragged into a war with Spain over the Protestant Netherlands, occupied at the time by the Spanish. To counter this, the Catholic faction attempted on 22 August to assassinate Coligny, but this was botched. Fearful of reprisals, Catherine – using her daughter Margaret's marriage to the Huguenot Henry, king of Navarre, as bait to lure her prey to Paris – persuaded Charles to sanction the murder of almost 200 leading Huguenots on the night of 24 August.

The assassinations escalated into a massacre. Over the next five days, mobs slaughtered 3000 Huguenots in Paris alone, with thousands more subsequently killed outside the capital as the unrest spread to the provinces. It was the worst religious massacre of the century – and one which Alba's master, Philip II, warmly praised. The dashing King Henry of Navarre narrowly survived to become Henry IV 'The Great' of France, founder of the Bourbon dynasty. Known as the 'Green Gallant' for his womanizing, he famously converted nominally to Catholicism to win control of France, saying 'Paris is worth a mass'.

Catherine de' Medici ranks as one of the most monstrous European female leaders. The massacre was encouraged by her son who ordered 'Kill them all!' But she was the mastermind.

The St Bartholomew's Day Massacre of 24 August 1572, as depicted in a contemporary painting by François Dubois. The painting shows the Huguenot leader Gaspard de Coligny being heaved out of the window of his house (top right). Catherine de' Medici, the instigator of the massacre, is the black-clad figure gazing at a pile of Protestant corpses (top centre).

Mary Tudor, queen of England and Ireland from 1553 until 1558, the first woman to rule England in her own right, was the notorious 'Bloody Mary' who placed her realm at the feet of the Spanish king and presided over a pitiless religious terror, burning dissidents at the stake, to enforce and restore Catholicism. Bitterly preoccupied with the past, she tried to reverse the Protestant Reformation started by her father, Henry VIII. Yet her own life was tragic, her marriage childless, her health ultimately fragile, her mind increasingly deranged; while her reign, both in her repression and foreign policy, failed utterly.

Bloody Mary 1516–58

'We shall never find any reign of any prince in this land or any other, which did ever show in it (for proportion of time), so many great arguments of God's wrath and displeasure, as were to be seen in the reign of this queen Mary.'

JOHN FOXE, PROTESTANT WRITER, 1563

The only surviving child of Henry VIII and his first wife, Catherine of Aragon, Mary remained a staunch Catholic throughout her life, despite being raised in the unforgiving world of Reformation England. Though plain, she was intelligent and vivacious and had delighted her parents as a child, but after the annulment of her mother's marriage to Henry, and the birth in 1533 of a daughter, Elizabeth, to his second wife, Anne Boleyn, Mary was increasingly ostracized. She was forbidden access to her parents and forced to act as lady-in-waiting to her infant half-sister. She never again saw her mother, and relations with her father became strained to breaking point. Yet Mary was nothing if not stubborn, and refused to give up her title of 'princess'. When Anne Boleyn was beheaded in 1536, Mary was reconciled to Henry, who eventually granted her the right of succession, next in line after her younger half-brother, the future Edward VI.

Queen Mary I, who earned the nickname 'Bloody Mary' for her persecution of English Protestants, depicted in a 1554 portrait by Anthonis van Dashorst. A visiting ambassador described her as being '. . . of low stature, with a red and white complexion, and very thin. Her eyes are white and large and her hair reddish.'

During Edward's reign, from 1547 to 1553, Mary retired from public life, refusing to conform to the new religion of the state, Protestantism, and instead openly practising the Latin Mass, which Edward had outlawed. When he tried to bring his sister to heel by summoning her to court in March 1551, she arrived in London in an ostentatious display of her faith, with over one hundred followers, each carrying rosary beads.

When Edward died, John Dudley, duke of Northumberland (son of Henry VII's official, executed by Henry VIII) led a Protestant coup, placing Henry VIII's great-niece, Lady Jane Grey, on the throne after marrying her to his son Guildford. Mary was forced to flee to East Anglia, but in a matter of days returned to the capital, backed by massive popular support, and ousted the pretender to her throne. Mary's coronation was greeted with a tremendous burst of gunfire, which contemporaries ominously compared to an earthquake. Ever the purist, she was anointed with holy oil imported from the continent to avoid the use of oil tainted by the Protestantism of Edward's reign. Northumberland was executed.

Mary I had one overriding obsession: to restore Roman Catholicism as the religion of the state. At first she proceeded cautiously, simply repealing some of the anti-Catholic legislation of Edward's reign, but then, encouraged by Cardinal Reginald Pole, she made plans to marry Philip II, the Catholic king of Spain, the son of her cousin, the Holy Roman Emperor Charles V. Through attaching England to a Catholic dynasty, she aimed to ensure it would never stray from Rome again.

'When I am dead and opened,' Mary declared, 'you shall find "Calais" lying on my heart.'

When the news of the betrothal became public in 1554, it created a surge of fear and xenophobia, culminating in a rebellion led by Sir Thomas Wyatt, aimed at putting the young Princess Elizabeth on the throne. Suppression of the revolt was swift and brutal. Nearly a hundred rebels suffered the grisly fate meted out to traitors in those days: hanging, drawing and quartering. Lady Jane Grey was beheaded, having earlier escaped death for her attempt to usurp the throne, even though she had no direct involvement in the rebellion. Elizabeth herself was held for a while in the Tower of London, in fear for her life.

The worst nightmares of the rebels were realized when, following Mary's marriage to Philip, draconian laws against heresy were immediately restored. For three brutal years, England felt the full ferocity of the Counter-Reformation. Close on three hundred men, women and children were burned at the stake between February 1555 and November 1558, including bishops Thomas Cranmer, Hugh Latimer and Nicholas Ridley. The first victim, the popular preacher John Rogers, was burned at Smithfield on 4 February 1555, in front of his eleven children. Church courts had the power to condemn heresy, but Mary alone could sign the death warrant.

To her ultimate humiliation, Mary never bore a child to carry on a line of Catholic monarchs in England. In November 1554 she became convinced she was pregnant – going so far as to hold a thanksgiving service in anticipation of the birth – but instead found she was suffering from cancer of the womb. Her standing was undermined further when, spurred on by Philip, she embarked on a disastrous war with France, leading to the loss of Calais in 1558, England's last foothold in continental Europe. 'When I am dead and opened,' Mary declared, 'you shall find "Calais" lying on my heart.' She died that same year, barren and lonely, Philip having left her to return Spain.

In the name of her faith, she sent innocent people to a slow and agonizing death, doing so with the callous zeal so typical of the doctrinaire fanatic. She well deserved her epithet of 'Bloody Mary'.

A HERETIC'S DEATH

Burning at the stake was the Church's chosen punishment for the crimes of heresy and witchcraft, because, unlike other forms of execution, it did not require the spilling of blood. It was introduced to England by Henry IV in 1401, as part of the persecution of the Lollards – a proto-Protestant group whose distaste for the wealthy and the privileged frightened the bishops and landowners of the realm. Although some of Henry IV's heresy laws fell into disuse, they were revived by Henry VIII and used by Bloody Mary to kill nearly three hundred people.

The larger the fire, the quicker the death – more merciful executioners would allow friends and family of the accused to feed the fire with wood, and the condemned would often scream for more flames. More commonly, however, the condemned was tied to a stake and a fire started among the small bundle of sticks placed at his or her feet, which would begin by charring the feet and ankles, then slowly lick up the calves. Amidst the screams, the victim would also suffer from slow suffocation from the smoke – contemporary observers noted how the mouth would visibly blacken, the lips thin

and the tongue swell. John Foxe's *Book of Martyrs* (1563) reports how, in some instances, the condemned, gasping for oxygen, would bang at their chest so hard that their arms would fall off as the flames reached the torso.

Some heretics astounded observers with displays of fortitude and calm adherence to their faith. When the bishops Nicholas Ridley and Hugh Latimer were burned by Queen Mary on 16 October 1555, Latimer spoke words that have echoed down the centuries: 'Be of good comfort, Master Ridley, and play the man; we shall light this day such a candle, by God's grace, in England, as I trust shall never be put out.'

Occasionally, however, when the religious authorities anticipated such an outburst, they would tie the tongue of the condemned in a gag or singe it before the burning began. This was the fate of Giordano Bruno (1548–1600), an Italian cosmologist and philosopher whose heretical views earned him the wrath of Pope Clement VIII, and who was burned at the stake in Rome on 17 February 1600, becoming one of the first martyrs to science.

The burning of Thomas Cranmer, Archbishop of Canterbury, in 1556, from Foxe's Book of Martyrs. Cranmer had earlier been forced by Mary to sign a document renouncing Protestantism. In a dramatic gesture, he thrust into the fire the hand with which he had signed the recantation, so that it would burn first.

Ivan IV of Russia, known as 'the Terrible', was a tragic but degenerate monster, both terrorized and damaged as a child, who grew up to be a successful empire-builder and shrewd tyrant. Ultimately he deteriorated into a demented, homicidal sadist who killed many thousands in a frenzied terror, impaling and torturing his enemies personally. By murdering his son, he hastened the demise of his own dynasty.

Ivan the Terrible

1530–84

> 'You shut up the Kingdom of Russia . . .
> as in a fortress of hell.'
>
> PRINCE KURBSKY, LETTER TO IVAN IV

Ivan was declared the 'Grand Prince of Muscovy' when he was just three years old, after the early death of his father. Five years later his mother too died. With both parents gone, the task of caring for Ivan fell to the boyar Shuisky family – members of whom also served as regents for the remainder of the prince's minority. The boyars formed a closed aristocratic class of around 200 families; Ivan complained that they bullied him, terrorized him, neglected him and were attempting to usurp his birthright.

Ivan's coronation took place in January 1547, and the early years of his reign were characterized by reform and modernization. Changes to the law code were accompanied by the creation of a council of nobles and local-government reforms. Efforts were also made to open up Russia to European trade and commerce. Ivan oversaw the consolidation and expansion of Muscovite territory. In 1552 he defeated and annexed the Kazan khanate, and the storming of the city of Kazan itself was followed by the slaughter of over 100,000 defenders. More military successes followed, and further territories, including the Astrakhan khanate and parts of Siberia, were brought under Russian sway. He built the gaudy St Basil's Cathedral in Red Square to celebrate the conquest of Kazan.

After a near-fatal illness in 1553, Ivan's personality appeared to undergo a transformation, and from that point he became ever more erratic and prone to bouts of rage. In 1560 his wife, Anastasia Romanovna, died from an unknown disease, an event that appears to have caused Ivan to suffer a breakdown. He convinced himself that the boyars had conspired to poison him – and he may have been right. If so, the plot led to the death of his beloved wife. He decided that the boyars would have to be punished and their power eradicated. The defection of one of his grandees, Prince Kurbsky, intensified his insane paranoia.

The result, on the one hand, was further administrative reform, aimed at augmenting the power of locally elected officials at the expense of the nobility. Such moves appeared to point the way towards a more rational and more competent form of government. Yet at the same time Ivan unleashed a vengeful terror against the unsuspecting boyars, and a wave of arrests and executions followed. Ivan devised peculiarly horrible deaths for some of them: Prince Boris Telupa was impaled upon a stake and took 15 agonizing hours to die, while his mother, according to one chronicler, 'was given to a hundred gunners, who defiled her to death'.

Worse was to come. In 1565 Ivan designated an area of Russia – dubbed the *Oprichnina* (meaning 'apart from') – within which the lands were to be directly ruled by the tsar.

Oprichniki squads crisscrossed the territory to implement Ivan's will. Dressed in black cloaks that bore the insignia of a severed dog's head and a broom (on account of their role in 'sniffing out' treason and sweeping away Ivan's enemies), the *oprichniki* set about crushing all alternative sources of authority. The boyars were singled out for especially harsh treatment.

Ivan embarked on an orgy of sexual adventures — both heterosexual and homosexual — while destroying his imagined enemies. He personally killed and tortured many. Ivan's savagery was shockingly varied in nature: ribs were torn out, people burnt alive, impaled, beheaded, disembowelled, their genitals cut off. His 'sadistic refinement' in a public bout of torturing in 1570 outdid all that went before and most of what came after.

In 1570 the tsar's agents perpetrated a frenzied massacre in the city of Novgorod, after Ivan suspected that its citizens were about to betray him to the Poles. Some 1500 nobles were murdered — many by being drowned in the River Volkhov — and an equal number of commoners were officially recorded as dead, though the death toll may have been far higher. The archbishop of Novgorod was sewn up in the skin of a bear, and a pack of hounds was set loose on him.

As the harsh internal repression took its toll on Russia's people, Ivan's fortunes went into steep decline. During the 1570s the Tartars of the Crimean khanate devastated large tracts of Russia with seeming impunity — even managing to set fire to Moscow on one occasion. At the same time, the tsar's attempts at westward expansion across the Baltic Sea succeeded only in embroiling the country in the Livonian War against a coalition that included Denmark, Poland, Sweden and Lithuania. The conflict dragged on for almost a quarter of a century, with little tangible gain. And all the while the *oprichniki* continued to engage in their wild bouts of killing and destruction; their area of operation, once the richest region of Russia, was reduced to one of the poorest and most unstable.

In 1581 Ivan turned his destructive rage against his own family. Having previously assaulted his pregnant daughter-in-law, he got into an argument with his son and heir, also called Ivan, and killed him in a fit of blind rage. It was only after Ivan the Terrible's own death — possibly from poisoning — that Russia was finally put out of its long agony.

A detail from a celebrated depiction of Ivan the Terrible's killing of his son, 16 November 1581, by the Russian artist Ilya Repin (1844–1930).

Ivan's second son, Fyodor, proved far less talented than the original heir apparent. In 1598 a former advisor to Ivan, Boris Godunov, seized control, and Ivan's bloodline was brought to an end.

The *oprichniki* inspired a later Russian tyrant, Josef Stalin, and served as a prototype for his secret police, the NKVD (see page 205). His own Terror was based on that of Ivan, whom he often called 'teacher'. 'Who now remembers the boyars wiped out by Ivan the Terrible?' he once said, 'His mistake was not to kill *all* the boyars'. Ultimately, Ivan the Terrible was mad as well as bad. As his best biographer, Isabel de Madariaga, wrote: 'Ivan was not like God, he tried to be God. His reign is a tragedy of Shakespearean proportions. His cruelty served no purpose . . . He is Lucifer, the star of the morning who wanted to be God and was expelled from the Heavens.'

THE INSANE CALIPH

Al-Hakim bi-Amr Allah, the sixth Fatimid caliph of Egypt, was another strange, dangerous and ultimately demented ruler. Aged just 11, he inherited an empire beset by problems – and proceeded to make things worse through outlandish decrees, such as prohibiting the eating of grapes and watercress and the game of chess. On another occasion he ordered that all dogs in Cairo should be slaughtered, and their bodies dumped in the desert. Deciding that people are most productive at night, he ordered that all work should be done during the hours of darkness. But he also ordered brutal massacres and eccentrically inconsistent and ever-changing religious oppression of, variously, Christians, Jews and other Muslim sects. In 1009 he ordered the destruction of the Church of the Holy Sepulchre in Jerusalem. Torture and murder on his orders became commonplace. In 1020, the caliph even ordered his armies to sack his own capital city, Cairo. His reign was finally brought to an end in 1021 when he rode out into the desert on a donkey without his guards and was never seen again. The donkey was found with blood on it – perhaps his sister, Sitt al-Mulk, ordered his assassination. Or did the mad caliph just disappear into the desert?

The destruction of the Church of the Holy Sepulchre in Jerusalem (1009) by forces of the deranged Fatimid caliph Al-Hakim, in a contemporary depiction.

Handsome, learned, headstrong and vain, the Elizabethan adventurer Humphrey Gilbert was a brutal English conquistador who sought to establish Ireland as an English colony, terrorizing men, women and children, sometimes creating a ghoulish pathway of bodyless heads to his own tent.

Humphrey Gilbert
c. 1539–83

'No one could come into his tent for any cause, but commonly he must pass through a lane of heads, which he used ad terrorem ... bringing great terror to the people, when they saw the heads of their dead fathers, brothers, children, kinsfolk and friends lie on the ground before their faces, as they came to speak with the said Colonel.'

THOMAS CHURCHYARD, WHO SERVED UNDER HUMPHREY GILBERT IN IRELAND

Gilbert was born in Devon, one of four children. After his father died, his mother remarried into the Raleigh family and bore two more sons, including Walter Raleigh, who was to become one of Queen Elizabeth's favourites. Gilbert was taken under the wing of Sir Henry Sidney, Lord Deputy of Ireland, and one of the most influential men in the realm. He studied at Eton and then Oxford, and learned to speak Spanish and French. He also acquired a knowledge of military strategy and navigation, and an interest in exploration. In 1566 he presented Queen Elizabeth with a pamphlet in which he outlined

Sir Humphrey Gilbert, soldier, adventurer and English colonizer in Ireland. As governor of Munster he subjected the province to a blood-soaked reign of terror.

his idea of finding a 'Northwest Passage' to China around the top of the American continent, to undercut the Spanish and Portuguese monopoly of trade with the East.

In 1562 Gilbert gained his first experience of warfare, serving under the earl of Warwick at the siege of Le Havre. He served under his mentor Sidney in Ireland in 1565, and returned there in 1569 as governor of the province of Ulster. He went on to plan an extensive English colonial settlement around Baltimore, near Cork, in the southern province of Munster, as part of the Elizabethan policy of replacing the independent Irish feudal lords with 'lord presidencies', military governors loyal to Elizabeth, a policy accompanied by the confiscation of land from local clans.

Gilbert's actions provoked the outbreak, in June 1569, of the first of the Desmond rebellions, led by the Fitzgerald earls of Desmond, who controlled much of Munster. Sidney ordered Gilbert to pursue the rebel leader James Fitzmaurice Fitzgerald, a devout Catholic who resented the incursions of Elizabeth's Protestant troops. Although Fitzgerald evaded capture by retreating into the hills and conducting a guerrilla war, Gilbert – now governor of Munster – pursued a policy of devastating the lands of the Desmonds. In December 1569 Sidney awarded Gilbert his knighthood, surrounded by the bloody corpses of his victims at an enemy camp that his troops had just decimated.

Gilbert's campaign was utterly relentless, the main plank of his strategy being to spread such terror through the Irish people that they wilted in the face of his advancing troops. Thus, without having to rely on the artillery normally needed in siege warfare, Gilbert obtained the surrender of nearly forty castles in the Kerry area in just three weeks. Gilbert himself fought with great personal bravery, but the terror conducted by his forces was deliberate, systematic, gruesome and undertaken with relish – as in their practice of severing the heads of dead corpses and placing them neatly on the ground, their faces visible, to form a corridor leading to Gilbert's tent. Thus, when his enemies came to discuss the terms of their surrender, they were confronted with the decapitated heads of their 'dead fathers, brothers, children, kinsfolk and friends'.

By early 1570 nearly all the rebels, Fitzgerald excluded, had surrendered, and Gilbert returned to England, where he became MP for Plymouth and drew up plans for an academy in London. In 1579 he was ordered back to Ireland to take on a resurgent Fitzgerald, but his fleet was so poorly navigated that it ended up in the Bay of Biscay. When he finally arrived at the port of Cobh in Munster, months off schedule, he resumed his worst behaviour, viciously beating a local around the head with the flat of his sword and murdering a merchant on the dockside.

In November 1578 Gilbert had made an attempt to sail to America, but was forced back by severe storms. He eventually established a colony in Newfoundland in June 1583, but drowned on the voyage home, when his ship went down in heavy seas. It was said that Gilbert had last been seen on deck reading Thomas More's *Utopia*. But in the end Gilbert would not be remembered for his learning or his courage or his imagination, but for setting the brutal pattern of English colonial rule in Ireland.

THE MASSACRE AT DROGHEDA

Humphrey Gilbert's massacre of innocent women and children characterized the worst excesses of the Elizabethan colonization of Ireland. Even in 16th-century warfare, the murder of non-combatants was prohibited by convention. However, the most notorious of English atrocities in Ireland came eighty years later, during Oliver Cromwell's campaign in the country in 1649–50.

Cromwell arrived in Ireland during the height of the English Civil War, fearing that the future Charles II would attempt to launch an invasion of England from Ireland, whose Catholic population was sympathetic to the Royalist cause. He determined to conquer the country as soon as possible, fearful of running out of funds and alarmed by the prospect of further political instability back in England.

One of Cromwell's first targets in his campaign was the garrison town of Drogheda, to the north of Dublin. Commanding the garrison of just over 3000 English Royalist and Catholic Irish troops was an English Royalist, Sir Arthur Ashton. On 10 September 1649 Cromwell ordered Ashton to surrender, or the town would face the consequences.

After some negotiations Ashton rejected the terms offered to him. Cromwell, at the head of a 12,000-strong army and impatient for a quick success, launched his attack on 11 September. Speaking to his soldiers, he 'forbade them to spare any that were at arms in the town'. As his men broke into Drogheda, all of the defenders were put to the sword – even those who quickly surrendered. Hundreds of civilians were also murdered. Catholic priests were systematically targeted, and those who had sought refuge from the fighting in St Peter's Church were burnt alive when the besiegers torched the building. Of the Royalist troops, Cromwell stated, 'I do not think thirty of their number escaped with their lives'. Those who did were promptly sold into slavery in Barbados. One estimate put the total death toll at 3500, of whom 2800 were soldiers and the rest clergy and civilians.

Modern research shows that the massacres have been exaggerated but, nonetheless, there is no doubt they were war crimes. Cromwell later accounted for himself before the English Parliament. 'I am persuaded,' he said, 'that this is a righteous judgment of God upon these barbarous wretches, who have imbued their hands in so much innocent blood and that it will tend to prevent the effusion of blood for the future, which are satisfactory grounds for such actions, which otherwise cannot but work remorse and regret.'

The Persecutions in Ireland, *attributed to Gerbrandt van den Eeckhout,* c. *1657. Cromwell's massacre at Drogheda in 1649 led to a flurry of popular images condemning British abuses in Ireland.*

In the 16th century a dark, damp cave on a wild stretch of coast in southwest Scotland was reputed to be the home of Sawney Beane, the head of an incestuous clan who lived off robbery, murder and the corpses of their victims. So terrifying were the stories of Beane's deeds that some historians have speculated that he might never have existed, but was rather dreamt up by the English as a way of demonizing the Scots as savage cannibals.

Sawney Beane
16th century

'*An incredible Monster who, with his Wife, lived by Murder and Cannibalism in a Cave. Executed at Leith with his whole Family in the Reign of James I.*'

THE COMPLETE NEWGATE CALENDAR, VOL. 1

The tale of Beane was made known to a popular audience in the 18th century in the *Newgate Calendar* (also called *The Malefactor's Bloody Register*), a series of sensationalist publications that described the details of notorious crimes, and so named from Newgate prison in London, where condemned prisoners were often held before their execution at Tyburn.

What the *Newgate Calendar* tells us is that Alexander Beane was born in East Lothian, about eight miles east of Edinburgh, sometime in the 16th century. His father was a ditch-digger and hedge-trimmer but Beane never showed any interest in hard work. As an adolescent he left home with an equally unpleasant woman from the local area and – unwilling to take conventional employment – traversed the country until he arrived at Bennane Head, on the borders of southern Ayrshire and Galloway. Here the couple set up home in a deep coastal cave, concealed from the view of passers-by.

Over the next 25 years, Beane and his partner raised an extensive family in his cave. At the time of his discovery, he was estimated to have produced 8 sons and 6 daughters, who had bred together to produce 18 grandsons and 14 granddaughters. According to the *Newgate Calendar*, the children were raised 'without any notions of humanity or civil society'. The clan survived by preying on anyone unfortunate enough to be travelling along this remote stretch of coast. They never robbed a victim whom they did not kill, and the bodies were then dragged back to the cave where they were dismembered and devoured. Leftover flesh was pickled, while unwanted bones and body parts were thrown into the sea.

The sight of these gruesome remains washed up on the shore shocked and perplexed the local population. But Beane and his clan, who worked by stealth and by night, avoided detection for many years. Instead, a number of local innkeepers and travellers were wrongly accused of responsibility and executed.

One fateful night, however, the Beane clan accosted a married couple. The man managed to fight off his assailants with his sword and pistol, but not before his wife had been knocked from her horse and immediately disembowelled. The savages then drank her blood as if it was wine. Having made good his escape, the man raised the alarm, and it was not long before King James VI of Scotland – later to become James I of England – was informed of the case.

Four hundred men and a pack of bloodhounds were dispatched to root out the cannibals. Beane's cave – well hidden in the cliff face, and totally inaccessible during high tide – might have avoided detection had not the dogs picked up the scent of human flesh. When the soldiers entered the cave they were met with a putrid smell and the horrific sight of dried body parts hanging from the walls, pickled flesh floating in barrels and heaps of jewellery, money and other valuables piled on the floor.

The wild-eyed Beanes made no attempt to escape. They were arrested and brought to Edinburgh, before being moved again – either to Leith or Glasgow – where they were executed without trial. The men of the clan had their hands, feet and genitals cut off, and were left to bleed to death. The women and children were forced to watch, before being burnt as witches. It was said that during the course of their reign of terror they had seen off over a thousand victims.

Cannibalism was not unknown in 16th-century Scotland, and – given that the *Newgate Calendar* gave considerable coverage to savageries perpetrated by English criminals – it seems unlikely that the tales about Sawney Beane were simply anti-Scots propaganda. The story of this figure from nightmare was regularly read to children in both Scotland and England throughout the 18th and 19th centuries as a stark warning of the consequences of indolence, and the inevitability of punishment should they go astray.

Alexander ('Sawney') Beane, as depicted in an engraving by James Basire from Lives of the Most Remarkable Criminals *(1735). Beane was the head of a Scottish family of some 50 members, who murdered and ate over 1000 people before being captured and executed.*

JEAN-BÉDEL BOKASSA

A world and an age away from Sawney Beane in his cold Ayrshire cave, Jean-Bédel Bokassa was the murderous tyrant of the Central African Republic with a taste for Napoleonic delusion and – it was rumoured – human flesh.

The son of a village chief, Bokassa was born in 1921 at the edge of a rainforest in Ubangi-Shari, part of French Equatorial Africa. He was orphaned at the age of 12 when his father was beaten to death by colonial forces for leading a revolt against the French forestry companies that dominated the tribes of the rainforest. His mother, heartbroken, killed herself shortly afterwards.

Educated in missionary schools, young Bokassa grew into a strong and stocky youth, and in 1939 joined the French colonial army as a private. Distinguishing himself during the Second World War, he soon rose up through the ranks. In 1960 Ubangi-Shari achieved independence as the Central African Republic, and in 1963 the new president, David Dacko, invited Bokassa to become chief of staff. On 31 December 1965 Bokassa led a coup against Dacko and declared himself president. He went on to abolish the constitution, and attempted to construct a cult of personality around his leadership.

Bokassa was a ruthless megalomaniac who was quick to purge even his closest allies if he thought they presented a threat. In 1972, despite his growing unpopularity and a number of assassination attempts, he declared himself president for life. He implemented law and order by savage means: thieves would have an ear cut off for a first offence, the other ear for a second offence, and a hand for a third. In 1977 Bokassa declared himself emperor of the 'Central African Empire' and wasted the country's entire aid budget of $200 million on a lavish ceremony in which he mimicked Napoleon by crowning himself.

In 1979 Bokassa had hundreds of schoolchildren arrested for refusing to wear uniforms made in a government factory. When he personally supervised the

The coronation of Emperor Bokassa, 4 December 1977. The African dictator consciously modelled his investiture ceremony on that of Napoleon Bonaparte in 1804.

massacre of a hundred of them by his Imperial Guard, there was an international outcry. Widely presumed to be on the verge of lunacy, Bokassa was forced out by a French-backed coup led by David Dacko. At his subsequent trial he was convicted of murder – though cleared of cannibalism – and sentenced to life imprisonment. He was released in 1993, dying of natural causes three years later.

'The Bloody Lady of Csejte', the Hungarian countess Elizabeth Báthory was Central Europe's most notorious female serial killer. Her sadistic torture and murder of scores or even hundreds of young women and girls was only stopped by her arrest and the trial of her accomplices. Her final prison was a walled-up room in her castle at Csejte, where she died alone.

Countess Elizabeth Báthory 1560–1614

'Elizabeth, you are like a wild animal . . . The shadows will envelop you and you will find time to repent your bestial life.'

COUNT THURZÓ'S JUDGMENT ON COUNTESS BÁTHORY AFTER HER ARREST

Elizabeth Báthory was born into a noble family from the Nyirbator region of eastern Hungary and grew up at Ecsed Castle. The Báthorys were one of the richest and most powerful aristocratic clans in the country.

In 1571, at the age of eleven, Elizabeth was engaged to Ferenc Nádasdy, a 16-year-old from another noble family. As was the custom for a bride-to-be, after their betrothal she moved to her husband's castle in the Sarvar region, and they were married in 1575. Her husband was a prominent figure at the royal court and became commander-in-chief of Hungary's armies during the country's successful war against the Ottoman empire.

With Nádasdy often away, the Countess was more than competent in caring for their domains. She was clearly intelligent, and fluent in at least three languages, at a time when even many nobles were barely literate. She soon showed herself to be a rigid disciplinarian – appearing to take pleasure in the task of punishing her servants for their misdemeanours. Stories emerged of her beating young servant girls with clubs for their transgressions, while others were forced outside naked into the snow and doused with cold water until they froze to death. This penchant for acts of sadism developed into a full-scale passion for torture and murder. Left to her own devices, in the absence of her husband, the dark side of the countess's character ran amok.

Countess Elizabeth Báthory, remembered as the 'Bloody Lady of Csejte'.

Young peasant girls were brought into the Castle, either on the lure of work, or through simple abduction by Elizabeth's aides. Once there, they were subjected to frightful forms of abuse and depravity. Victims were beaten, mutilated and burnt; all part of a sustained and bloody pattern of torment. A witness at her later trial reported how Elizabeth had once been too ill to get out of bed, and had ordered a female servant to be brought to her. When the young girl appeared, the countess attacked her, biting her and tearing flesh away from the screaming victim's cheek, shoulders and breasts. There seemed no limit to her sadistic enjoyment of such cruelty, especially if plenty of blood was involved. Indeed, it was this that led to the legend of later centuries that the countess regularly bathed in the blood of virginal girls in an effort to maintain her youth.

Her husband Ferenc Nádasdy died in 1604, and she moved to another family castle at Csejte, in modern Slovakia. Now, not only peasant girls but the daughters of the local, lesser nobility were also targeted; and Elizabeth grew ever more brazen. Bodies were dumped regardless of the risk of their being discovered and traced back to the countess. In one infamous incident, four girls were thrown from the Castle ramparts in full view of horrified villagers. With such open displays of inhuman cruelty growing ever more frequent, it was a matter of time before Elizabeth's reign of terror came to an end.

Between 1602 and 1604, rumours of the nefarious activities on the Nádasdy estates became more public, in part by the agitations of a Lutheran priest, István Magyari. Initially, the Hungarian government was slow to respond to the growing volume of accusation being levelled at the countess, out of deference to her husband. After his death people began to take a closer look at the countess, but it was not until 1610 that King Matthias ordered the Palatine of Hungary, Count György Thurzó, to investigate.

As he realized the scale of the atrocities, Thurzó was keen to avoid a scandal involving so prominent a noble family, to whom he was himself related. The authorities opted to confine Elizabeth to house arrest, rather than put her on trial. Thurzó arrived at Csejte Castle on 29 December 1610 and arrested the countess, together with four servants who were deemed to be accomplices. Elizabeth's horrifying exploits were still evident. Thurzó discovered one girl who was already dead and another who was close to dying; many more were being held within the compound. Though, as had been agreed, Elizabeth avoided trial, the case against her four co-conspirators came quickly to court on 7 January 1611, and many of the details of what had taken place at Csejte came to light. Three of the accused were convicted and executed; the fourth was found guilty and sentenced to life imprisonment. Elizabeth remained confined to one room in her castle. The windows and door were bricked up – the only gaps were to allow ventilation and food to be passed in to her. She died in August 1614, at the age of fifty-four.

Bram Stoker's novel *Dracula*, published in 1897, has led people fascinated by blood to speculate that the career of 'The Blood Countess' of Transylvania was the core inspiration for the vampire genre, at least as much as the life of Vlad the Impaler (see page 107). But the sadistic pleasures and depraved deeds of the real Elizabeth Báthory ensure her place as one of history's monsters.

HISTORY'S MOST EVIL FEMALE SERIAL KILLERS

• MARIE, MARQUISE DE BRINVILLIERS (1630–76): a Parisian woman who poisoned as many as 50 people, including her father and two brothers.

• GESCHE GOTTFRIED (1785–1831): a German poisoner whose 16 victims included her parents, sons, two husbands and several friends.

• BELLE GUNNESS (1859–1931): an American who killed at least 20 people, including her own children, two husbands and numerous male suitors.

• MARGIE VELMA BARFIELD (1932–84): an American (and the first woman to be executed by lethal injection), who burnt her first husband to death while he slept, and poisoned a further six husbands, several boyfriends and her own mother.

• MYRA HINDLEY (1942–2002): the 'Moors murderer' who, together with her partner Ian Brady, abducted, sexually abused and murdered five children between July 1963 and October 1965.

• GENENE JONES (b.1950): an American nurse who murdered at least 11 children and possibly as many as 46.

• ROSEMARY WEST (b.1953): an Englishwoman who, together with her husband, Fred, was responsible for the torture, abuse and murder of at least 10 young women at their home in Gloucester.

• BEVERLEY ALLITT (b.1968): the 'angel of death', Allitt was a paediatric nurse who killed four children (and attempted to kill several others) using poisonous injections.

• AILEEN CAROL WUORNOS (1956–2002), an American lesbian prostitute executed for killing at least seven men, claiming they had attempted to rape her.

A scene from the death sentence of the Marquise de Brinvilliers, carried out on 17 July 1676. The notorious poisoner was forced to drink 16 pints of water, beheaded and burned at the stake.

Manic-depressive, self-obsessed and prone to violent outbursts, Don Carlo Gesualdo, Prince of Venosa, was a gifted Renaissance composer who murdered his wife and her lover in the most gruesome fashion. His music provides an insight into a wildly passionate and unpredictable mind, capable of creating great beauty, but also ridden with gloom and pain.

Don Carlo Gesualdo, Prince of Venosa
1566—1613

'Guilt and remorse . . . pursued him for the rest of his life, as did the fear of eternal damnation. He died in 1613, by all accounts a miserable, neurotic figure, yet having composed some of the most boldly inventive, complex and idiosyncratic vocal music of the Renaissance.'

FROM *PRINCE OF PAIN: THE STRANGE CASE OF CARLO GESUALDO* BY CHRIS BLACKFORD

The Gesualdos were a prominent Italian noble family who owned large swathes of land in southern Italy, including a castle at Gesualdo and a palace in Naples. Portraits of Don Carlo himself show a slim and angular figure, with a downcast and joyless countenance, receding black hair, a furrowed brow, a thin moustache and a pointed beard.

From his youth, Gesualdo's first passion was for music, and he was an accomplished singer as well as expert on the lute and the harpsichord. Contemporary accounts suggest that his second passion was for men, and it was rumoured that he had a number of homosexual affairs, which continued throughout his two marriages.

Gesualdo's first bride, whom he married in 1586, was Donna Maria D'Avalos, his beautiful and charming cousin, who, although only 30, had already been twice widowed. It was rumoured, probably unfairly, that Donna Maria's first husband had died in a vain attempt to satisfy her. It was not long after her marriage to Gesualdo that Donna Maria gave him an heir. Having done his dynastic duty, Gesualdo then turned his attentions to music once again.

Donna, who craved attention but who was regularly rebuffed by the intense and aloof Gesualdo, soon found solace in the arms of another man, the dashing Don Fabrizio Carafa, Duke of Andria, who was himself already married. Over the course of a torrid, two-year affair, Donna and Don Fabrizio lived dangerously, risking hurried assignations and bribing Gesualdo's servants to keep their secret. Meanwhile, Gesualdo's uncle, Don Giulio, had also set his sights on his nephew's wife, only to have his advances rejected. He then vindictively revealed the details of Donna's affair to Gesualdo.

Gesualdo was furious, but his plans for revenge were cold-blooded and meticulous. On 16 October 1590 he told his wife that he was leaving Naples to go hunting, leaving her free to contact her lover. Instead, he waited secretly inside the palace until Don Fabrizio arrived, and then, with the help of his servants, smashed down the door of Donna's bedroom, catching the lovers naked in each other's arms and murdering them both in a frenzied attack. Don Fabrizio died from a combination of stabbing and a shot in the head, while Donna suffered a horrific succession of stab wounds to her stomach and genitalia. Long after his wife had expired, Gesualdo continued his assault on her corpse, screaming 'She's not dead yet!'

As a final humiliation the naked bodies were taken out into the street and displayed to the public; it was rumoured that Donna's body was taken down and further desecrated by a depraved Dominican monk. It was also said that Donna may have been pregnant at the time of an attack, or that she left behind her an infant boy, whom Gesualdo then also slaughtered, believing the child was not his.

After the double murder, Gesualdo spiralled down into a period of guilt-induced depression. In February 1594, however, he married again. His second wife was Eleanora d'Este, niece of Alfonso II d'Este. The d'Este family seat was in Ferrara, where Gesualdo moved for two years, enjoying the lively musical scene in the city. Although this was a period in which Gesualdo produced some of his best music, the marriage was a deeply unhappy one, for both parties. The compositions he produced during this time were indicative of his state of mind, characterized as they were by sudden changes in tempo, dramatic exclamations and an emotionalism that oscillated between anger, eroticism and doom-laden introspection.

Gesualdo manipulated and bullied Eleanora, both physically and mentally, periodically beating her, then demanding that she return to his side, despite the fact that he openly maintained a mistress. Eleanora complained of the abuse to her brother, and the d'Este family attempted to instigate divorce proceedings. Meanwhile, Gesualdo – who had returned to the family seat at Gesualdo in 1596 – became increasingly reclusive and manic, rarely leaving the castle and engaging in bizarre masochistic ceremonies, such as ordering his servants to flog him, sometimes while they held him down, sometimes while he was defecating.

Gesualdo died in Naples on 8 September 1613. He was clearly a mentally disturbed man, prone to rage and melancholy, and with strong sadomasochistic tendencies. It was these passionate excesses that gave his music its enduring quality, but, at the same time, he was living proof that great art can be created by the vilest, most despicable and inadequate of men.

Carlo Gesualdo, composer, lutenist and murderer of his first wife and her lover. He is depicted in this painting with his uncle Carlo Borromeo, the celebrated Counter-Reformation cardinal (right).

Perhaps the most mysterious death of a musician was that of Jean-Marie Leclair (1697–1764), a French baroque composer. In 1764 he was found dead in his house in Paris, having been stabbed to death by an unknown assailant. The killer was never found, though suspicion pointed at Leclair's nephew.

Another French baroque composer, Jean-Baptiste Lully, was killed by his own vocation, so to speak. In 1687, while conducting a *Te Deum* by beating the time on the floor with a staff, he inadvertently pierced his toe. The wound became infected, and in a matter of weeks he was dead.

During the Second World War, the Nazis murdered a trio of brilliant Czech composers of Jewish background. Viktor Ullmann (1898–1944) was a Christian convert who was confined in the Bohemian concentration camp of Theresienstadt before being moved on to Auschwitz and murdered in 1944. Pavel Haas (1899–1944) was a Bohemian-born composer who had moved to Prague to seek his fame, only for the Nazis to arrest him and send him to Auschwitz, via Theresienstadt. The third and youngest of the three, Gideon Klein (1919–45), was a prodigious talent who performed in clandestine concerts in Nazi-occupied Prague, until he was identified, interned at Theresienstadt and died doing hard labour in a coalmine called Fürstengrube, three days before it was liberated.

The Austrian composer Anton Webern (1883–1945) managed to escape persecution by the Nazis, despite the fact that his music was denounced by them as pro-Bolshevist. Shortly after the end of the war he was shot by an American soldier, having stepped outside during a curfew to smoke a cigar.

Jean-Baptiste Lully, depicted in a contemporary portrait by Pierre Mignard. His career as court composer to Louis XIV was ended by a self-inflicted blow from the baton with which he was conducting a Te Deum in honour of the Sun King's recent recovery from illness.

Wallenstein was a blood-spattered if charming warlord, a politically brilliant and brutally ambitious mercenary captain who became so meteorically powerful and rich that he held emperors to ransom, mastered colossal estates, was raised to his own dukedom and principality, and almost joined the ranks of kings himself. But he overreached himself – his rise and fall was a tragedy of greed and megalomania.

Albrecht von Wallenstein

1583–1634

> 'The Duke of Friedland [Wallenstein] has up to now disgusted and offended to the utmost nearly every territorial ruler in the empire ...'
>
> ANSELM CASIMIR VON WAMBOLD, ELECTOR OF MAINZ, IN 1629

Wallenstein was born in Hefimanice, Bohemia, into a family of minor Protestant aristocrats. His military career began in 1604 when he joined the forces of the Habsburg Holy Roman Emperor, Rudolph II. Two years later he converted to Catholicism – the religion of his new master – and this paved the way for his marriage in 1609 to an extremely wealthy widow from Moravia.

Wallenstein put the riches and estates he had gained by his marriage towards the furtherance of his own career in the service of the Habsburgs. In 1617 he came to the aid of the future emperor Ferdinand II by raising a force for the latter's war against Venice. When the Protestant nobles of Bohemia came out in revolt in 1618 at the start of the Thirty Years' War, and proceeded to confiscate Wallenstein's estates, the warlord raised a force to fight under the imperial standard. He went on to earn distinction on the

Albrecht Wenzel Eusebius von Wallenstein, supreme commander of the armies of the Habsburg emperor Ferdinand II, as portrayed by Julius Schnorr von Carolsfeld, after an original by Sir Anthony van Dyck.

battlefield, and not only reclaimed his estates but also took over the lands of the Protestant nobles he defeated. He went on to incorporate these into a new entity called 'Friedland', over which he was made count palatine and in 1625 a duke.

With the onset of the Danish War in 1625, Wallenstein raised an army of over 30,000 men to fight for the imperial Catholic League against the Protestant Northern League. A grateful Ferdinand – now emperor – immediately appointed him commander-in-chief. Wallenstein went on to achieve a series of brilliant victories, and Ferdinand rewarded him with the principality of Sagan and the duchy of Mecklenburg.

Power and success now seem to have gone to Wallenstein's head. He was no longer satisfied to remain the emperor's most dependable lieutenant; he wanted to be master of his own destiny. And to this end he opened negotiations with his erstwhile enemies – the Protestant Hanseatic ports of northern Germany. The growing cleavage between Wallenstein – who now styled himself 'Admiral of the North and the Baltic Seas' – and the emperor was confirmed by the latter's Edict of Restitution in 1629. This declared that all Catholic lands that had, since 1552, fallen under Protestant control were to be restored to their former owners. For a man keen to build his own personal empire by means of deals with the Protestant nobles of northern Germany, the edict was anathema, and Wallenstein opted to disregard Ferdinand's orders. He had already aroused the jealousy of much of the imperial aristocracy, and they now took the opportunity to press for his dismissal – which came about in 1630. Wallenstein retired to Friedland and plotted his revenge.

With King Gustavus Adolphus of Sweden, a leading enemy of the emperor, Wallenstein hatched a plot that would have given him control of all Habsburg dominions. Ferdinand discovered Wallenstein's treachery, but his military reversals made him so desperate that he asked Wallenstein to return to his service – for a suitably high price – to help him fight the Swedes and their Saxon allies. Wallenstein agreed, and in 1632 gave battle to the Swedes at Lützen. Although Gustavus Adolphus was killed, the Swedes won the day.

Having revealed his military fallibility, Wallenstein was aware that his position was vulnerable. Determined to avoid a second dismissal, he refused to disband his army, and, worse, he did nothing to stop the Swedes securing further victories in Germany. At the same time, he attempted to negotiate with the emperor's enemies – Saxony, Sweden and France. Such double-dealing proved inconclusive, however, and Wallenstein resumed the offensive against these powers in late 1633.

But word of Wallenstein's latest treachery had reached the imperial court at Vienna. At this point Wallenstein resolved on one last throw of the dice, and in January 1634 prepared to come out in open revolt against the emperor. However, as he found the support of his subordinates ebbing away, he tried to cut one final deal: he would resign in return for a substantial pay-off. This offer was rejected, and Wallenstein fled to the Saxons and Swedes in a fresh effort to link up with them against the Habsburgs. That enterprise was doomed to failure, however, and in February 1634 Wallenstein was assassinated by troops from within his own army.

MERCENARIES

In the ancient world, most leaders – including the biblical kings David and Solomon and the Egyptian pharaoh Rameses the Great – used mercenaries (those who fight solely for money rather than for their country). The Persians employed numerous Greek mercenaries, Darius the Great and his son Xerxes relying on them heavily in the Greco-Persian wars. In 401 BC, 10,000 Greek mercenaries fought their way from Mesopotamia to safety in the epic March of Xenophon. Ten thousand Greeks fought for King Darius III in the battles of Granicus River (334 BC) and Issus (333 BC) against Alexander the Great. Alexander used Greek mercenaries in turn, as did the Carthaginians – notably Hannibal – during the Punic Wars, while the Romans regularly used Numidians, Balearics, Gauls, Iberians, Cretans and, later, Germans.

Flemish mercenaries fought for William the Conqueror against the English in 1066, while in 1346 Genoese mercenary crossbowmen fought for Philip VI of France at the Battle of Crécy. Byzantine emperors regularly hired barbarian mercenaries, sometimes with disastrous results, as in 1071 when the Varangian Guard helped to oust Emperor Romanus Diogenes and install his brother, Michael VII, on the throne. During the 14th and 15th centuries, Italy – racked by city-state feuding – was dominated by mercenary bands whose condottiere (leaders) hired out their services to the highest bidder. When one such group – Roger de Flor's 2500-strong Catalan Company, employed by the Byzantine emperor Michael IX Palaeologus – were decimated by another group – the Alans – it laid waste to Thrace and Macedonia in what became known as the Catalan Revenge. Another condottiere – the English-born Sir John Hawkwood (1320–94) – commanded the White Company (one of numerous contemporary 'Free Lance' bands) in France and Italy, having previously served in the Hundred Years' War.

Between 1618 and 1626, one of Wallenstein's chief opponents was the German mercenary Ernst von Mansfeld. Despite being a Catholic, he defected to the Protestant side after a perceived snub from Archduke Leopold.

Irish soldiers, as part of the Treaty of Limerick in 1691, left en masse (14,000 soldiers and 10,000 women and children) to serve as mercenaries in France in the so-called 'Flight of the Wild Geese'. The term 'Wild Geese' – the title of a 1978 film about mercenaries in Africa – was subsequently used of Irish mercenaries who served in continental European armies in the 17th and 18th centuries.

Famous mercenaries of the 20th century include the psychopathic former British soldier 'Colonel' Callan (real name Costas Georgiou), who fought in the Angolan civil war (executed 1976), and Morris 'Two-Gun' Cohen (1887–1970), a one-time Jewish soldier who became bodyguard to the Chinese leader Sun Yat-sen and later his head of intelligence. Today, mercenaries market themselves as private military companies, most notably Blackwater Worldwide, founded in 1997 as Blackwater USA in North Carolina and now contracted by the US government to provide security services in Iraq.

Sir John Hawkwood, England´s most notorious mercenary, in an equestrian fresco by Paolo Uccello (1397–1475) housed in Florence Cathedral.

Aurangzeb, known as *Alamgir* ('world-seizer'), was the last of the great Mughal emperors of India, expanding his empire and ruling for almost half a century, but his cruelty to his father was shameful even by the standards of dynastic rivalries and his intolerant repression and imposition of Muslim orthodoxy undermined the admirably tolerant tradition of his great predecessors, the emperors Babur and Akbar the Great. He thus alienated his millions of Hindu subjects, weakened his empire and started the rot that led to the British conquest.

Aurangzeb 1618–1707

> '*I have sinned terribly, and I do not know what punishment awaits me.*'
>
> Aurangzeb's alleged death-bed confession

The third son of Shah Jahan and Mumtaz Mahal, in the dynasty descended from Tamerlane, the Mongol conqueror, Aurangzeb was a pious Muslim from an early age. As a young man he proved himself a capable administrator and proficient soldier in his father's service, but resented the fact that Shah Jahan nominated his eldest and favourite son, Dara Shikoh, his heir, leaving Aurangzeb out of the line of succession. This led to a rift between father and son, and a growing rivalry between Aurangzeb and Dara Shikoh.

The rivalry between the two brothers became increasingly bitter after their father fell ill in 1657. Shah Jahan's second son, Shah Shuja, also claimed the imperial throne, as did a fourth brother, Murad Baksh. Yet the real struggle remained that between Aurangzeb and the original heir apparent. To this end, Aurangzeb allied himself with Murad against Dara Shikoh, whom he defeated in 1658. As Dara Shikoh fled, Aurangzeb had their father placed under house arrest. In a stunning act of betrayal, he then attacked and defeated Murad, and had him executed. Even as he did so, he attempted to buy off Shah Shuja by offering him a governorship. But it was not long before Aurangzeb made a move against the ill-prepared Shah Shuja, who was defeated, forced into exile and later disappeared – presumed murdered at the hands of Aurangzeb's agents. After once more defeating Dara Shikoh, Aurangzeb had his last surviving brother brought back to Delhi in chains. In 1659, against the backdrop of Aurangzeb's own coronation, Dara Shikoh was publicly executed and the head delivered to his grieving and shocked father in an act of grievous filial cruelty rarely matched in history.

With his brothers mercilessly disposed of, Aurangzeb set about expanding his dominions by means of military might, culminating three decades later with victories over the rulers of Bijapur and Golconda, which brought the Mughal empire to its greatest extent. But the problems that would in the end fatally weaken this great empire began to emerge as soon as Aurangzeb assumed the throne. Immediately life at court became markedly more austere, in line with the more rigid and puritanical interpretation of Islam followed by the new emperor. Music was banned, while works of art – such as portraits and statues – that could be considered idolatrous were proscribed. Of greater consequence, the *jizya* tax on non-Muslims, which had been allowed to lapse under his predecessors, was now reinstituted, while non-Muslim worship was actively discouraged, and a large number of Hindu temples were destroyed.

Unsurprisingly, such measures provoked violent resistance. A Pashtun revolt erupted in 1672 and was only suppressed with difficulty. In 1675 Aurangzeb provoked a major Sikh rebellion after having

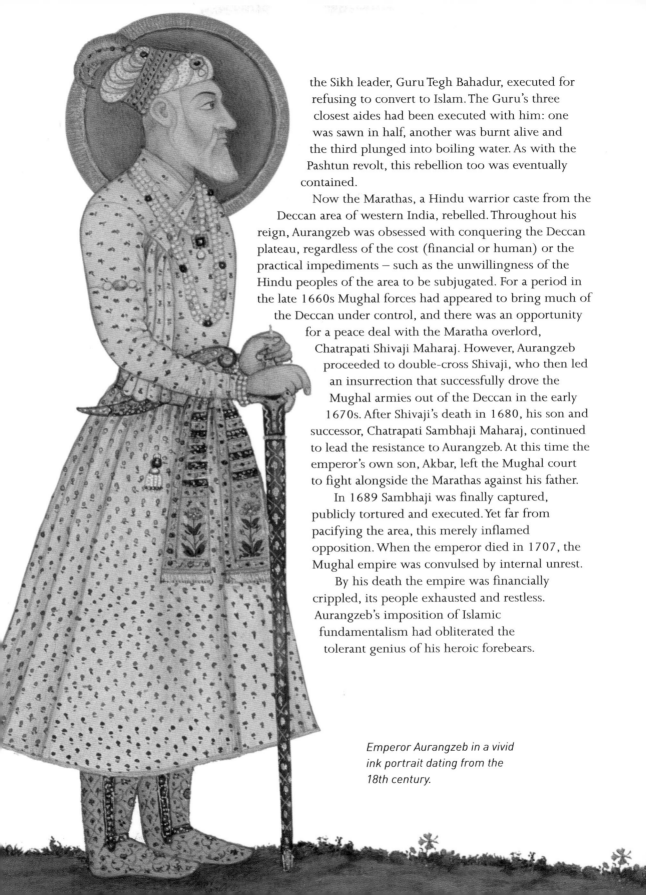

the Sikh leader, Guru Tegh Bahadur, executed for refusing to convert to Islam. The Guru's three closest aides had been executed with him: one was sawn in half, another was burnt alive and the third plunged into boiling water. As with the Pashtun revolt, this rebellion too was eventually contained.

Now the Marathas, a Hindu warrior caste from the Deccan area of western India, rebelled. Throughout his reign, Aurangzeb was obsessed with conquering the Deccan plateau, regardless of the cost (financial or human) or the practical impediments – such as the unwillingness of the Hindu peoples of the area to be subjugated. For a period in the late 1660s Mughal forces had appeared to bring much of the Deccan under control, and there was an opportunity for a peace deal with the Maratha overlord, Chatrapati Shivaji Maharaj. However, Aurangzeb proceeded to double-cross Shivaji, who then led an insurrection that successfully drove the Mughal armies out of the Deccan in the early 1670s. After Shivaji's death in 1680, his son and successor, Chatrapati Sambhaji Maharaj, continued to lead the resistance to Aurangzeb. At this time the emperor's own son, Akbar, left the Mughal court to fight alongside the Marathas against his father.

In 1689 Sambhaji was finally captured, publicly tortured and executed. Yet far from pacifying the area, this merely inflamed opposition. When the emperor died in 1707, the Mughal empire was convulsed by internal unrest.

By his death the empire was financially crippled, its people exhausted and restless. Aurangzeb's imposition of Islamic fundamentalism had obliterated the tolerant genius of his heroic forebears.

Emperor Aurangzeb in a vivid ink portrait dating from the 18th century.

THE BLACK HOLE OF CALCUTTA

Fifty years after the emperor Aurangzeb, British influence in India was such that the last independent Nawab of Bengal, Siraj-ud-Dawlah, believed they were conspiring to oust him – a fear compounded by the governor of Calcutta's repeated refusal to stop extending fortifications to Fort William in the heart of the city. Legend has it that, in June 1756, Dawlah's men attacked Calcutta and, after taking the local garrison of the British East India Company, swiftly forced its surrender, locking the defeated troops into a tiny, windowless room reserved for petty criminals, 18 feet (5.5m) long and 14 feet (4.3m) wide. According to the subsequent testimony of the commander of the garrison, a man named John Holwell, in his book *A Genuine Narrative of the Deplorable Deaths of the English Gentlemen and others who were suffocated in the Black Hole*, 146 people were imprisoned within this tiny and almost airless space, 123 of whom died from the ordeal. The fable of the 'black hole of Calcutta' was born.

In 1915, however, in an article by J. H. Little entitled 'The Black Hole – The Question of Holwell's Veracity', serious question marks were raised over Holwell's reliability as a witness, not least because it was shown that 146 people could not possibly have been confined within a room of the stated dimensions. Survivors also disagreed over whether or not the room had a window. Later in the 20th century, a revised account was produced, which stated that 64 prisoners were interred in the room (of whom 21 survived) – still making for a horrific experience, but one considerably less shocking than the original tale. Later analysis, such as the 1959 study by Indian scholar Brijen Gupta, has questioned whether the incident happened at all, suggesting rather that it was invented as part of a propaganda drive by the East India Company to de-legitimize the Bengali ruler, deliberately making him out as a savage barbarian. The most recent research has concluded that the Black Hole did indeed happen – albeit on a scale smaller than that claimed by Holwell – but it was probably the result of administrative ineptitude rather than deliberate brutality.

The Black Hole of Calcutta, where the Nawab of Bengal is said to have held British troops after the fall of Fort William in 1756. A legend quickly grew up that only 23 of the 146 British prisoners survived, but this story has now been shown to be a myth.

Conspirator, perjurer, thief, fantasist and the most notorious liar in English history, Titus Oates was directly responsible for the execution of over thirty men and the torture and ruin of many others. Oates's invention of the 'Popish Plot' in 1678 plunged England into a frenzy of anti-Catholic hysteria, and for a time he was hailed as a national hero. As Oates manipulated the fears of the country for his own aggrandizement, one contemporary observed that 'his greatest pleasure was to be feared by everyone and to harm as many as possible'.

Titus Oates 1649–1705

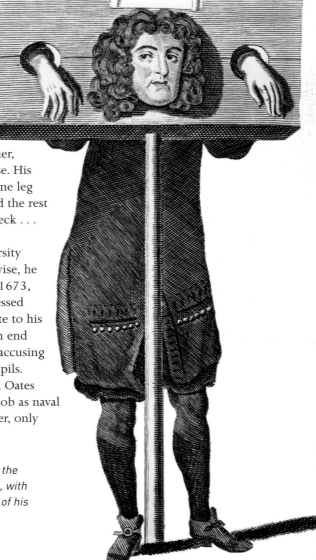

'If he be a liar, he is the greatest and adroitest I ever saw, and yet it is a stupendous thing to think what vast concerns are like to depend upon the evidence of one young man who hath twice changed his religion.'

SIR HENRY COVENTRY, 1678, AS TITUS OATES GAVE EVIDENCE BEFORE THE PRIVY COUNCIL

Oates, who was raised by a violent and unloving father, was prone to convulsions, dribbling and a runny nose. His personal appearance was equally unfortunate, with one leg shorter than the other, 'his face a rainbow colour, and the rest of his body black', with 'slouching ears . . . a short neck . . . a thin chin, and somewhat sharp'.

In 1667 Oates matriculated at Cambridge University but left without achieving a degree. Claiming otherwise, he briefly worked as a preacher at a vicarage in Kent in 1673, but was forced to resign after his congregation expressed alarm at his violent temper. His second job, as a curate to his father in Hastings, was also short-lived, coming to an end when he received a summons for perjury for falsely accusing the local schoolmaster of sodomy with one of his pupils. Thoroughly discredited and on the run from the law, Oates fled to London and managed to bluff his way into a job as naval chaplain on board the ship *Adventure*, bound for Tangier, only to be sacked in 1676 for homosexual activities.

Convicted of perjury for his role in fabricating evidence of the Popish Plot of 1678, Titus Oates stands in a wooden stock, with the words Testis ovat *('the witness rejoices', an anagram of his name) above his head.*

In March 1677, having thoroughly exhausted the patience of all the Protestants with whom he had come into contact, and without the slightest hint of sincerity, Oates decided to change his religion. He sought out Father Berry, a mentally unstable priest, and was accepted into the Roman Catholic Church. After a brief period spent begging and stealing from his new Catholic colleagues, he was granted a place at the English Jesuit College at Valladolid in Spain. It was here that he assumed a new identity, the pious convert 'Titus Ambrose of Ambrosius', and began to collect some of the information that he would later use to concoct his stories of papist treachery. Within months, Oates had reinvented himself again as 'Samson Lucy', speciously claiming to have attained a degree from the University of Salamanca, and moved to another Catholic seminary, at Saint-Omer, in northern France.

At Saint-Omer, Oates's fellow students quickly lost patience with his foul temper, one of them even breaking a pan over his head. Expelled in 1678, Oates sought out an old acquaintance, Dr Israel Tonge, a fire-and-brimstone Protestant preacher who was obsessed with the belief that the Jesuits were plotting against England. Having run out of favour with the Catholic establishment, Oates now claimed to have first hand evidence of a 'Popish Plot' to murder King Charles II and to replace him on the throne with his Catholic brother, James, duke of York.

Tonge, having engineered a brief meeting with the king, passed on Oates's allegations to the authorities in 1678. In the ensuing atmosphere of panic, despite the fantastical nature of his claims, Oates was summoned to appear before the House of Commons. Under cross-examination, his story became more confused and contradictory, but he was adept at lying, playing to the anti-Catholic prejudices of his audience. His 'evidence' prompted a wave of arrests, mainly of innocent Jesuit priests but also of a number of prominent Catholic lords. Many suspects were horribly tortured. In all, over thirty men were found guilty of treason and executed. As a reward for his endeavours, Oates was given a pension and a room in Whitehall. With no sign of humility, he gloried in the thanks of Parliament, wearing ecclesiastical dress and presenting himself as the saviour of the nation.

In the end, Oates overplayed his hand, even implicating the queen in the plot. Flailing in the face of legal scrutiny and with his privileged position unravelling before his eyes, he began to feign illness and faint during cross-examination. By 1684 the groundless allegations had completely collapsed and the duke of York sued for libel, winning £100,000 damages from Oates. The following year, after the duke of York came to the throne as James II, Oates was arrested, tried, imprisoned for life and forced to wear an inscription on his head, referring to his 'horrid perjuries'. As part of his punishment he received five lashings a year and was placed in the pillory, where he was pelted with eggs and rotten fruit.

Oates never showed any remorse for the victims of his web of lies. After the flight of James II in 1688 and the restoration of a Protestant monarchy, Oates was released from prison, but soon squandered the pension he was awarded by William III. He died in 1705, a bankrupt. Oates's story reveals as much about the sectarian prejudices of late 17th-century England — to which he so effectively pandered — as it does about his own cold-hearted mendacity.

THREE NOTORIOUS CONSPIRACY THEORIES

Even in our rational modern age of the internet and 24-hour news, irrational myths can be more influential than scientific facts. Like many other conspiracy theories in history, Oates's alleged Popish Plot gained so much traction because it played upon people's existing fears and hopes.

The most famous conspiracy theory in history was the document known as the *Protocols of the Elders of Zion*, purportedly the minutes of a meeting of Jewish leaders at the first Zionist Congress in Basel in 1897, revealing their plans for world domination.

In reality it was forged in Paris sometime between 1895 and 1899 by Pytor Ivanovich Rachovsky, an agent of the Okhrana (Russian secret police), who stole the idea from a far-fetched 1868 novel called *Biarritz* by Hermann Goedsche, a German civil servant and rampant anti-Semite. The Russian forgery was intended to boost support for Tsar Nicholas II by presenting his critics as Jewish conspirators.

Apart from causing an upsurge in anti-Semitism in Russia, which lasted for many years, the forgery had an even more poisonous legacy. In *Mein Kampf* Adolf Hitler cited the *Protocols* to support his diatribe against the Jews, despite the fact that an English journalist had already exposed it as a forgery. To this day, it is taken to be authentic by anti-Semitic groups such as the Ku Klux Klan and extreme Islamists such as President

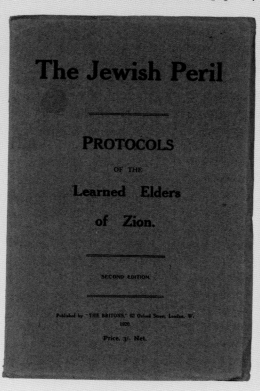

The first British edition, published in 1920, of The Protocols of the Elders of Zion, *a 19th-century Russian forgery purporting to show that Jews were planning to take over the world. Translations of* The Protocols *are still in print in many Middle Eastern countries, where the book is regarded as genuine.*

Ahmadinejad of Iran, who has even questioned the reality of the Holocaust.

Another conspiracy theory with anti-Semitic overtones was the Dreyfus Affair in France. In 1894 Captain Alfred Dreyfus, a Jewish army officer working at the war ministry, was arrested on suspicion of providing military information to the Germans. Dreyfus was made a scapegoat by French right-wingers, who saw him as the tool of those they regarded as France's deadly enemies – the Germans, the socialists and the Jews. Dreyfus was found guilty and sent to Devil's Island, a French penal colony in South America – despite a campaign for his release led by the novelist Emile Zola, who was forced to flee France and seek political exile in England. It was not until 1906 that Dreyfus was finally pardoned, long after incontrovertible evidence of his innocence had emerged.

In our own times, many deluded conspiracy theorists, mainly in the Arab world but also in the West, choose to believe that the 9/11 mass-murderous terrorist attacks by al-Qaeda against America were either the work of the US government (to justify wars against Muslim Afghanistan and Iraq), or of the mysterious powers of international Jewry, which brings us back full circle to the insane anti-Semitism of the *Protocols of the Elders of Zion*.

Nader Shah of Iran was the self-made military and political genius and empire-builder who dominated his native country, defeated the Mughal emperors and Ottoman sultans, conquered vast new territories, stole the Peacock Throne for himself, overthrew the Safavid dynasty to raise himself from enslaved orphan and freebooting bandit to the throne of King of Kings. But he sank into paranoid brutality, frenzied killing and finally the insanity that led to his murder. Known as 'the Second Alexander', he was the tragic and murderous 'Napoleon of Iran'.

Nader Shah 1688–1747

'Nader of Isfahan invaded [the Mughal Empire] with his troops resembling the waves of the sea, and put all the natives of the provinces of Kabul, the Punjab and Delhi at once to the sword.'

MUHAMMAD MUHSIN SADIKI, JEWEL OF SAMSAM (C. 1739)

Nader was a member of a Turkmen tribe that inhabited a northern area of Iran. He began life in obscurity. His father died when he was young, and Nader and his mother were subsequently abducted and pressed into slavery by a band of raiding tribesmen. Nader, though, soon escaped and entered the military service of a local chieftain, a position in which he distinguished himself and rose rapidly through the ranks. But in due course the headstrong Nader abandoned the chieftain and embarked on a life of banditry. By the mid-1720s he could count on some 5000 followers.

This flouting of central authority was scarcely surprising; this was, after all, a time of deep unrest within Persia. Nader's home tribe had always given fealty to the Safavid shahs who had ruled the country for the previous two hundred years. Yet, by the early 18th century, the Safavid empire was in terminal decline. In 1719 it had been challenged by its former Afghan subjects who had invaded Persia proper, and within three years the shah, Soltan Hossein, had been deposed. In response, Nader had initially yielded to the Afghan conquerors, but he later opted for rebellion. He now allied himself with Tahmasp, the son of Soltan Hossein, who was attempting to regain his father's throne. Nader's military capabilities were soon recognized, and in 1726 he was appointed supreme commander of Tahmasp's forces.

By 1729 Nader had decisively defeated the Afghans and restored Tahmasp to the throne. He proceeded to attack the Ottoman Turks and reconquer the territory they had seized from Persia in Azerbaijan and Mesopotamia. But he was diverted by a domestic rebellion, and while he dealt with this, Shah Tahmasp attempted to bolster his own military credentials by launching a new assault on the Ottoman empire. It proved to be a disastrous move, and most of Nader's work was now undone. Incandescent with rage at Tahmasp's incompetence, in 1732 Nader deposed him and replaced him with his infant son, Abbas III – although Nader, as regent, wielded the real power.

By 1735 Nader had once more regained the territory lost to the Ottomans. But such battlefield accomplishments were no longer enough for Nader. In January 1736 he convened an assembly of Persia's most prominent political and religious figures and 'suggested' that the youthful shah be deposed and he, Nader, be appointed in his place. Unsurprisingly, the assembled notables gave their consent.

Nader now embarked on a spree of conquest that would earn him the epithet 'the Second Alexander'. In 1738 he attacked Kandahar, the last redoubt of the Afghans. The city was levelled and a new town, Naderabad, named after the new shah, was built in its place. Nader also sent his navy across the Persian Gulf, where he subjugated Bahrain and Oman. Then in 1739 he launched the campaign for which he would become most infamous: his assault on the Mughal empire in India.

The main Mughal armies were obliterated at the Battle of Karnal in February 1739, leaving the way open to Delhi, the Mughal capital. On arriving at the city, Nader ordered a massacre of its inhabitants, resulting in the deaths in a single day of between 20,000 and 30,000 people. The city was then ransacked and all manner of treasures carried back to Persia – including the Peacock Throne, which would thereafter symbolize the shah's authority. But Nader's appetite for conquest was not yet satiated, and, as he pushed into Central Asia, he took on Ottomans, Russians and Uzbeks.

In 1741 Nader was the subject of an assassination attempt, after which he became ever more paranoid. Convinced that his eldest son, Reza Qoli Mirza, had been involved in the attempt on his life, he had him blinded, while the alleged fellow-conspirators were put to death. The growing severity of Nader's rule, far from crushing dissent, served only to provoke fresh bouts of unrest. These uprisings were met with ever more ferocious reprisals, and Nader was reputed to have had towers of skulls constructed as a demonstration of the price of disloyalty. At the same time, the ruthless discipline he imposed on his own soldiers grew increasingly harsh. This inclination towards cruelty was ultimately to prove fatal, for in 1747, whilst on his way to confront yet another rebellion, Nader was murdered by disgruntled troops.

Thousands died at his hands; his taxes and wars had ruined his own people and at his death, his empire fell to pieces. And his savage cruelty spawned a dark legend. Yet his was an astonishing achievement. He was as brilliant as he was brutal: centuries later, Stalin studied Nader Shah as a man to admire for his flawed but pitiless grandeur.

Nader Shah (1688–1747), shah of Persia (1736–47) and founder of the Afsharid dynasty (1736–96), as portrayed by an anonymous 18th-century Persian artist. He created the largest and most powerful Iranian empire since the Sassanids, encompassing Iran, northern India and parts of Central Asia.

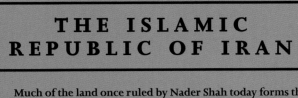

THE ISLAMIC REPUBLIC OF IRAN

Much of the land once ruled by Nader Shah today forms the Islamic Republic of Iran, established in 1979 following the popular revolution that forced the abdication of the shah, Reza Pahlavi. His fall and exile saw the return of Ayatollah Ruhollah Khomeini, who oversaw the creation of a Shi'a-dominated theocracy that fused a populist socio-economic programme with fundamentalist Islamism. Virulent hatred of 'The Great Satan' America and the West (as demonstrated by the 1979–81 US embassy hostage crisis in Tehran and the death-penalty *fatwa* issued in 1989 against British author Salman Rushdie for his supposedly blasphemous work, *The Satanic Verses*), and anti-Zionism, provided the glue that held together the Republic. Whilst adhering to some democratic forms, Khomeini established a rigid theocratic leadership which ruthlessly stamped out opposition, establishing a vice-like grip over political activity that has never been relinquished. The Supreme Leader, an ayatollah, backed by the elite Revolutionary Guard and a vicious secret police, controls all policy and outranks the elected president and assembly.

Shortly after the Islamic revolution, Iran was plunged into crisis by Saddam Hussein's invasion of its oil-rich province of Khuzestan (see page 302), the repelling of which proved hugely costly in terms both of human lives and resources. The Republic has since become a bastion of anti-Western militancy in the Middle East, sponsoring terrorist groups – notably Hezbollah in Lebanon and Hamas in Gaza – from the early 1980s onwards and funding suicide attacks on Israeli and American targets. It has also attempted to establish itself as the leading Islamic power – its allegiance to the Shi'a brand of Islam constituting a major challenge to the more numerous Sunni countries in the region, and Saudi Arabia in particular. Since 2003 Iran has flourished as a regional superpower in the vacuum caused by America's bloody war in Iraq.

Khomeini was succeeded as Supreme Leader by Ayatollah Ali Khamenei who stymied a weak 1990s 'reform' movement and backed the 2005 election of Iran's current president, Mahmoud Ahmadinejad, a radical demagogue and rabid anti-Semite who has denied the Holocaust, declared he wishes to exterminate Israel, and whose pursuit of an Iranian nuclear arsenal, in defiance of the West, may yet bring the world to nuclear catastrophe.

Mahmoud Ahmadinejad was elected president of Iran in 2005 on a populist Islamist platform. He gained notoriety in April 2006 when he called for Israel to be 'wiped off the map'.

Robespierre was the first prototype for the modern European dictator: his sanctimonious vision of republican virtue and terror, and the brutal slaughter he unleashed in its name, were studied reverently by the Russian Bolsheviks and helped inspire the totalitarian mass-killings of the 20th century. Known as 'the Sea-green Incorruptible', his name has become a byword for the fatal purity and degenerate corruption of the 'Reign of Terror' which followed the French Revolution of 1789 and climaxed with the execution of King Louis XVI on 21 January 1793. The Terror illustrated not only the corrupt dangers of utopian monopolies of 'virtue', but how ultimately such witch hunts consume their own children.

Maximilien Robespierre 1758–94

'That man will go far, he believes everything he says.'
COMTE DE MIRABEAU ON ROBESPIERRE AT THE OUTSET OF THE REVOLUTION

Born in the Artois region of northern France, Robespierre's family was financially secure, but his childhood was not a happy one. His father was a drunk and his mother died when he was just six. Nonetheless, the young Maximilien won a place to study law at the prestigious Lycée Louis-le-Grand in Paris and soon made his name as a populist, defending the poor against the rich.

Like many of the other young professionals who were to drive the French Revolution – such as the fanatical lawyer Louis de Saint-Just (later nicknamed the 'angel of death') or the radical journalist Jean-Paul Marat – Robespierre eagerly absorbed the theories of the Swiss philosopher Jean-Jacques Rousseau, whose notion of a 'social contract' held that a government had to be based on the will of the people to be truly legitimate.

Although fussy about his appearance, often wearing the powdered wigs associated with the profligate aristocrats of ancien régime France,

An unattributed 18th-century caricature of Maximilien Robespierre straining money from the French people.

165

Robespierre – with his weak voice, small stature and pallid complexion – did not cut an imposing figure. But as the comte de Mirabeau said of him at the outset of the Revolution: 'That man will go far; he believes everything he says.'

In the wake of the storming of the Bastille in July 1789, the event that triggered the Revolution, Robespierre aligned himself politically with the far left. As the representative for Artois in the Constituent Assembly, set up in July 1789 to decide on a new constitution, he became closely involved with the radical faction called the Jacobins, rivals of the more moderate Girondins. His ideas gained a sympathetic hearing among the Parisian bourgeoisie, and he rose swiftly, in 1791 becoming Public Accuser (giving him the power of life and death over all citizens, without recourse to trial or appeal) and then first deputy for Paris a year later.

An implacable paranoia about potential enemies of the Revolution haunted him and in December 1792, when Louis XVI was brought to trial, Robespierre – a fierce critic of the king – insisted that 'Louis must die, so that the country may live'.

Above all, it was as a leading member of the 'Committee of Public Safety' that Robespierre forged his reputation in blood. Set up by the National Convention in April 1973, this was a revolutionary tribunal invested with unlimited dictatorial powers. Robespierre was elected a member in July 1793 and swiftly instigated the so-called 'Terror'. Tens of thousands of 'traitors' – ostensibly those who had expressed sympathy with the monarchy or who thought the Jacobins had gone too far in their relentless pursuit of 'enemies of the people' – were rounded up without trial and lost their heads on the guillotine. In reality, anyone Robespierre counted an enemy was liquidated, the apparatus of the state ruthlessly employed to silence them. Robespierre himself personally ensured that his rivals Georges Danton and Camille Desmoulins were executed in April 1794.

Robespierre and his allies turned their attention to growing opposition to the Revolution in Lyon, Marseilles and the rural Vendée in western France. After more than 100,000 men, women and children had been systematically murdered on Robespierre's orders the revolutionary general François Joseph Westermann wrote in a letter to the Committee: 'There is no more Vendée. I crushed the children under the feet of the horses, massacred the women . . . exterminated. The roads are sown with corpses.' For Robespierre, revolutionary virtue and 'the Terror' went hand in hand. As he put it in February 1794: 'If the spring of popular government in time of peace is virtue, the springs of popular government in revolution are at once virtue and terror: virtue, without which terror is fatal; terror, without which virtue is powerless.'

Increasingly alienated by his tyranny, the National Convention turned decisively against him when he accused them of a conspiracy to oust him. A warrant was issued for his arrest and he retreated to his power base at the Hôtel de Ville in Paris. As troops entered the building to seize him, Robespierre, surrounded by his henchmen Georges Couthon, Louis de Saint-Just, Philippe Le Bas, and François Hanriot, sustained a bullet wound (almost certainly self-inflicted) that ripped apart his jaw. Bleeding heavily, he was quickly taken away and finished off at the guillotine, suffering the fate of so many of his opponents before him.

Some see Robespierre as one of the founding fathers of social democracy, his revolutionary excesses occasioned by his championing the cause of the people. Many more though view him as a brutal dictator who manipulated the Parisian mob for his own ends – a hypocritical despot whose terror was the precursor of the totalitarian butchery of Hitler and Stalin in modern times.

TORTURE AND EXECUTION

During the French Revolution public beheadings became something of a spectator sport. The device used for such industrial-scale executions was the guillotine, a tall wooden frame down which a slanted blade would be dropped onto the neck of the victim. Observers reported that the severed head would sometimes remain alert for a few seconds, displaying an expression of either bewilderment or indignation.

Ironically, the introduction of the guillotine in late 18th-century France was designed to deliver a painless death. Initially called the *louison*, the Parisian press dubbed it 'Madame Guillotin' after Dr Joseph-Ignace Guillotin, a member of the French National Assembly and a professor of anatomy who, in 1791, had argued that all condemned persons should suffer the same mode of execution, regardless of social class.

The guillotine was kind compared to earlier methods of capital punishment, such as disembowelment, dismember-ment, impalement, crucifixion, burning at the stake, boiling in oil and flaying alive. One tortuous procedure, originating in ancient Greece and commonly practised across medieval Europe, was the Catherine wheel – named after the martyr Saint Catherine of Alexandria. The victim was fastened to a large wooden wheel, which was then rotated as the executioner fractured each of his (or her) limbs with blows from a cudgel. As an act of mercy, the final blows – from which the expression, 'coup de grâce' derives – was delivered to the head and chest. After death the victim's lifeless limbs were woven around the spokes and raised onto a pole for the crows to feed on. A variety of this torture – breaking on the wheel – was practised in France until the Revolution. The word 'roué' (originally meaning 'broken on the wheel', from the

French word *roue*) is derived from it. But the most appalling death of all was the Chinese 'Lingchi', or 'death by a thousand cuts', an execution by minute slicing, last conducted before a crowd in Beijing in 1904 at the execution of multiple killer Wang Weiqin and twice in 1905 before its abolition later that year.

Another slow and gruesome method of execution, favoured by the Spanish Inquisition, involved the victim being stretched, sometimes by as much as 12 inches, on a rack by a system of pulleys. As joints popped and bones cracked, the executioner would tear off the victim's nipples, tongue, ears, nose and genitals with red-hot pincers. Other popular methods included the garrotte, a mechanical device in which a wire or rope or metal band was fastened around the victim's neck and then gradually tightened, causing slow strangulation.

In 1888 Harold Brown – a dentist and an employee of Thomas Edison, the inventor of the light bulb – came up with the electric chair, first used the following year in New York. 'Old Sparky' has now been retired in most US states, as victim's heads had the unfortunate tendency to burst into flames. Nowadays lethal injection is the preferred method – although the fact that several recent executions using lethal injection have been both protracted and painful has led to calls for it to be abandoned. In China, which tops the league in terms of numbers executed each year, the victim is simply shot in the back of the neck – and his family is sent the bill for the bullet.

China executed 470 people in 2007 – but probably many more. China, Iran, Saudi Arabia, Pakistan and the USA perform 88 per cent of known executions annually.

Shaka was the founder-conqueror of the Zulu empire and the creator of the Zulu nation. A military genius of astonishing energy, he was also a vicious, paranoid, vindictive, cruel and self-destructive tyrant.

Shaka 1787–1828

'It became known to us that Shaka had ordered that a man standing near us should be put to death for what crime we could not learn: but we soon found it to be one of the common occurrences in the course of the day.'

RECOLLECTIONS OF A SURGEON VISITING SHAKA IN 1824

Shaka was raised with an absent father and a strong, devoted and wronged mother in an atmosphere of instability, violence and fear. His father, Senzangakona, was chief of the Zulu tribe, but, unusually, opted to marry a lower-class woman from the neighbouring eLangeni clan. The marriage broke up when the young Shaka was six, and his mother took him back to the eLangeni; however, she was ostracized there because of her marriage. Not only did the future leader spend the rest of his youth without a father, he also had to deal with the social stigma that resulted from a marriage that brought 'disgrace' upon his mother. Unable to cope, his mother went into exile, eventually finding a home with the Mtetwa clan in 1802.

Shaka's fortunes began to change when, at 23 – already tall, muscular and striking – he was called up to perform military service by Dingiswayo, a chief of the Mtetwa. As a warrior Shaka soon achieved a reputation for brilliance and bravery, and he helped the Mtetwa establish their dominance over many smaller clans, including the Zulus. He also witnessed, at first hand, Dingiswayo's efforts to reform the organization and attitude of the armed forces – lessons he did not forget.

In 1816 news arrived that Shaka's father had died. Dingiswayo now released him from his service so that he might return and claim his birthright as Zulu chief. Although the Zulu were, at that time, one of the smaller clans on the east coast of southern Africa, Shaka had big plans for the future.

On his return, he immediately crushed internal opposition to his rule. He then set about remodelling the Zulu into a warrior people. The army was re-equipped and re-organized, embracing the horned 'buffalo' battle formation that would become its trademark. When deployed, the objective of this formation was always the same: the annihilation of the enemy's troops.

At a time when most 'battles' were little more than skirmishes, with little sense of strategic direction, Shaka's disciplined and ruthless approach constituted a revolution in clan warfare. His armies quickly established a terrifying reputation, and Shaka began to use them to redraw the map of southern Africa.

The first to feel his wrath were those clans closest to the Zulu along the eastern seaboard, including the eLangeni. Shaka brought down a terrible vengeance on those who had inflicted misery on his mother when he had been a boy, impaling the clan's leaders on wooden stakes cut from their own fences.

Other victories followed, and after each one Shaka incorporated the men of the vanquished clans into his own armies. Within a year he had quadrupled the size of the forces at his command. When in 1817 Dingiswayo – still Shaka's nominal overlord – was murdered by a rival, Chief Zwinde of the Ndwandwe clan, the way was clear for untrammelled Zulu expansion.

Thereafter, one clan after another was conquered and their lands devastated. Those who lay within Shaka's path faced a stark choice: submit, flee or die. The major clans in the area, including the Ndwandwe, were overwhelmed, as were numerous smaller clans to the south of the Zulu. By 1823 Shaka had devastated much of southeastern Africa.

It was not just those who came into immediate contact with Shaka and his forces who were affected. The flight inland of thousands who feared Shaka's marauding armies tore up the established clan structure and social framework of the African interior. In the 'Mfecane' ('crushing') that followed, as many as 2 million people may have died as this internal 'scramble for Africa' spiralled out of control.

The worst was yet to come. In 1827 Shaka's mother died, and the warrior-chief abandoned all sense of restraint. He was no longer concerned with establishing a huge Zulu empire, but instead sought to inflict the pain he himself felt at his mother's death on as many others as possible. In the first phase of this public 'mourning' process, some 7000 Zulus were slaughtered. Pregnant women were killed, along with their husbands, whilst even cattle were butchered by the agents of Shaka's rage.

Death and destruction now became the only phenomena that gave meaning to Shaka's life, and he unleashed his armies to carry fire and slaughter far and wide. The violence only ended when Shaka was assassinated by his half-brothers Dingane and Mhlangana in 1828. A life that had promised so much ended in dishonour: stabbed to death with spears, the once great chief was buried without ceremony in a pit.

At time of his death, Shaka governed over 250,000 people and could raise an army of 50,000. He had built a huge kingdom out of almost nothing, but the price paid by ordinary Africans was vast. Millions had died as a consequence of Shaka's unbridled ambition.

Shaka, the brutal Zulu chief, carries a large shield and a spear, and wears an outfit made from grass or feathers with a tall feather in his headband, in an illustration from Nathaniel Isaacs' Travels and Adventures in Eastern Africa *(1836).*

THE FALL OF THE ZULU EMPIRE

Prior to his death, Shaka had established friendly relations with the British, but not with the Afrikaaners (Boers), and under his half-brother successor, Dingane, the first armed clashes occurred with Boer settlers in Natal. After an initial victory, a Zulu force of several thousand suffered a decisive defeat at the hands of a much smaller contingent of Boers at the Battle of Blood River in December 1838 – an event that triggered a Zulu civil war with Mpande – another of Shaka's half-brothers – who formed an alliance with the Boers and succeeded in overthrowing Dingane. Over the following couple of years, much of the Zulu empire fell under Boer control, but Britain's formal annexation of Natal in 1843 led to the restoration of these lands to the Zulus.

Thereafter, until the second half of the 19th century, the British made no concerted effort to confront the Zulus. Indeed, government policy was to safeguard the integrity of the Zulu empire from Boer expansionism. All this changed, however, in January 1879 when, to placate the Akrikaanèrs after the annexation of the Transvaal two years earlier, the British instigated the Zulu War, aiming to seize Zululand as an area ripe for Afrikaaner settlement. They ordered the Zulu king Cetshwayo – Mpande's son – to disband his army within 30 days; when he failed to comply, hostilities began.

By September 1879, Cetshwayo had been captured and the territory brought under British control (though not before the British had suffered a famous defeat at the Battle of Isandhlwana and been pinned down at the siege of Rorke's Drift – an incident forever commemorated in the 1964 film Zulu). Though unrest continued in the years that followed, prospects for an independent Zulu homeland had suffered fatal damage. In 1887, Zululand was formally annexed to the crown – a move that signalled the permanent dissolution of the Zulu empire.

The legendary defence of Rorke's Drift, 22/23 January 1879, as depicted by Alphonse-Marie-Adolphe de Neuville (1880). Ninety-five members of B Company, 2nd Battalion 24th Warwickshire Regiment, successfully defended their garrison against an intense assault by some 4000 Zulu warriors.

Behram was the leader of India's Thuggee cult, a shadowy network of secret societies who practised multiple killings in which ritual, theft and sadism played equal parts. The Thuggees – who gave the English language the word 'thug' – remain something of a mystery; indeed, some have even questioned their very existence, suggesting that they might have merely been the product of an overactive British colonial imagination. Such doubts aside, however, the Thuggees appear to have endured for centuries, until they were extirpated by the British in the 1830s and 1840s. Behram was a chieftain in the final years of the cult's existence, and it is thought that he and his gang may have been responsible for as many as a thousand murders.

Behram d. 1840
and the Thugs

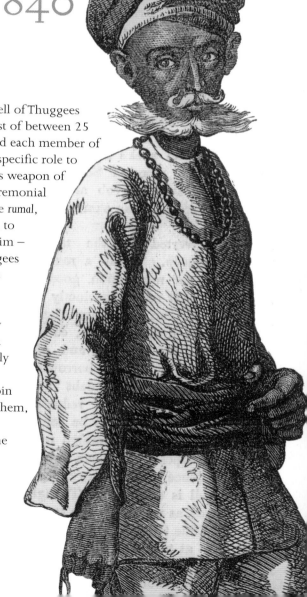

'The one certain thing in the whole process was that those travellers marked for death by Thugs would die. Treasure bearers and merchants, nobles and sepoys all fell to the grim efficiency of the stranglers, befriended and lured to a favoured spot, their suspicions assuaged, then seized and murdered so swiftly that few even had time to cry out.'

MIKE DASH, *THUG: THE TRUE STORY OF INDIA'S MURDEROUS CULT* (2005)

An individual cell of Thuggees tended to consist of between 25 and 50 men, and each member of the gang had a specific role to play. The group's weapon of choice was a ceremonial yellow cloth, the *rumal*, which was used to strangle the victim – hence the Thuggees were sometimes referred to as *phanseegurs*, or 'stranglers'. They usually picked on travellers – preferably wealthy ones – as victims, the reason being that those on the road would be less likely to be missed if they suddenly 'disappeared'.

Having identified their target, the Thuggees would join their quarry on their journey on the pretext of assisting them, so winning their confidence. When they arrived at a pre-selected spot the group would camp for the night, and the

A Thuggee cult member, as depicted in an 1858 issue of the Illustrated London News. *No portrait of Behram himself is known to exist. The Thuggees committed multiple murders in their worship of the goddess of death, Kali.*

intended victims, tired after the day's exertions, would be lulled into a false sense of security – perhaps with some form of music or other distraction. Suddenly, without warning, the designated assassin – the *bhurtote* – would strike. The *rumal* was slipped over the head of the victim and, while a *shumsheera* ('hand-holder') stifled any attempts to struggle, the victim was strangled. It was all over in a matter of seconds. Any travelling companions were dealt with in a similarly ruthless fashion.

Afterwards, the Thuggees ransacked the deceased's possessions and the bodies were then disposed of – often into unmarked graves, which had been prepared in advance by other members of the gang. On occasion, the victims would be hacked up – their bones crushed and their stomachs slit open to ease the burial process and prevent a build up of gas that could give away the grave site. With the clear-up operation complete the band would then melt away, taking their spoils with them and leaving little evidence that anything untoward had occurred.

The motivation for Thuggee killings remains uncertain. Obviously, the prospect of robbing and stealing from wealthy travellers carried a clear financial incentive. Yet it is possible there were also more spiritual inducements. Thuggees were devotees of Kali, the Hindu goddess of death and destruction, and legend has it that they believed every murder they committed delayed the return of the goddess – an event that was thought to carry apocalyptic consequences – by a millennium. The whole process surrounding the killing was attended by elaborate rites and prescribed modes of behaviour. There were thus clear rules about who could and who could not be killed; it was, for instance, only towards the end of the Thuggees' existence that women came to be seen as legitimate targets – and even then this was not universal across the entire network. By the same token, particular importance was attached to the issue of who should be murdered first if a group of several travellers was being attacked. Everything was invested with symbolic significance; this was not mindless banditry and slaughter in the manner of the Dacoits (see page 173).

Such was the organization, then, of which Behram was a *jemadar* or leader. His career as a Thuggee lasted some four decades, until he was betrayed by a British informer (or 'approver' as they were then known) and arrested in 1837. During that time, the cell that he had headed appeared to have been uniquely proficient. In 1838 Behram admitted to 'being present' at some 931 murders, although a year earlier, shortly after his arrest, he had stated: 'I may have strangled with my own hands about 125 men, and I may have seen strangled 150 more.' Perhaps knowing he was doomed to die, he began to exaggerate the extent of his crimes.

Behram was hanged by the British in 1840. The man who had overseen the deaths of so many men and women – most of them with the trademark Thuggee scarf wrung around their necks – found that the noose had finally caught up with him.

THE DACOITS

James Paton – from whom we know much about Behram – worked for the 'Thuggee and Dacoity Office' of British India's colonial administration in the 1830s. The Dacoits comprised a loose network of 'armed robbers' who, like their Thuggee counterparts, specialized in targeting travellers in the vast untamed interior of India. Unlike the Thuggees, however, they were never successfully suppressed by the British (or by later Indian authorities).

Several Dacoits achieved notoriety – none more so than Dau Maan Singh, a bandit responsible for some 1112 robberies and 185 murders between 1939 and 1955 in the Madhya Pradesh region of north-central India. He was hailed by some as a Robin Hood figure who targeted the rich and shared his wealth with the poor, though there is little evidence that he shared his swag with anyone.

Another famous Dacoit was Phoolan Devi (1963–2001), remembered romantically as the 'Bandit Queen'. Her kidnap by a Dacoit gang in the late 1970s saved her from an abusive marriage to a man 20 years her senior, and she later became a consort to the group's leader and member of the band, famously returning with them to her village, where she publicly murdered her former husband.

After a split within the group relating to caste distinctions, Devi was held prisoner by a hostile faction in the village of Behmai, where gang members repeatedly raped her before she managed to escape. Reinstalled later at the head of her own gang, she took her revenge through the Behmai massacre of 1981, in which 22 men were lined up and shot in the village – an incident that prompted a public outcry and a massive manhunt. Though Devi evaded arrest, with her health failing she negotiated her own surrender in 1983. Amazingly, after her release on parole in 1994, she went on to become a politician, serving as an MP from 1996 to 1998 and from 1999 until her assassination in 2001 – most likely by those seeking vengeance for events in Behmai two decades earlier. Immortalized in the 1994 film *The Bandit Queen* – the accuracy of which she hotly disputed, successfully filing a suit against the filmmakers – she remains one of the most famous women in India over the last half century.

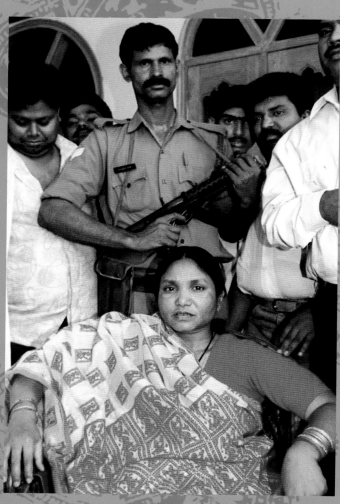

Phoolan Devi, the so-called 'Bandit Queen', backed by a bodyguard and supporters, during her election campaign in Mirzapur, in the northern Indian state of Uttar Pradesh, in 1996. In 2004 Sher Singh Rana, the principal defendant in the sensational July 2001 murder of Phoolan Devi, was sprung from a high-security prison in New Delhi, apparently by a group of bandits dressed as police.

Jack the Ripper stalked the dingiest areas of Victorian London, preying on the most vulnerable and ostracized members of society: prostitutes. In a frenzied bout of blood lust, he murdered at least five women from August to November 1888. The Ripper, also known the 'the Whitechapel murderer' or 'the leather apron', remains the most infamous murderer never to be caught and the first serial killer to achieve an international profile. 'Horror ran through the land,' reads one account from the period. 'Men spoke of it with bated breath, and pale-lipped women shuddered as they read the dreadful details.'

Jack the Ripper

All of the Ripper's murders took place in or around the poverty-stricken Whitechapel area of east London. His victims were street prostitutes. Although they were not raped, in nearly every case their throat was cut and lower torso mutilated in such a way as to suggest a depraved sexual motive for the murder and an obsession with wombs. Such was the surgical precision with which the bodies were maimed that police felt the killer must have had at least some knowledge of either anatomy or butchery.

On 7 August 1888, Martha Tabram was stabbed 39 times in the stairwell of a block of flats in Whitechapel, and left with her lower body exposed. Whether the Ripper was responsible is disputed, but he was unquestionably behind the murder of Mary Ann Nichols, found in a cobbled alleyway in Whitechapel on 31 August, strangled and then repeatedly stabbed in the throat, stomach and genitalia. Detective Inspectors Frederick George Abberline, Henry Moore and Walter Andrews were brought in to assist local enquiries (later supplemented by the city police under Detective Inspector James McWilliam) and separate suspects were questioned concerning both murders, but nothing came of their investigations. Then, on 8 September, a pattern began to emerge, as the body of Annie Chapman was found in Spitalfields, with her throat cut and some of her organs ripped from her body.

The killer clearly thrived on the fear he was creating. On 30 September, after killing his next victim, Elizabeth Stride, outside the International Working Men's Club in Dutfield's Yard, he boldly walked eastwards to Aldgate, probably passing the police patrols that were passing every 15 minutes, where he accosted Catherine Eddowes near a warehouse. Just discharged from a local police station for being intoxicated, she was found lying on her back with her throat cut, stomach opened and organs removed. The last victim of the Ripper was Mary Jane Kelly, another local prostitute, murdered in her room in Spitalfields and chopped into tiny pieces on 9 November.

On 27 September, mid-way through the killings, the Central News Agency received a poorly written confession, in red ink, signed 'Jack the Ripper'. Although this may have been a hoax, on 16 October a local committee set up to keep vigil in the area was sent what appeared to be half a human kidney, apparently from one of the murder victims. As news of a serial killer stalking the streets appeared in the press, so fear escalated into hysteria, and the London police commissioner, Sir Charles Warren, was forced to resign.

Who was the Ripper? Wilder speculation has alleged political motives on his part. Was he a social reformer – perhaps even Thomas Barnardo – eager to bring the squalid conditions of areas such as

Whitechapel to public attention? Could he have been a twisted Irish nationalist: perhaps their leader in the House of Commons, Charles Stewart Parnell, who, known to walk the streets of Whitechapel, was followed for a time by police before being ruled out as a suspect? The writer George Bernard Shaw seemed to give some credence to the idea when he wrote, in September 1888: '[while] we conventional Social Democrats were wasting our time . . . some independent genius has taken the matter in hand . . . by simply disembowelling four women'.

The most controversial suggestion was that Prince Albert Victor, the duke of Clarence and eldest son of the Prince of Wales, was involved in the killings, and that the government and royal family covered up the crimes to prevent a scandal. The idea has intrigued conspiracy theorists in particular, not least because the prince was known for his dissipated lifestyle, but the weight of evidence suggests he was elsewhere when several of the murders were committed.

Suspicion fell for a time on the sizeable Jewish community in east London, as old prejudices flared up during the killings, with rumours of ritual religious murder. The Ripper had left some body parts after the double murder of 30 September, and chalked a message in a stairwell claiming that 'The Juwes are men that will not be blamed for nothing'. Aaron Kosminski – a Polish Jew who worked as a hairdresser in London before being committed to a lunatic asylum in 1891 – was later named chief suspect by Assistant Chief Constable Sir Melville Macnaghten, but no charges were ever brought, despite Robert Anderson (head of CID) and Chief Inspector Donald Swanson (whom he temporarily entrusted with the case) also considering Kosminski the chief suspect. Others, though, claim the cryptic message on the wall points to a Masonic connection, the Juwes representing Jubela, Jubelo and Jubelum, ritually killed, according to Masonic tradition, for murdering Grand Master Hiram Abif.

Macnaghten also named three other possible suspects: Montague Druitt, a barrister and teacher with an interest in surgery, who was believed to be insane and later found dead; Michael Ostrog, a Russian-born thief and conman who was detained in asylums on several occasions; and Francis Tumblety, a physician who fled the country under suspicion for the Kelly

From Hell, *a gory 2001 film directed by Albert and Allen Hughes, is one of many fictionalized portrayals of the mysterious figure of the Ripper.*

murder. Other suggestions have included Jacob Isenschmid, an insane Swiss pork butcher, and Severin Klowoski, a Polish surgeon who poisoned three wives. According to crime novelist Patricia Cornwell, however, the most likely candidate was in fact a German-born artist named Walter Richard Sickert, whose paintings included numerous misogynistic images of violent assaults on women, though criminologists had previously dismissed Sickert as a credible suspect.

Why did the Ripper murders suddenly stop? Was the perpetrator consigned to a mental institution and thus prevented from continuing his killing spree. Did he die from syphilis or perhaps even commit suicide? Could it be that, having made his grotesque point, he was content to retire again into the shadows? Did he move elsewhere when the police presence in London became too much to handle? Or did he not stop at all but simply change his modus operandi, being guilty of not just 5 but 11 murders in Whitechapel between 3 April 1888 and 13 February 1891. No one can say for sure, but the slaughter ended as abruptly as it had begun.

The Ripper has been portrayed, based on a few alleged sightings, as a tall man, wearing an apron and carrying a black doctor's bag full of surgical knives, but *The Star* newspaper, reporting at the time, captures far more powerfully the awfulness of his crimes and the sheer terror he provoked. 'A nameless reprobate — half beast, half man — is at large,' it wrote. 'Hideous malice, deadly cunning, insatiable thirst for blood — all these are the marks of the mad homicide. The ghoul-like creature, stalking down his victim like a Pawnee Indian, is simply drunk with blood, and he will have more.'

NOTORIOUS SERIAL KILLERS

TED BUNDY (1946–89). American. Confessed to murdering 30 young women. Executed.

AMY ARCHER-GILLIGAN (1873–1928). American. Found guilty of poisoning her husband and five residents of her nursing home; may have killed many more. Declared insane.

LUIS GARAVITO (b. 1957). Colombian. Admitted to the murder and rape of 189 young boys. Imprisoned.

H.H. HOLMES (1860–96). American. Confessed to murdering 27 guests at his Chicago hotel, but may have killed hundreds. Executed.

BRUNO LÜDKE (1908–44). German. Convicted (probably wrongly) of the murder of 51 people, but declared insane because of his mental disability. Killed by lethal injection.

DELFINA AND MARÍA DE JESÚS GONZÁLEZ. Mexican. Convicted in 1964 of the murder of 80 prostitutes and 11 clients in the brothel they ran.

FRED WEST (1941–95). British. Tortured, raped and murdered at least 12 young women. Committed suicide. His wife Rosemary (b. 1953) was jailed for her involvement in 10 of the murders.

GARY LEON RIDGEWAY (b. 1949). American. Pleaded guilty to the murders of 48 women. Imprisoned.

DR HAROLD SHIPMAN (1946–2004). British. Thought to have murdered at least 215 of his patients. Committed suicide.

Serial killer Ted Bundy in a fit of rage at his trial for the murder of Kimberly Leach, December 1987.

William Walker was the most notorious of the American freebooters who in the 19th century sought to carve out private empires for themselves in Latin America. Walker – who for a brief time was the self-declared president of Nicaragua – was an adventurer and opportunist of merciless ambition and greed, who attempted to extend the slavery system of the Deep South into Central America, and whose campaigns were responsible for the deaths of thousands of Latin Americans.

William Walker
and the Filibusters   1824–60

> '... had this man with the plain name, the name that to-day means nothing, accomplished what he adventured, he would ... have established an empire in Mexico and in Central America, and, incidentally, have brought us into war with all of Europe.'
>
> RICHARD HARDING DAVIS,
> REAL SOLDIERS OF FORTUNE (1906)

Walker was born in Nashville, Tennessee, into a wealthy family of Scottish descent. He studied at the University of Nashville and also in Edinburgh, Heidelberg and Paris. During his time in Europe he qualified as a doctor, and also witnessed the Revolutions of 1848. On his return to America he practised medicine in Philadelphia before moving to New Orleans, where he studied law and briefly owned and edited a newspaper.

Walker was an upholder of the system of slavery that underpinned the economy of the Southern states of the USA, but which was opposed by the North. Like many other supporters of slavery, he also believed that the United States was bound, by 'manifest destiny', to take control of Central and eventually South America. These men believed

Freebooting adventurer General William Walker built his own private empire in Nicaragua before being court-martialled and sentenced to death in 1860. He is shown here praying with a priest shortly before his execution.

that Mexico was not strong enough to hold off the ambitions of the great powers, and that the United States must establish itself as the dominant force in the region before the French or the British intervened.

In 1850 Walker moved to California, which was at this time a magnet for hundreds of adventurers who – without the sanction of the US government – cast envious eyes towards the Spanish-speaking lands to the south. Such men were referred to as 'filibusters', a word derived from the Spanish *filibustero*, a pirate or freebooter. Walker soon became the most notorious of these filibusters. Although little over five foot tall and slightly built, to his admirers he was 'the grey-eyed man of destiny'.

On 15 October 1853 Walker sailed from San Francisco with a force of fewer than fifty mercenaries, intent on seizing control of the Mexican territories of Sonora and Baja California. Landing at La Paz in Baja California, he proclaimed the 'Republic of Lower California', set up a government, declared English to be the first language, and introduced the constitution of Louisiana, which permitted slavery.

Mexico was quick to respond to Walker's challenge to its sovereignty and sent troops to La Paz, obliging Walker to move his headquarters to Ensenada, where he declared the Republic of Sonora. By May 1854, however, Walker and his men had been forced back to the United States, where he was tried but acquitted of breaking the country's neutrality laws.

Unperturbed, Walker raised money and troops for another colonial foray, and in May 1855, despite the opposition of the federal authorities, he sailed from San Francisco, bound for Nicaragua, which had been in the midst of a power struggle. The faction that was on the losing side had invited Walker – who now had an international reputation as a ruthless mercenary – to rescue their cause. Walker proceeded to rout the Nicaraguan army, and was granted the title of generalissimo. He received further funding from supporters of slavery in the United States, awarded himself a monopoly on Nicaragua's maritime trade and reversed the country's 30-year-old anti-slavery laws.

On 12 July 1856 Walker reached the peak of his power when he became president of Nicaragua. He was officially recognized by the United States and even began to gather recruits for further conquests in Guatemala, El Salvador, Honduras and Costa Rica. However, a coalition of these countries mounted a successful military campaign against him – at the cost of thousands of lives – and in May 1857 he was forced to throw himself on the mercy of the United States navy, which took him home.

In November 1857, having gathered yet another force, this time at Mobile in Alabama, Walker landed in Nicaragua again, but was soon apprehended by the United States navy and repatriated once more. Having again escaped prosecution, in 1860 he led his fourth and final assault on Central America, but was captured by the Royal Navy on his arrival in Honduras. Handed over to the Honduran authorities, Walker was tried by court martial and executed on 12 September 1860, aged just 36.

Walker's hubris was inextinguishable. Throughout his life, his ego led him into dangerous situations – during his time in California he fought three duels in the name of honour, in all of which he was wounded. A renegade who believed that he was destined to conquer and rule a great empire, he failed to accept the mounting obstacles against him. In reality, his missions were doomed, and his pride – in trying to impose his will on Latin America – was his downfall.

GENERAL NORIEGA

Manuel Antonio Noriega ruled Panama from 1983 to 1989 as a brutal military dictator, initially with the support of the USA.

In the 1960s and 1970s, as a prominent commander in Panama's National Guard, he had led a ruthless campaign against guerrillas fighting the country's military government, and was also thought to be responsible for the 'disappearance' of hundreds of political dissidents. At the same time, his support had been periodically enlisted by the CIA.

In 1983 Noriega seized power, and went on to give the United States favourable trading rights in Panama. He also gave assistance to the US-backed rightwing factions in the conflicts then going on in Nicaragua and El Salvador. In October 1984 he attempted to attain some democratic legitimacy by calling presidential elections, but when he realized that defeat was imminent he simply called a halt to the electoral process and continued his military rule. Hundreds of critics of the regime were tortured or 'disappeared' by the 'Dignity Battalions', Noriega's personal paramilitary force. When in 1985 the Panamanian opposition figure, Hugo Spadafora, attempted to return from exile in Costa Rica, he was seized at the border, then tortured and beheaded.

Meanwhile, the United States had begun to look askance at Noriega, suspecting him of being a double agent and passing valuable information to Fidel Castro of Cuba. The US also suspected Noriega of assisting Pablo Escobar's drug-smuggling Medellín Cartel (see page 310), and in 1988 indicted him for trading in narcotics. Within Panama, Noriega's position grew weaker as the opposition movement, known as the Civic Crusade, became more difficult to suppress.

In 1989, after Noriega ignored the results of another election, President George Bush Snr ordered the invasion of Panama. Noriega took refuge in the Vatican embassy, but was eventually forced out on 3 January 1990 after US forces played loud rock music outside the building day and night, in an effort to dislodge him. Taken to Miami, Noriega was tried and imprisoned for drug trafficking, racketeering and money laundering, and was sentenced to 40 years in jail, later reduced to 30. Both France and Panama, where he was convicted of murder in *absentia*, have asked for his extradition.

Panamanian military leader General Manuel Noriega at a conference of Central American and Caribbean countries.

Francisco Solano López was the vainglorious dictator of Paraguay who, in the name of honour and national prestige, led his country to almost total destruction at the hands of Brazil, Argentina and Uruguay. Capable of great personal cruelty, López was a deluded popinjay, an inept psychopath and a mass-murdering megalomaniac who was obsessed with dreams of grandeur and believed that he could become the Napoleon of South America. But he overplayed his hand disastrously, with fatal consequences for himself, his family and the country that he claimed to love.

Francisco López 1827–70

López was the eldest son of President Carlos Antonio López, a merciless tyrant who ruled Paraguay from 1844 until his death in 1862. The younger López had been groomed to succeed his father, promoted to brigadier general at just 18.

He became an increasingly proud and preposterous young man, and liked to have himself pictured on horseback or in military uniform, with a profusion of ribbons and insignia, his thick black beard covering a somewhat portly face. From his teenage years he was an avid womanizer, capable of oleaginous charm and eloquence, but likely to become forceful if his advances were rejected.

In 1853 young López travelled to France on a diplomatic mission on behalf of his father. In Paris he became intoxicated with the political pomp, imperial ceremony and military showmanship of Emperor Napoleon III. He studied the campaigns of the first Napoleon and believed that he himself had a talent for strategy. While in Paris he also met Eliza Lynch, a beautiful Irish girl whom he took back to Paraguay and who was to become his mistress for the rest of his life.

On his father's death in 1862, López seized power quickly, imprisoning potential rivals and being duly elected president by the Paraguayan congress. While on his deathbed, his father was reported to have warned him of the dangers of foreign aggression. But despite growing up so close to the centre of Paraguayan politics, López showed little sensitivity to the precarious nature of the balance of power in the region, determined to become the Napoleon III of South America. Foolishly, in 1863, just one year into his reign, he allowed Paraguay to become embroiled in the civil war that was taking place in nearby Uruguay, in which both Brazil and Argentina – the most powerful nations in South America – had a stake.

Puffed up with his own sense of self-importance, López believed that he could act as the arbiter between these contending powers and thereby establish himself as the dominant warlord of South America. Accordingly, in November 1864 he declared war on Brazil, and sent his troops over the border. By December they had taken the province of Mato Grosso, known for its valuable diamond mines, but instead of consolidating his position López then demanded the right to station troops in Corrientes, a province of Argentina that was strategically important in his campaign against Brazil. In April 1865, after Argentina refused, López launched a disastrous invasion.

On 1 May 1865 Brazil, Argentina and Uruguay set aside their differences and united together against Paraguay. A foolish incursion into Uruguay in 1865 stretched López's forces to

breaking point, and in May 1866 his army suffered a terrible defeat at the hands of the allies at Tuyuti. By July 1867 López was in full retreat, and his enemies chased and harried him back into Paraguay.

As Paraguay's fortunes in the 'War of the Triple Alliance' rapidly began to decline, López turned his rage on his fellow Paraguayans. By the middle of 1868 he had become convinced that his own family were plotting against him, and ordered the execution of his brothers and brother-in-law, and even had his own mother and sisters flogged. In what became known as the San Fernando massacres, López tortured and slaughtered men and their entire families – many thousands of them – including ministers, judges, senior civil servants and even foreign diplomats. All were executed without trial on suspicion of being deserters or traitors.

Such actions were the signs of a desperate man. As his enemies closed in, López was driven northward with the ragged remnant of his army towards the frontier of Paraguay and Brazil. Here, on 1 March 1870, he was killed by Brazilian troops as he tried to escape by swimming a river.

Karl Marx once wrote of Napoleon III, when comparing him to his uncle, the great Napoleon I, that all historical episodes occur twice, the first time as history and the second time as farce. The life of Francisco Solano López might suggest that they can occur for a third time, with farce mixed with tragedy in equal measure. Some Paraguayans have seen López as a national hero, prepared to stand for the honour of his country at any cost. That cost, however, included the lives of between a third and a half of the population of Paraguay, murdered by López or killed in his wars.

Francisco Solano López, the corrupt and megalomaniacal ruler of Paraguay from 1862 to 1870, depicted here in a contemporary engraving by Emile Bayard.

ELIZA LYNCH

To this day Paraguayans are divided over the figure of Eliza Lynch. Those who see Francisco López's presidency as a noble episode in Paraguayan history have placed his Irish moll on a pedestal as Paraguay's version of Evita Perón – a captivating visionary and a regenerator of the country. On the other hand, for the many who regard López's presidency as a disaster, brought about by sadism and hubris, Lynch was a gorgeous, profane, blood-spattered seductress, the Latin-Celtic Jezebel who stoked her lover's ego, encouraging him to embark on his disastrous military adventures, who turned him against his own family and encouraged him to kill

Eliza Alicia Lynch was born on 30 June 1835 in County Cork in Ireland, to a Protestant physician, John Lynch, and his wife, Adelaide Schnock. In 1847 the family moved to Paris, and in 1850, when she was just 15, Eliza married a French military surgeon.

The marriage ended in divorce, and Eliza was already working as a courtesan when she was introduced to López in 1853. To the thickset, chubby-faced López she must have seemed an exotic beauty, with her tall, voluptuous figure, her long red hair, her blue eyes and her porcelain skin. Their love affair developed quickly and by the time that López had to return to Paraguay, Lynch was pregnant. Besotted, López left her funds to follow him to South America. She gave birth to the first of five sons in October 1855, not long after she arrived in Buenos Aires.

Soon settled in Asunción in palatial splendour, Eliza simultaneously delighted and horrified Paraguayan high society with her charm, Parisian affectations and impish behaviour – not to mention her importation of French cuisine, music, perfume, fashions and art.

During the war López made his mistress the largest landowner in Paraguay by handing her huge swathes of land, including a number of profitable ranches and over twenty homes for her personal use. But her fortune was tied in with his, and within days of his death she had all her lands confiscated. She fled to back to Paris – but not entirely empty-handed, as she took with her thousands of pounds worth of jewels and cash. When she later returned to Paraguay to reclaim her land, she was swiftly deported back to Paris, where she died in 1886.

Eliza Alicia Lynch, known as 'Madame Lynch,' the beautiful and deadly Irish mistress of Paraguayan dictator Francisco Solano López, in a likeness dating from 1855.

Beautiful, cunning and cruel, Empress Dowager Cixi was the archetypal 'dragon lady'. She rose from obscurity to become the effective ruler of China for 47 years, during which time she presided over a humiliating decline in the country's fortunes. In the second half of the 19th century, the Qing dynasty that had ruled China for more than 250 years struggled to cope with the challenges posed by modernization and increasing pressure from the European powers. Having suffered military defeats at the hands of its foreign rivals, and faced with growing internal unrest, China's last imperial dynasty finally fell in 1911. No one had contributed more to this collapse than the empress dowager herself.

Empress Dowager Cixi
1835–1908

'After this notice is issued to instruct you villagers ... if there are any Christian converts, you ought to get rid of them quickly. The churches which belong to them should be unreservedly burned down. Everyone who intends to spare someone, or to disobey our order by concealing Christian converts, will be punished according to the regulation ... and he will be burned to death to prevent his impeding our programme.'

BOXER POSTER, 1900

When she entered Emperor Xianfeng's household as his concubine in 1851, the future empress dowager was known as 'Lady Yehenara, daughter of Huizheng'. She was renamed 'Yi' soon after, and then 'Noble Consort Yi' following the birth of her son Zaichun in 1856. When the emperor died in 1861, Zaichun assumed the throne, and to reflect her new position as 'Divine Mother Empress Dowager', Yi was given the title 'Cixi', meaning 'motherly and auspicious'.

Before his death, Xianfeng had charged eight 'regent ministers' to govern during his son's minority, but a palace coup saw power pass instead to the late emperor's consort, Mother Empress Dowager Ci'an,

Cixi as a young woman. She served both as empress and empress dowager, and effectively ruled China from 1861 until her death in 1908. The imperial Qing dynasty collapsed three years later.

and the Divine Mother Empress Dowager Cixi. Aided by the ambitious Prince Gong, they were to enjoy a 12-year period of shared rule, exercising power 'from behind the curtain'.

Zaichun, renamed Tongzhi (meaning 'collective rule'), was belatedly allowed to begin his 'reign' in 1873, but the two matriarchs, having gained a taste for power, had no intention of quietly slipping into retirement. Cixi in particular continued to dominate the young emperor, cowing him into accepting her authority.

After just two years, Tongzhi died, but the accession of Cixi's four-year-old cousin, Emperor Guangxu, saw the two women restored as regents. Six years later, in 1881, Empress Ci'an died suddenly, leading to rumours that Cixi had poisoned her. Ci'an's death opened the way for Cixi to exercise unfettered power, reinforced in 1885 when she stripped Prince Gong of his offices.

By this time the empress dowager had accumulated a huge personal fortune. At a time of growing financial crisis for China, she built a string of extravagant palaces and gardens, and a lavish tomb for herself. Meanwhile, she stifled all efforts at reform and modernization. In 1881, she banned Chinese nationals from studying abroad because of the possible influx of liberal ideas. When proposals were brought forward for a vast new railway that would open up much of China, she vetoed the plans, claiming it would be 'too loud' and would 'disturb the emperors' tombs'.

The young Emperor Guangxu was due to assume the reins of power in 1887. At her instigation, various accommodating court officials begged her to prolong her rule, due to the emperor's youth. 'Reluctantly' she agreed, and a new law was passed that allowed her to continue 'advising' the emperor indefinitely.

Even after she finally handed over power in 1889 – retiring to the massive Summer Palace she had built for herself – Cixi continued to overshadow the imperial court. She forced the new emperor to marry his niece, Jingfen, against his will. When he later snubbed his wife to spend more time with Consort Zhen – known as the 'Pearl Concubine' – Cixi had Zhen flogged.

In the mid-1890s the empress dowager insisted on diverting funds from the Chinese navy to pay for extensive refurbishments to her Summer Palace for the celebration of her 60th birthday. When Japan launched a war against China in 1894, the latter's armed forces were defeated. The reformers won the confidence of Emperor Guangxu, and in 1898 he launched his 'first hundred days' of measures.

The empress dowager was unwilling to cede an inch. In September 1898 she organized a military coup that effectively removed Guangxu from power. He nominally continued as emperor until 1908, but was declared 'not fit' to rule the country in an edict she herself authored.

Cixi's undoing proved to be the Boxer Rebellion of 1900. Her announcement of support for the Boxer movement, which she saw as a bulwark of traditional Chinese values against Western and liberal influences, prompted the Western powers to march on Beijing and seize the Forbidden City. Cixi was forced to flee, and imperial authority was only restored after the emperor signed a humiliating treaty. Cixi died in November 1908, leaving Puyi as emperor, aged 2. Overthrown by the Revolution of 1911, briefly reinstated in 1917, set up as puppet emperor of Manchukuo by the Japanese from 1932 until 1945, he was China's last monarch. Cixi had proven the gravedigger of the Chinese empire.

THE BOXER RISING

The Boxer Rising, begun in 1900, was led by a clandestine group, the Righteous and Harmonious Fists (the Boxers), which taught its members martial arts (and even claimed it could train them to be immune from bullets). It began life in Shandong province and gained a following among the rural poor. It produced mass propaganda accusing Catholic missionaries of acts of sexual abuse and Western immigrants of trying to undermine China. Violent attacks against both became commonplace.

Believing the movement might help her retain power, Cixi endorsed the rebellion as an expression of Chinese popular culture. Thereafter, anti-Western riots and the destruction of foreign property escalated and in the summer of 1900 a Boxer 'army' laid siege to Western embassies in Beijing. The Chinese imperial army was complicit in the assault, doing little to relieve the defenders. It took the arrival of international troops to lift the siege (after which the city was looted), and several more months for the rising itself to be quelled.

Ironically, the rebellion increased foreign interference in China. The Boxer Protocol of 1901 not only forced the Chinese Government to accede to a huge reparations bill, but also gained Western countries major trade concessions and allowed them to station forces permanently in Beijing – a further insult to the sense of wounded national pride upon which the abortive rebellion had been predicated.

An illustration in Le Petit Journal *depicts the decapitated heads of rebels on display during the Boxer Rebellion of 1900.*

Leopold II, king of the Belgians, was the hypocritical and ambitious colonist who developed the vast and lucrative central African colony of the Congo at a terrible human cost. He carved himself a colossal personal empire, exploiting and killing millions, to build his fortune – turning the heart of Africa into Joseph Conrad's *Heart of Darkness*.

Leopold II and the Congo
1835–1909

'Many were shot, some had their ears cut off; others were tied up with ropes round their necks and bodies and taken away.'

ROGER CASEMENT, REPORTING TO THE BRITISH FOREIGN SECRETARY ON THE TREATMENT OF THE NATIVES IN LEOPOLD'S CONGO FREE STATE

Leopold succeeded his father, Leopold I, in 1865. He studiously avoided involving Belgium in the Franco-Prussian War of 1870–1, realizing that his small country had no influence in the power politics of Europe. But European neutrality did not amount to high-mindedness; instead, Leopold's ambitions extended beyond Europe, and in 1876 he confided in his ambassador in London: 'I do not want to miss a good chance of getting us a slice of this magnificent African cake.'

Leopold set his sights on the untapped natural resources of the river basin of the Congo, covered in dense rainforest and eighty times the size of Belgium. In 1876 he formed the Association Internationale Africaine to promote the exploration and colonization of Africa, and two years later commissioned the British-American explorer Henry Morton Stanley to explore the Congo region. By buying off local tribes for a pittance and duping them into signing away their lands to European control, Stanley requisitioned massive portions of the Congo for Leopold. Thus was created the 'Congo Free State', for which Leopold gained international recognition at the Conference of Berlin of 1884–5.

The Congo Free State was free only in name. It was not even a Belgian colony, but rather Leopold's personal property, from which he squeezed profits as he plundered the area's rich natural resources, notably rubber and ivory. Leopold never visited the Congo, preferring to govern it through a series of agents, whose own profits were gleaned from commission.

Order in the Congo Free State was maintained by the Force Publique, a notoriously cruel mercenary force of 20,000 men, officered by Europeans but relying on badly paid Africans as foot soldiers. The Force Publique was charged with the collection of the 'rubber tax', an oppressive levy that effectively required forced labour: arriving in tribal villages, Leopold's agents seized the women and children and refused to release them until the men went into the rainforest and brought back the requisite quantity of rubber, which was then sold on, all the time swelling Leopold's coffers.

In order to stop them wasting ammunition on hunting wild animals, the Force Publique were ordered to account for every bullet they fired by bringing back the right hand of their victim. The hands of thousands of innocent Congolese were cut off by the mercenaries, whether they were dead or alive. Villages were burned down, inhabitants tortured and some reports even suggested that members of the Force Publique engaged in cannibalism. The headquarters of Leon Rom, the barbaric Belgian soldier in

charge of the Force Publique, was surrounded by hundreds of severed heads.

These atrocities caused the death of an estimated 10 million people, half the population of the Congo, either at the hands of the Force Publique or through hunger and deprivation. Meanwhile, Leopold presented himself to the rest of Europe as a humanitarian, determined to liberate the area from the scourge of the Arab slave trade, and spreading European 'civilization'. But the Christian missionaries who penetrated into the heart of the Congo told a very different story, and reports of awful abuses began to filter back to Europe.

In the first decade of the 20th century there were a number of tribal rebellions. These were brutally suppressed, but they did serve to provoke further scrutiny into conditions in the Congo Free State. In 1900 Edmund Dene Morel, an English trader, began to campaign against the horrific conditions in the territory, and in 1903 the British Foreign Office commissioned the diplomat Roger Casement to go to the Congo to find out what was going on. Casement's detailed eyewitness report did much to stir up international outrage, and writers such as Arthur Conan Doyle, Joseph Conrad and Mark Twain joined in the campaign. In 1908 the Belgian parliament finally voted to annex the Congo from their own king, ending his control of the region.

It was not until 1960 that Congo achieved full independence, but the brutal legacy of Leopold II still continues to haunt the country, which has suffered from years of civil war in which millions have been killed. Leopold died on 17 December 1909, a shamed and hated figure, who justified his behaviour in the Congo to the very end of his life. Mark Twain wrote that the ageing king was a 'greedy, grasping, avaricious, cynical, bloodthirsty old goat', while for Arthur Conan Doyle the rape of the Congo was simply 'the greatest crime in history'.

Leopold II, king of the Belgians, in a photograph taken in 1905.

HEART OF DARKNESS

Leopold II declared that his aim in colonizing the jungles of Africa was to 'open to civilization the only part of our globe which it has not yet penetrated, to pierce the darkness which hangs over entire peoples'. The appalling hypocrisy of Leopold's claim was mercilessly dissected in Joseph Conrad's 1899 novella *Heart of Darkness*, which exposed the evil then being perpetrated in the Congo in the name of civilization.

Conrad (1857–1924) – born Józef Teodor Konrad Korzeniowski in Poland and living there until he was 16 – is widely regarded as one of the finest novelists in the English language and a master of prose, an extraordinary achievement given that he only learned to speak English fluently in his early 20s while working as a seaman on British vessels. Although the Congo is not named directly, *Heart of Darkness* is based on his experiences on a steamship on the River Congo in the 1890s. Much of the narrative is told through Marlow, a steamship captain, but the central character of the book is Kurtz, a corrupt, crazed ivory trader, possibly loosely based on Leon Rom, the leader of the Force Publique in the Congo.

Kurtz – who has taken part in unspeakable atrocities and established himself as the leader of the local tribes – embodies the paradoxes of the colonial experience. He has been an intellectual, a poet and an enthusiastic proponent of 'colonial civilization', only to become a savage head-hunter, who now scribbles 'Exterminate all the brutes.' On his deathbed, having succumbed to fever, his face wears an 'expression of sombre pride, of ruthless power, of craven terror' as he cries out 'The horror! The horror!' – a damning verdict on the legacy of colonialism.

The finest of Conrad's many works are reckoned to be *Lord Jim* (1900), *Nostromo* (1904), *The Secret Agent* (1907) and *Under Western Eyes* (1911). Many have been adapted into films, including *The Secret Agent* twice (Alfred Hitchcock's 1936 *Sabotage* and the eponymous 1996 film featuring Bob Hoskins, Patricia Arquette and Gérard Depardieu); and 'The Duel' (1908), in Ridley Scott's *The Duellists* (1977). *Heart of Darkness* was the inspiration for Francis Ford Coppola's classic movie *Apocalypse Now* (1979), set in the context of the Vietnam War and starring Marlon Brando as an American Colonel Kurtz.

A view of the Congo River, setting for Joseph Conrad's novella Heart of Darkness.

Jacob H. Smith, the American general known as 'Hell Roaring Jake' or 'Howling Jake', became notorious for his atrocities against civilians in the Philippine–American War (1899–1902). Comparable to later outrages such as the My Lai Massacre in Vietnam (1968) and the Haditha killings in Iraq (2005), Smith's actions in the Philippines indelibly stained the reputation of the United States military.

Jacob H. Smith and the Philippine–American War

1840–1918

> 'The more you kill and burn, the better it will please me.'
>
> GENERAL JACOB SMITH, 1901

Not much is known about Smith's early life, but he came to prominence during the American Civil War, fighting for the Union, and was reputed to have been one of the most successful officers tasked with recruiting blacks into the Union armies. He was later indicted for using money set aside for new recruits to fund a personal sideline in whisky, gold and diamond speculation, and as a consequence was removed from his position as an army judge advocate.

In the decades that followed, there were several instances of Smith's volatile temperament landing him in difficulty – often with those of superior rank. On one occasion in the mid-1870s he got into trouble for insulting a colonel, and in 1885, following an incident in a bar in Texas, he was court-martialled for 'conduct unbecoming an officer and a gentleman'. Smith was also involved in several civilian court cases – most of which were the result of his failure to repay gambling debts.

As the 19th century drew to a close there was little to suggest that Smith would be remembered as anything other than a dissolute good-for-nothing. But his fortunes were to be transformed by the outbreak of the Spanish–American War in 1898, which ended with the transfer of a number of Spanish colonies to the USA. One of these colonies, the Philippines, was unwilling to swap Spanish for American rule and – having previously waged a successful insurgency against their Spanish overlords – the Filipinos made a bid for independence, launching a three-year struggle in June 1899. Among the US troops dispatched to the Philippines was Jacob H. Smith, now a colonel.

Faced by the superior firepower and training of the American troops, the Filipinos opted to fight a guerrilla campaign. In one notorious incident on the island of Samar in 1901, 40 American troops were killed in a single attack in what became known as the 'Balangiga Massacre'. The episode caused an outcry back in the United States, and President Theodore Roosevelt ordered the military governor of the Philippines, Major General Adna Chaffee, to bring the islands back under control.

In response, Chaffee promoted Smith to the rank of brigadier general and put him in command of the 'Samar Campaign'. Smith outlined his strategy to one of his subordinates, Major Littleton Waller. 'I want no prisoners,' he declared. 'I wish you to kill and burn; the more you kill and burn, the better it will please me . . . The interior of Samar must be made a howling wilderness.' Waller was ordered to ensure that anyone capable of bearing arms against the United States – i.e. anyone over the age of ten –

A press cartoon of 5 May 1902 showing General Jacob ('Howling Jake') Smith's order to 'KILL EVERY ONE OVER TEN', one of the most infamous episodes of the Philippine–American War. The bottom caption reads, 'Criminals Because They Were Born Ten Years Before We Took the Philippines'.

was put to death. The reprisal killings that followed claimed between 2000 and 3000 lives. In an attempt to break Filipino resistance, Smith also deployed a scorched-earth policy and interdicted the food supply to Samar.

Incredibly, Smith could see nothing wrong in what he had done; on the contrary, he actually boasted of his efforts to journalists, claiming that such measures were appropriate when fighting 'savages'. Yet revelations over what had occurred on Samar caused outrage when they became public, and Smith was once more put before a court martial, for 'conduct to the prejudice of good order and military discipline'. In May 1902 he was found guilty, reprimanded and forced to resign his commission.

Smith – now known as 'The Monster' – died in 1918. A year earlier, after the USA had entered the First World War, he had volunteered to serve in the trenches. But there was to be no way back for Smith. Not only was he far too old, but, more significantly, his conduct while in American uniform had proven a major embarrassment to the government. Indeed, the atrocities his troops committed on Samar continue to cast a shadow over relations between the United States and the Philippines to this day.

THE INVENTION OF
THE CONCENTRATION CAMP

During the Philippine–American War (1899–1902), the United States built a concentration camp on the island of Marinduque. Concentration camps were invented, however, by the British – specifically by Lord Kitchener, who established the first during the Second Boer War (1899–1902). The conflict had evolved into an insurgency pitting Boer 'commandos' against regular British troops. Kitchener responded by ordering that all non-combatant Boers should be 'concentrated' within specially created camps – partly to guarantee their safety as he initiated a 'scorched-earth' policy in the Transvaal and Cape Colony, but also to deny Boer guerrillas the 'water' in which they 'swam'. Although Kitchener was a notably tough general, he was no monster. But the concentration camps were run incompetently: 28,000 of the Boer inmates died in epidemics, leading to scandal, enquiries and the discontinuation of a bad policy.

In Nazi Germany and the Soviet Union under Stalin, camps were the centrepieces of state policies of genocide and terror. An estimated 15,000 labour and extermination camps were established in Nazi-occupied countries, including Bergen-Belsen (70,000 estimated deaths), Buchenwald (56,000), Dachau (31,591), Flossenbürg (30,000), Neuengamme (55,000), Ravensbrück (90,000) and Sachsenhausen (100,000) in Germany; Auschwitz-Birkenau (2.5 million), Belzec (600,000), Chelmno (320,000), Gross-Rosen (40,000) Majdanek (360,000), Plaszów (9000) Sobibór (250,000), Stutthof (65,000)

and Treblinka (870,000) in Poland; Mauthausen-Gusen (95,000) in Austria; Sajmište (100,000) in Serbia; Salaspils (101,000) in Latvia; Theresienstadt (Terezin) (35,000) in Czechoslovakia; and Maly Trostenets (65,000) in Belarus.

In the Soviet Union, Stalin established thousands of gulags – 'corrective' labour camps – in at least 476 separate complexes, including Kolyma, Norilsk and Vorkuta, each located north of the Arctic Circle. At any one time between 1929 and 1953 the gulags held an estimated 7 million prisoners, of whom around 700,000 died each year. Eighteen million people passed through them under Stalin. The gulags were officially abolished in 1960.

More recently, camps as places of imprisonment, torture and murder have reappeared in Europe, with the brutal 'ethnic cleansing' of the Balkan conflicts of the 1990s. The 677 camps in Bosnia, housing mainly Bosnians Muslims and Bosnian Croats, included Omarska (7000 prisoners; 5000 killed), Keraterm (3000; 300), Trnopolje (6000; unknown), Heliodrom (6000; unknown) and Manjača (3737; unknown).

Boer families in a British concentration camp during the Second Boer War (1899–1902), in an image from Le Petit Journal, *20 January 1901. Some 28,000 Boer internees died in camps such as this, the first ever to be established for the confinement and control of civilians in wartime.*

Lothar von Trotha issued one of the first historically documented orders for genocide. On his command some 90 per cent of the Herero tribe of German South-West Africa (present-day Namibia) were exterminated – a deliberate act of annihilation that was to provide inspiration for other genocidal racists throughout the remainder of the 20th century.

Lothar von Trotha
and the Namibian massacres
1848–1920

'I wipe out rebellious tribes with streams of blood and streams of money. Only following this cleansing can something new emerge.'

LOTHAR VAN TROTHA

By the time he arrived in Africa in 1894, Adrian Dietrich Lothar von Trotha was a veteran of the Austro-Prussian and Franco-Prussian wars. His first African posting was as commander of colonial forces in German East Africa (today's mainland Tanzania, Rwanda and Burundi), and while there he carved out a reputation as someone who would brook no opposition from the natives. A short stint in China followed, during which he played an important role in helping to put down the anti-Western Boxer Rebellion (see page 185).

In May 1904 von Trotha was made commander in chief in German South-West Africa, which was then in the grip of a major rebellion, led by the Herero tribe. He arrived in the colony at the head of 10,000 heavily armed men, determined to solve the 'Herero problem'. First he ordered his forces to make a broad sweep, driving the Herero into a single location. His men then surrounded the Herero on three sides. The spot was well chosen, as the only way out was into the Kalahari Desert.

At the Battle of Waterberg in August 1904 von Trotha attacked the encircled Herero – who numbered around 50,000, of whom around 6000 were warriors – with some 2000 men. Though the Herero held a numerical advantage of three to one, they simply could not compete with the modern rifles, machine guns and artillery of the German forces. In defeat, the survivors opted to flee into the arid Kalahari – as von Trotha had hoped they would. With his trap sprung, he now ordered his men to poison the any water holes they came across. Meanwhile, fences were erected all along the desert boundary, with intermittent guard posts to watch for any who attempted to escape the barren wilderness; those who did were to be shot on sight.

Lest anyone be in any doubt as to what he had planned, von Trotha then issued his notorious 'Extermination Order':

All the Herero must leave the land. If they refuse, then I will force them to do it . . . Any Herero found within German borders, with or without a gun, with or without cattle, will be shot . . . No prisoners will be taken. This is my decision for the Herero people.

In a slight relenting of this draconian order, not all of the Herero were shot on sight. Some were sent to labour camps or pushed into slavery. The effect was largely the same, however, as thousands of Herero died from overwork, disease or starvation. Many of the women were victims of sexual abuse. By the time von Trotha was done scarcely 15,000 out of an initial population of over 80,000 Herero remained alive.

A number of Herero were the subject of medical experimentation by a genetic scientist, Eugene Fischer. Fischer's work, which pointed to the supposed inferiority of the Africans, later stimulated the ideas of one Adolf Hitler, who read Fischer's book while in prison in 1923 and declared himself impressed.

In April 1905 von Trotha was faced with another uprising – this time from the Nama people. Once more he resorted to the methods that had proved so devastating against the Herero. A public decree was issued, the terms of which make for chilling reading:

> The Nama who chooses not to surrender and lets himself be seen in the German area will be shot, until all are exterminated. Those who, at the start of the rebellion, committed murder against whites or have commanded that whites be murdered have, by law, forfeited their lives. As for the few not defeated, it will fare with them as it fared with the Herero, who in their blindness also believed that they could make successful war against the powerful German Emperor and the great German people. I ask you, where are the Herero today?

In the slaughter that followed this edict, some 10,000 Nama perished; a further 9000 were interned in concentration camps.

Back in Germany, von Trotha's activities prompted a burst of public condemnation when they became known in late 1905. To quell the disquiet, the Kaiser recalled von Trotha to Europe, but he was not punished for his actions, and remained within the senior ranks of the German military. He served throughout the First World War, and died of natural causes in 1920.

On von Trotha's watch, the Herero and Nama tribes of South-West Africa had been all but consigned to oblivion. He thus set the pattern that culminated in the unimaginably large-scale genocide of the Holocaust. In recognition of this, in August 2004 the German government officially acknowledged von Trotha's activities, accepted 'historic and moral responsibility' for them, and apologized to the people of Namibia.

Lothar von Trotha, commander-in-chief of the German expeditionary force in South-West Africa, photographed in 1906. Von Trotha was responsible for the near-extermination of the Herero people of Namibia.

DISAPPEARED PEOPLES

Conquest and colonization across the centuries, as far back as the annihilation of the Amalekites in biblical times (1 Chronicles 4:42–3), have robbed many cultures of their identity, driven some to near-extinction and obliterated others altogether.

Why some ancient cultures – such as the Hittites, Philistines, Trojans and Minoans – vanished from history is unclear. Likewise the mighty Mayan civilization of Central America mysteriously died out by the 10th century, though survivors later formed city-states until crushed by colonizing Spaniards. The Mayan language, however, survives, spoken by descendants in the region today. The arrival of the conquistadors, coupled with 'Old World' diseases such as smallpox, measles and typhoid, devastated other indigenous peoples in Central and South America. Between 1520 and 1580 the mighty Aztec and Inca empires were all but wiped out, any survivors assimilated into the new population. In Brazil the indigenous population fell after colonization from 3 million to around 300,000, estimates suggesting that, in all, 95 per cent of South American natives have been lost.

North American Indians suffered likewise. The Arawaks had vanished by the mid-17th century and the Mohawks and Iroquois were devastated by smallpox, followed over subsequent centuries by the Indians of the Plains and West Coast. Forced removal to reservations – such as that of 17,000 Cherokees in 1830 in the so-called 'Trail of Tears' – coupled with wholesale massacres as of the Sioux at Wounded Knee in 1890, dealt a further blow to North American Indian culture. Today, Native Americans of the Navajo, Cherokee, Choctaw, Sioux, Chippewa, Apache, Lumbee, Blackfeet, Iroquois, and Pueblo survive, but nearly nine out of ten have mixed blood.

In Australia there were about 600 different Aborigine peoples when the Europeans arrived, but massacres and disease reduced their numbers by an estimated 90 per cent between 1788 and 1900. In New Zealand it could have been a similar story. The numbers of indigenous Maoris were halved between 1840 and 1900, but the population recovered. In both New Zealand and Australia indigenous peoples today are increasingly reasserting their culture and rights.

Herero prisoners in chains following the uprising of 1904–5. The Herero were victims of the 'scramble for Africa', when various European powers competed to plunder the riches of the African continent.

Rational and mild-mannered, Hawley Harvey Crippen – the original doctor of death – made history as the first criminal to be apprehended using the new wireless telegraph. In a grisly crime that shocked Edwardian Britain, he poisoned his wife and cut her into pieces, boiling her organs, throwing her head into a canal and burying her torso under the floor of their marital home.

Dr Crippen 1862–1910

'...that they did, at 39 Hilldrop Crescent, feloniously and wilfully, of their malice aforethought, kill and murder one Cora Crippen, otherwise Belle Elmore.'

FROM THE WARRANT ISSUED FOR THE ARREST OF
DR CRIPPEN AND HIS MISTRESS IN 1910

Hawley Harvey Crippen was born in 1862 in Coldwater, Michigan. After qualifying as a doctor and studying homeopathy, he moved to New York City, entrusting his infant son, Otto, to the care of his parents after the death of his first wife around 1890. Six months later, he met Cora Turner (stage name Belle Elmore), a 19-year-old aspiring music-hall performer. Loud and confident, with dark curly hair, generous hips and a voluptuous figure, she could not have been more different from the gently spoken, slightly built Crippen.

Cora had hoped the marriage would bring financial security to pursue her stage career, but an economic downturn forced Crippen to take a job with a homeopathic mail-order business, and in 1897 he moved to London to open up a new office for the firm. Cora stayed in America at first, pursuing a string of affairs, and when she

The Edwardian murderer Dr Harvey Crippen in an undated – and heavily retouched – photograph.

finally joined Crippen in 1900, she wasted no time immersing herself in the social whirl of the London theatrical scene. The couple moved house a number of times, and while living at 39 Hilldrop Crescent in Camden Town, Cora conducted an affair with their student lodger.

In 1901, Ethel Le Neve, a quiet 18-year-old secretary, joined Crippen's office, and the two began a liaison, as yet unconsummated. The Crippens' marriage was disintegrating rapidly, and towards the end of 1909, Crippen resolved to dispose of his wife, deliberately telling a colleague he had concerns about her health. On 17 January 1910, he ordered five grains of hyoscine hydrobromide – a drug used as a sedative – from a chemist on Oxford Street. Cora Crippen was last seen alive on 31 January 1910. Although friends and neighbours were suspicious about her disappearance, Dr Crippen reassured them she had returned to the United States on family business, subsequently claiming she had died from pneumonia. Within a matter of weeks, he had moved Ethel into the house.

On 30 June 1910, Scotland Yard were informed about Cora's disappearance and Crippen was interviewed by the police. He lied again, coolly telling Inspector Walter Drew that his wife had left him and that he had been too embarrassed to tell his neighbours. After days of being interviewed, he and Ethel fled to Antwerp, where they boarded the SS *Montrose*, a transatlantic liner bound for Montreal.

On 14 July, shortly after the couple had fled, 39 Hilldrop Crescent was searched again and the remains of a female torso were found in the coal cellar. The body, which turned out to be Cora

DNA AND THE FORENSICS OF DETECTION

DNA evidence is not the only development to have transformed the forensics of detection. For the best part of a century, fingerprints were the most important tool.

Early research on fingerprints was conducted in 1823 by the Czech physiologist Jan Evangelista Purkyně (1899–1902), in the 1870s by the British doctor Henry Faulds and in the following decade by the British anthropologist Sir Francis Galton, who in his influential book, *Fingerprints*, established the massive odds against two fingerprints being the same. The first fingerprint files were compiled in 1892 by the Argentine police official Juan Vucetich, who also was the first to identify a criminal through their use: Francisca Rojas, who left a bloody print on a doorpost after murdering her two sons. Five years later, the world's first fingerprint bureau was established in Calcutta, two Indian experts developing the Henry system of fingerprint classification (named after their supervisor, Edward Henry, Bengal's inspector-general of police) – a system still used today. In July 1901, a fingerprint branch was set up at New Scotland Yard, London, fingerprint use spreading to America the following year.

Recent years have seen the advent of DNA profiling (sometimes called genetic fingerprinting), first used in a murder case to convict Colin Pitchfork in 1987 for the so-called Enderby murders. DNA is a nucleic acid containing genetic code found in all living organisms, and in 1985 the British scientist Sir Alec Jeffreys discovered that each human, with the exception of identical twins, has a unique DNA pattern that can be 'read' off from sections of non-coding DNA. At a crime scene, DNA can be extracted from traces of blood, semen, skin, saliva or hair and matched against samples from suspects. Less dependable, though frequently used to identify skeletal remains, is the use of mitochondrial DNA, which though not unique to individuals can help reinforce other evidence (including circumstantial evidence.).

Profiling has allowed the reopening and solving of numerous cases, years after the crimes were perpetrated. The first American convicted using DNA evidence was Tommie Lee Andrews, sentenced in 1987 to 22 years in prison for the rape of a woman in Florida. In 1999, following mitochondrial DNA comparison, Hadden Clark was charged with the murder and cannibalization in 1986 of Michelle Dorr, whose skeletal remains had recently been discovered. Anthony Balaam, known as the Trenton Strangler, was convicted in 2000 for rape and murder after his DNA matched that in semen taken from

Crippen's, had been mutilated so that it would fit into the small space. Crippen had removed her spine and rib cage and burned them in the kitchen hearth, boiled her organs in acid, and cut off her head, which he had thrown into a local canal. An arrest warrant was immediately issued.

Meanwhile, on board the *Montrose*, Crippen was travelling under the name Robinson, and Ethel had disguised herself as a young boy, supposedly Crippen's son. However, the captain of the ship, Harry Kendall, had been alerted to the hunt for the two fugitives, and, unconvinced by Ethel's disguise, sent a message back to England – via the new medium of wireless telegraphy – that he had the suspects on board. Inspector Drew quickly boarded the SS *Laurentic*, a much faster ship, which overtook the *Montrose*, arriving in Montreal a day earlier. As the *Montrose* docked, Drew boarded the ship and arrested Crippen and Ethel, then took them back to London.

At his trial, Crippen protested his innocence and, wishing to protect her, refused to allow Ethel to stand as a defence witness on his behalf. The prosecution argued he had tried to poison Cora, then shot her in the head after this failed. Crippen was found guilty of murder and hanged on 23 November. His mistress was found not guilty of being an accessory after the fact. In October 2007, forensic scientist David Foran cast doubt on the conviction, claiming that mitochondrial DNA evidence showed the body parts found in Crippen's home to belong to someone other than Cora Crippen, adding another twist to this gruesome tale.

two of his victims. In 2004, DNA evidence was used against Derrick Todd Lee – the infamous Baton Rouge serial killer.

In Britain, too, DNA profiling has helped solve many crimes, including that of Ian Simms, convicted in 1989 of the murder of Helen McCourt, despite her body never being found. National tests on prisoners with mental disorders in 2003 led to 64 cold cases being solved – including a 1997 murder in London and a 1994 rape in South Yorkshire. In 2006, DNA evidence helped secure the conviction of Steve Wright for the murder of five prostitutes in Ipswich.

Despite the apparently compelling nature of the DNA evidence, the lengthy and controversial trial of the actor and former American football star O. J. Simpson (1994) ended with his acquittal.

Profiling can prove innocence as well as guilt. In 1993, Kirk Bloodsworth became the first American to be freed from death row after DNA tests exonerated him from the 1984 murder of nine-year-old Dawn Hamilton (DNA evidence later helping to identify the real killer, Kimberly Ruffner). In December 2000, Frank Lee Smith was likewise cleared of murder after 14 years on death row, while in 2003, DNA evidence revealed that two murders for which David Allen Jones had been convicted had in fact been carried out by the Los Angeles serial killer Chester Turner.

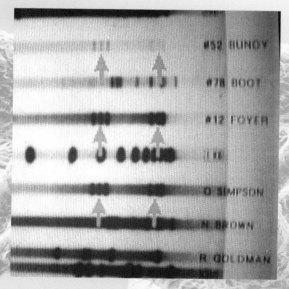

The DNA strand used as evidence in the 1994 O.J. Simpson murder trial in Los Angeles, which according to biochemist Robin Cotton linked Simpson to the murders of his ex-wife and Ronald Goldman. The black smudges, reflecting the banding patterns of Simpson's genetic material, highlighted by the arrows, show that blood taken from O.J. Simpson matches samples taken at the crime scene and the foyer of Simpson's residence.

Lenin was the gifted, ruthless, fanatical, yet pragmatic Marxist politician who created the blood-soaked Soviet experiment that was based from the very start on random killing and flint-hearted repression, and which led to the murders of many millions of innocent people. Lenin was long revered in communist propaganda and in naïve Western liberal circles as the kind-hearted and decent father of the Soviet peoples, but we now know that he relished the use of terror and bloodletting and was as frenziedly brutal as he was intelligent and cultured. He was, however, one of the political titans of the 20th century, and without his personal will there would have been no Bolshevik Revolution in 1917.

Vladimir Lenin
1870–1924

'One out of ten of those guilty of parasitism will be shot on the spot … We must spur on the energy of the terror … shoot and deport … launch merciless mass terror against kulaks, priests, and white guards …'

LENIN IN 1918

Unimpressive in person but exceptional in personality, Vladimir Ilych Ulyanov, known as Lenin, was small and stocky, prematurely bald, and had a bulging, intense forehead and piercing, slanted eyes. He was a genial man – his laughter was infectious – but his life was ruled by his fanatical dedication to Marxist revolution, to which he devoted his intelligence, pitiless pragmatism and aggressive political will.

Lenin was raised in a loving family, and was descended from nobility on both sides. His father was the inspector of schools in Simbirsk, while his mother was the daughter of a wealthy doctor and landowner; further back his antecedents included Jews, Swedes and Tartar Kalmyks (to whom he owed his slanting eyes). Lenin possessed the domineering confidence of a nobleman, and as a young man he had even sued peasants for damaging his estates. This helps to explain Lenin's contempt for old Russia: 'Russian idiots' was a favourite curse. When criticized for his noble birth, he replied: 'What about me? I am the scion of landed gentry . . . I still haven't forgotten the pleasant aspects of life on our estate . . . So go on, put me to death! Am I unworthy to be a revolutionary?' He was certainly never embarrassed about living off the income from his estates.

The rustic idyll on the family estate ended in 1887 when his elder brother Alexander was executed for conspiring against the tsar. This changed everything. Lenin qualified as a lawyer at Kazan University, where he read Chernychevsky and Nechaev, imbibing the discipline of Russian revolutionary terrorists even before he embraced Marx and became active in the Russian Socialist Workers' Party. After arrests and Siberian exile, Lenin moved to western Europe, living at various times in London,

Cracow and Zurich. In 1902 he wrote *What Is to Be Done?* which defined a new vanguard of professional and ruthless revolutionaries and led to the break-up of the party into the so-called majority faction – the Bolsheviks under Lenin – and the more moderate Menshevik minority.

'Trash', 'bastards', 'filth', 'prostitutes', 'Russian fools', 'cretins' and 'silly old maids' were just some of the insults Lenin heaped on his enemies. He had enormous contempt for his own liberal sympathizers, whom he called 'useful idiots', and mocked his own gentler comrades as 'tea-drinkers'. Revelling in the fight, he existed in an obsessional frenzy of political vibration, driven by an intense rage and a compulsion to dominate allies – and to smash opposition.

Lenin cared little for the arts or personal romance: his wife, the stern, bug-eyed Nadya Krupskaya, was more manager and amanuensis than lover, but he did engage in a passionate affair with the wealthy, liberated beauty Inessa Armand. Once in power, Lenin indulged in little flings with his secretaries – at least according to Stalin, who claimed Krupskaya complained about them to the Politburo. But politics was everything to Lenin.

During the 1905 Revolution, Lenin returned to Russia; but the Bolshevik uprising in Moscow was suppressed by Tsar Nicholas II and Lenin had to escape back into exile. Desperately short of money and always pursuing factional ideological feuds that split the party further, Lenin used bank robberies and violence to fund his small group. During these escapades, Stalin caught Lenin's eye and he consistently promoted him even when other comrades warned him of Stalin's violent propensities: 'That's exactly the sort of person I need!' he replied. By 1914 the Bolsheviks had almost been crushed by the tsarist secret police, and most were in exile or prison: as late as 1917 Lenin – who spent the war in Cracow, then Switzerland – was wondering if the Revolution would happen in his own lifetime.

But in February 1917 spontaneous riots brought down the tsar. Lenin rushed back to Petrograd (St Petersburg), invigorated the Bolsheviks into an energetic radicalism, and through his own personal will created a programme that promised peace and bread, and so popularized his party. Despite huge opposition from his own comrades, Lenin – backed by two gifted radicals, Trotsky and Stalin – forced the Bolsheviks to launch the October coup that seized power in Russia and changed history.

From the moment Lenin took power as premier – or chairman of the Council of People's Commissars – the new Soviet Republic was threatened on all sides by civil war and foreign intervention. Lenin made peace with Germany at Brest-Litovsk and introduced the New Economic Policy to encourage some un-Marxist free enterprise, but pursued victory in the Russian Civil War with War Communism, brutal repression and deliberate terror. 'A revolution without firing squads is meaningless,' he said. In 1918 he founded the Cheka, the Soviet secret police, and encouraged pitiless brutality. Between 280,000 and 300,000 people were murdered under his orders; this only came to light when the archives

Vladimir Ilyich Lenin makes a celebratory speech as head of the first Soviet government in Red Square on the first anniversary of the 1917 Russian Revolution.

were opened in 1991. 'We must . . . put down all resistance with such brutality that they will not forget it for several decades,' he wrote.

After Lenin himself was shot and almost killed in an assassination attempt in August 1918, the 'Red Terror' was intensified. His most energetic and talented protégés, Stalin and Trotsky, were also the most brutal. When the peasantry opposed his policies and millions perished in famines, Lenin said, 'Let the peasantry starve.' By 1920 the Soviet Revolution was safe, but Lenin himself was exhausted, and he never really recovered from the bullet wounds he had received in 1918. In 1922 he promoted Stalin to general secretary of the party, but when Stalin insulted other comrades and then Lenin's own wife, Lenin tried to remove him from his position. It was too late. Lenin was felled by a series of strokes, but managed to record a testament in which he attacked all his potential successors, including Trotsky and especially Stalin, whom he said was 'too rude' for high office. But his health collapsed and he died in 1924. He was embalmed, displayed in a mausoleum in Red Square, and worshipped like a Marxist saint.

In the Soviet Union, Leninism and Stalinism were one and same: a utopian totalitarian creed, founded on repression, bloodletting and the destruction of personal freedom. Thanks to Lenin, this ideology took the lives of over 100 million innocent people in the 20th century.

Lenin's Campaign Against the Kulaks

In 1918 Lenin initiated the 'Red Terror' against all those considered enemies of the people – such as the kulaks (wealthy peasants). The following order, issued in 1918, is typical:

Comrades! The insurrection of five kulak districts should be pitilessly suppressed.

The interests of the whole revolution require this because the last decisive battle with the kulaks is now under way everywhere.

An example must be demonstrated.

1. Hang (and make sure that the hanging takes place in full view of the people) no fewer than one hundred known kulaks, rich men, bloodsuckers.

2. Publish their names.

3. Seize all their grain from them.

4. Designate hostages in accordance with yesterday's telegram.

Do it in such a fashion that for hundreds of kilometres around the people might see, tremble, know, shout: they are strangling and will strangle to death the bloodsucking kulaks.

Telegraph receipt and implementation.

Yours, Lenin.

PS: Find some truly hard people.

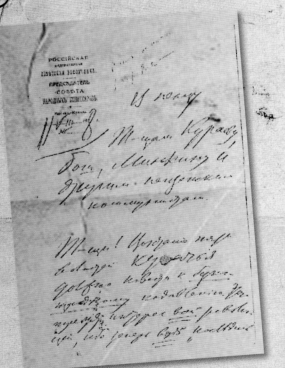

Lenin's infamous 'hanging order' of 11 August 1918, when he ordered the execution of 100 kulaks.

Dubbed *El Centauro del Norte* ('The Centaur of the North'), Pancho Villa has acquired a quasi-romantic reputation as a Mexican folk-hero that masks his true legacy. Villa's intelligence, charisma and military effectiveness made him a major player in the revolutionary politics of his day, but his violence, ambition and cold-blooded brutality mark him out as the archetype of the South American caudillo.

Pancho Villa 1878–1923

> 'It is better to die on your feet than to live on your knees!'
> — EMILIANO ZAPATA

Born as Doroteo Arango, somewhere near San Juan del Río, Durango, in 1878, Pancho Villa hailed from peasant stock. After working as a sharecropper in his late childhood, he moved to the city of Chihuahua when he was 16, hoping to make his fortune, but when a landowner from his village sexually assaulted his sister, he returned home immediately and killed her assailant in cold blood. With that one act, he consigned himself to a life of banditry and fled for the Sierra Madre mountains. For the next 17 years, he was to terrorize those living within or passing through his mountain fiefdom, cattle rustling, bank robbery and murder becoming his specialities.

Mexico at the time was ruled by the corrupt dictator, Porfirio Díaz. Much of the country's land was ruthlessly exploited by the wealthy owners of large estates (haciendas), leaving the bulk of the population to labour under political repression and grinding poverty. In 1910, the long-serving Díaz stood for 're-election' as president. Opposition to his rule, however, had crystallized around Francisco Madero, the 'apostle of democracy', supported by volunteers known as *antirreeleccionista* (anti re-electionists). When Díaz inevitably claimed victory, Madero proclaimed his 'Plan of San Luis Potosi', declaring the election fraudulent and calling for an armed uprising. The Mexican Revolution had begun. Villa threw in his lot with the revolution, capturing the towns of both Chihuahua and Ciudad Juárez for the Maderoists. Though he claimed a political

Regarded by some as a brutal, modern-day version of Robin Hood, Pancho Villa spent most of his life as a violent renegade and outlaw with a price of 100,000 pesos on his head.

'awakening', it is hard to tell whether he believed in the cause or simply sensed which way the wind was blowing, but the revolution proved to be a turning point in his life.

By 1911, Díaz had been swept from power and forced into exile. Hopes for the establishment of genuine democracy in Mexico, however, were dashed when, in 1913, President Madero was assassinated by loyalists to the old regime and Victoriano Huerta, the head of the Mexican armed forces, seized power in a bloody coup. Formerly allies in the Maderoist cause, Huerta and Villa were by now bitter enemies, Huerta having even conspired in Villa being sentenced to death for stealing and insubordination. Only Madero's personal intervention had prevented that sentence from being carried out.

Villa unsurprisingly committed himself to support the forces of Venustiano Carranza – leader of the opposition to Huerta – and secured a string of military victories, defeating Huerta's forces at Ciudad Juárez, Tierra Blanca, Chihuahua, Ojinaga, Torreón, Saltillo and and Zacatecas. These successes played a major part in bringing about Huerta's eventual downfall in July 1914, and made Villa a hero of the revolution. They came, however, at a cost. At Zacatecas, for instance, some 7000 people were killed and a further 5000 injured – many of them civilians. Concerns surfaced that Villa revelled unduly in the task of killing and was reluctant to accept any authority other than his own.

By 1915, Villa – once the darling of the revolution – had become an erratic renegade. He declared open revolt against Carranza and aligned himself ever more closely with the extremist fringe of the revolution around Emiliano Zapata, a leading figure in the struggle against President Díaz. In Carranza's chief general, Álvaro Obregón, though, Villa had met his military match. He was defeated in two battles at Celaya in 1915, Obregón's more modern techniques and weapons of war proving decisive.

Villa withdrew to Chihuahua and there instituted a reign of fear, imposing his own brand of law and recruiting new members (however reluctant) for his bandit brigades. Faced with growing economic problems, he ruthlessly requisitioned funds from the once loyal people of the region – a move that served only to impoverish them further. He even issued his own money, anyone who refused to accept the currency being shot for 'betraying the revolution'.

Hemmed in by government forces, and increasingly enraged by what he saw as American interference (President Woodrow Wilson had opted to back Carranza's government as the most likely way of establishing stable government in Mexico), Villa turned his attentions to the United States. A January 1916 raid on a train on the Mexico North Western Railway, near Santa Isabel, Chihuahua, killed 18 Americans. A cross-border assault on Columbus, New Mexico, followed in March, killing 10 soldiers and 8 civilians.

In response, President Wilson sent some 6000 troops into Mexico under General John 'Black Jack' Pershing, but this 'punitive expedition' to find Pancho Villa proved unsuccessful. Villa remained a fugitive until 1920, when he finally negotiated a 'peace deal' with Carranza's successor, President Adolfo de la Huerta. For three years afterwards he lived in semi-retirement on his estates in Chihuahua, before he was assassinated in 1923.

Many Mexicans today remember Villa with pride for the part he played in the revolution, and for standing up to the American superpower. Yet, this is to ignore the reality that Villa was a homicidal warlord for whom the revolution served as a convenient excuse to justify his crimes. At his death, Villa was reputed to have said, 'Don't let it end like this. Tell them I said something.'

ZAPATA

The life of Pancho Villa was intertwined with that of another famous Mexican revolutionary – Emiliano Zapata. Like Villa, Zapata gained a reputation as a populist who was prepared to use force to achieve his aims; and, again like Villa, he took the side of Madero in the struggle to overthrow the dictator, Porfirio Díaz.

When Madero's regime proved too conservative for Zapata, he refused to disband the force of guerrillas he had first assembled to take on Díaz. Instead, in 1911 he proclaimed the 'Plan de Ayala' and promised to carry forward the 'revolution'. The plan called for radical land reform in Mexico to improve the lot of the ordinary peasant. Zapata wanted to break down the estates by returning the land to Mexico's impoverished indigenous communities. The ethos of his programme was summed up in its rallying cry, 'Tierra y Libertad!' ('Land and Freedom!'), which came to define Zapata and his supporters.

After Madero had been deposed by General Huerta, Zapata took part in the struggle against the

Pancho Villa with fellow revolutionary Emiliano Zapata. Villa is sitting on the presidential throne in the Palacio Nacional.

new dictatorship. When Huerta was in turn ousted, to be replaced by the constitutionalist Carranza, history repeated itself. Zapata again found himself in opposition to the government, and once more resolved that the agrarian revolution he desired could only be secured by armed struggle. Lands were burned and opponents murdered by the rampaging 'Zapatistas' – now styling themselves the 'Liberation Army of the South'.

In response, Carranza had a sizeable bounty placed on the revolutionary's head and, following Pancho Villa's defeat, Zapata became increasingly isolated. In April 1919 he was assassinated. He remains an even more iconic figure than Villa in revolutionary circles around the world, especially in Mexico. In the 1990s, when indigenous Mexicans from the Chiapas province again turned to violence to protest against their living conditions, it was Zapata's name that they called on – with the new 'Zapatistas' claiming the ideological legacy of Emiliano and his followers.

Stalin was the Soviet dictator who defeated Hitlerite Germany in the Second World War, expanded the Russian empire to its greatest extent, industrialized the USSR and made it a nuclear superpower. During a reign of terror lasting thirty years, this monstrous mass-murderer was responsible for the annihilation of more than 25 million of his own innocent citizens, and confined 18 million to slave-labour camps.

Josef Stalin 1878–1953

> 'He sought to strike, not at the ideas of his opponent, but at his skull.'
>
> LEON TROTSKY, 1936

Josef Djugashvili was born in Gori, a small town in Georgia in the Caucasus, the son of an alcoholic cobbler called Beso and his clever, forceful wife, Keke. Poor, unsure of his real paternity, with a pockmarked face, webbed feet and one shorter arm, young Soso (as he was known) grew up to be a highly intelligent, super-sensitive, emotionally stunted child possessed of both an inferiority complex and an overweening arrogance. His mother managed to win him a place at the seminary in Tiflis, where he studied for the priesthood, learned Russian, studied the classics and published romantic poetry. But after his conversion to Marxism, he became a fanatical and pitiless revolutionary and joined Lenin's Bolsheviks. He was a born conspirator who dominated his comrades, undermined and betrayed his rivals, murdered suspected police spies, always pushing towards the extremes. He was repeatedly arrested but repeatedly escaped, returning from exile in Siberia for the 1905 Revolution. He became the leading financier of the Bolsheviks through bank robberies and extortion (see page 206).

His violent escapades having drawn the attention of Lenin, Stalin was elected to the party's central committee. He was arrested for the last time in 1912 and exiled to the Arctic Circle, where he spent most of the First World War. When the tsar was unexpectedly overthrown in March 1917, Stalin returned to Petrograd, where he was later joined by Lenin. After his seizure of power in the October Revolution, Lenin recognized that the brilliant, showy Leon Trotsky and the morose, ruthless Stalin were his two most competent henchmen, and promoted them to his ruling executive committee, the politburo. With the outbreak of the Civil War, Lenin maintained power by terror, deploying Stalin as a brutal troubleshooter. But Stalin proved to be unimpressive as a military leader compared with Trotsky, whom Stalin constantly tried to undermine.

In 1922 Lenin, keen to balance Trotsky's prestige, promoted Stalin to the post of party general secretary. Before long, however, Lenin became outraged by his protégé's arrogance and tried to sack him – but it was too late. After Lenin suffered a fatal stroke in 1924, Stalin allied himself with Lev Kamenev and Grigory Zinoviev against Trotsky, who was defeated by 1925, sent into exile in 1929 and assassinated by one of Stalin's hitmen in 1940. After Trotsky's exile, Stalin swung rightwards, allying himself with Nikolai Bukharin to defeat Kamenev and Zinoviev.

In 1929 Stalin was hailed as Lenin's successor, and thenceforth became the subject of a frenzied cult of personality. Jettisoning Bukharin, Stalin embarked on a ruthless push to industrialize the backward USSR and collectivize the peasantry. When the peasantry resisted, Stalin launched a quasi-war against the better-off peasants, known as 'kulaks', shooting many, exiling more, and continuing to sell grain abroad even as ten million were shot or died in a famine he himself had created. It was one of Stalin's greatest crimes.

In 1934, despite a triumphant party congress, there was a plot to replace Stalin with his young henchman, Sergei Kirov, who was later assassinated in Leningrad. Stalin may or may not have ordered the killing, but he certainly used it to launch the Great Terror to regain control and crush any dissent. With the aid of the NKVD secret police, Stalin subjected those he regarded as his leading political enemies to a series of show trials, extracting false confessions by torture. Zinoviev, Kamenev and Bukharin were all found 'guilty' of fabricated crimes and shot, as were two successive leaders of the NKVD, Yagoda and Yezhov. But the show trials were just the tip of the iceberg: in 1937–8 Stalin drew up secret orders to arrest and shoot thousands of 'enemies of the people' by city and regional quotas. The politburo and central committee were purged; 40,000 army officers were shot, including three of the five marshals. Even Stalin's closest friends were not immune: he signed actual death lists of 40,000 names. Soviet society was terrorized and poisoned. In those years approximately 1 million were shot, while many millions more were arrested, tortured and exiled to the labour camps of Siberia, where many died.

In 1939, faced with a resurgent Nazi Germany and distrusting the Western democracies, Stalin put aside his anti-Fascism and signed the Non-Aggression Pact with Hitler. Poland was partitioned between Germany and the USSR, and 28,000 Polish officers were murdered in the Katyn Forest on Stalin's orders. Stalin also seized and terrorized the Baltic States, and launched a disastrous war against Finland.

Stalin ignored constant warnings that Hitler was planning to attack the USSR. The invasion came in June 1941, and within days the Soviet armies were retreating. Stalin's inept interference in military matters led to colossal losses – some 6 million soldiers – in the first year of war. But by late 1942 he had finally learned to take advice, and his generals scored a decisive victory over the Germans at Stalingrad. This was the turning point in the war, and by the time Berlin fell to the Red Army in May 1945, the Soviets controlled all of eastern Europe – and were to maintain a steely grip on it for the next 45 years. Stalin was indifferent to the cost of victory: some 27 million Soviet citizens – both soldiers and civilians – perished during the war, during the course of which Stalin had ordered the deportation of entire peoples to Siberia, including 1 million Chechens, of whom half died in the process.

Generalissimo Stalin as world arbiter and conqueror of Berlin at the Potsdam Conference, July–August 1945.

Stalin's last years were spent in glorious, paranoid isolation. Soon after the end of the war he relaunched his reign of terror. In 1949 two of his own chosen heirs were shot in the Leningrad case, along with many others. In 1952, apparently convinced that all Jews in the USSR were in alliance with America, he planned to execute his veteran comrades, implicating them in a fabricated 'Doctors' Plot', alleging that Jewish doctors were conspiring to assassinate the old Soviet leadership. Stalin died after a stroke in March 1953.

A master of brutal repression, subtle conspiracy and political manipulation, this cobbler's son became both the supreme pontiff of international Marxism and the most successful Russian tsar in history. Stalin and the Bolsheviks, along with his great foes Hitler and the Nazis, brought more misery and tragedy to more people than anyone else in history.

Tiny in stature, with inscrutable features, honey-coloured eyes that turned yellow in anger, Stalin was gifted but joyless, paranoid to the point of insanity, utterly cynical and ruthless, yet a fanatical Marxist. A terrible husband and father who poisoned every love relationship in his life, he believed that human life was always expendable and physical annihilation was the essential tool of politics. 'One death,' he is meant to have said with characteristic gallows humour, 'is a tragedy; a million is a statistic.' Stalin had no illusions about his brutality: 'The advantage of the Soviet model,' he said, 'is that it solves problems quickly – by shedding blood.'

One of history's most pitiless monsters, he nonetheless remains a hero to many: a textbook presented by President Vladimir Putin himself in 2008 hailed him as 'the most successful Russian leader of the 20th century'.

BANDIT AND LOTHARIO

After the crushing of the 1905 Revolution, Stalin created his own outfit of gangsters and hitmen who killed police agents and raised cash for Lenin in a series of outrageous, bloody bank robberies, protection rackets, train heists and piratical hold-ups on the Black Sea and the Caspian. Stalin's career as an outlaw culminated in the Tiflis bank robbery in June 1907, in which his gangsters killed 50 people and got away with 300,000 roubles. Stalin then moved his outfit to oil-rich Baku, always on the run, always spreading violence and fear.

At this time Stalin was married to Kato Svanidze, with whom he had a son, Yakov, but Kato died in 1907. Contemptuous of a settled existence, he enjoyed affairs with many women, became engaged to many of them, fathered illegitimate children – and abandoned all of them heartlessly. He married again in 1918, but failed to make his new wife, Nadya Alliluyeva, any happier than his other women. She committed suicide in 1932, leaving Stalin two legitimate children, Vasiliy and Svetlana.

Stalin in his twenties, when he was living the life of a Marxist bandit, revolutionary and serial womanizer.

Mehmed Talat Pasha was one of the 'Young Turks', the nationalistic reformers who seized power in the Ottoman empire in 1908, but as one of the 'Three Pashas' who dominated the Turkish government he was the key architect of the Armenian massacres perpetrated between 1915 and 1916, which cost the lives of over 1 million people.

Talat Pasha 1881–1922
and the Armenian massacres

'What on earth do you want? The question is settled. There are no more Armenians.'

TALAT PASHA RESPONDING TO QUESTIONING ABOUT THE ARMENIANS FROM THE GERMAN AMBASSADOR, 1918

Talat was a civil servant in the post office until he was sacked for his membership of the Young Turks – officially the Committee of Union and Progress (CUP). After the Young Turk revolution of 1908, and the restoration of parliament, Talat was elected a deputy for Edirne, and subsequently became minister for interior affairs. After the assassination of prime minister Mahmud Sevket Pasha in July 1913, Talat, working alongside Enver Pasha and Djemal Pasha, became one of the 'Three Pashas', the junta of triumvirs who dominated the Ottoman government until the end of the First World War, leading it into a disastrous war. As interior minister, Talat organized the deportation and killings of Armenian people.

At the beginning of the 19th century, the predominantly Christian Armenians had still been referred to as the Millet-i Sadika – the 'loyal community'. However, Russian expansion into the Caucasus helped stimulate Armenian nationalism. The Ottoman empire contained far fewer Christians after the 1878 Congress of Berlin, exposing the Armenians to Muslim resentment as outsiders and traitors; ordinary Turks

Mehmed Talat Pasha, the Turkish politician held responsible for the Armenian killings, photographed around 1915. Pasha was assassinated in 1921 by an Armenian student seeking revenge for the massacre.

envied Armenian mercantile wealth. Many Turks came to see the rise of Armenian nationalism as a threat to the very existence of the Ottoman state.

Already, in the final years of the 19th century, Sultan Abdul Hamid II and others had acquiesced in a series of pogroms against Armenians: possibly hundreds of thousands died in 1895–6, while the Adana massacre of 1909 cost an estimated 30,000 lives.

After the Ottoman empire entered the First World War in 1914 on the side of the Central Powers, it attempted to retake territories lost to Russia during the Russo-Turkish War of 1877–8. The endeavour was to end in total failure. However, Russia armed Armenian insurgents. When Russian/Armenian forces took Van in mid-May 1915, setting up an Armenian mini-state, the Three Pashas immediately laid the blame at the door of the supposedly 'disloyal' Armenians. Talat prepared the state's revenge.

On 24 April 1915, the security forces rounded up over 250 Armenian intellectuals and community leaders in Istanbul, deported them to the east and then murdered them. The ground had been prepared, however, since the beginning of the year with the disarming of Armenians serving within the Ottoman military. After the initial deportations in April, the programme was soon extended to the entire Armenian community. Men, women and children were sent on forced marches – without food or water – to the provinces of Syria and Mesopotamia. On 27 May, the Three Pashas passed the Deportation Law, confirmed by act of parliament. The Special Organization, a paramilitary security force, was allegedly set up under Enver Pasha and Talat to carry out deportations and massacres.

During the deportations, men were routinely separated from the rest of the population and executed. Women and children were obliged to march on, and subjected to intermittent beatings and massacres. Those who survived the journey were herded into concentration camps. Conditions there were appalling. Many prisoners were tortured, made the subject of gruesome medical experiments or slaughtered. Many more died from hunger and thirst. Some of the worst excesses in the camps were recorded by the American ambassador, Henry Morgenthau, who reported how the guards would 'apply red-hot irons to his [an Armenian's] breast, tear off his flesh with red-hot pincers, and then pour boiled butter into the wounds. In some cases the gendarmes would nail hands and feet to pieces of wood – evidently in imitation of the Crucifixion, and then, while the sufferer writhed in agony, they would cry: "Now let your Christ come and help you!"'

Talat Pasha was reported to have told an official at the German embassy in 1915 that the Ottoman government was 'taking advantage of the war in order to thoroughly liquidate its internal enemies, the indigenous Christians . . . without being disturbed by foreign intervention'. Between 1 and 1.5 million Armenians, out of a population of just under 2.5 million, perished in this period, whether this was an officially ordered genocide or a disorderly series of massacres.

Talat then focused more of his attention on the deteriorating military position, and in 1917 was appointed grand vizier of the Sublime Porte (i.e. Ottoman prime minister). But he failed to stem the tide of military defeats, and resigned in October 1918, fleeing Turkey aboard a German submarine. In 1919, the world's first war crimes trials were held under Allied auspices. The CUP leadership were found guilty and Talat, as the mastermind of the massacres, was sentenced to death. The Turks appealed to Germany for his extradition, but before this could happen Talat was murdered in Berlin in March 1921. His assassin was a survivor of the massacres who had seen his sisters raped and murdered by Turkish troops.

The persecution of the Armenians that Talat initiated provided the inspiration that others would draw on later in the century. Thus, as he contemplated his slaughter of the Jews, Hitler remarked, 'Who, after all, speaks today of the annihilation of the Armenians?' Even to this day, to mention the Armenian massacres in Turkey is interpreted as the crime of 'insulting Turkishness', and is punishable by imprisonment.

GENOCIDE

The 20th century saw the emergence of two chilling terms: genocide and democide. The first – a combination of the Greek *genos* ('race') and Latin *caedere* ('to kill') – was coined by the US lawyer Raphael Lemkin in 1944, writing about the Holocaust. Defined as an attempt to destroy, wholly or in part, any national, ethnic, racial or religious group, it was subsequently formalized as a crime by the United Nations in 1948. The more embracing term 'democide' was invented in 1992 by US professor R. J. Rummel to cover government-sanctioned murder of people or individuals, genocide or otherwise.

Besides the Holocaust, the 20th century witnessed other well-documented democides, including the Armenian massacre of 1915, Stalin's 1932–3 forced famine in the Ukraine, Kazakhstan and southern Russia, the Japanese 'Rape of Nanking' (1937), Pol Pot's killing fields in Cambodia and 'ethnic cleansing' in Bosnia during the 1992–5 Balkan conflict and the massacres of 300,000 people by the Sudanese government in Darfur since 2003. Often forgotten, but equally horrific, was the mass killing that took place in Rwanda in 1994, when over 800,000 Tutsis were murdered.

The Tutsis – though comprising just 10 per cent of Rwanda's population – had once subjugated the Hutu majority, but independence from Belgium in 1962 saw the Hutus gain power and Tutsis flee en masse. They returned, however, in 1990 with a rebel army – the Rwandan Patriotic Front – forcing Hutu president Juvénal Habyarimana to agree to shared power, but the ceasefire was fragile, extremist Hutus of the National Republican Movement for Democracy and Deve'

and Coalition for the Defence of the Republic already drawing up death-lists.

A UN peacekeeping force was despatched to the area after neighbouring Burundi's Hutu president was assassinated in 1993, his successor, Cyprien Ntaryamira, subsequently joining Habyarimana in negotiations with Tutsi leaders, but when both men were killed on 6 April – their plane shot down as they returned from talks – the carnage began. The UN force, numbering just 2500, could do little to stop the murderous Interahamwe and Impuzamugambi militias of the Hutu, and all bar 200 were evacuated following the murder of 10 Belgian soldiers. Tutsis were less fortunate, up to 10,000 being killed each day, clubbed, shot or hacked to death with machetes. Massacres – encouraged by the media and state propaganda – occurred even in churches and hospitals, 1200 being slaughtered as they sheltered in a church in Musha. Eventually the UN Security Council – which to sidestep intervention had studiously avoided using the term genocide – agreed to send a 5000-strong force, though this arrived too late to stop the killing, it being left to the Rwandan Patriotic Front finally to halt the genocide in July. More than one-tenth of the population had been killed.

A Tutsi survivor of the genocide in Rwanda lies in his bed at Gahini hospital. Hutu militias seeking to rid Rwanda of Tutsis brutally murdered 800,000 people. between early April and mid-July 1994.

Benito Mussolini, the dictator of Italy from 1922 to 1943, was the father of fascism – a domineering autocrat whose totalitarian politics paved the way for Nazism. Ruthlessly suppressing any form of dissent at home, he was also an avaricious colonialist with Roman imperial delusions, directly responsible for the death of over 30,000 Ethiopians in his infamous Abyssinian campaign as well as complicit, through his alliance with Adolf Hitler, in the atrocities of Nazi Germany.

Benito Mussolini
1883–1945

'. . . the Fascist conception of the State is all embracing; outside of it no human or spiritual values can exist, much less have value.'

MUSSOLINI, THE DOCTRINE OF FASCISM, 1932

Benito Amilcare Andrea Mussolini was born on 29 July 1883 in Predappio, central northern Italy. His father was a blacksmith and his mother a schoolteacher, a profession he took up but then swiftly abandoned. After an unsuccessful year trying to find employment in Switzerland in 1902 – during which he was imprisoned for vagrancy – he was expelled and sent back to Italy for military service.

In his twenties, following in the footsteps of his father, Mussolini was a committed socialist, editing a newspaper called *La Lotta di Classe* (*The Class Struggle*) before, in 1910, becoming secretary of the local Socialist Party in Forli, for which he edited the paper *Avanti!* (*Forward!*). He also wrote an unsuccessful novel called *The Cardinal's Mistress*. Increasingly known to the authorities for inciting disorder, he was imprisoned in 1911 for producing pacifist propaganda after Italy declared war on Turkey. Unsurprisingly, he initially opposed Italy's entry into the First World War, but – perhaps believing a major conflict would precipitate the overthrow of capitalism – he changed his mind, a decision that saw him expelled from the Socialist Party. He swiftly became captivated by militarism, founding a new paper, *Il Popolo d'Italia*, as well as the pro-war group Fasci d'Azione Rivoluzionaria, although his own military service was cut short in 1917 following injuries sustained after a grenade explosion in training.

Mussolini was now a confirmed anti-socialist, convinced that only authoritarian government could overcome the economic and social problems endemic in post-war Italy, as violent street gangs (including his own Fascisti) battled for supremacy. To describe his decisive, personality-driven politics, he coined the term 'fascismo' – from the Italian word *fascio*, meaning 'union', and the Latin *fasces*, the ancient Roman symbol of a bundle of rods tied around an axe, denoting strength through unity. In March 1919, the first fascist movement in Europe crystallized under his leadership to form the Fasci di Combattimento. His black-shirted supporters, in stark contrast to the flailing liberal governments of the period, successfully broke up industrial strikes and dispersed socialists from the streets. Though Mussolini was defeated in the 1919 elections, he was elected to parliament in 1921, along with 34 other fascists, forming the National Fascist Party later that year. In October 1922, after hostility between left- and right-wing groups had escalated into near anarchy, Mussolini – with thousands of his Blackshirts – staged the so-called 'March on Rome' (in fact he caught the train) but he presented himself as the only man who could restore order. In desperation, King Victor Emmanuel III fatefully asked him to form a government.

The new regime was built on fear. On 10 June 1924, Giacomo Matteotti, a leading Socialist Party deputy, was kidnapped and murdered by Mussolini's supporters after criticizing that year's elections, which saw fascists take 64 per cent of the vote. By 1926, Mussolini (calling himself Il Duce – the leader – and initially supported by the liberals) had dismantled parliamentary democracy and stamped his personal authority on every aspect of government, introducing strict censorship and a slick propaganda machine in which newspaper editors were personally handpicked. Two years later, when he placed executive power in the hands of the Fascist Grand Council, the country had effectively become a one-party police state.

In 1935, seeking to realize his dreams of Mediterranean domination and a North African empire, Mussolini ordered the invasion of Ethiopia, his use there of mustard gas, followed two years later by the vicious suppression of a rebellion against Italian rule, leading the League of Nations to impose sanctions on Italy. Increasingly isolated, he left the League and allied himself with Hitler in 1937 – the same year in which he granted asylum and support to the brutal Croatian fascist Ante Pavelić – emulating the Führer in pushing through a raft of anti-Semitic laws. It soon became clear, however, that Mussolini was the minor partner in the relationship, Hitler failing to consult him on almost all military decisions.

After Hitler invaded Czechoslovakia in March 1939, putting paid to hopes of peace sparked by the Munich Agreement of the previous year, Mussolini ordered the invasion of neighbouring Albania, his troops brushing aside the tiny Albanian army of King Zog. In May, Hitler and Mussolini declared a Pact of Steel, pledging to support the other in the event of war – a move that sent shudders of fear across Europe.

Italy did not enter the Second World War until the fall of France in June 1940, when it looked like Germany was on course for a quick victory, but the Italian war – beginning with a botched assault on Greece in October, then humiliating routs in North Africa – was an unmitigated disaster. For all the puffed-up militarism of his regime, Mussolini's army was disastrously unprepared for a war on this scale, haemorrhaging troops in the Balkans and Africa.

Following the Anglo-American arrival on the shores of Sicily in June 1943, Mussolini's fascist followers abandoned him and had him arrested, only for German commandos to rescue him from imprisonment and place him at the head of a puppet protectorate in the north of Italy. On 27 April 1945, as the Allies closed in, Mussolini – disguised as a German soldier – was captured by Italian partisans at the village of Dongo, near Lake Como. He was shot the following day, along with his mistress. Their bodies were taken to Milan and hung upside down from meathooks in Piazza Loreto.

Benito Mussolini, bare-chested, speaks from the platform of a threshing machine in the newly built town of Aprilia in the Pontine Marshes, 1938.

THE ABYSSINIAN CAMPAIGN

In October 1935, Mussolini invaded Abyssinia (modern-day Ethiopia), using air power and chemical weapons (mustard gas) in a barbaric campaign that lasted seven months and involved the systematic murder of captured prisoners, either at public gallows or thrown from aircraft mid-flight. The campaign resulted in the annexation of Ethiopia into Italian East Africa, along with Eritrea and Somaliland.

Mussolini had dreams of empire but the campaign was also to avenge Italy's humiliation of March 1896, when Ethiopia had defeated an Italian army at Adowa. The 1935 invasion – for which the Italians used a border dispute as a specious pretext – pitted Italian tanks, artillery and aircraft against Emperor Haile Selassie's ill-equipped and poorly trained army.

Making steady progress towards the Ethiopian capital, the Italians looted the Obelisk of Axum, an ancient monument, and firebombed the city of Harar, eventually taking the capital Addis Ababa on 5 May 1936, forcing Haile Selassie to flee the country. Mussolini's victorious commander Marshal Badoglio was absurdly named the Duke of Addis Ababa. Along the way, in a flagrant violation of the Geneva Protocol of 1925, they dropped between 300 and 500 tonnes of mustard gas, even gassing the ambulances of the Red Cross.

Meanwhile, from the safety of Rome, Mussolini ordered that 'all rebel prisoners must be killed', instructing his troops to 'systematically conduct a politics of terror and extermination of the rebels and the complicit population'. In February 1936, after a failed assassination attempt on the colonial governor, Italian troops went on the rampage for three days.

The Italian military establishment had warned Mussolini that a challenge to British and French influence in Africa and the Middle East might provoke Britain into a war that 'would reduce us to Balkan level', but Britain – under Neville Chamberlain – and France were pursuing a policy of appeasement in this period, and Mussolini correctly calculated they would not act decisively, which encouraged Hitler. However, Italy's Ethiopian empire was short-lived, liberated by Britain in 1941. Haile Selassie reigned until 1974 – and it was Badoglio who replaced Mussolini in 1943 and made peace with the Allies.

Ethiopians in the captured Tigray province pay their respects, Italian fashion, to a huge likeness of the 'Great White Father'.

General Hideki Tojo, nicknamed 'the Razor', was prime minister of Japan during much of the Second World War, the architect of its imperial aggressions, and the force behind its appalling policy of aggrandizement and brutality that cost the lives of millions and destroyed his own country. Tojo, the son of a general, embarked on a military career at a young age, serving as an infantry officer, a military attaché and an instructor at the military staff college. By 1933 he was a major general. Prior to this Tojo had become a member of a hard-right militaristic group that expounded fanatical ultra-nationalism. However, during the attempted coup by ultra-nationalists on 26 February 1936 Tojo remained loyal to Emperor Hirohito and assisted in its suppression.

Hideki Tojo
1884–1948

'The Greater East Asian War was justified and righteous.'
HIDEKI TOJO, AFTER HIS FAILED SUICIDE BID IN SEPTEMBER 1945

Tojo's loyalty was rewarded in 1937 when he was named chief of staff of the Kwantung Army in Manchuria. In this position he played an important role in launching the Second Sino-Japanese War – an eight-year conflict that would leave millions dead as the Japanese military ignored both human decency and the laws of war in pursuit of imperial conquest in China. Non-combatants – men, women and children – were deliberately targeted, resulting in such atrocities as the so-called 'Rape of Nanking', in which, between December 1937 and March 1938, Japanese troops butchered between 250,000 and 350,000 Chinese civilians.

As the war in China progressed, the Japanese army tightened its control over the civilian government, and Tojo became more deeply immersed in politics. In May 1938

General and Prime Minister Hideki Tojo, pictured here in full military regalia in 1942, was one of the principal architects of Japanese aggression during the Second World War.

he was appointed deputy minister of war in the government of Prince Fumimaro Konoe. In that role he was one of the more vocal advocates of a pact with Nazi Germany and Fascist Italy, and also pushed for a preventive strike against the Soviet Union.

In July 1940 Tojo became minister of war, and proceeded to oversee Japan's formal entry into the Axis alliance with Germany and Italy. By July 1941 Tojo had convinced Vichy France to endorse Japanese occupation of several key bases in Indo-China – a move that paved the way for US sanctions against Japan and increased tensions between the two countries. When Fumimaro Konoe was finally pushed into retirement in October 1941, Tojo, while holding on to his portfolio as minister of war, stepped up to replace him as prime minister. He immediately declared his commitment to the creation of a 'New Order in Asia'. Initially, he supported the efforts of his diplomats to bring this about through agreement with the United States. But as it became clear that no deal was possible with the USA on the terms desired, he authorized the attack on the American naval base at Pearl Harbor on 7 December 1941 that unleashed the war in the Pacific.

Victorious Japan overran Singapore, Malaysia, much of China, the Philippines, Indonesia and a vast swathe of the Pacific, pushing towards India through Burma, but the US navy destroyed the Japanese fleet at the Battle of Midway in June 1942 and thereafter gradually retook the Pacific under General MacArthur. Tojo assumed almost dictatorial powers, but in the aftermath of the American capture of the Marianas in July 1944 he resigned.

Tojo bore responsibility for the Japanese conduct of the war, which was almost as barbaric as that of the Nazis in Europe. Recent research has shown that Emperor Hirohito was not the pawn of the militarists but enthusiastically supported and directed them. Hirohito must share some of the responsibility shouldered by Tojo for Japan's war crimes. During the Sook Ching massacre of February–March 1942, for instance, up to 50,000 ethnic Chinese were systematically executed by Japanese forces in Singapore. At the same time, the Japanese embarked on the 'Three Alls' policy in China – by which Japanese troops were ordered to 'Kill all, burn all and loot all' in order to pacify the country, resulting in the killing of 2.7 million civilians. Even after Tojo had stepped down, the barbaric rules that he had helped create, in which human life was deemed valueless, endured – resulting in such atrocities as the Manila massacre of February 1945, in which 100,000 Filipino civilians were slaughtered.

Alongside the killing, the Japanese carried out hideous medical experiments on captured prisoners and subject populations. Biological and chemical weapons were tested on selected victims; others were operated on without anaesthetic, or exposed to the elements to see how their bodies reacted. International conventions on the treatment of prisoners of war were disregarded, and POWs were forced to work in appalling conditions, deprived of food and medicine, and tortured and executed without restraint.

Japan resisted defeat with brutality and suicidal determination. As American forces approached Japan itself and Soviet troops attacked Japanese Manchuria, US nuclear bombs were dropped on Hiroshima and Nagasaki, bringing surrender.

To this day, the character and scale of what took place on the authority of Hideki Tojo remains difficult to comprehend. In the wake of Japan's unconditional surrender in August 1945 Tojo tried to commit suicide. However, in April 1946, he was placed on trial for war crimes. He was found guilty, and hanged on 23 December 1948.

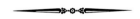

THE BATAAN DEATH MARCH

After a three-month struggle for the Bataan Peninsula in the Philippines, some 75,000 Allied troops (comprising around 64,000 American and 11,000 Filipino troops) formally surrendered to Japanese forces on 9 April 1942. They were then forced to undertake a march to a prison camp 60 miles away. On the journey, many were executed – stopping without permission was taken as a sign of insubordination and met with instant retribution. Many more died from the conditions they endured. Here is the testimony of one POW, Lester Tenney, who experienced the 'Death March' and lived to tell the tale:

The Japanese soldiers arrived in our area at 6:00 a.m. on April 10, 1942, and after a few minutes of hollering and seeking cigarettes, they herded us together and forced us to walk to the main road on Bataan and we took with us only those possessions we had on our bodies at that time. Many had no canteen and no head covering. So we marched for the first four days without food or water . . . We walked from sun up to sun down. No lunch break, no dinner, and sleeping was in a large warehouse that could easily hold 500 men but was crowded with 1200 men who had little if any space to lay down. And when you had to remove your body waste you were forced to do it on the floor where you slept . . . I saw with my own eyes a POW being killed with a bayonet into his back because he stopped at a free flowing artesian well for a cup of water. Killed for a drink of water. And what about the Caribou wallows that lined every road in the Philippines where the animals sat during the hot days. The water in those wallows was filthy, and contained among other things, animal dung. But when you are thirsty and without water for days on end, a desire for water takes over your sense of right and wrong and you leap from the line of marchers and push the scum on top of the water away so you could get a drink of this so-called water. Dysentery was the end result, and death followed closely behind.

After the war, the Japanese commander in charge of the march, Lieutenant-General Masaharu Homma, was executed for war crimes.

The strain shows on the faces of US POWs Samuel Stenzler, Frank Spear and James McDonald Gallagher, Bataan, April 1942.

In 1920, Baron Roman Ungern von Sternberg, a sadistic, mystical Russian warlord obsessed with Genghis Khan, Buddhism and anti-Semitism, conquered Mongolia with a ramshackle army of Russian and Mongol cavalry. The crazy reign of this psychotic Mongolian–Baltic Colonel Kurtz – 'the Bloody Baron' – is one of the most grotesque stories of modern times and personifies the murderous tragedy of the Russian Civil War in which millions perished.

Baron Ungern von Sternberg 1886–1921
and the Russian Civil War

Born in the Austrian city of Graz, Ungern was a Baltic nobleman of German descent, raised in Tallinn, capital of Estonia, then part of the Russian empire. He joined the Russian army, serving in the disastrous Russo-Japanese War and earning demotions for thuggery. Aristocratic connections repeatedly saved him. His service in the Far East sparked his fascination with Buddhism, albeit of a kind far removed from the trendy peacenik version of film stars today; it was already linked to the anti-Semitism that would attract the then Dalai Lama to Nazi racial theories.

In the First World War Ungern rose to cavalry general, and when the Bolsheviks seized power he joined the Whites in the Far East and fought under another fascinating psychopath, the Cossack *Ataman* (chief) Semenov, backed by Japan. He was given command of a division of Asian cavalry within Semenov's self-declared 'Mongol-Buryats Republic'. Though resolutely anti-Bolshevik, the two men enjoyed a fractious relationship with the other White armies opposed to the Reds, defying the authority of Admiral Kolchak, Supreme Ruler of the Whites, and operating independently.

Ungern governed a small town, Dauria, where he presided over a hellish crew of bloodthirsty torturers who killed any Bolsheviks or Jews. Turning against Semenov, he created a private army of Buryats, Tartars, Cossacks and Tsarist officers that resembled a medieval host. Ungern personifies the tragic brutality of the Russian Civil War (1918–21), in which Communist commissars, savage White warlords, generals, anarchists, nationalists, Cossacks and cut-throat anti-Semites managed to kill (by massacre or starvation) 10–20 million people.

Ungern was obsessed with his role in history: to restore monarchy under Nicholas II's brother, Grand Duke Michael (actually already killed by Bolsheviks), in Russia and restore Genghis Khan's glory and the rule of the living god-king, the perverted Bogd Khan, in Mongolia. In a savagely inept campaign, Ungern managed to expel Chinese troops, take the Mongolian capital Urga (now Ulan Bator), and restore the Bogd Khan with himself as dictator (aided by Tibetan troops lent by the Dalai Lama).

His reign was a surreal fiesta of tyranny, torture and murder. Unfortunate victims – whether Communist, Jewish or merely the well-off – suffered frenzied beatings ('Did you know men can still walk when flesh and bone is separated?'), beheading, burning alive, dismemberment and disembowelment,

exposure naked on ice, or being torn apart by wild animals. Some were dragged by a noose behind moving cars, hunted through streets by Cossacks, forced naked up trees until they fell out and were shot, or tied between bent-back branches, which when released would rip their bodies apart.

Ungern had long adhered to a quasi-religious mysticism that for many – with the Revolution and the Civil War – took on a millenarian bent, anticipating a coming apocalypse, the collapse of society and the creation of a 'new world order'. Ungern came to see himself as the reincarnation of Genghis Khan. He hated Jews, whom he killed wherever possible, claiming 'the Jews are not protected by any law . . . neither men nor women nor their seed should remain'. Even women and children were not spared.

In June 1921, Ungern's armies were defeated by the Bolsheviks. He himself was seriously wounded, and, as he attempted to flee, his surviving troops mutinied and attempted to kill him. They failed, but in August handed him over to the Bolsheviks. The 'Bloody Baron' was transported back to Russia in a cage, given a public show trial in the city of Novosibirsk, and executed by firing squad on 15 September 1921.

The sadistic and demented anti-Bolshevik warlord Roman Ungern von Sternberg.

Adolf Hitler is the embodiment of the historical monster, the personification of evil and the organizer of the greatest crimes of mass-murder ever committed, responsible for a world war, in which more than 70 million died, including 6 million in the Holocaust. No other name has earned such opprobrium or come to typify the depths to which humanity can sink. Amidst the horrors of history, the crimes of the Nazi Führer continue to occupy a unique place.

Adolf Hitler 1889–1945

'If one day the German nation is no longer sufficiently strong or sufficiently ready for sacrifice to stake its blood for its existence, then let it perish and be annihilated by some other stronger power . . .'
ADOLF HITLER, 27 NOVEMBER 1941

Born in Braunau am Inn in Austria, Hitler left school at 16 without any qualifications. He suffered disappointment when his application to study to be an artist in Vienna was twice rejected. He struggled to survive in Vienna on the strength of his painting, imbibing nationalism and anti-Semitism.

In 1913 Hitler moved to Munich, and in August 1914 joined the German army, subsequently fighting on the Western Front and reaching the rank of corporal. When in November 1918 the German government agreed to an armistice, Hitler – and many other nationalistic Germans – believed that the undefeated German army had been 'stabbed in the back'. He was appalled by the Treaty of Versailles, under which Germany lost much territory and most of its armed forces.

After the war, Hitler joined the German Workers' Party (DAP), impressed by its fusion of nationalism, anti-Semitism and anti-Bolshevism. Before long he won a reputation as a rabble-rousing orator, and in 1921 he became leader of the National Socialist German Workers' Party (NSDAP) – the Nazi Party, evolving a cult of power worship, cleansing violence and wanton killing, racial superiority, eugenics and brutal leadership. He created a paramilitary wing, the SA (Sturmabteilung, or 'Storm Division'), headed by Ernst Röhm.

Inspired by Mussolini's example in Italy, Hitler resolved to seize power, and in November 1923 in Munich launched an attempted putsch against the democratic Weimar Republic. This failed and he was arrested and sentenced to five years in prison – but served only a few months, during which period he wrote Mein Kampf ('My Struggle'), which exuded rampant anti-Semitism, anti-communism and militant nationalism. He also changed tactics, deciding to seek power through the ballot box – and then to replace democracy with an autocratic state.

Hitler's opportunity came with the arrival of the Great Depression. In subsequent elections, as the economy deteriorated, the Nazi Party increased its vote, becoming the largest party in the Reichstag (German parliament) in July 1932, a position confirmed by elections in November. On 30 January 1933 Hitler was sworn in as chancellor.

After the burning down of the Reichstag in February 1933, Hitler suspended civil liberties and passed an 'Enabling Act', which allowed him to rule as dictator. Opposition was crushed. Hitler even turned the repression inwards: the 'Night of the Long Knives' in June 1934 saw the murder of Röhm and the SA leadership by the SS (Schutzstaffel or 'Protection Squad'). Two months later Hitler, backed by henchmen such as Hermann Goering and Joseph

Adolf Hitler was chancellor of Germany from 1933 to 1945. His belligerent re-armament programme and his territorially aggressive policies led to worldwide conflict on an unprecedented scale.

Goebbels, achieved absolute civil and military power when he became Führer ('leader') and head of state.

The Nazis initiated an economic recovery, reducing unemployment and introducing ambitious new schemes such as the building of the brand-new autobahn (motorway) network. Many of Hitler's erstwhile opponents were prepared to give him the benefit of the doubt. Yet the economic 'miracle' was largely achieved via a huge rearmament drive, in violation of the Treaty of Versailles – the first phase in Hitler's broader determination to launch a deliberately barbaric European and racial war.

In March 1936 Hitler reoccupied the demilitarized zone in the Rhineland. He carefully noted the response of the international community – nothing. This encouraged him. In March 1938 he annexed Austria; in September he secured the German-speaking Sudeten area of Czechoslovakia; and in March 1939 he occupied the remainder of Czechoslovakia. In each instance, he experienced little resistance from the other European powers. He had fulfilled his core pledge: Versailles had been reduced to nothing more than a 'scrap of paper'.

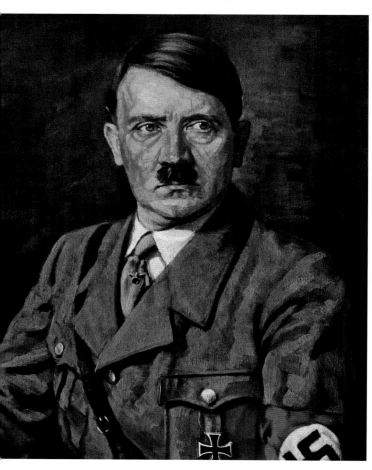

Adolf Hitler in party uniform with swastika armband. This official portrait dates from 1933, when the National Socialist party seized power in Germany.

Hitler signed the Molotov–Ribbentrop Pact with the Soviet dictator Josef Stalin which partitioned eastern Europe between these two brutal tyrants. In September 1939 Hitler conquered Poland, a move that triggered British and French declarations of war. But in the spring of 1940 the German armies turned west, conquering Norway, Denmark, the Low Countries and France in a lightning campaign. In 1941 both Yugoslavia and Greece fell, and only Britain remained undefeated. Hitler now dominated his barbaric continental empire and appeared impregnable.

In June 1941, Hitler launched a surprise attack on Stalinist Russia in Operation Barbarossa, the largest and most brutal conflict in human history in which 26 million Soviets alone died. He moved east to command his greatest enterprise from military headquarters in eastern Poland (the 'Wolf's Lair'). German forces won a series of astonishing victories at the start of the Barbarossa campaign, almost taking Moscow, the Soviet capital, and capturing some 6 million prisoners.

Meanwhile another even more horrific project was gathering steam within Nazi-occupied Europe. *Mein Kampf* had spoken darkly of Hitler's intentions towards the Jews, and the Nuremberg Laws of 1935–6, which deprived Jews of their civil rights in Germany, had hinted at worse to come. As the war clouds gathered towards the end of the decade there were more ominous signs: Kristallnacht (the 'Night of Broken Glass') in

November 1938 had brought a wave of attacks on Jewish homes and properties across Germany.

Hitler was initially content to enslave and starve the Slavs and drive the Jews out of German lands; they were interned in ghettoes and concentration camps across occupied Poland. But he now ordered a policy of extermination, using *Einsatzgruppen* ('Task forces') to shoot a million Jews. Barbarossa served as the trigger and excuse for the 'Final Solution of the Jewish Question'. Under Hitler's orders to SS Reichsführer Heinrich Himmler, Jews were dispatched to extermination camps to be slaughtered in gas chambers on an industrial scale. The Holocaust, as it became known, claimed 6 million Jewish lives, as well as the lives of many more minorities hated by the Nazis, including Gypsies, Slavs and homosexuals. It remains a crime of unparalleled magnitude.

But the Soviets defeated the Germans at Stalingrad in 1942–3. After their victory at Kursk in the summer of 1943, the Soviets slowly but inexorably destroyed Hitler's empire, advancing all the way to Berlin. In June 1944, the Allies invaded northern France in the D-Day landings and started to fight their way to meet the Soviets in Germany itself. Yet an ever more deluded, brutal Hitler refused to countenance reality, demanding that his soldiers fight to the last man. As Germany was slowly crushed between the Red Army in the east and the British and Americans in the west, he fled to the *Führerbunker* in Berlin, where on 30 April he committed suicide, responsible for 70 million dead.

THE LAST DAYS OF HITLER

Hitler fled to the *Führerbunker* in Berlin on 16 January 1945, along with support staff and, later, Eva Braun and the Goebbels family. On 16 April the Red Army launched the Battle of Berlin, attacking in a pincer movement that swiftly smashed into the city.

Hitler spent his time ordering non-existent armies to launch non-existent offensives, denouncing his potential successors Goering and Himmler as traitors, and holding twee tea parties with his devoted female secretaries. Elsewhere in the bunker, his SS guards and female staff held wild drunken orgies. On 28 April, hearing of Himmler's attempt to broker peace, Hitler furiously had SS officer Hermann Fegelein (Eva Braun's brother-in-law and Himmler's 'golden boy') shot in the Chancellery garden.

On 29 April Hitler married Eva Braun in a civil ceremony in the *Führerbunker*. The next day, Braun and Hitler swallowed cyanide capsules – previously tested on his dog, Blondi – and Hitler shot himself in the right temple. Scotching rumours that he escaped to South America, eyewitness claims that his body was burned were substantiated when officers of SMERSH (the Red Army counter-intelligence unit) discovered remains near the bunker, confirmed by dental records as Braun's and Hitler's. His skeleton was buried under the Magdeburg Soviet airbase in East Germany, then dug up and incinerated in 1970 on the orders of KGB chief Yuri Andropov. In 2000 part of the skull was put on display in the Federal Archives Service in Moscow.

The Croatian fascist Ante Pavelić was the 'Butcher of the Balkans' – indeed his killing was so barbarous that even the genocidal Nazis regarded it as excessive. During the Second World War Pavelić, an admirer of Adolf Hitler, created an independent state of Croatia, and purged the country of all non-Croatians in a feverish genocide against local Jews and Serbian Orthodox – an orgy of slaughter that killed 700,000 people.

Ante Pavelić 1889–1959

'With help from God and our great friends . . . [there] arises the free and Independent State of Croatia, in which, Croatian peasants, all land and all authority will be in your hands, in which law and fairness will rule, and in which all weeds will be eradicated, which were planted by the foreign hand of our enemies.'

PAVELIĆ'S RADIO ADDRESS TO CROATIA, 5 APRIL 1941

Pavelić was born in 1889 in the village of Bradina in Bosnia, which was then part of the Austro-Hungarian empire. His parents hailed from the Croatian town of Lika, and from an early age he displayed a strong interest in Croatian folk tales and national stories. While studying at the university in Zagreb, the Croatian capital, he began to espouse the cause of Croatian nationalism, of which he soon became a fanatical exponent.

In 1912 he was arrested following the attempted assassination of the Austro-Hungarian viceroy of Croatia-Slavonia.

The Kingdom of the Serbs, Croats and Slovenes (later known as Yugoslavia) was formed after the First World War, in the wake of the collapse of the Austro-Hungarian empire. Pavelić opposed the centralizing government of the new state and continued to campaign for Croatian independence. In 1927 he was elected to the federal parliament in Belgrade as a representative of the hard-line Croatian nationalist faction.

In January 1929 King Alexander of Yugoslavia announced the creation of a 'Royal Dictatorship'. Pavelić responded by creating the Ustaše Croatian Liberation Movement. Based in Zagreb, this group aimed to 'liberate' Croatia from 'alien occupation' and establish a 'free and independent state over the whole of its national and historic territory'. The Ustaše was immediately proscribed, and Pavelić fled to Vienna, being sentenced to death in absentia for publicly advocating the overthrow of the state. Subsequently expelled by the Austrian government, he found refuge in Mussolini's Italy, where he set up Ustache training camps. The Ustaše launched a terrorist campaign against the Yugoslav regime, and in 1934 Pavelić was implicated in the assassination of King Alexander. Afraid of the consequences of this act of international terrorism, Mussolini moved to suppress the Ustaše, and Pavelič himself was imprisoned until 1936. For a while Pavelić maintained a low profile, but the outbreak of the Second World War transformed his prospects.

On 6 April 1941 Germany invaded Yugoslavia. Four days later the 'Independent State of Croatia' was declared by a supporter of Pavelić in Zagreb. Pavelić was declared the *Poglavnik* ('leader') and he and his fellow Ustaše exiles were now sent back to their homeland by Mussolini, who had reached an agreement with them that Italy was to annex a section of the Dalmatian coast of Croatia once they had attained power.

The new government formed by Pavelić consciously modelled itself on the Nazi dictatorship in Germany. The death penalty was swiftly instituted for a wide range of offences against 'the honour and interests of the Croatian nation', and laws were passed to preserve 'Aryan blood and honour' by prohibiting marriage between Croats and Jews. Further anti-Semitic legislation followed.

At a meeting at the Berghof in Germany, Hitler told Pavelić that it might require fifty years' work to attain a homogenous Croat state. Pavelić set about the task with relish, and Serbs, Jews and Gypsies were rounded up and sent to extermination camps. By 1945 over 80 per cent of the Jewish population in Bosnia and Croatia (totalling just under 40,000 people) had been murdered, along with around 29,000 Gypsies and half a million Serbs, with a further 300,000 deported to Serbia in such atrocious conditions that even the German SS killers themselves complained about the condition of the arriving refugees and the disorderly conduct of the killing. Those who remained were forced to choose between death or conversion to Catholicism (most Serbs were Orthodox). On one occasion in 1941, hundreds of Serbs were ordered to attend a church in the village of Glina for conversion, but once they were inside the doors to the building were barricaded and the church was set alight. None survived.

The predations of the Ustaše fuelled the Yugoslav Resistance, which came to be dominated by Josip Tito's communist Partisans. The withdrawal of German military support precipitated the collapse of the Ustaše regime, and in May 1945 Pavelić and thousands of his supporters fled. Some 80,000 Ustaše members were slaughtered by the vengeful Partisans, with perhaps a further 30,000 Croat civilians also killed in the carnage. The bloody retribution continued into the first years of the new Federal People's Republic of Yugoslavia established by Tito.

Pavelić himself managed to escape, first to Austria and then to Italy, where, it has been suggested, the Allied occupying powers were aware of his presence but failed to arrest him. By 1948 he had made his way to Argentina, where he acted as an adviser to President Juan Perón. In 1957 he was the target of an assassination attempt by Yugoslav agents that left him badly wounded, and he subsequently fled to Franco's Spain, where he died in 1959.

The after-effects of Ante Pavelić and his wartime regime have been felt ever since. When the Balkans exploded into fresh conflict in the 1990s, the shadow of the Ustaše continued to linger over the region, as nationalist fanatics, both Croatian and Serb, revived Pavelić's murderous policies under the guise of 'ethnic cleansing'.

Croatian fascist leader Ante Pavelić, photographed in 1941 with the German foreign minister Joachim von Ribbentrop (right).

QUISLINGS

Ante Pavelić of Croatia was just one of the monstrous non-German collaborators who helped Hitler in his dystopic racial mass-murder across Nazi-occupied Europe. Some – the so-called 'Quislings' – were placed in power by Hitler himself, notably Vidkun Quisling (1887–1945; executed), a Norwegian Nazi sympathizer appointed president of Norway in 1942, his name subsequently synonymous with collaboration; Jozef Tiso (1887–1947; executed), a priest who, as premier of the Slovak Republic following Hitler's annexation of the Sudetenland, deported thousands of Jews to the death camps; and Anton Mussert (1894–1946; executed), Dutch National Socialist leader and declared 'Führer of the Dutch People' in 1942.

Some already in power allied themselves with Hitler, including his chief ally, Benito Mussolini; Marshal Pétain (1856–1951; died in prison), the French premier who surrendered much of France to the Nazis; Pierre Laval (1883–1945; executed), former French prime minister who became leader of the Vichy government he helped the Germans establish; Marshal Ion Antonescu (1882–1946; executed), the vehemently anti-Semitic and anti-Russian *conducător* of Romania, who forced King Carol II to abdicate, supported the Germans on the Eastern Front, and oversaw the murder of 380,000 Jews and 10,000 Gypsies; Boris III, tsar of Bulgaria (1894–1943; possibly poisoned), who agreed to deport 13,000 Jews from recently re-annexed territories though protected those in Bulgaria; Admiral Miklós Horthy (1868–1957), Regent of Hungary who collaborated with the Nazis through fear of com-munism, but eventually broke with Hitler; and generals Georgios Tsolakoglou (1886–1948), Konstantinos Logo-the topoulos (1878–1961) and Ioannis Rallis (1878–1946), Nazi puppets in Greece.

Other pro-Nazi collaborators included Staf De Clercq (1884–1942) and Hendrik Elias (1902–73) of the Flemish National League, who cooperated in deporting Jews; Frits Clausen (1893–1947), leader of the Danish Nazi Party, and Léon Degrelle (1906–94), head of the Rexist Movement in Belgium; General Andrey Vlasov (1900–46; executed), who in 1944 established the anti-Soviet Russian Liberation Army; and Bronislav Kaminski (1899–1944), commander of the Kaminski Brigade (of the Russian National Liberation Army) who, with henchmen Konstantin Voskoboinik and Yuri Frolov, oversaw the slaughter on Nazi orders of 10,000 citizens during the 1944 Warsaw Uprising. Kaminski was then shot by the SS themselves for depravity beyond even Hitler's standards. Of the Quislings, apart from Pavelić, the Romanian Antonescu, who ordered the frenzied massacres of Odessan and Romanian Jews, was Hitler's most murderous ally: 'The Jew', he said, 'is Satan.'

Vidkun Quisling (left) with the SS leader Heinrich Himmler (see page 246), on a visit to Berlin. The word 'Quisling' has come to mean 'a traitor who assists the enemy'.

General Francisco Franco, the generalissimo of Spain from 1939 to 1975, is in some ways the forgotten tyrant, his deeds overshadowed by Adolf Hitler and Josef Stalin, yet he was truly one of history's monsters. In the 1930s, this fascistic warlord won power with brutality and terror in a savage civil war, aided by his ally Hitler, and proceeded to terrorize the civilian population of Spain for 25 years. As democracy thrived in the rest of Western Europe following the Second World War, his brutal military dictatorship continued to crush dissent, and to shoot and torture his supposed enemies.

Francisco Franco

1892–1975

'I am responsible only to God and history.'
GENERAL FRANCO

Franco was born in northwest Spain in 1892, in the naval city of Ferrol. His mother was a pious and conservative upper-middle-class Catholic; his father a difficult and eccentric man who expected his son to follow him into the navy. Due to naval cutbacks, however, at just 14 years old, Franco entered the army instead. Fiercely professional, he soon carved out his reputation as a brave and driven soldier, becoming a captain in 1916 and the youngest general in Spain in 1926, aged 34.

General Francisco Franco, fascist dictator of Spain from 1939 to 1975. He is pictured here on 1 October 1936, leaving Spanish military headquarters after being proclaimed head of state and 'generalissimo' of the armies. The Nationalist commander General Emilio Mola, who coined the term 'fifth column', can be seen in the background.

Although staunchly loyal to the monarchy, Franco was not overtly involved in politics until 1931, when the Spanish king abdicated, leaving the government in the hands of left-wing republicans. When the conservatives won power back two years later, they identified Franco as a powerful potential ally and promoted him to major-general, instructing him to suppress an uprising by Asturian miners in October 1934. Election victory for the left-wing Popular Front in 1936, however, saw Franco effectively demoted and sent to the Canary Islands, but just months later the right-wing Spanish nationalist bloc called on the army to join them in rebellion against the government, which had failed to stabilize the country. The Spanish Civil War had begun.

In a radio broadcast from the Canary Islands in July 1936, Franco declared he would join the rebels with immediate effect and, after mixed fortunes for Nationalist forces in Morocco and Madrid, he was declared generalissimo, effectively the leader of the Nationalist cause during the three years of war that followed.

Franco's wartime campaign was notorious for his indiscriminate brutalizing of civilian populations, aided on occasions by German and Italian fascist governments. Franco organized a White Terror in which 200,000 people were murdered. The most infamous atrocity was the 1937 market-day bombing of the Basque town of Guernica by the German Condor Legion. Though it was not a military target and had no air defences, the Luftwaffe pounded the town throughout the day and swooped over outgoing roads to mow down fleeing civilians as the town was engulfed in a fireball. An estimated 1654 people were slaughtered.

Victory, when it finally came, was not enough for Franco. 'The war is over,' he declared in 1939, 'but the enemy is not dead.' He had drawn up lists of 'reds' during the conflict: alleged communists to be arrested. Now in control of the state, he set about rounding up and liquidating his enemies. Hundreds of thousands of republicans fled the country as, between 1939 and 1943, anything between 100,000 and 200,000 non-combatants or surrendering troops were summarily and systematically executed.

Repression characterized every aspect of Franco's regime. He nominally re-established the monarchy without appointing a king – but retained all executive powers in his own hands. Democracy was abandoned, criticism regarded as treason, imprisonment and abuse of opponents rife, parliament a mere puppet to the executive, rival political parties and strikes banned, the Catholic Church given a free rein over social policy and education, the media muzzled, creative talent strangled by strict censorship and any dissent ruthlessly suppressed by his secret police, who practised widespread torture and murder right up to Franco's death in 1975. Dismissive of international criticism, Franco himself insisted on personally signing all death warrants until his death while his family married into the aristocracy and amassed colossal wealth.

A true mark of the regime was Franco's shameful decision to grant asylum to Ante Pavelić, the fascist dictator of Croatia during the Second World War – a man thought to be responsible for over 600,000 deaths. Franco also during that time repaid Hitler and Mussolini's support during the Civil War by sending troops – albeit limited in number – to assist the Nazis in their fight against the Soviets. But he survived by resisting Hitler's request for him to join the war and then posing as an anti-communist after 1945.

The ghost of Franco has yet to be completely exorcized from Spanish politics, as recently as 2004 a commission having been set up to compensate his victims and oversee the exhumation of the mass graves. His crimes may pale in comparison to dictators such as Hitler, Mussolini and Stalin, yet few have pursued the liquidation of their own people with such remorseless determination as this evil autocrat.

SPAIN'S WHITE AND RED TERRORS

As Generalissimo Francisco Franco signed his death-lists, he would place 'E' for execute for those to die, 'C' for those spared and, most macabre and revealing of all, 'GARROTE Y PRENSA' ('GARROTTE WITH PRESS COVERAGE') next to the names of certain well-known people. Nothing so sums up the miserable wickedness of the victors of the Spanish Civil War. Franco resembled the 19th-century Spanish general who on his deathbed was asked if he forgave his enemies. 'I have none,' he replied, 'I had them all shot.'

For a generation of left-wing intellectuals, the struggle of Republican Spain to defend itself against Franco's Nationalists epitomized the struggle between socialist progress and fascist reaction. Idealistic intellectuals such as George Orwell, Ernest Hemingway and the French novelist André Malraux flocked to Spain to fight for the Republican cause. In total, about 32,000 foreign volunteers from Europe and America fought in the campaign, while Nazi Germany and Fascist Italy pumped money and troops into Franco's army – and dropped bombs on the civilian populations in Republican-dominated areas.

In support of the Republic, Stalin's USSR supplied 331 tanks and 600 planes, together with a large number of pilots, in return for Spanish gold reserves. The Red Terror in Spain, according to recent historical research, accounted for the deaths of somewhere between 40,000 and 100,000 people. Precise figures are unknown.

During the bloody summer of 1936, 8000 suspected Nationalists were massacred in Madrid, and another 8000 in Catalonia – both Republican-controlled areas. Wealthy farmers, industrialists and those associated with the Catholic Church received particularly brutal treatment at the hands of the various Republican factions. Nearly 7000 clerics, including nearly 300 nuns, were killed, despite being non-combatants.

Some Republicans defended these massacres on the grounds that the other side was worse. Others tried to stand back. Commenting on the atrocities committed by his own side, the anarchist intellectual Federica Montseny noted 'a lust for blood inconceivable in honest men' before the war.

One of the ironies of history is that while the Stalinist terror within the Republicans is as notorious as the Red Terror that slaughtered supposed rightists, Franco and the Nationalists killed many, many more: some 200,000 were murdered by Franco in his White Terror during the war, while another half million remained in his torture chambers and camps afterwards. Franco really delivered on his associate General Queipo's promise 'For every person you kill, we will kill ten.'

An execution during the Spanish Civil War. Both sides dealt ruthlessly with prisoners and civilians.

Chairman Mao, revolutionary, poet and guerrilla commander, was the Communist dictator of China whose brutality, egotism, utopian radicalism, total disdain for human life and suffering, and insanely grandiose schemes led to the murder of 70 million of his own citizens. Born manipulator and ruthless pursuer of power, this monster was happy to torment and murder his own comrades, to execute millions, permit millions more to starve and even risk nuclear war, in order to promote his Marxist-Stalinist-Maoist vision of a superpower China under his own semi-divine cult of personality.

Mao Zedong 1893–1976

'I look at Mao, I see Stalin, a perfect copy.'

NIKITA KHRUSHCHEV

Mao was born in the village of Shaoshan in Hunan province on 26 December 1893. Forced to work on the family farm in his early teens, he rebelled against his father – a successful grain dealer – and left home to seek an education at the provincial capital, Changsha, where he participated in the revolt against the Manchu dynasty in 1911. He flirted with various careers, but never committed to anything until he subsequently joined the recently formed Chinese Communist Party in 1921. He married Yang Kaihui in 1920, by whom he had two sons (later marrying He Zizhen in 1928 and well-known actress Lan Ping – real name Jiang Qing – in 1939). At 24, he recorded his amoral philosophy: 'People like me only have a duty to ourselves . . .' he worshipped 'power like a hurricane arising from a deep gorge, like a sex-maniac on the heat . . . We adore times of war . . . We love sailing the sea of upheavals . . . The country must be destroyed then reformed . . . People like me long for its destruction.' In 1923, the Communists entered an alliance with the Kuomintang (Nationalist Party). Sent back to Hunan to promote the Kuomintang, he continued to foment revolutionary activity, predicting that Chinese peasants would 'rise like a tornado or tempest – a force so extraordinarily swift and violent that no power, however great, will be able to suppress it'.

In 1926, the Kuomintang leader Chiang Kai-shek – the toothless military strongman whose vicious, corrupt and utterly inept gangster-backed regime would enable Mao and the Communists ultimately to triumph and conquer China – ordered the so-called Northern Expedition to consolidate the fragmented government power. By April 1927, having defeated over 30 warlords, he slaughtered the Communists in Shanghai, being named Generalissimo the following year, with all China under his rule. Mao, meanwhile, had retired to a base in the Jinggang Mountains, from where, emerging as a Red leader, he embarked on a guerrilla campaign. 'Political power grows from the barrel of a gun,' he said.

In 1931, Mao became chairman of the Chinese Soviet Republic in Jiangxi. Happy to murder, blackmail and poison his rivals – killing 700,000 in a Terror from 1931–5 – he displayed the same political gifts as Stalin: a will for power, ruthlessness, an addiction to turmoil and an astonishing ability to manipulate. Like Stalin also, he destroyed his wives and mistresses, ignored his children and poisoned everyone whose lives he touched: many went insane.

In 1933, after several defeats, Chiang launched a new war of attrition resulting in a dramatic turnaround that prompted the Communists to sideline Mao and, on the advice of Soviet agent Otto Braun, launch a disastrous counterattack, leading in 1936 to a full-scale retreat that became known as the Long March. By the late 1930s, using gullible Western writers like Edgar Snow and Han Suyin, Mao had created his myth as a peasant leader, poet and guerrilla-maestro, the March portrayed as an epic journey in which he heroically saved the Red Army from Nationalist attack. In fact, much was invented to conceal military ineptitude and his deliberate wastage of armies to discredit Communist rivals.

In 1937, Japan launched a full-scale invasion of China. Chiang was forced by Zhang Xueliang, the 'Young Marshal' who kidnapped the Generalissimo, to combine forces with Mao. Secretly Mao strove to undermine Chiang's war effort, even briefly cooperating with Japanese intelligence. By 1943, he had achieved supremacy in the Communist Party, poisoning and purging rivals and critics with brutal efficiency. He continued to court Soviet support for the Communists, whose future was assured when Stalin helped defeat Japan in 1945.

Chiang's militarily incompetent kleptocracy, heavily backed by America, collapsed as Mao, backed by massive Soviet aid and advice from Stalin, gradually drove the Kuomintang off the mainland. In 1949, Mao declared the People's Republic of China, embarking on an imperial reign of wilful caprice, ideological radicalism, messianic egotism, massive incompetence and mass-murder: 'We must kill. We say it's good to kill,' ordered this 'man without limits'. Three million people were murdered that year.

In 1951–2, Mao subjected China to his so-called 'Three-Anti' and 'Five-Anti' campaigns to eliminate China's bourgeoisie. Spies infiltrated everywhere, informing on supposed transgressors, who were heavily fined, sent to labour camps or executed. Mao ruled like a Red Emperor, paranoid about his security, always on the move, shrewdly manipulating his henchmen and pitilessly sacrificing old comrades to maintain power at all costs. He constantly declared: 'Too lenient, not killing enough.' While he lived like an emperor on 50 private estates using military dancing-girls as 'imperial concubines', he drove China to become a superpower, deploying Chinese troops against America in the Korean War as a way of persuading Stalin to give him military, especially nuclear, technology. It would not matter, he mused, 'if half the Chinese were to die' in a nuclear holocaust.

Mao continued to wage war on his people throughout the 1950s. The 1958–9 Anti-Rightist Campaign – through which over half a million people were labelled 'rightists' – saw hundreds of thousands consigned to years of hard labour or execution. The Great Leap Forward of 1958–62,

A portrait of Chinese Communist leader Mao Zedong (1967). Architect of the Cultural Revolution and the Great Leap Forward, Mao is reckoned to have extinguished the lives of 70 million of his own citizens.

THE CULTURAL REVOLUTION

The great proletarian Cultural Revolution now unfolding is a great revolution that touches people to their very souls ... Our objective is to struggle against and crush those persons in authority who are taking the capitalist road, to criticize and repudiate the reactionary bourgeois academic "authorities" and the ideology of the bourgeoisie and all other exploiting classes and to transform education, literature and art and all other parts of the superstructure that do not correspond to the socialist economic base, so as to facilitate the consolidation and development of the socialist system.

The Decision of the Central Committee of the Chinese Communist Party, 8 August 1966, which launched the Cultural Revolution. It was a decision that would lead to millions of deaths.

A Red Guard holds aloft the thoughts of Mao in this cover design for an edition of the Little Red Book.

massive drive to increase steel production, encouraged villagers to create useless little forges, coupled with a move to collectivize China's peasantry into rural communes. Emulating Stalin with his manmade 1932–3 famine, Mao sold food to buy arms even though China starved in the 'the greatest famine in history': 38 million died. When defence minister Marshal Peng Dehuai criticized his policies. Mao purged him but his anointed successor, President Liu Shaoqi, managed to claw back some power from Mao in 1962.

Denouncing Liu, who was destroyed and allowed to die in poverty, Mao avenged himself by getting control of the army and state through his chosen successor, the talented, neurotic Marshal Lin Biao and supple chief factotum Premier Zhou Enlai. He masterminded another Terror, the 'Cultural Revolution', in which he asserted his total domination of China by attacking the party and state, ordering gangs of students, secret policemen and thugs to humiliate, murder and destroy lives and culture. Three million were killed between 1966 and 1976; millions more were deported or tortured.

The ageing Mao fell out with Lin Biao, creator of the Little Red Book, who died in a plane crash while fleeing in 1971. This left Mao in the hands of his grotesque, vicious wife Jiang Qing and the Maoist radicals known as the 'Gang of Four'.

Having fallen out with Moscow, Mao pulled off one last coup: US President Richard Nixon's visit to China in 1972. Dying, Mao restored, then again purged, the formidable pragmatist Deng Xiaoping. Mao died in 1976 and Deng emerged as the paramount leader and architect of today's China who liberated the economy but not the people of China, and enforced Communist power in the Tiananmen Square massacre. Mao's Communists still rule China.

Yezhov was the dwarfish Soviet secret policeman who organized and coordinated Stalin's Great Terror, during which a million innocent victims were shot and millions more exiled to concentration camps. Such was the frenzy of arrest, torture and killing under Yezhov's sometimes meticulous, sometimes drunken control that this murderous witch-hunt was known as 'the Meatgrinder'.

Nikolai Yezhov

1895–1940

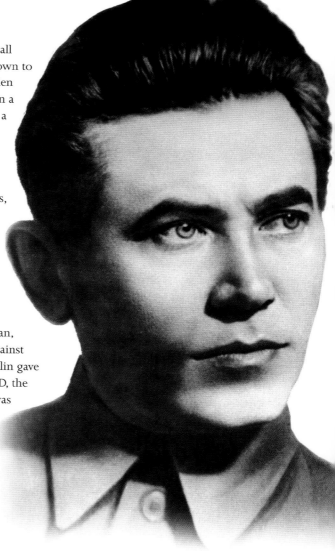

'If during this operation, an extra thousand people are shot, that's not such a big deal.'
NIKOLAI YEZHOV, 1937

Born in a small Lithuanian town to a forest warden (who also ran a brothel) and a maid, Yezhov only had a few years' schooling before going to work in a factory. He joined the Red Army after the Revolution and served during the Civil War. He was a shrewd, able, tactful and ambitious party administrator and personnel expert. By the early thirties, he was close to Stalin, in charge of all party personnel appointments and a central committee secretary. A colleague noted that 'I don't know a more ideal worker. After entrusting him with a job, he'll do it. But he doesn't know when to stop.' But this suited Stalin, who called his new favourite 'my blackberry' – a play on the word *yezhevika*.

In 1934 the assassination of Stalin's closest henchman, Sergei Kirov, allowed him to unleash the Great Terror against 'enemies of the people', real and imagined. In 1935 Stalin gave Yezhov a special responsibility for supervising the NKVD, the secret police. The chief of the NKVD, Genrikh Yagoda, was out of favour; Yezhov aimed to destroy him and take his place. But Yezhov's first task was to take over the case against Stalin's former allies, Zinoviev and Kamenev. Yezhov supervised their interrogations, threatening to kill their families, turning up the

Nikolai Ivanovich Yezhov was made leader of the NKVD by Stalin in 1936, and unleashed a frenzy of repression in the Stalinist Soviet Union.

heating in their cells in midsummer – but also promising them their lives if they confessed to absurd crimes at the first show trial. They finally agreed. The show trial, staged in 1936, was a success, but despite Yezhov's promises, Zinoviev and Kamenev were shot in his presence. Yagoda had the bullets dug out of their brains so he could keep them in his desk; later Yezhov found the bullets, and kept them in his own drawer. In September 1936 Stalin sacked Yagoda and promoted Yezhov to people's commissar of internal affairs (NKVD).

As Yezhov supervised the spread of the Terror, arresting ever-larger circles of suspects to be tortured into confessing imaginary crimes, the Soviet press worked the population up into a frenzy of witch-hunting against Trotskyite spies and terrorists. Yezhov claimed that Yagoda had tried to kill him by spraying his curtains with cyanide. He then arrested most of Yagoda's officers and had them shot. Then he arrested Yagoda himself. 'Better that ten innocent men should suffer than one spy get away,' Yezhov announced. 'When you chop wood, chips fly!'

On Stalin's orders, in May 1937 Yezhov arrested Marshal Mikhail Tukhachevsky, the most talented Red Army officer, together with many other top generals. The idea was to break the independent power of the army, but the generals had to confess their 'crimes' to convince the other Soviet leaders that they were guilty of crimes against the state. Yezhov personally supervised their savage torture: when Tukhachevsky's confession was found in the archives in the 1990s it was covered in a brown spray that was found to be the blood spatter of a human body in motion. The generals were all shot in Yezhov's presence. Stalin, who never attended torture sessions or executions, questioned him on their conduct at the final moment. In all, some 40,000 officers were shot.

Yezhov now expanded the Terror in a bizarre way, clearly on Stalin's orders, by initiating random killing by numbers, giving each city and region a quota of two categories: category one was to be shot and category two to be exiled. These quotas constantly expanded, until approximately a million were shot and many millions more deported to hellish labour camps in Siberia. Wives of the more prominent victims were arrested and usually shot too. Children aged between one and three were to be confined to orphanages, but children older than that could be shot. 'Beat, destroy without sorting out,' Yezhov ordered, adding, 'Better too far than not far enough.'

By 1938 the Soviet Union was in a turmoil of fear and killing, all supervised by Yezhov. Stalin kept a low profile, but Yezhov was now everywhere, hailed as the hero-avenger of a society in which enemies were omnipresent. He was now almost as powerful as Stalin, worshipped in poems and songs, with towns named in his honour. Yezhov devised special execution chambers at Moscow's notorious Lubyanka Prison and elsewhere; the chambers had a sloping concrete floor like an abattoir, wooden walls to absorb bullets and hoses to drain the blood.

But by now Yezhov was cracking up and losing control. He constantly toured the country arresting and killing; he worked all night, torturing suspects and drinking heavily; he was becoming more and more paranoid, fearing that at any moment Stalin would turn against him. He had many of his close friends, ex-girlfriends and his own godfather shot. The stress ate at him: he boasted drunkenly that he ruled the country, he could arrest Stalin. As the third show trial starring Bukharin and Yagoda opened in Moscow, even Stalin became alarmed by the uncontrolled nature of the Terror he had unleashed. It had served its purpose, and now he needed a scapegoat. Stalin was hearing about Yezhov's excesses, drunkenness, debauchery, bisexual promiscuity and boasting. He ordered Yezhov to kill his top lieutenants, including his deputy, who was chloroformed in Yezhov's own office and then injected with poison. As he felt Stalin's disapproval, Yezhov started to kill anyone who could incriminate him – a thousand were killed in five days without Stalin's permission.

In the autumn of 1938 Stalin promoted another protégé, Lavrenti Beria, to become Yezhov's deputy. In October the politburo denounced the management of the NKVD. In November Yezhov appeared for the last time for the annual parade on Lenin's Mausoleum. He was sacked from the NKVD on 23 November, though he remained officially as commissar of water transport. But he barely turned up for work, instead losing himself in a series of drunken homosexual orgies, waiting for the knock on the door. When it came, and the inevitable trial and death sentence followed, Yezhov collapsed. On the way to the execution chamber he himself had designed, he wept, got hiccups and fell to the floor. He had to be dragged to his death.

Yezhov was a typical half-educated but diligently ambitious Soviet bureaucrat, but finding himself with an almost absolute fiat over life and death, empowered by Stalin himself, he revelled in the hunt, the details of administering murder and the slaughter itself, and personally spent nights torturing his victims. Stalin's 'Bloody Dwarf' became the second most powerful man in the Soviet Union, but the stress almost drove him mad, and he ended as a victim of his own Meatgrinder. A degenerate monster, a slavish bureaucrat, a slick administrator, a sadistic torturer yet also a broken reed, Yezhov pioneered a new sort of mass-production totalitarian slaughter for the mid-20th century. 'Tell Stalin,' he announced at his trial, 'I shall die with his name on my lips.'

THE LIFE AND LOVES OF STALIN'S 'BLOODY DWARF'

'I may be small in stature,' Yezhov once said, 'but my hands are strong – Stalin's hands!' Yezhov was so tiny – just 5 feet (151 cm) tall – that as a young man he had been rejected by the tsarist army. He was also unstable, sickly, sexually confused, frail and skinny, but at the same time jovial, hard-drinking and possessed of a puerile sense of humour (including a taste for farting competitions). With his handsome face, blue eyes and thick dark hair, and his fondness for dancing, singing and playing the guitar, he was a popular figure, especially with women – although, unusually, for the Soviet leadership, he was promiscuously bisexual.

His first wife was a party comrade called Antonina, whom he divorced to marry a glamorous and promiscuous Jewish woman named Yevgenia, who held a salon for writers and film stars. At the time of Yezhov's downfall, his successor Beria began to investigate Yevgenia's sexually adventurous antics. Yezhov tried to divorce her in time, probably to save her and their adopted daughter Natasha, but possibly to save himself too. All her lovers, including the brilliant writer Isaac Babel, were arrested and shot. Yevgenia committed suicide.

Vyacheslav Molotov (left), Sergo Ordzhonikidze (second left), Nikolai Yezhov (second right) and Anastas Mikoyan (right) rank amongst Stalin's most murderous henchmen, along with Georgi Malenkov, Lazar Kaganovich, Andrei Zhdanov, Klim Voroshilov and Nikita Khrushchev.

Khorloogin Choibalsan was the Stalin of the Mongols who brutally ruled over the Mongolian People's Republic as a puppet state of the Soviet Union. He orchestrated the murder of tens of thousands of his own people, suppressing an ancient culture, shooting his rivals, purging Buddhist priests and promoting himself in a grotesque cult of personality.

Marshal Choibalsan
1895–1952

'They die one after another. Shcherbakov, Zhdanov, Dimitrov, Choibalsan . . . die so quickly!'

STALIN LAMENTS THE DEATH OF HIS MONGOLIAN ALLY, 1952

Choibalsan regarded himself as a communist, but also dreamed of uniting the Mongolian tribes under one government. Like Stalin and many other top Russian Bolsheviks, he studied for the priesthood – Buddhist, in Choibalsan's case – until, as a young man, he became intoxicated with Marxism and embraced radical atheism. He made contact with Bolshevik revolutionaries during a trip to Siberia and founded his own Soviet-style revolutionary organization in Mongolia in 1919. In 1921, he was one of the founder members of the Mongolian People's Revolutionary Party.

From March 1921, Mongolia had briefly been controlled by Baron Ungern von Sternberg, a White Russian warlord (see page 216). Within months, however, the Soviet-assisted armies of Damdin Sükhbaatar had defeated Ungern's forces, and the Mongolian People's Republic was established. Choibalsan – already commissar of the Mongolian Red Army – was appointed deputy war minister. During the 1920s, he distinguished himself with his zealously pro-Soviet behaviour, and led violent purges of those moderate revolutionaries who had fought for Mongolia's liberation.

A small and ferocious man with a shaved head and military bearing, Choibalsan caught the eye of Stalin, who recognized in his Mongolian ally a ruthless and reliable fanatic with few quibbles about taking human life to impose Marxism-Leninism even in the rustic Buddhist culture of Mongolia. In the mid-1930s, Stalin became frustrated with the existing leader of the Mongolian communists, Peljidiyn Genden, especially after Genden met him in 1935 and resisted the 'red imperialism' of purges of the Lamas (priests) and aristocracy along with Soviet collectivization. In 1936, Stalin engineered Genden's fall, ensuring that Choibalsan replaced him. Genden was arrested and shot in Moscow as a Japanese spy.

Elevating himself to the rank of marshal, Choibalsan henceforth dominated Mongolia as chairman of the council of peoples' commissars, promoting himself as a flawless genius in a cult based on that of Stalin. Cities took his name and he even renamed a mountain after himself.

Choibalsan maintained a strong working relationship with Stalin, whose tactics and policies he mimicked. His first priority was to eliminate potential rivals and critics from within the party, so in the late 1930s he orchestrated a series of brutal purges of those he designated 'enemies of the people', such as intellectuals and landowners, many of whom he accused of spying for Japan. Above all, it was the Buddhist monks who suffered at his hands, despite his own early training as a monk. All religious practice was suppressed, and an estimated 700 temples destroyed. Over 35,000 people were shot, perhaps as many as 100,000, of whom 18,000 were monks. Tens of thousands more were rounded up and interned.

In the 1940s, Stalin allowed Choibalsan to dream of uniting the Mongolian people under his rule. Thus Choibalsan encouraged ethnic tensions in Eastern Xinjiang, an area of Inner Mongolia under Chinese control. However, although the Soviets assisted with a brief invasion of Inner Mongolia, Stalin wanted to avoid conflict with China and subsequently signed a peace agreement, forcing Choibalsan to rein in his ambitions.

When Choibalsan became ill, he went to Moscow to seek treatment from Russian doctors in the special Kremlin clinic, but they could not help him, and he died on 26 January 1952. The marshal's death was one of a series among Stalinist grandees at the Kremlin clinic – deaths that Stalin exploited, claiming that the mainly Jewish doctors were trying to murder the Soviet leadership in the so-called 'Doctors' Plot'. He planned to use this as an excuse to liquidate likely successors among his comrades, but he died before he could fully unleash the purge.

Choibalsan was embalmed and displayed in a mausoleum in Ulan Bator, his body subsequently cremated after this was demolished in 2005 to make way for a memorial to Genghis Khan. Since the establishment of democracy in 1990, some of the dreadful secrets of Choibalsan's murderous regime have emerged, including mass graves filled with the bodies of priests – with bullet holes in their skulls. No doubt more atrocities will be unearthed. Though Choibalsan modernized Mongolia and significantly improved its infrastructure, he did so at a terrible cost to his country. He ranks as one of the forgotten monsters of Stalinism who almost succeeded in destroying his ancient culture.

Khorloogin Choibalsan was the Soviet puppet leader of Mongolia from 1936 until his death in 1952.

THE BURMESE JUNTA

The country of Burma (now Myanmar) has been ruled by a military junta since a coup in 1962 led by Ne Win, who established a one-party state, dissolved parliament, curtailed civil rights, arrested opponents, nationalized business and set about marginalizing ethnic minorities. Ruthlessly crushing protests, riots and – in 1976 – an attempted coup, he handed over the presidency in 1981 to San Yu, but remained firmly in control as chairman of the Burma Socialist Programme Party, handpicking army officers and ministers.

Obsessed with numerology, Ne Win bizarrely revised the currency in 1987 into tender divisible by his lucky number – 9 – destroying the savings of millions. Mounting unrest led to his resignation as party chairman in July 1988. In the same year, the Four Eights Uprising, a massive pro-democracy protest, was crushed in a coup that saw a 21-strong military junta – the State Law and Order Restoration Council (SLORC) – take control, led by General Saw Maung. Up to 10,000 protestors, mostly students and Buddhist monks, were killed, causing outrage in a country where the latter are revered as spiritual leaders. The SLORC subsequently instigated a twin programme of deforestation – to accommodate mass opium production – and systematic genocide against groups such as the Karen, Karenni, Shan, Kachins (Jingpo), Mons, Rohingyas, Wa and Chin (Zomis). Rape, torture, forced relocation, slave labour and murder have led to over 650,000 people – including 250,000 Karen – being displaced in eastern Burma alone, and around 2,000,000 fleeing to Thailand.

Multiparty elections were allowed in 1990, contested by activist Aung San Suu Kyi, but humiliating defeat saw the result ignored. The following year Suu Kyi (later awarded the Nobel Peace Prize) was placed under house arrest – twice temporarily lifted but later reimposed – for 'endangering the state'. A courageous and tireless campaigner for democracy, she is still held today. In 1992 Than Shwe replaced Saw Maung as chairman of the SLORC (later renamed the State Peace and Development Council) and commander-in-chief of the Tatmadaw (armed forces).

In 2002, after an alleged coup attempt by his son-in-law and three grandsons, Ne Win died in disgrace, a brief press obituary making no mention of his rule. In 2003, new prime minister Khin Nyunt unveiled a 'road map to democracy' but he was replaced the following year by hard-line Soe Win. Two years later, around 100,000 protestors led by Buddhist monks demonstrated in Rangoon against massive fuel-price increases. Close to 3000 were arrested, and at least 13 monks killed. The same year (2005), work started on a lavish new capital city – Naypyidaw ('Abode of Kings') – 300 miles north of Rangoon, which includes the fortress-like home of General Than Shwe, who continues to rule the country. The city was officially named on 27 March 2006, the annual Armed Forces Day.

Graphic proof of the regime's paranoia, intransigence and contempt for human life came in May 2008 after Cyclone Nargis struck the country, claiming over a 100,000 lives, decimating Burma's infrastructure and leaving hundreds of thousands homeless. For weeks the junta refused to allow relief supplies or foreign-aid workers into the country, massively intensifying the suffering and misery of its people. It finally bowed to international pressure but continued to hamper an effective response to the crisis.

A pro-democracy protester raises a placard during a demonstration outside the Burmese embassy in Kuala Lumpur, Malaysia, in 2007.

A kleptomaniac, fantasist and certified lunatic, Dr Marcel Petiot – nicknamed 'Dr Satan' – was also a cold, calculating fraudster, guilty of at least 60 murders and possibly many more. During the Second World War, he set himself up as the organizer of an escape route out of Nazi-occupied Paris, selling his services to anyone who wanted to flee. But it was a hideous trick: Petiot simply robbed his victims, and then killed them.

Dr Marcel Petiot
1897–1946

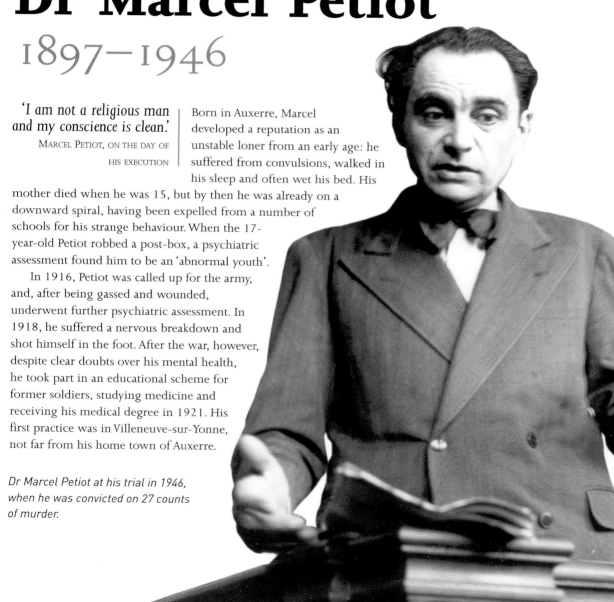

'I am not a religious man and my conscience is clean.'
MARCEL PETIOT, ON THE DAY OF HIS EXECUTION

Born in Auxerre, Marcel developed a reputation as an unstable loner from an early age: he suffered from convulsions, walked in his sleep and often wet his bed. His mother died when he was 15, but by then he was already on a downward spiral, having been expelled from a number of schools for his strange behaviour. When the 17-year-old Petiot robbed a post-box, a psychiatric assessment found him to be an 'abnormal youth'.

In 1916, Petiot was called up for the army, and, after being gassed and wounded, underwent further psychiatric assessment. In 1918, he suffered a nervous breakdown and shot himself in the foot. After the war, however, despite clear doubts over his mental health, he took part in an educational scheme for former soldiers, studying medicine and receiving his medical degree in 1921. His first practice was in Villeneuve-sur-Yonne, not far from his home town of Auxerre.

Dr Marcel Petiot at his trial in 1946, when he was convicted on 27 counts of murder.

Notwithstanding occasional signs of insanity, Petiot seems to have achieved a certain degree of popularity, becoming mayor of Villeneuve-sur-Yonne in 1926 after a controversial campaign. That same year, however, although never prosecuted, he was linked to the murder of a woman, rumoured to be his lover. It was a sign of things to come. In 1927, he married Georgette Lablais, daughter of a wealthy landowner, who bore him a son, but three years later he was investigated in relation to another woman's murder, again said to be his lover. Once more, the police took no action, despite the fact that the only witness died in Petiot's presence. He likewise escaped imprisonment despite numerous accusations of embezzlement and fraud, and other brushes with the authorities.

Petiot was finally forced to resign as mayor in 1931, and in 1933 he moved with his family to Paris, where he built up a successful practice. But beneath his respectable exterior, he was also selling morphine and heroin to prostitutes and drug dealers. In 1934, a female patient died of a morphine overdose, and in 1936 his wife admitted him to a mental institution for a year after he was convicted of shoplifting and assaulting a police officer.

After the fall of France to the Nazis in 1940, Petiot began posing as an agent of the French Resistance, promising those who wanted to flee the occupation, including genuine Resistance fighters and Jews fearing deportation to the East, safe passage out of the country. Demanding a price of 25,000 francs for every escapee, he would lure his victims to an elegant three-storey house on Rue Le Sueur that he had purchased especially for the scheme. There, he would administer a lethal injection, telling his victims he was vaccinating them against diseases endemic to their supposed destination, South America. He disposed of their bodies by dissolving them in a pit of quicklime or dismembering them and throwing the pieces into the Seine. In a macabre twist, at the height of the operation in 1943, he was arrested and interrogated by the Gestapo, who suspected him of helping Jewish families flee their clutches.

With so many bodies to dispose of, Petiot became impatient and, in March 1944, made the mistake of trying to burn them in the furnace of the house on Rue Le Sueur. So rank was the resultant smell that the Parisian police and fire brigade arrived at the property and discovered the carnage. Petiot was arrested, but after claiming he was a Resistance fighter and that the bodies were those of Nazis or collaborators, he was released and went on the run. Apparently believing his own story of heroic resistance, his arrogance led to his capture when he responded to the French newspaper *Résistance*, which had denounced him as a Nazi sympathizer – police tracing him through the letter.

Once the French authorities had unravelled Petiot's elaborate fantasy, they charged him with the murder of 27 people between 1941 and 1944. At his trial, he admitted to only 19 of the 27 murders, while actually claiming to have killed more than 60, all in the name of patriotic resistance. Indeed, the true figure may have been even higher – over 80 partially dissected bodies were removed from the Seine between 1941 and 1943.

Guillotined on 26 May 1946, Petiot – cool, smiling and unrepentant to the last – was clearly a man suffering from serious mental illness. But his campaign of murder was as calculating as it was cruel, involving rational planning and providing him with a constant source of profit. Whatever his state of mind, he consciously preyed on the most vulnerable people he could find, while placing himself on a pedestal as a national hero.

PSYCHOLOGICAL PROFILING OF SERIAL KILLERS

The term 'serial killer' was first used in the mid-1970s by FBI agent Robert Ressler, who also helped pioneer the science of psychological profiling following the horrific crimes in America of Ted Bundy and David Berkowitz. Bundy confessed to the rape and murder of at least 30 women between 1974 and 1978, though some put the number of his victims – who were bludgeoned and then strangled – much higher. Berkowitz – who fantasized about a bizarre satanic cult – confessed to killing six people and wounding seven others in New York between 1976 and 1977.

Some trace the development of psychological profiling back to New York psychoanalyst Dr Walter C. Langer who, in 1943, was asked to 'profile' Adolf Hitler. The first recorded instance in a criminal context was in 1956, when police asked Dr James Brussel (dubbed 'the Sherlock Holmes of the Couch'), to profile the so-called 'Mad Bomber'. In the 1960s, his profile of the notorious Boston Strangler led to the arrest of Albert DeSalvo.

Such work led to the founding of the FBI's Behavioural Science Unit in 1972, two of its pioneers, Howard Teten and Patrick Mullany, identifying and employing behavioural characteristics in solving violent crimes. They were followed, among others, by FBI agent (and, later, horror writer) John Edward Douglas, who in 1988 published *Sexual Homicide: Patterns and Motives*, followed in 1992 – in partnership with Robert Ressler and Ann and Allen Burgess – by the *Crime Classification Manual*. In Britain, police called in psychologist Dr David Canter to assist in the 'Railway Rapist' case, his work leading to the arrest and conviction of John Duffy and David Mulcahy in 1988. Canter went on in 1994 to establish the Centre for Investigative Psychology at the University of Liverpool. More recent influential publications include Eric Hickey's *Serial Murderers and Their Victims* (1991) and Helen Morrison's *My Life among the Serial Killers: Inside the Minds of the World's Most Notorious Murderers* (2004).

Characteristics of serial killers are disputed but many list the following: abuse as a child, unusual aggression in early years (fire raising, cruelty to animals or other children), stunted personality and emotions, compulsive and fluent lying, above-average intelligence and a complete lack of conscience. Typically, they are socially and/or sexually dysfunctional, preying on strangers, usually women and children. Once they start their killing spree, the pattern of murder intensifies, usually following a particular fetishistic pathology, whether in the selection of victims, the displaying of the bodies, or the method of killing. Most serial killers are manipulative, seeing rape and murder as the ultimate expression of control.

Some of the more infamous serial killers in the UK have included John George 'Acid Bath' Haigh, John Christie, Beverley Allitt (the Angel of Death), Ian Brady and Myra Hindley (the Moors Murderers), Donald Neilson (the Black Panther), Harold Shipman, John Straffen, Dennis Nilsen, Peter Sutcliffe (the Yorkshire Ripper), Fred and Rosemary West and, more recently, Steve Wright (the Suffolk Strangler), while the US has seen, among countless others, Henry Lee Lucas, John Wayne Gacy, William Bonin (the Freeway Killer), Randy Kraft (the South Californian Strangler), Charles Manson, Eddie Gein and Michael Lee Lockhart. The most prolific killer of all, with over 300 estimated victims, may well be the Colombian Luis Alfredo Garavito Cubillos, fittingly nicknamed 'The Beast'.

Albert DeSalvo, who confessed to strangling 13 women in the Boston area, is held by police, moments after he was captured following his escape from a mental hospital in 1967.

Al 'Scarface' Capone epitomized the murderous American Mafia mobsters who ran their rackets with impunity during the Prohibition era. Ironically, despite his deep involvement in organized crime and murder, the only charge he was ever convicted of was income-tax evasion.

Al Capone 1899–1947

Born in Brooklyn, New York, Alphonse 'Al' Capone was the son of Gabriele Capone, an Italian barber who had arrived in America with his wife Teresina in 1894. Al embarked on his career in organized crime when he left school aged just 14, and fell under the influence of a gangster boss, Johnny 'the Fox' Torrio. From there he graduated to the 'Five Points Gang' in Manhattan. It was during this period that he was slashed in the face after a bar-room brawl, leaving him with the scar by which he would later be known. He was also suspected of involvement in two killings, though witnesses refused to come forward and nothing was ever proven.

Capone's mentor Torrio had left New York for Chicago in 1909 to run a brothel racket. Ten years later he sent for his protégé, and it was probably Capone who was responsible for the murder in 1920 of Torrio's boss, 'Big Jim' Colosimo, with whom Torrio had fallen out. Torrio subsequently emerged as the undisputed kingpin of crime in the Windy City.

The introduction of Prohibition in 1920 endowed America's gangsters with a gold mine of opportunities. Trade in smuggled alcohol became big business, and speakeasies 'where bootlegged liquor was readily available' became the defining image of the era. But behind the relaxed jollity of the speakeasy and the gangster glamour lay violence, wanton sadism and psychopathic brutality.

In 1923 a reform-minded mayor, William E. Dever, was elected in Chicago on a platform of reining in the mobsters. As a result, Torrio and Capone opted to relocate much of their business to the satellite town of Cicero. The following year, with council elections scheduled for Cicero, Capone was determined to ensure that his candidates won, by whatever means. In the resulting violence, his brother Frank was killed and an election official was murdered, amid a wave of kidnappings, ballot-box theft and general intimidation. When it was all over Capone had won in Cicero, in one of the most dishonest elections ever seen.

Within weeks Capone, apparently believing himself impregnable, shot dead a small-time gangster called Joe Howard who had insulted a friend of his in a bar. The crime made Capone a target for William McSwiggen – the 'hanging prosecutor' – and though he failed to pin any charges on Capone, McSwiggen did succeed in putting the gangster firmly in the public spotlight, setting Capone on the road to becoming America's 'public enemy number one'.

In 1925 Torrio retired after an attempt on his life by a rival concern, the North Side Gang run by Dean O'Banion, George 'Bugs' Moran and Earl 'Hymie' Weiss. Capone now took over from Torrio as the leading figure in the Chicago underworld. Thereafter, he developed an increasingly public persona, ostentatiously attending major sporting occasions, such as baseball games, and even the opera, presenting himself as an honest, successful businessman, with a flair for the common touch. In truth everyone knew the real source of Capone's wealth.

Protection rackets, illegal gambling, bootlegging and prostitution – wherever there was a quick buck to be made, Capone had a hand in it. His eye for profit was combined with a ruthless approach to dealing with possible rivals – and the greatest threat to his hegemony, in Capone's view, was the North Side Gang, the hoodlums who had earlier attacked Johnny Torrio.

The result was the 1929 St Valentine's Day Massacre. Disguising his men as policemen, Capone sent them to Moran's warehouse at 2122 North Clark Street, where they lined seven of the North Siders up against a wall and machine-gunned them in cold blood. Several of the victims were also blasted with a shotgun in the face. The gang leader, Moran, escaped, but with his key lieutenants dead his operation went into steep decline. Capone was left as Chicago's undisputed Mr Big.

But outrage over the killings generated pressure for more action on the part of the authorities against Capone. It was this that led the FBI to launch its ingenious bid to pursue Capone for income-tax offences. Aware that he was unlikely ever to be indicted for any of his more violent activities (both because of the distance he now kept between himself and specific actions and because of the fear of reprisals that kept any potential witnesses from testifying), the federal government appointed a Treasury agent, Eliot Ness, and a hand-picked team of agents – the 'Untouchables' – to go after Capone.

As a strategy it proved to be a stunning success. In June 1931

The infamous gangster and racketeer Al Capone defiantly smoking his trademark cigar on the train carrying him to the federal penitentiary in Atlanta, where he began serving an 11-year sentence for income-tax evasion in 1932.

Capone was formally charged with income-tax evasion, and that October he was found guilty and sentenced to 11 years in prison. Initially sent to Atlanta penitentiary, in 1934 he was transferred to the maximum-security facility at Alcatraz. In 1939 he was released early, owing to ill health. But he was never able to regain control over his criminal empire. A shadow of his former self, Capone retreated into obscurity – finally dying of syphilis in 1947, a forgotten figure.

THE MAFIA IN THE USA

The New York underworld of the early 1900s, dominated by Jewish and Irish gangs, changed with the arrival of the Mustache Petes, Sicilian Mafiosi Joe 'the Boss' Masseria and Salvatore Maranzano. They infuriated young bucks such as 'Lucky' Luciano, associate of Jewish mobsters 'Bugsy' Siegel and Meyer Lansky.

In 1929 – having been recruited by Masseria after running a bootlegging racket with Vito Genovese and Frank Costello – Luciano was left for dead during the Castellammarese War between Masseria and Maranzano. He took his revenge in 1931, having both assassinated, taking over their empires and organizing the Five Families of New York – the Bonannos, Colombos, Gambinos, Lucchese and Genovese – into the National Crime Syndicate, which included the Brooklyn Boys (dubbed Murder Inc.) – hired thugs headed by Albert 'Mad Hatter' Anastasia who carried out gangland murders – and the Commission, a 'court' that settled disputes.

Luciano's reign – supported by Lansky, the mob's banker, and blue-eyed film-star-like Benjamin Siegel, whose psychopathic violence earned him the nickname 'Bugsy' – was short-lived, as he was convicted and imprisoned in 1936, then deported to Italy.

In 1946 Siegel founded his own city, Las Vegas, persuading Mafia bosses to invest in the Flamingo Hotel, but costs forced closure. The mob exacted retribution: Siegel was gunned down at his Beverly Hills home in June 1947 but Bugsy's own city flourished. Lansky took over the Flamingo and went on to dominate gambling in Vegas and Havana, Cuba, his worldwide empire inspiring the *Godfather* films. In 1970, threatened with tax-evasion charges, he fled to Israel, escaping conviction after he was forced to return.

The 1950s and 1960s was a 'golden age' for the US Mafia, and for a new generation – including Mickey Cohen, Salvatore Giancana, and the Boiardo and DeCavalcante families who inspired the Soprano family in David Chase's TV drama. Giancana was also instrumental in J.F. Kennedy's 1960 election as president through his control over key Chicago wards and union votes, and even shared a mistress with him, Judith Campbell Exner, introduced to them both by Frank Sinatra. However, the 1970 Racketeer Influenced and Corrupt Organizations Act (RICO) – which led in 1992 to the conviction of the last Mafia showman, Gambino boss John Gotti, thanks to the testimony of his hitman, underboss Sammy 'the Bull' Gravano – diminished Mafia power.

The bloody aftermath of the St Valentine's Day Massacre, 14 February 1929, in which seven members of 'Bugs' Moran's North Side Gang were gunned down by Al Capone's men in Chicago, Illinois.

Beria was a sinister Soviet secret policeman, psychopathic rapist and enthusiastic sadist who ordered the deaths of many and took a personal delight in the torture of his victims. The personification of the criminal monstrosity of the Soviet state, he was a coarse, cynical intriguer, a vindictive cut-throat, a deft courtier and a perverted thug. Yet he was also a highly intelligent, enormously competent and indefatigable administrator with the vision ultimately to reject Marxism and propose the sort of liberal programme that Mikhail Gorbachev brought to fruition years later.

Lavrenti Beria 1899–1953

'Let me have one night with him and I'll have him confessing he is the King of England.'

LAVRENTI BERIA

Beria was born in Georgia in 1899 to a very religious mother but of uncertain paternity – he was probably the illegitimate son of an Abkhazian nobleman. In Baku during the Russian Civil War he worked as a double agent, serving both the anti-Bolshevik regime and the Bolsheviks. Once Baku was retaken by the Bolsheviks, he proved a shrewd politician, and in 1921 he joined the new secret police, the Cheka, rising quickly to become head of the Georgian branch. He first met Stalin, a fellow Georgian, in 1926, and always behaved towards him not like a Bolshevik comrade (as was then the fashion) but like a medieval liege to his king. Stalin decided to use him against the old Georgians who ran the Caucasus, promoting him against their protests to first secretary of Georgia, and then of the entire Caucasus. When Stalin made his courtiers garden with him, Beria used an axe and told Stalin he would use it to tear out any weeds that he was ordered to extract. Beria understood Stalin's vanity and produced a book on the history of the Communists in the Caucasus that inflated Stalin's importance before the Revolution.

Stalin's local ally in the Caucasus was Abkhazian boss Nestor Lakoba, who had helped to promote Beria. But now Lakoba and Beria clashed, and in

A formal portrait of Lavrenti Beria, Stalin's sinister and sadistic secret police chief.

1936 Stalin allowed Beria to destroy his old friend which he did by poisoning Lakoba after an evening at the opera in Tiflis. Then, in what was to become a typical pattern, Beria set about destroying the entire Lakoba family, killing his brothers, young children and friends. When the Great Terror really started, Beria killed and tortured his way through the Caucasus, murdering far more victims than his quota.

In late 1938 Stalin brought Beria to Moscow and promoted him to 'assist Yezhov' (see page 232), the head of the NKVD, the secret police. Beria had been friendly with Yezhov, but now his role was to destroy him. On 25 November he was made boss of the NKVD in Yezhov's place, and set about restoring order to the frenzied chaos of Yezhov's killing machine. The Terror was officially over – but it never ended, it simply became secret, as Beria set about purging more Soviet leaders and generals. He liked to torture them himself, and beat one victim so hard that he knocked out one of his eyes. Stalin and Beria enjoyed coming up with imaginatively lurid ways of destroying their enemies. When Beria had found out that Lakoba's wife feared snakes above anything else, he drove her to insanity by placing snakes in her cell. He kidnapped and murdered his comrades' wives and killed other comrades in faked car crashes.

After Stalin signed the Non-Aggression Pact with Hitler in 1939, allowing him to annex eastern Poland, the Baltic States and Moldavia, Beria supervised the brutal killing and deportation of hundreds of thousands of innocent people suspected of anti-Soviet tendencies. In 1940 Beria, on Stalin's orders, presided over the execution of 28,000 Polish officers in the Katyn Forest. Following Hitler's invasion of the Soviet Union in 1941, Beria became ever more powerful. Promoted to commissar-general of security and made a marshal of the Soviet Union, he was one of the key administrators on the new state defence committee though which Stalin ran the war. Running the vast Gulag camp system as well as much of the country's industrial production, Beria continued to run the secret police and terrorize the generals on Stalin's behalf. In 1941 Beria proposed the deportation of the Volga Germans, and later, in 1944, the deportation of the Chechens, Karachai, Kalmyks, Balkars and Crimean Tartars. Hundreds of thousands were killed or perished en route. In 1945 Beria accompanied Stalin to Yalta, where President Roosevelt, spotting Beria at a dinner, asked his identity: 'That's Beria,' replied Stalin. 'My Himmler.'

During the Potsdam Conference, President Truman informed Stalin about America's new nuclear weapons. Stalin immediately placed Beria in charge of over 400,000 workers, including many brilliant scientists, tasked with developing a Soviet atom bomb. In 1946 Beria became a full member of the politburo. But Stalin had started to distrust him, sensing his cynicism about Marxism itself and his increasing dislike of his master. Stalin removed him from the ministry of internal affairs in 1946, purged his protégés and promoted Abakumov, another ruthless thug, to be minister of state security, independent of Beria. Yet Beria still managed to wield considerable influence. In 1949, to Stalin's delight, Beria delivered the Soviet atom bomb. In the same year, Beria managed to turn Stalin against two of his chosen heirs, and both were shot in the Leningrad Case.

By the early 1950s Stalin was in decline, forgetful, more and more paranoid, and never more dangerous. He now loathed 'Snake-eyes' Beria, who, in turn, hated Stalin and his system, even though he himself was one of its monsters. When Stalin died in March 1953, Beria emerged from the deathbed as the strongman of the new regime. Although his title was first deputy premier, he dominated the nominal premier, the weak Malenkov, and took charge of the ministry of internal affairs. He disdained the coarse, clumsy but shrewd Khrushchev, whom he fatally underestimated. Freed of the hated Stalin, Beria overconfidently proposed the freeing of millions of prisoners, liberalization of the economy and the loosening of Soviet hegemony over eastern Europe and the ethnic republics. Yet at the same time he was still arresting his personal enemies and intimidating his rivals. No one trusted him, everyone feared him. Three months after Stalin's death, Khrushchev orchestrated a palace coup backed by Marshal Zhukov and the Soviet military. Beria was arrested, and secretly confined in a military bunker. Here he begged for his life, writing pathetic letters to his ex-comrades, but to no avail: at his trial he was sentenced to death.

On the day he was due to die, he cried and collapsed until his executioner, a Soviet general, stuffed a towel in his mouth and shot him through the forehead.

Short, squat, bald and increasingly fat, Beria had a flat face with large fleshy lips, greeny-grey skin, and, behind his glinting pince-nez, grey, colourless eyes. At the same time, he was energetic, witty, quick, curious and an avid reader of history. 'He was enormously clever with inhuman energy,' said Stalin's deputy Molotov. 'He could work for a week with one night's sleep.' According to one of his henchmen, 'Beria would think nothing of killing his best friend.' Several of his colleagues observed that if he had been born in America, he would have been head of General Motors. Yet — with his love of intrigue, poison, torture and killing — he would also have flourished at the court of the Borgias.

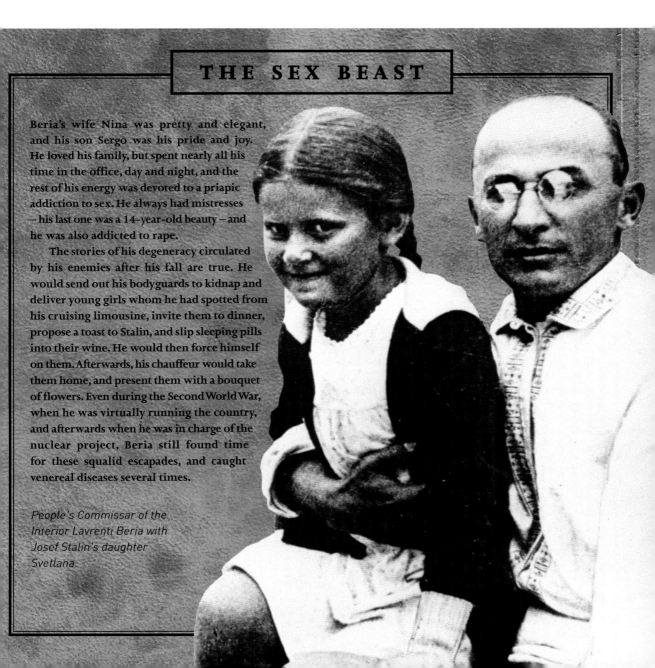

THE SEX BEAST

Beria's wife Nina was pretty and elegant, and his son Sergo was his pride and joy. He loved his family, but spent nearly all his time in the office, day and night, and the rest of his energy was devoted to a priapic addiction to sex. He always had mistresses — his last one was a 14-year-old beauty — and he was also addicted to rape.

The stories of his degeneracy circulated by his enemies after his fall are true. He would send out his bodyguards to kidnap and deliver young girls whom he had spotted from his cruising limousine, invite them to dinner, propose a toast to Stalin, and slip sleeping pills into their wine. He would then force himself on them. Afterwards, his chauffeur would take them home, and present them with a bouquet of flowers. Even during the Second World War, when he was virtually running the country, and afterwards when he was in charge of the nuclear project, Beria still found time for these squalid escapades, and caught venereal diseases several times.

People's Commissar of the Interior Lavrenti Beria with Josef Stalin's daughter Svetlana.

Heinrich Himmler was the chief organizer of the greatest crime in human history – the industrialized murder of 6 million Jews by execution squads, gas chambers and crematoria. Under his master Adolf Hitler, Himmler was the second most powerful man in the Third Reich, amassing huge powers as Reichsführer-SS, police chief and interior minister, and masterminding not just the Holocaust but also the massacre of Gypsies and homosexuals and the brutal enslavement of Slavs and other *Untermenschen* – 'subhumans'.

Heinrich Himmler

1900–45

'I also want to mention a very difficult subject before you here, completely openly. It should be discussed amongst us, and yet, nevertheless, we will never speak about it in public. I am talking about the Jewish evacuation: the extermination of the Jewish people.'

HEINRICH HIMMLER, 4 OCTOBER 1943

Heinrich was born in Munich to Gebhard Himmler, a respectable headmaster and tutor of Wittelsbach royalty, and his wife Anna Maria. Slightly built and preferring chess and stamp-collecting to the sports field, he was the antithesis of the Aryan ideal. He did eventually marry following a chance meeting with divorcée Margarete Siegroth in a hotel lobby. The couple had one daughter, Gudrun.

Himmler met future Nazis in the right-wing paramilitary Freikorps after the First World War. Supporting Hitler from the start and joining the Nazi Party in 1925, his unflinching loyalty, coupled with his administrative abilities and utter ruthlessness, led to his appointment in 1928 as Reichsführer-SS, head of the *Schutzstaffel* (SS). After Hitler became Chancellor of Germany in 1933, Himmler created the non-uniformed intelligence service, the SD

Heinrich Himmler as leader of the SS in 1933. The second most powerful man in Germany throughout much of the war, Himmler oversaw all police and security forces and organized the murder of 6 million Jews.

(*Sicherheitsdienst*), and the following year he organized the Night of the Long Knives in which Ernst Röhm and the leadership of the SA – *Sturmabteiling* ('Stormtroops') – were murdered. By 1936, he controlled the plainclothes political police, the dreaded Gestapo, and all uniformed police.

The outbreak of war in 1939 saw Himmler appointed Commissioner for the Consolidation of the German Race, charged with eliminating 'inferior' people from the Reich, and he set about expanding his concentration camps to detain opponents, and inferior races, Slavs and Jews. In September, Reinhard Heydrich – his talented protégé, head of both the SD and Gestapo – ordered the forcible eviction of Jews from across the Reich into ghettos in Poland, where thousands were executed, starved or died from disease.

In May the next year, following further mass deportations of Jews and Gypsies, Himmler put before Hitler plans to rid Europe of all Jews through 'forced evacuation to the East' – their euphemism for physical extermination – the 'final solution to the Jewish problem'. Hitler approved. In June 1941, following the invasion of the Soviet Union, Himmler – delegated to carry out 'special tasks' – despatched special killing squads, his SS *Einsatzgruppen*, who murdered a million Jews, Gypsies and communists. Himmler himself personally witnessed executions, and when, in August 1941, brains from one of the victims spattered his SS uniform, he demanded that concentration camps be equipped with gas chambers as a more efficient way of killing, more humane for the executioner.

The following January, Heydrich – who was assassinated later that year by Free Czech agents – spelt out to Nazi officials at the Wannsee Conference (see page 248) plans to deport all European Jews to new modern death factories – the extermination camps, mainly in the East. Numerous such camps – including Bergen-Belsen, Auschwitz-Birkenau, Belzec and Treblinka – were hastily constructed. Bergen-Belsen held over 60,000 Jews, of whom over 35,000 died of starvation, overwork, disease and medical experiments. Dachau – built in March 1933 to house political prisoners – served as a labour camp and centre for horrific medical experiments, those too sick to work being summarily executed or sent to the nearby Hartheim killing centre. Meanwhile, 3 million Russian prisoners of war were deliberately starved to death on Hitler/Himmler's orders.

Most notorious of death camps was Auschwitz-Birkenau, established by Himmler in May 1940, and by 1942 equipped with seven gas chambers in which an estimated 2.5 million were murdered, roughly 2 million of whom were Jews, Poles, Gypsies and Soviet POWs. Only about 200,000 people survived, the rest cremated or piled into mass graves.

In June 1942, Himmler ordered the deportation of 100,000 Jews from France and approved plans to move 30 million Slavs from Eastern Europe to Siberia. The following month he ordered the 'total cleansing' of Jews from the Polish General Government – 6000 a day from Warsaw alone were transported to the death camps.

In 1943, Himmler was appointed minister of the interior. The following year Hitler disbanded the military intelligence service (the *Abwehr*) and made Himmler's SD Nazi Germany's sole intelligence service. In 1944, as the Allies advanced from the west, Himmler failed completely as military commander of Army Group Vistula.

Recognizing defeat was inevitable, Himmler desperately attempted to destroy evidence of the death camps, then attempted to seek peace with Britain and America. Hitler ordered his arrest. Himmler fled in disguise but was arrested in Bremen, after which he swallowed a cyanide capsule.

A chinless, bespectacled ex-chicken-farmer who suffered from nervous ailments, he built a second family with his mistress, his ex-secretary whom he called 'Bunny' – but the attic of their house contained furniture and books made from the bones and skins of his Jewish victims. He was a meticulous administrator who organized the systematic extermination of 6 million Jews (two-thirds of the Jewish population of Europe), 3 million Russians, 3 million non-Jewish Poles, 750,000 Slavs, 500,000 Gypsies, 100,000 of the mentally ill, 100,000 Freemasons, 15,000 homosexuals and 5000 Jehovah's Witnesses – murder on a scale never before imagined.

The Wannsee Conference

On 20 January 1942, Himmler's deputy, Reinhard Heydrich, convened a meeting of the 15 leading Nazi bureaucrats, many of them lawyers and 8 of them possessing doctorates, in a large house in an affluent suburb of Berlin, near a picturesque lake called the Wannsee.

Over a million Jews had already been murdered by the mobile *Einsatzgruppen*, but the work was considered too slow and demoralizing. The purpose at Wannsee was to convey directives from the Führer regarding the 'Final Solution' of the Jewish Question and create an administrative and legalistic framework for mass-murder. 'Europe was to be combed of Jews from east to west,' and those present charged with the capture, transportation and industrial extermination of the estimated 11 million European Jews.

'Another possible solution of the problem has now taken the place of emigration, i.e. the evacuation of the Jews to the East,' said Heydrich. The notes, kept by Adolf Eichmann, carefully avoid direct reference to extermination but 'evacuation' was the accepted euphemism for slaughter, as Heydrich made clear:

> Under proper guidance, in the course of the final solution the Jews are to be allocated for appropriate labour in the East. Able-bodied Jews, separated according to sex, will be taken in large work columns to these areas for work on roads, in the course of which action doubtless a large portion will be eliminated by natural causes. The possible final remnant will, since it will undoubtedly consist of the most resistant portion, have to be treated accordingly, because it is the product of natural selection and would, if released, act as the seed of a new Jewish revival.

Building of the extermination camps of Belzec, Treblinka and Auschwitz was complete within the year. No one present expressed dissent and, unsettlingly, few of the participants were punished appropriately. Their respective fates were:

- HEYDRICH: assassinated later that year in Prague
- ROLAND FREISLER: killed in an air-raid in Berlin, February 1945
- RUDOLF LANGE: killed in action, February 1945
- ALFRED MEYER: committed suicide, April 1945
- HEINRICH MÜLLER: disappeared in Berlin, 1945
- MARTIN LUTHER, died in Berlin, May 1945
- KARL EBERHARD SCHÖNGARTH: executed for war crimes (killing British POWs), May 1946
- FRIEDRICH WILHELM KRITZINGER: acquitted of war crimes, died 1947
- JOSEF BÜHLER: executed for war crimes, 1948
- ERICH NEUMANN: briefly imprisoned, died 1948
- WILHELM STUCKART: released for lack of evidence, 1949; died in car crash, 1953
- ADOLF EICHMANN: hanged in Israel, 1962
- GEORG LEIBBRANDT: released 1950; died June 1982
- OTTO HOFMANN: pardoned 1954; died December 1982
- GERHARD KLOPFER: released for lack of evidence; worked as tax advisor; died January 1987

Half-starved slave labourers lying in wooden bunks, including future chronicler of the Holocaust Elie Wiesel (centre bunk seventh from left), look amazed as their liberators, US troops of the 80th Army Division, enter their barracks in Buchenwald concentration camp, 16 April 1945.

Rudolf Hoess was a mild-mannered figure who rarely lost his temper. He was also cold, calculating and remorseless. As the commander of the Auschwitz extermination camp, he was arguably the biggest mass murderer in history, coordinating and proudly keeping a record of the slaughter of approximately three million people, the vast majority of them European Jews. After spending the day overseeing the slaughter of thousands of people, he would return home to the warm welcome of his family, kissing his wife and tucking his four children into bed while the smoke from the burning bodies of his victims plumed into the air, visible from his window.

Rudolf Hoess 1900–47
and Auschwitz

'It took from 3 to 15 minutes to kill the people in the death chamber, depending upon climatic conditions. We knew when the people were dead because their screaming stopped.'
RUDOLF HOESS'S SIGNED CONFESSION TO THE NUREMBERG WAR CRIMES TRIBUNAL

Born into a strict Roman Catholic family in Baden-Baden, Hoess was a lonely child with few friends. During the First World War, aged only 14, he joined the German army. By the time he was 17 he had become the army's youngest non-commissioned officer, and was eventually awarded the Iron Cross first and second class. In 1922, after hearing Adolf Hitler speak in Munich, he left the Catholic Church and joined the Nazis. He was sentenced to ten years in prison following the murder of a communist school teacher in 1924, but released in 1928. Hoess joined the SS in 1933, and a year later he was appointed to the staff at the SS concentration camp at Dachau. In 1938 he was promoted to adjutant at the Sachsenhausen camp, and in 1940 was appointed commandant of Auschwitz in Nazi-occupied Poland, a position he held until November 1943.

In 1941 Heinrich Himmler informed Hoess of Hitler's plans for a Final Solution to the Jewish question, which, he was left in no doubt, meant the complete extermination of the 11 million Jews

(previous page) The entrance to the Auschwitz concentration camp near the town of Oświęcim in southern Poland, surmounted by the slogan 'Arbeit macht frei' ('work will make you free').

then estimated to live in Europe. Speaking to a camp commandant at Treblinka, Hoess learned how 80,000 Jews, principally from the Warsaw Ghetto, had been liquidated in the course of half a year through carbon monoxide poisoning. But Hoess believed that mass extermi-nation needed more efficient methods so, when he built the extermination unit at Auschwitz, he used Zyklon B, a crystallized form of cyanide. It was dropped through the ceiling of the locked chambers where the victims had been told they were to take a shower.

Hoess later explained how he had tested Zyklon B on prisoners in their cells, donning a gas mask and releasing the gas. He was impressed with the swiftness of death, and in September 1941 ordered a larger-scale trial, killing 850 prisoners in one go. By mid-1942, mass killings of Jews were taking place every day. With such large numbers, the gas took longer to take effect, some victims surviving in agony for as long as 15 minutes. Hoess and his SS men knew everyone was dead when the screaming stopped. At that point, the guards would arrive in the chamber and remove gold rings and rip out gold

THE NUREMBERG TRIALS

After the Second World War, the major Allied powers – the United States, the USSR and Britain – established a court in which to try those Nazis who had been accused of war crimes. The 24 most important figures were tried first, between 14 November 1945 and 1 October 1946. The trials of lesser figures such as doctors and judges who had participated in the Nazi regime were to follow.

The trials took place at the Palace of Justice in Nuremberg, a city chosen for its symbolic significance, for it was here that the Nazis had held some of their most famous rallies before the war. The defendants sat before a panel of judges handpicked from each of the three major Allies.

Among the more notorious figures on trial were Hermann Goering, *Reichsmarschall* and Hitler's longtime deputy and heir apparent, Martin Bormann (secretary of the Nazi Party and Hitler's right-hand man; he was tried in absentia), Hans Frank (Reich law leader and governor general of occupied Poland), Wilhelm Frick (minister of the interior who had passed the Nuremberg race laws), Rudolf Hess (Hitler's deputy who had attempted to make a secret peace deal with Britain in 1941), Ernst Kaltenbrunner (the highest surviving member of the SS leadership), Wilhelm Keitel (head of the high command of the armed forces), Joachim von Ribbentrop (minister for foreign affairs), Alfred Rosenberg (Nazi racial theorist), Fritz Sauckel (slave-labour chief), Arthur Seyss-Inquart

(former Austrian chancellor and commissioner for the occupied Netherlands) and Julius Streicher (anti-Semitic publisher).

The testimony of the participants was shocking to the outside world and brought home the extent of the murderousness and brutality of the Nazi regime. Julius Streicher was unrepentant about his warped views to the last, stating on 16 December 1945 that 'The Jews are making a mistake if they make a martyr out of me; you will see. I didn't create the problem; it existed for thousands of years.' Hermann Goering claimed that 'The four real conspirators are missing: the Führer, Himmler, Bormann, and Goebbels.'

At the conclusion of the trial, 12 death sentences were read out by the judges, 10 of which were carried out on 16 October 1946 by hanging (Bormann was believed to be in hiding, and Goering committed suicide on the eve of his execution). Those who were given prison sentences were sent to Spandau prison in Berlin. Nonetheless, the majority of the monstrous criminals who perpetrated the Holocaust escaped punishment.

Senior Nazis on trial at Nuremberg. Front row from left: Hermann Goering (committed suicide), Rudolf Hess (imprisoned), Joachim von Ribbentrop (hanged), Wilhelm Keitel (hanged). Back row from left: Karl Doenitz (imprisoned), Erich Raeder (imprisoned), Baldur von Schirach (imprisoned), Fritz Sauckel (hanged), Alfred Jodl (hanged).

teeth from the corpses, before they were shovelled into ditches, or placed on large grids and burned.

Driving his comrade Adolf Eichmann around the 20,000-acre site on an official visit, Hoess boasted that he had the capacity to gas 10,000 people in one day. According to his own estimate, in his signed statement to the Nuremberg War Crimes Tribunal, 2.5 million Jews were gassed or burned to death at Auschwitz – along with an estimated 200,000 Russian prisoners of war – while another half a million inmates died of starvation and disease. Between 70 and 80 per cent of those who entered the camp died. In the summer of 1944, although no longer commander, Hoess returned to Auschwitz to supervise the murder of more than 400,000 Hungarian Jews. In fact, Hoess's methods had been so pleasing to the Nazi hierarchy that he was made chief inspector of all the concentration and extermination camps.

As Soviet troops approached Auschwitz, Hoess fled, disguising himself as 'Franz Land' and going into hiding. But British troops discovered his wife Hedwig and interrogated her for six days, which led to his arrest. After giving evidence at the Nuremberg Trials, Hoess was handed over to the Polish authorities. Tried and sentenced to death, on 16 April 1947 he was hanged on a gallows specially built for him beside the former crematorium at Auschwitz.

An ambitious, bland and manipulative pen-pusher, Adolf Eichmann, Hitler's 'expert on Jewish affairs' at the Central Office of Reich Security, was the Nazi bureaucrat of death who committed mass murder by organizing and planning the registration, transport and cremation of 6 million Jews.

Adolf Eichmann
1906–62

'If I have to, I will go to the grave with a smile, for the knowledge of having five million Jews on my conscience gives me a feeling of great satisfaction.'

ADOLF EICHMANN

Eichmann was born to a middle-class family in the industrial city of Solingen in Westphalia, the eldest of five children. The family moved to Linz in Austria, where Eichmann – although possessed of steel-blue eyes – was labelled 'Ziggy' or 'Jew boy' by his schoolmates on account of his dark complexion.

A failure at school, Eichmann went on to work as a door-to-door salesman. In 1932 he attended a Nazi Party meeting in a beer hall in Linz, where he was approached by a young lawyer and acquaintance of his father called Ernst Kaltenbrunner, who was later to be Gestapo chief and his boss at the Central Office of Reich Security. Eichmann was never an ideologue, but he did relish following orders – so when Kaltenbrunner instructed him that he was to join the party, he promptly obeyed.

After Hitler came to power in Germany, Eichmann moved to Bavaria, where he joined the SS intelligence service. In this role he became adept at keeping detailed records of potential 'enemies of the Reich', first focusing on Freemasons before moving to the Jewish department. He began to read widely on the subject, learning some Hebrew and making a research trip to Palestine in the summer of 1937.

In March 1938 Eichmann was sent back to Austria – now under German control – to help coordinate forced Jewish emigration. Moving into a house that had been confiscated from the Rothschild family – and making ample use of its wine cellar – he presented himself as a polite and reasonable figure, willing to make compromises with Jewish leaders. These compromises involved confiscating their estates in return for safe passage. His statistics for emigration soon outran those of his counterparts in Germany.

Encouraged by his mentor Reinhard Heydrich, Eichmann soon became known as the key Nazi expert on Jewish emigration. As the Second World War began, he was transferred to Berlin, and in October 1940 presided over the first mass deportation of Jews from German territory.

During the first two years of the war Eichmann concentrated on deporting Jews to ghettos in Poland. In the late summer of 1941 Heydrich informed him of the Führer's desire for a 'Final Solution' to the Jewish question. Eichmann witnessed some of the mass shootings in Poland that marked the beginning of the Holocaust, and visited Auschwitz on a number of occasions, where he discussed more efficient modes of execution, advocating the use of poison gas. In January 1942 he took the minutes at the Wannsee Conference (see page 248), in which the plans for the Final Solution were drawn up.

Eichmann had personal control of his own concentration camp, at Theresienstadt (Terezin) in Poland, which he opened to inspectors from the International Red Cross, presenting it as a model prison. In fact, Theresienstadt was merely a staging post on the way to the gas chambers of Auschwitz. On 20 July 1942, organizing deportations from occupied France, Eichmann gave orders that not even children were to be spared. He visited Auschwitz again that summer, where the sight of mass burnings of corpses made him feel sick, but failed to prick his conscience.

When the German army arrived in Hungary in the spring of 1944, Eichmann moved his operation to Budapest, where he set about rounding up the country's 400,000 Jews, circulating forged letters and postcards among the Jewish community telling of the fair conditions in the Jewish 'work camps' of Poland, and encouraging fellow Jews to move there voluntarily. Even though the war was clearly lost, the Nazis diabolic plan to destroy the Jews had to continue. When the Allies bombed the train lines from Budapest, Eichmann sent 40,000 Hungarian Jews on a 'death march' to Austria, to prevent them being liberated by the Allies.

Trying to flee Austria at the end of the war, Eichmann was accosted by an American patrol, which, however, failed to identify him. Acquiring false papers, he remained in Germany for five years, and then, in July 1950, he fled to Argentina. But there were those who were determined to bring the perpetrators of the Holocaust to justice, and in 1960 Eichmann was finally tracked down by the Israeli intelligence service Mossad. He was abducted by a team of agents and taken to Jerusalem to face justice in an Israeli court.

At his trial, Eichmann claimed that he would have killed his own father if ordered to do so. To Hannah Arendt he personified the 'banality of evil'. Blindly obedient to some of the most evil men in history, he was in fact an enthusiastic and monstrous mass-murderer: he was truly the devil of the details. Sentenced to death, he was hanged on 1 June 1962.

Adolf Eichmann, SS-Obersturmbannführer, and from 1939 leader of the Jewish unit of the Central Office of Reich Security, responsible for organizing the transport of Jews to concentration camps. Eichmann is pictured here during his trial in Jerusalem (1961).

REINHARD HEYDRICH

Tall, slim, athletic, blue-eyed and blond, though with broad feminine hips, Heydrich was a Nazi, a fanatic and killer, a master of espionage and the chief organizer of the secret but colossal slaughter of Europe's Jews. He specialized in clandestine intrigues, running a brothel to bug well-known patrons and using concentration-camp prisoners, murdered with injections, to provide the pretext for Hitler's invasion of Poland. Heydrich was born of musical parents in the city of Halle, near Leipzig, in 1904. His father was a Wagnerian opera singer and his mother, who was extremely strict and regularly beat her son, was a talented pianist. Like his protégé Adolf Eichmann, young Heydrich was never popular among his peers, who nicknamed him 'Moses' because of rumours that he had Jewish ancestry.

Deeply sensitive about these rumours, in his teens Heydrich became fanatically obsessed with the supposed inherent superiority of the Germanic people. In 1931, aged 27, he joined the SS, impressing Heinrich Himmler during his interview. In 1933 he was promoted to brigadier general and given the responsibility of setting up the SD, the SS security service. where he identified the administrative talents of Adolf Eichmann.

In 1939 Heydrich was put in charge of the Reich Main Security Office, and after the invasion of Poland formed five SS *Einsatzgruppen* ('task forces') to round up political enemies, dissidents, aristocrats and Jews in the occupied territory. With the invasion of the Soviet Union in 1941, more *Einsatzgruppen* were sent east, shooting an estimated 1,300,000 Jews by the end of the war. In January 1942 Heydrich convened the Wannsee Conference in Berlin, which organized the Final Solution in which six million Jews were killed on an industrial scale (see page 248).

In September 1941 Heydrich was appointed *Reichsprotektor* of Bohemia and Moravia (formerly part of Czechoslovakia), where he instituted repressive measures and became known as *Der Henker* ('the Hangman'). On 27 May 1942, as he rode without an escort in an open-top green Mercedes, he was ambushed by two British-trained Free Czech fighters and died later of his wounds. In retaliation, the Nazis wiped out the entire Czech village of Lidice. Heydrich, along with his successor Ernst Kaltenbrunner, ranks with the most grotesque monsters of human history.

Reinhard Heydrich, chief of the Reich Main Security Office and Reichsprotektor *of Bohemia and Moravia.*

Dr Hastings Banda was the father of Malawian independence, a shrewd political manipulator and a popular opponent of colonialism who created a one-party state, a vainglorious cult about his own person, and a savage repressive terror to maintain his own dictatorship.

Dr Hastings Banda
c. 1906–97

'I am too busy to die.'

HASTINGS BANDA, WHO WAS SAID TO HAVE BEEN OVER ONE HUNDRED WHEN HE DIED

Although his official birthday was stated as 14 May 1906, Hastings Banda is believed to have been born some time towards the end of the 19th century. The son of a peasant, he was baptized into the Church of Scotland and attended a local mission school, where he showed himself to be a talented student. After spending several years working as miner, in 1925 he moved to the United States to study, and in 1937 received a medical degree from the University of Tennessee. In 1941 he achieved further medical qualifications at the University of Edinburgh, and moved to the north of England and then London, where he practised medicine from 1945 to 1953 specializing in the sexually transmitted diseases of soldiers and sailors.

From 1949, despite living in London, Banda increasingly turned his attention towards the plight of his homeland, particularly after white settlers tried to extend their influence by federating his native Nyasaland with Rhodesia in 1953. That year he returned to Africa and worked as a doctor in the Gold Coast (now Ghana), and became increasingly well known to black nationalists in Nyasaland. In 1958 he finally returned home to become president of the Nyasaland African Congress, touring the country and leading the opposition to the federation of Nyasaland with Rhodesia.

In 1959 a state of emergency was declared in Nyasaland, and Rhodesian troops were flown in to restore order, arresting Banda in March 1959. However, on his release in April 1960, the British invited Banda to London where they accepted his demands for constitutional changes, and in 1961 Banda and his allies won a sweeping election victory. Banda became the minister of natural resources and local government and then, in 1963, prime minister, a position he maintained as Nyasaland finally achieved independence as Malawi on 6 July 1964. At first Banda was universally acclaimed as a hero of independence, but soon many of his former supporters were criticizing his autocratic ways. In August 1964, just a month after independence, he dismissed four of his ministers after discovering that they were attempting to curb his power under the new constitution. Fearing for their lives, they fled the country. In 1966 Banda succeeded in changing the constitution to increase his own powers and declared himself president of the new Republic of Malawi. Five years later he tightened his stranglehold even further by making himself president for life and adopting the name 'Great Lion'.

Banda's regime was austerely authoritarian, and he tried to impose his own personal control on all important government offices. Dissent was forbidden and critics of the government were jailed or executed – many being fed to the crocodiles. Under the 1971 constitution the only party legally permitted to operate was Banda's Malawi Congress Party (MCP), and each Malawian adult was expected to be a member and to carry their membership card at all times. Every public building and business

Dr Banda at his birthday celebrations on 14 May 1992. Banda, a hero of independence, went on to become a symbol of brutal dictatorship and eccentric autocracy.

was ordered to display a picture of the president, which was to be positioned higher than anything else on the wall. Television was banned, and all other media outlets, including cinema and radio, were severely censored and heavily laced with the image or voice of the president, while mail was opened and phones were tapped. Study of the history of the country before the late 1960s was discouraged, books were burned, and a number of tribes were prohibited from speaking their own language.

Even when it came to the smallest details, Banda was an obsessive disciplinarian. Although he presented himself as an advocate of women's rights, both Malawian and foreign females were strictly prohibited from showing their thighs, or wearing shorts or jeans. Men were ordered to be clean-shaven and short-haired, and specific directives were given to prohibit the entry of 'hippies' to the country.

Banda's policies were largely pro-Western and often unpopular; he sought friendly relations with apartheid South Africa in order to improve the country's trade and infrastructure, at which he had some initial success. However, the withdrawal of Western aid in 1993 undermined this strategy, and that year he was forced to legalize rival political parties in order to stem the tide of dissent. In 1994, in the first proper elections for 30 years, he was defeated by the opposition leader, Bakili Muluzi.

In January 1996 Banda was acquitted, along with his former aide John Tembo, of charges relating to the assassination of four political opponents in 1983, although few disputed the fact that his dictatorship had been based on the suppression of political opponents, in which the threat of violence was, at the very least, always under the surface. He died in November 1997 in a hospital in South Africa; he may have been over one hundred years old.

Banda's polite, gentlemanly exterior and medical 'bedside manner' disguised an ambitious and ruthless man.

DOC-TATORS AND DOC-TERRORISTS

One of the stranger phenomena of 20th-century tyranny was the political rise of medical doctors, who qualified in and even practised medicine, taking the Hippocratic Oath to save life and heal disease, yet became brutal dictators or murderous terrorists.

Dr Hastings Banda of Malawi and Dr François Duvalier of Haiti were the quintessential doc-tators. Like other ambitious young men in Third World countries, they trained to be doctors as a way of getting an education, but Duvalier went further, employing the image of surgical incision and saving by killing to promote his rise to power: 'A nation's ills demand a doctor,' he said. 'A doctor must sometimes take a life to save it.'

The first of the doc-tators was William Walker (see page 177), the American warlord and Nicaraguan dictator responsible for many murders, who qualified as a physician and practised briefly. Félix Houphouët-Boigny, born of royal heritage in Ivory Coast, practised medicine for 15 years before becoming its first president, ruling autocratically and self-indulgently for 33 years between 1960 and 1993. Known as the Grand Old Man of Africa, he was the doc-tator *par excellence*. Dr Radovan Karadžić, the president of the Bosnian Serb Republic and henchman of President Milošević (see page 302), studied medicine and practised as a psychiatrist, even working with the Serbian soccer team. Indicted for the murder of 7500 Muslim men and boys at Srebrenica in 1995 and the shelling of Sarajevo, he was finally captured in Belgrade in July 2008. Dr Che Guevara, the legendary revolutionary, was another medical doctor (trained at Buenos Aires University) who embraced repressive politics: in the early years of the Cuban Revolution, he was an enthusiastic and personal participant in the execution of class enemies. Bashar al-Assad, the Syrian dictator, allegedly responsible for atrocities and murders in Lebanon, is an eye-doctor, having qualified as an ophthalmologist in London and Damascus before succeeding his father in 2000.

Doctors have proved even more ubiquitous in terrorism. Dr Ayman al-Zawahiri, an Egyptian surgeon, is deputy leader of al-Qaeda and was the mastermind behind the killing of 3000 innocents on 9/11. Dr George Habash, a Palestinian physician, was the leader of the brutal terrorist faction, the PFLP, during the 1970s. Dr Abdel al-Rantissi, co-founder of Hamas, the Palestinian terrorist organization, trained as a paediatrician in Alexandria yet devoted himself to organized suicide bombings, killing many innocent Israeli civilians: 'We will kill Jews anywhere,' he said.

A poster in the streets of Havana of the Argentinian-born revolutionary and medical doctor Che Guevara, based on Alberto Korda's iconic 1960 photograph entitled Guerrillero Heroico *('Heroic Guerrilla').*

François Duvalier, the president of Haiti for 14 years, was a corrupt and brutal autocrat who brought to heel a proud but unstable nation – the first free black republic – through his ghoulish paramilitary death squads, the Tonton Macoutes. With his violent acolytes he plundered the country and terrorized opponents of the regime. Coming to prominence as a medical doctor with a genuinely popular appeal, he resorted to corruption, kleptocracy and a Voodoo mysticism in which he saw himself as a semi-divine figure, half-Christ, half-Voodoo hero, Baron Samedi.

François 'Papa Doc' Duvalier 1907–71

'I am the Haitian flag. He who is my enemy is the enemy of my fatherland.'

FRANÇOIS 'PAPA DOC' DUVALIER

François Duvalier was born on 14 April 1907 in Port-au-Prince, Haiti's capital. His mother, who was mentally unstable, worked in a bakery and his father was a teacher, journalist and justice of the peace. The couple nicknamed their son 'Papa Doc' after he qualified to practise medicine at the University of Haiti in 1934. In 1939, as a successful young professional, he married Simone Ovide Faine, a nurse, and went on to have four children, three girls and a boy, Jean-Claude, born in 1951, who would later succeed his father in 1971. Duvalier spent a year at the University of Michigan and, with American assistance, won national recognition for his public-health work against tropical diseases such as yaws and malaria, which had claimed countless lives in Haiti.

In 1938, Duvalier formed 'Le Groupe des Griots', a group of black intellectuals – influenced by the ethnologist and Voodoo scholar Lorimer Denis – which aimed to awaken black nationalism and Voodoo mysticism in Haiti. In 1946, after the Second World War, he joined the government of President Dumarsais Estimé, becoming director general of Haiti's public health service and then, in 1948, minister of public health. In 1950, however, the government was overthrown by a military coup led by Paul Magloire, who identified Duvalier as a key opponent of the new regime, forcing him into hiding from 1954.

Haiti was notoriously unstable, however, and Duvalier re-emerged in December 1956 after Magloire was compelled to resign. Over the next nine months, the country experienced six governments, Duvalier and his followers participating in them all. Finally, in September 1957, he was elected president in his own right, on a populist platform, promising to end the control of the mulatto elite – those of mixed Latin American and European origin – and claiming to be a Voodoo priest.

Despite the fact that the generals had helped to rig his election, Duvalier did not trust the army and, with the help of his chief aide, Clément Barbot, he decreased its size and created the Tonton Macoutes, or Volunteers for National Security, as a counterweight. The Volunteers, soon known as the Bogeymen, were a thuggish militia, loyal to the president and numbering between 9000 and 15,000. Without an official salary, they were instead given free rein by the government to help themselves through extortion, racketeering and crime – in return, they kidnapped, intimidated and murdered opponents of the regime, as many as 30,000 during Duvalier's reign. They dressed in quasi-military clothing, wore dark glasses and mimicked the demons of the Voodoo tradition, preferring to use machetes and knives rather than firearms to dispose of their victims, whom they would leave strung up as a warning to others. No rivals were to be tolerated in Duvalier's regime, as his aide Barbot discovered to his cost after he temporarily assumed the reins of government when the president suffered a heart attack in May 1959. On Duvalier's recovery, he was promptly imprisoned and, after plotting against his former friend on his release, killed in 1963. Others considered a threat were sent to Fort Dimanche, where they were tortured to death.

Having fought off an attempted invasion by Haitian exiles – assisted by Cuban guerrillas – in August 1959, Duvalier soon resumed control. In 1961, a sham election saw his term as president unanimously extended to 1967, Haiti as a result becoming increasingly isolated, as potential allies such as the United States – which had backed him against the 1959 invasion attempt – began to ostracize the regime. This isolation, however, gave Duvalier more room to stamp his cult of personality on the regime, manipulating the Voodoo traditions of the island and portraying himself as the embodiment of the nation. He imposed his image on the rural population by mimicking Baron Samedi, a sinister spirit figure in Voodoo associated with death, depicted in top hat and tuxedo, with dark glasses and skull-like face. At the same time, despite having been excommunicated by the Vatican in 1964 for harassing the clergy, he associated himself closely with the figure of Christ, one notorious propaganda image depicting Jesus with his hand on Duvalier's shoulder declaring, 'I have chosen him.'

In 1964, Duvalier became president for life in a quasi-monarchical regime, amending the constitution to ensure that his son, Jean-Claude, became president following his death. 'Baby Doc' Duvalier duly took over the country in 1971 at just 19 years of age, his ostentatious displays of wealth incurring the wrath of the impoverished nation, which remained largely illiterate while the corrupt elite siphoned off the country's remaining assets. 'Baby Doc' ruled until 1986, when he was overthrown by the military.

Leader of the world's first black republic and Haiti's longest-serving ruler, Duvalier brought misery and turmoil to his people. His regime of murder, greed and superstition – epitomized by the Bogeymen – wreaked terror and bloodshed upon an unsuspecting nation. Despite his populist message, he was concerned only with serving his own ends, embezzling millions of dollars and leaving the country destitute.

Francois Duvalier, the corrupt, Voodoo-obsessed dictator who ruled Haiti for 14 years, photographed here in 1969.

VOODOO

Voodoo, which derives from the word 'vodun', meaning spirit, is an ancient religious practice that originated in West Africa, perhaps as much as 10,000 years ago. It is still practised by more than thirty million people worldwide, despite once being suppressed and denounced as black magic by Christian colonialists.

Haiti is regarded as the home of Voodoo, where it is an officially sanctioned religion under the state's constitution. It was imported into Haiti along with thousands of slaves who were seized in West Africa and forced to work in the French colony. In August 1791, a Voodoo ceremony involving the sacrifice of a black pig was one of the sparks for the Haitian Revolution, which saw the establishment of an independent Haitian republic in 1804.

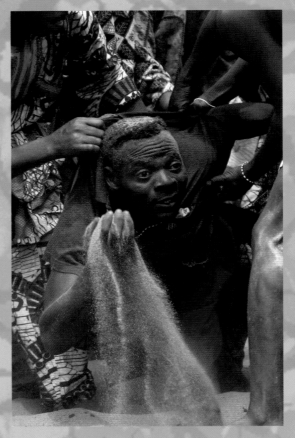

A Voodoo dancer possessed by Voodoo magic goes into a trance in Ouidah, Republic of Benin.

collectively as Loa. Baron Samedi, whom Papa Doc imitated, was one of the most famous of these spirits. Associated with sex and resurrection, he was said to stand at the crossroads of the spiritual world, watching the souls of the dead pass by.

One feature of Voodoo ceremonies is 'possession', in which a subject is purportedly inhabited by spirits from whom the priest or priestess extracts information concerning other spirits or future events. Uniquely, the religion holds that not only humans have souls; all natural phenomena are of holy significance.

Despite negative perceptions encouraged by critics of Voodoo, neither fear of zombies nor the use of sinister Voodoo dolls – models of the souls

Voodoo is famed for its flamboyant religious ceremonies, which involve singing, dancing and animal sacrifice, run by a priest or priestess, often known as 'Papa' or Mama'. In Voodoo culture, everything in the universe is interconnected and nothing – human, animal or object – is an independent entity. Voodoo practitioners pay homage to a supreme deity, known as *Bon Dieu* ('Good God'), but there are also hundreds of lesser spirits and angels organized into families and influencing every aspect of life – from health to wealth and love and happiness – known

of others, to whom harm can be done through inserting pins and casting spells – are prominent features of mainstream Voodoo. It is often mistakenly confused with Louisiana Voodoo, also known as New Orleans Voodoo, a bastardized form of the tradition that emerged among the French- and Creole-speaking African-American population of Louisiana. Here greater emphasis is placed on charms and folk legends, such as the Gris-Gris, an amulet (normally a small cloth bag containing potions of herbs, hair and other personal effects) that protects the wearer from evil or brings luck.

Enver Hoxha was intellectually sophisticated, handsome and charming, but a paranoid, rigidly dogmatic and murderous Stalinist tyrant of Albania who in a 40-year reign isolated and impoverished his country, tormented and murdered his own people and ran the government apparatus with sinister, sometimes tragicomic, violence, killing many of his own comrades in faked accidents, suicides and executions. By his death, he had turned his country into a failed state on the brink of collapse.

Enver Hoxha 1908–85

'Stalin was not at all what the enemies of communism accused and accuse him of being. On the contrary, he was just and a man of principle … We Albanian communists have successfully applied the teachings of Stalin … His rich and very valuable experience has guided us on our road and in our activity.'

ENVER HOXHA, MEMOIRS

Hoxha was the son of a well-off cloth merchant, and during the 1920s and 1930s he spent several periods abroad, studying and working in France (he attended philosophy lectures at the Sorbonne) and Belgium, before returning to teach French in a school in the town of Korcë. When Fascist Italy invaded Albania in 1939, Hoxha refused to join the newly established Albanian Fascist Party, and was sacked from his job as a consequence. A year later, he opened a tobacco shop where in 1940, he helped found the Albanian Communist Party, which began an insurgent campaign against Italian occupation, drawing on the assistance of Tito's Partisans in neighbouring Yugoslavia. After liberation in 1944, Enver Hoxha became both the new prime minister and minister of foreign affairs but really ruled as First Secretary of the Albanian Party of Labour.

Hoxha was a loyal and devoted Stalinist, savagely purging personal and class enemies. Stalin and Hoxha met frequently, enjoying long discussions on history and linguistics, later retold in Hoxha's surprisingly fascinating memoirs. In 1949, after Marshal Tito's split with the Soviet Union, Hoxha severed relations with

Enver Hoxha was dictator of Albania from 1944 until his death in 1985, turning the tiny Balkan state into a brutal outpost of Stalinist tyranny. He is pictured here at the 5th National Games of Albania in 1985.

Yugoslavia – even though Albania was much indebted to its far larger neighbour. He also executed his defence minister Koci Xoce for Titoism. Fearful lest his people be 'contaminated' by exposure to the Titoist 'deviance', Hoxha ordered the construction of guard posts along the entire length of the country's border – which became one of the most intensely monitored frontiers in the world. Later he ordered the building of 750,000 one-man concrete bunkers and 700,000 pillboxes to defend the country against invaders, an absurd and bizarre decision that still disfigures the Albanian littoral.

Behind his Balkan curtain, Hoxha embarked on a Stalinist-style exercise in social engineering. He sought the creation of an urban working class worthy of the name (hitherto, Albania had been a clan-based peasant society) and the socialization of national life. Forced industrialization followed, while agriculture was reorganized on the Soviet collective-farm model. At the same time, all of Albania gained access to electricity for the first time, life expectancy rose, and illiteracy rates plummeted. Yet the human cost of this social revolution was enormous.

Hoxha's secret police, the Sigurimi, were brutal and ubiquitous: hundreds of thousands were tortured and killed. Hoxha's prime minister Mehmet Shehu spoke openly at a Party Congress about their methods: 'Who disagrees with our leadership in some point, will get a spit into his face, a blow onto his chin, and, if necessary, a bullet into his head.' Out of three million Albanians, one million were at some point either arrested or imprisoned in his perpetual terror.

Hoxha also added his own individual and quixotic touches. Private car ownership was banned, as were beards, which were seen as a rural throwback. Xenophobia was encouraged as the Albanian communists fused their adherence to the strictures of Marxist-Leninism with a glorification of various national myths. The central focus of such propaganda was the man heralded as the greatest Albanian of all time – Hoxha himself. However, Hoxha was careful to share his cult of personality with that of Stalin, who remained an object of forced reverence in Albania for the next four decades.

After the Sino-Soviet split of 1960, Hoxha allied himself with Beijing against Khrushchev's Soviet Union, which he believed to be abandoning the true path towards socialism laid down by Comrade Stalin. This realignment led to a precipitous decline in Albanian standards of living, as the country had been highly dependent on Soviet grain, and on the USSR as its principal export market. To quell any possible dissent, Hoxha decided to emulate his new Chinese friends and launched an Albanian 'Cultural Revolution'. From 1967, Albania was officially declared an 'atheistic' state with all mosques and churches closed and clerics arrested. All private property was confiscated by the state, and the numbers of arrests increased exponentially.

After a brief and highly constrained cultural liberalization during the early 1970s, a further wave of repression and ideological purification followed in 1973. Then, in 1978, two years after Mao's death and following the rise of the more moderate Deng Xiaoping, Hoxha broke with China, leading his country into yet further seclusion.

Hoxha survived numerous efforts to depose him – by loyalists of the exiled King Zog, by the British government, and by Khrushchev. Awareness of these threats fuelled his already considerable paranoia, which manifested itself in a series of internal purges. Those at the apex of the system found themselves under the greatest threat: members of the politburo and central committee were regularly arrested and executed for allegedly treasonable activities, and the seven successive interior ministers responsible for carrying out his purges were all themselves purged. In 1981 Hoxha's most trusted henchmen, the long-serving Mehmet Shehu, prime minister since 1954, challenged his plan for the succession and his isolationism. Shehu officially 'committed suicide' after being accused of involvement with 'war criminals', the CIA and the KGB, and suffering a nervous breakdown, itself illegal. Various accounts claimed the ageing Hoxha had personally murdered Shehu or more likely had him shot.

Hoxha himself died in office in 1985. Embalmed and displayed in a mausoleum, he was later reburied in a humbler grave.

THE 'LITTLE STALINS' OF EASTERN EUROPE

The Red rulers of Europe were murderous tyrants in their own right. Leader of the German Democratic Republic (GDR) from 1950 to 1971, Walter Ulbricht (1893–1973) oversaw the construction in 1961 of the Berlin Wall, supported by his eventual successor, Erich Honecker (1912–94). Their Stasi secret police were notoriously brutal and often absurd in their meticulous surveillance.

Poland became a model Soviet republic under Boleslaw Bierut (1892–1956), president from 1947 until dying mysteriously in Moscow. Opponents of his regime were systematically executed after secret trials.

Hungary endured repression under Mátyás Rákosi (1892–1971), nicknamed the 'bald murderer' for his ruthless purges. Appointed leader in 1947, he ruled until 1956 when the Soviets suppressed the Hungarian Revolution; ultimately succeeded by János Kádár, who ruled 1956–88.

Gheorghe Gheorghiu-Dej (1901–65) led the ruthless Stalinist Romanian regime from 1948 with Ana Pauker (1893–1960) until her arrest in 1952, and then ruled on his own as a dictator until his death.

From 1946 the premier of Bulgaria was Georgi Dimitrov (1882–1949), but he died in Moscow amid rumours of poisoning. His hard-line successor, Vulko Chervenkov (1900–80), implemented purges until he was deposed in 1954 and replaced by Todor Zhivkov (1911–98), who ordered the murder of dissidents such as Georgi Markov in London.

In Czechoslovakia after the 1948 coup d'état, Klement Gottwald (1896–1953) implemented a Stalinist terror, but died five days after attending Stalin's funeral. He was succeeded by Stalinists Antonín Novotný and – after Soviet suppression of the 1968 Prague Spring – Gustáv Husák, who ruled 1969–87.

Democracy now rules Europe. The tyrants are all gone except for one: Alexander Lukashenko, despotic president of Belarus since 1994, who rules brutally with his KGB secret police and an appalling human rights record to this day.

An East Berlin mural of GDR leader Erich Honecker and Soviet leader Leonid Brezhnev. The graffiti reads: 'God help me to survive this deadly love.'

ГОСПОДИ ! ПОМОГИ МНЕ ВЫЖИТЬ

СРЕДИ ЭТОЙ СМЕРТНОЙ ЛЮБВИ

MEIN GOTT. HILF MIR. DIESE TÖDLICHE LIEBE ZU ÜBERLEBEN

MOSKAU KUNSTLERAGENTUR   BRODOWSKI, BERLIN 1034, PSF 29

Mengele was the German Nazi SS doctor, known as the 'Angel of Death', who ran a Frankenstein-like laboratory at the Auschwitz death camp, conducting hideous racist experiments. In a sickening betrayal of the Hippocratic Oath – in which healing and saving life are the essence of the medical profession – he was directly responsible for the deaths of thousands of innocent children and countless adults, particularly twins. Escaping justice until his death in 1979, he personified the terrifying fusion between tribal barbarism and a warped scientific modernity that characterized the worst excesses of Nazism.

Dr Josef Mengele
1911–79

'We were people who'd been given a death-sentence, though it wasn't carried out straightaway. Instead of killing us there and then, they made guinea-pigs of us, doing what is done these days in laboratories with cats or rats.'

AUSCHWITZ TWIN, MENASHE LORINCZI

The eldest of three children, Mengele was born on 16 March 1911 in the village of Günzburg, Bavaria, to upper middle-class parents Karl and Walburga, both devout Catholics. He grew up in the atmosphere of humiliation and betrayal that infected Germany after the First World War, defeat being attributed to a 'stab in the back' in which Germany's Jewish community was alleged to have played a leading part. In 1931, like many other disillusioned young men, Mengele joined a fascist paramilitary organization, the *Stahlhelm* ('Steel Helmets'), but he was more than a simple thug, attaining a degree in medicine from the University of Munich in 1935.

As a talented and well-educated young man, with strong fascist credentials – he briefly served as a Brownshirt in the *Sturmabteilung* (SA) in 1934 before resigning due to a kidney complaint – Mengele was well placed for promotion under the Nazi regime following Hitler's appointment as Chancellor of Germany on 30 January 1933. In 1937, he became a researcher at the new Third Reich Institute for Heredity, Biology and Racial Purity at Frankfurt – working under Professor Otmar Freiherr von Verschuer, a pet of the Nazi regime – and in 1938 he became a Blackshirt, a member of the elite *Schutzstaffel* (SS). The following year he married Irene Schoenbein, with whom he would have a son, Rolf, in 1944.

During the first three years of the war, Mengele served as a medical officer with the Waffen SS, first in France and then the Soviet Union, where he distinguished himself, winning the Iron Cross First Class in January 1942 after being wounded pulling two soldiers out of a burning tank while under enemy fire. Declared unfit for combat, he was reposted at the end of the year to the Race and Resettlement Office in Berlin, and promoted to Hauptsturmführer (captain).

Meanwhile, the Nazi hierarchy had secretly completed plans for the 'Final Solution': the extermination of those regarded as racially inferior to the Ayran race, such as Jews, Gypsies, Slavs and the mentally and physically disabled. In May 1943, Mengele was appointed by Heinrich Himmler, the architect of the 'Final Solution', as a medical officer at Birkenau, a new annex to the Auschwitz extermination camp in southern Poland.

Suavely dressed, handsome and smiling, Mengele's role in deciding the fate of prisoners earned him the nickname 'Angel of Death'. Coolly inspecting them as they shuffled off the trucks, he would signal 'left' or 'right' with a casual wave of the riding crop held in his gloved hand. Left – reserved for those in good health between 18 and 35 – meant survival, albeit slave labour. Right – to which went the old, sick and weak, together with babies and their mothers (who, as Mengele coldly observed, 'won't work well if they know their children are dead') – meant the gas chamber, where 400,000 were sent during his time at Auschwitz. Occasionally Mengele's urbane mask would slip and, in a fit of rage, he would beat the nearest prisoner to death, shooting them in the head or ordering they be hurled, dead or alive, into pits of burning gasoline. When one mother resisted an attempt to separate her from her 13-year-old daughter, he drew his gun and shot them both before sending all those from their truck to be gassed.

A select few – dwarfs, those with genetic abnormalities and, above all, twins (who became known as 'Mengele's Children') – were taken to Block 10, the 'Zoo', where Mengele could fulfil his sickest scientific fantasies, one twin often being made to hold down the other as he conducted a hideous range of experiments, including blood tests and transfusions, radiography, castration and dissection. Others had dye injected into their eyes, often causing blindness, or organs transferred, usually without anaesthetic. On one occasion, he injected chloroform into the hearts of fourteen Gypsy twins, meticulously dissecting each one afterwards. When twins died, Mengele would keep select body parts on the wall of his office as a trophy.

Auschwitz was liberated by Soviet troops in January 1945, but Mengele had already fled from the Soviet advance before the troops had arrived. He moved briefly to the Gross-Rosen concentration camp in Silesia, then fled again, only to be captured by Allied troops in Munich. However, posing as another doctor – whose papers he had stolen – he was released in August, after which, as the Nuremberg trials began in November, he went into hiding, working for the next four years as a stableman in Bavaria. Still undetected, he escaped on an Italian ocean liner in 1949 to Buenos Aires, Argentina, possibly with the help of the ODESSA network (see page 266). He was tracked down by the West Germany authorities in 1959, but evaded extradition proceedings by moving to Paraguay, and then on to Brazil, assuming the identity of Wolfgang Gerhard, a fellow Nazi crony. Although Mossad, the Israeli intelligence service, came close to tracking him down, he was never brought to justice, dying in 1979 after suffering a stroke while swimming near São Paulo in Brazil.

Mengele was tried in absentia in Jerusalem in 1985, but it was scant consolation to the survivors of his heinous crimes, conducted, outrageously, in the name of science. In the context of the many horrors of the Holocaust, Mengele stands out as one of its most horrifying figures.

Dr Josef Mengele (centre) pictured in 1944 with Auschwitz commandant Richard Baer (left) and former commandant Rudolf Hoess (right; see page 249).

ODESSA

ODESSA – standing for *Organisation der ehemaligen SS-Angehörigen* (Organization of Former Members of the SS) – is the name sometimes given to a clandestine network established towards the end of the Second World War, which offered protection and assistance to senior Nazis and other European fascists as they tried to avoid capture and prosecution by the victorious Allies. Its existence was first suggested by the Nazi-hunter Simon Wiesenthal, and it was the subject of a best-selling novel by Frederick Forsyth. How far ODESSA was a structured organization is debated; it more likely involved various groups working independently after the war to smuggle high-ranking Nazis out of Allied-occupied territory into sympathetic South American countries, particularly Paraguay and Argentina.

A key figure in establishing these networks was Otto Skorzeny (1908–78), an Austrian Nazi who served in the Waffen-SS during the war. Handpicked by Hitler to lead the commando raid in Italy that released Benito Mussolini from captivity in July 1943, towards the end of the war he turned to establishing 'ratlines' (escape routes) to help Nazis escape. To fund these, he used the treasure that rich Nazis and German industrialists had asked him to hide away, much of it hidden in the mountains of Bavaria. In May 1945, he gave himself up to the Allies, but his trial for war crimes collapsed and he escaped in 1947, continuing his ODESSA work from safe sanctuary in Francoist Spain.

Another prominent ratline was established by Bishop Alois Hudal, a Nazi sympathizer responsible for the pastoral care of Germans in Italy, including many of those in prisoner-of-war camps. Using these contacts, Hudal established an escape route to South America through Italy, subsequently helping Franz Stangl (the commanding officer of the extermination camp at Treblinka) and even Adolf Eichmann (the architect of the Holocaust) to escape. A network of Croatian Franciscan priests, led by Father Krunoslav Draganović, ran a similar project.

What is so striking about these operations is the open complicity of national leaders. President Juan Domingo Perón denounced the Nuremberg Trials and welcomed Nazi war criminals to Argentina, offering them passports and citizenship. Some estimates suggest that as many as ten thousand suspected Nazis and other fascists and war criminals escaped via ratlines. As late as July 1979, individuals claiming to represent ODESSA exploded a bomb in France, in an attempt to assassinate the Nazi-hunters Serge and Beate Klarsfeld.

The Red Cross passport used by Adolf Eichmann in 1950 (see page 261), when he escaped to Argentina under the alias 'Ricardo Klement'.

Brutal, murderous, repressive and deluded by his own propaganda, Kim Il Sung was the self-styled 'Great Leader' and long-time dictator of North Korea. He led his country on a path to war, international isolation and economic collapse, and during his half century in power North Korea became arguably the most totalitarian and surreal regime in the world. Indeed, long after his death he remains 'the President' of his insane, bizarre and hellish country.

Kim Il Sung

1912—94

'The oppressed peoples can liberate themselves only through struggle. This is a simple and clear truth confirmed by history.'

KIM IL SUNG

Kim Il Sung was born Kim Sung Ju, the eldest of three sons of a Christian father. Japan had invaded Korea in 1910 and Kim grew up under Japanese rule until, in the 1920s, his family moved to Manchuria in northeast China, where he learnt Chinese and became interested in communism. After the Japanese invaded first Manchuria and then the rest of China, Kim joined the anti-Japanese resistance movement. During the Second World War he fled to the Soviet Union, where he underwent further military training and political indoctrination.

After Japan's defeat in 1945, Korea was divided into two zones of occupation, with the Soviets in the north and the Americans in the south. In 1946 the Soviets set up a satellite Communist state in the north, with Kim as its

Kim Il Sung, the founder of the Democratic People's Republic of Korea, ruled over his isolated and impoverished Stalinist fiefdom from 1949 until his death in 1994. He is shown here in an official propaganda photograph.

head. While the south of the country proceeded with free elections, Kim immediately began imposing a repressive Stalinist totalitarian system; this included the creation of an all-powerful secret police, concentration camps, the redistribution of property, suppression of religion and killing of 'class enemies'.

In June 1950 – despite warnings from Stalin urging patience – Kim ordered his troops to invade South Korea in order to reunite the country, thereby triggering the Korean War. North Korea received logistical, financial and military support from China and the Soviet Union, while the South received backing from the UN, who sent an international force, mainly composed of US troops. Despite initial successes, the North Korean troops were soon beaten back. Kim was only rescued by massive Chinese intervention. After three years the conflict – which cost between 2 and 3 million lives – ended in a stalemate.

At home, Kim tightened his grip, banishing outside influence and liquidating internal enemies. An attempted coup by eleven party members in 1953 – the first of a number of such attempts – ended in a Stalinist show trial of the participants, who were swiftly executed. A purge of the party followed, and tens of thousands of Koreans were sent to labour camps – still a feature in North Korea.

Kim promoted an all-pervasive cult of personality centred around the 'Juche' (or 'Kim Il Sungism'), a political philosophy based on his own supposedly god-like qualities. According to the state media, Kim was the flawless 'Eternal Leader' or 'Supreme Leader'. In 1980 he announced his intention of creating a dynasty of dictators when he named his son, Kim Jong Il, as his successor.

HEREDITARY DICTATORS

One of the more surprising and ironic developments of recent times has been the resurgence of hereditary autocracies in self-declared socialistic republics that nominally despise inherited power but have in fact created modern monarchies. In 1980, Kim Il Sung decreed his decadent if ruthless son, Kim Jong Il, 'the great successor to the revolutionary cause'. Kim Jong Il acceded to the throne of the Kims in 1994 and called the West's bluff by becoming a nuclear power while his people starved.

Another hereditary dictator is Ilhan Aliyev, president of Azerbaijan – who, in 2003, succeeded his father Gaidar Aliyev, ex-member of the Soviet politburo and Azeri dictator since 1993.

Syria is nominally a republic, ruled by the secular, socialistic Ba'athist Party. Its president from 1971 to 2000 was Hafez al-Assad, a shrewd and merciless dictator known as the 'sphinx of Damascus', but, on his death, he was succeeded by his son Bashar al-Assad, who had been rapidly promoted within the Ba'ath Party after the death of his elder brother, and his father's chosen heir, Basil.

In 2001, at the age of 29, Joseph Kabila, president of the Democratic Republic of Congo, acceded to power just ten days after the murder of his father Laurent-Désiré Kabila. Elected president in 2006, he has since repressed his opposition.

In Togo, Faure Essozimna Gnassingbé reigns as president. In 2005, he succeeded his father Gnassingbé Eyadéma, who had ruled as dictator from 1967 to his death.

In Cuba, Fidel Castro seized power in Cuba in 1959 with his brother Raul as defence minister. He brought the world to the brink of nuclear annihilation in the Cuban Missile Crisis of 1962, and, on retirement in 2008 due to ill health, was the longest-serving dictator in the world: he was succeeded as president by his brother Raul.

These are not the first hereditary dictators. In 1972, Chiang Kai-shek, the corrupt, inept Generalissimo of China (1926–49) – who on losing his country to the Communists fled to Taiwan, where he became dictator – was succeeded as premier by his son Chiang Ching-kuo, who subsequently became president in 1978, ruling until his death in 1988. In Haiti, Francois 'Papa Doc' Duvalier was succeeded by

Meanwhile, with military spending taking up nearly a quarter of the country's budget, poverty became rife. In the 1990s food shortages led to famine, in which as many as 2 million people may have perished. The country maintained its utter isolation. Korea came to be seen as a rogue state and a sponsor of terrorism, particularly against its southern neighbour: North Korea was responsible for the assassination in 1983 of 17 South Korean officials who had been on an official visit to Burma, and for the downing in 1987 of a South Korean commercial jet, resulting in the deaths of 115 people. North Korea went on to develop its own nuclear arsenal.

After surviving another coup attempt in 1992, Kim Il Sung finally died on 8 July 1994, officially of a heart attack. His son and successor, Kim Jong Il, the self-styled 'Dear Leader', has continued his father's megalomaniac policies – and is also rumoured to have large sums of his country's money stashed away for his own use in Swiss bank accounts. Embalmed and worshipped to this day, Kim was a homicidal dictator responsible for the deaths of millions and the impoverishment of North Korea.

his son, Jean Claude 'Baby Doc' Duvalier, aged 19, in 1971 (see page 259). In the 19th century, the López father and son ruled dynastically in Paraguay (see page 180). In Nicaragua, Anastasio Somoza ruled as dictator from 1936 until he was murdered in 1956, when he was succeeded by his two sons, Luis Somoza and Anastasio Somoza Debayle, who reigned until the latter was overthrown by the Sandinistas in 1979.

In today's Libya and Egypt, Colonel Gadaffi, the flambayant radical dictator who has ruled since 1969, and President Mubarak, who has ruled since 1981, are both grooming their sons for the succession. It is hard though for sons to equal their fathers and few such strongmen succeed in founding long-lasting dynasties. In England, the rule of the Lord Protector Oliver Cromwell ended in 1658 with the succession of his hapless son, Richard Cromwell, nicknamed Tumbledown Dick because he was soon overthrown: King Charles II was restored in 1660.

Kim Jong Il, eldest son of Kim Il Sung. He succeeded his father as leader of North Korea upon the latter's death in 1994.

Alfredo Stroessner, who dubbed himself *El Excelentissimo*, 'The most Excellent', ruled Paraguay for 35 cruel years, marked by murder, torture and dread stability. He remains the prototype of the brutal and greedy South American general in power.

Alfredo Stroessner
1912—2006

'I do insist that in Paraguay there was order; the judiciary had the power of complete independence; justice was fully exercised.'

ALFREDO STROESSNER

The son of a German immigrant and a wealthy Paraguayan mother, Stroessner was born in Encarnación, Paraguay. In 1932, after attending the military college in Asunción, he joined the army, and went on to distinguish himself in the 1932–5 Chaco War against Bolivia. Although married with three children, Stroessner, with his meticulously trimmed moustache and confident appearance in uniform, had numerous mistresses and is said to have fathered up to fifteen illegitimate children.

Stroessner the commander distinguished himself in the Paraguayan civil war of 1947, in which he sided with Federico Chávez. In 1951, Chávez, now president, appointed Stroessner as commander-in-chief of the armed forces. But in May 1954, as Paraguay struggled in the face of an economic crisis, Stroessner overthrew Chávez in a coup. In order to rubber-stamp his presidency, he called an election in which he was the only candidate permitted to stand. His image was soon plastered across Paraguay, and he even named a city, Puerto Presidente Stroessner, after himself.

Throughout his presidency, Stroessner maintained a defensive posture, arguing that the country was always in a 'state of siege' and needed to be constantly vigilant against imagined enemies. As a staunch anti-communist he received assistance from the United States in the earlier years of his regime, and he had some success in stabilizing the economy.

However, in order to prop up his regime he spent swathes of the national budget on 'maintaining order'. And while he made token gestures to the rural and urban working classes, in reality his regime was propped by the interests of business and the large landholders. Corruption was rife, members of his Colorado Party were given privileged treatment in business and health care, and the country became a sanctuary for smugglers, arms dealers and drug barons.

Stroessner's regime was a dictatorship in all but name. Paraguay's parliament continued to meet, but it was dominated by his supporters. In 1967, and again in 1977, he had the country's constitution specially modified so that he could continue as president for longer and he was 'elected' eight times. Every five years he called an election, but the voting was marred by fraud and sustained intimidation of any potential opponents.

In the 1960s and 1970s, as pressure grew from the United States for Stroessner to introduce some democratic reforms, he permitted a semblance of opposition to emerge. This was merely a token gesture, however, as critics of the regime lived in constant fear of Stroessner's secret police, who were trained by escaped Nazi SS torturers.

Over the course of Stroessner's reign hundreds of thousands of Paraguayans were imprisoned for political offences (in a prison known as 'la Técnica') and thousands disappeared. Stroessner even ordered the arrest of elected senators, one of whom survived to recount how needles were inserted under his fingernails. More details came out after Stroessner fell from power: former dissidents described how they were beaten and tortured with electric shocks, and how their screams would be recorded and played down the phone to their families, or their bloodstained garments sent to their homes. Sometimes the family of a murdered dissident was asked to pay to receive the corpse. According to some accounts, Stroessner would, on occasions, personally oversee the interrogation and torture of his opponents. In 1987 his police tear-gassed a gathering of Women for Democracy.

Stroessner was also involved in oppression beyond the borders of Paraguay. He participated in Operation Condor, a clandestine plot – backed by the CIA and involving a number of other South American rulers – designed to assassinate leftwing elements on the continent. At the same time, Stroessner turned Paraguay into a haven for deposed dictators, such as Anastasio Somoza Debayle of Nicaragua, and many Nazi war criminals, most notoriously Josef Mengele (see page 264).

In 1988 Stroessner was elected to an eighth successive term as president, only to be forced out the following year in a bloody coup led by his former aide and ally General Andrés Rodriguez. Stroessner, fearing prosecution, was permitted to go into exile in Brazil. For many years, Paraguay unsuccessfully demanded his extradition on charges relating to Operation Condor and the other crimes committed during his regime. He died at the age of 93 in a Brasilia hospital, having failed to recover from a hernia operation.

Stroessner boasted that he had brought stability and wealth to a country that had suffered from a lack of both. In reality, the wealth was shared around a few cronies, and any criticism of his regime was likely to result in torture and murder. The true cost of the 'stability' that Stroessner brought to Paraguay has been revealed by the discovery of masses of documents and tape recordings – now referred to as the 'archives of terror' – which detail the systematic torture committed by his secret police.

Paraguayan dictator General Alfredo Stroessner seen during a gala reception in Asunción.

TRUJILLO THE GOAT

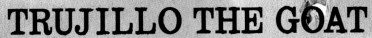

Rafael Trujillo (1891–1961) ruled the Dominican Republic for 31 years with a savage brutality and flamboyant personality cult, epitomizing the murderous military strongman (caudillo) and military clique (junta) that have dominated South American politics until the very recent rise of democracy in countries such as Chile, Argentina and Brazil. Trujillo rose to commander of the Dominican army, overthrew the president and held power from 1930 to 1938 and again from 1942 to 1952 when he handed over the presidency to his brother Hector. As army supremo, 'the Chief' (also known as 'the Goat') ruled in an absolute tyranny, backed by a savage secret police, the SIM (Military Intelligence Service). He covered himself in medals (hence his nickname, 'Bottlecaps'), renamed the capital Trujillo City and the highest mountain Mount Trujillo, killed and tortured thousands of opponents and stole millions of dollars. In 1937 he ordered his troops to kill all dark-skinned 'Haitians' – 20,000 were slaughtered with machetes in what became known as 'the cutting' or the 'Parsley Massacre' (those who couldn't pronounce the word perejil – the Spanish word for Parsley – were murdered).

Though he admired Hitler, Trujillo remained neutral in the Second World War and accepted Jewish refugees, yet he continued to murder his enemies, awarding himself the titles 'Great Benefactor of the Nation' and 'Father of the New Dominion'. But by the 1950s, Dominicans – and the US – were sickened by his excesses. After a plot against him was uncovered, Trujillo tortured and murdered the implicated Mirabal sisters; their fate – dramatized in the film *In the Time of the Butterflies* (2001) – horrified everyone. CIA-backed plotters finally assassinated Trujillo in his car in 1961, a story retold by Peruvian novelist Mario Vargas Llosa in his book *The Feast of the Goat* (2000). But the dictator's playboy son Ramfis Trujillo seized power and tortured suspected plotters to death before his uncles, Hector and Jose Trujillo, returned to take over. Finally, the USA ended the monstrous reign of the Trujillo dynasty, whose members fled into exile in November 1961.

Rafael Leónidas Trujillo y Molina was dictator of the Dominican Republic from 1930 to 1961. His fondness for gaudy uniforms and medals earned him the nickname 'Bottlecaps'.

Most of the Communist Party leaders who ruled the countries of Eastern Europe on behalf of their Soviet masters in the decades after the Second World War were pliant stooges. Nicolae Ceauşescu of Romania was different. Not only did he make a break with the USSR, but he promoted his own cult of personality as self-declared 'Genius of the Carpathians' and diverted his poverty-stricken country's resources to vast monuments to his own glory while using his Securitate secret police to murder his enemies. He and his wife Elena ruled as a grotesque partnership. When the communist Eastern Bloc collapsed in 1989–90, they were the only two of the ousted leaders to be shot.

Nicolae and 1918–89
Elena Ceauşescu 1916–89

'He always claimed to act and speak on behalf of the people, to be a beloved son of the people, but he only tyrannized the people all the time.'

PROSECUTOR AT THE OPENING OF THE TRIAL OF NICOLAE AND ELENA CEAUŞESCU, DECEMBER 1989

Born into a peasant family, Ceausescu joined the fledgling Romanian communist movement in the early 1930s. At the time Romania was a conservative monarchy, and being a communist was illegal. In 1936 Ceausescu was jailed for two years, and in 1940 was interned in a concentration camp. Here he met Gheorghe Gheorghiu-Dej, the leader of the Romanian Communist Party, and escaped with him in 1944. That same year a broad-based anti-fascist 'liberation' government – including Dej – was set up with Soviet assistance. In 1947 he married ploughman's daughter Elena.

In 1947 the Communists ousted their erstwhile allies from government, and in 1952 Dej became *de facto* dictator of Romania. With the elevation of his mentor, Ceausescu was able to secure his own position, and when Dej died in 1965, Ceauşescu became party leader and head of state. Many Romanians hoped their new leader would inaugurate a period of greater liberalization and reform. In August 1968 such expectations intensified after Ceauşescu's denunciation of the Soviet invasion of Czechoslovakia, and his defiant line made him a genuinely popular figure within Romania, and earned plaudits from the West. Nevertheless, he was quick to assure the Soviets that his country would remain a loyal member of the Eastern Bloc.

Early optimism started to dissipate as Ceauşescu began to fantasize about turning Romania into a world industrial power house; and as he did so, prospects for liberalization receded. Instead, Ceauşescu became obsessed with shoring up his monopoly of power, and to this end he introduced a process of continual job rotation by which functionaries at every level were ordered to change position regularly, with the intention that no one would be able to build up a power base to challenge him. The fact that the system also led to administrative chaos does not seem to have troubled Ceauşescu, who in March 1974 assumed the ability to rule by decree alone. His wife Elena became increasingly powerful as vice-premier, politburo member and self-declared 'Mother of the Nation': the Ceauşescus ruled as a gruesome partnership and stories of her greed, ruthlessness and vainglory abounded.

The role of the secret police, the infamous Securitate, or State Security Department, also expanded. By 1989 it had an estimated 24,000 members, and right across society a climate of fear was inculcated in which everyone was encouraged to spy on everybody else; failure to do so resulted in confinement in prison or a labour camp. At the same time, Ceauşescu became intoxicated with the notion that Romania needed to build an image as a modern socialist utopia, culminating in the 1980s with the construction of the gigantic palace in the heart of Bucharest. This monstrous piece of architecture was built on the back of what was effectively slave labour, and required the eviction of 40,000 people from their homes in order to make space for it.

Ceauşescu determined to combine the values of socialism with an ever more strident Romanian nationalism. This resulted in an increasingly bizarre series of campaigns aimed at cementing Romania's national greatness. In March 1984, for example, concerned at the country's low birth rate, Ceauşescu decreed that women of child-bearing age were required to have monthly gynaecological examinations under the watchful eye of the Securitate, and if they were not pregnant had to justify why not.

By the 1980s, as the country faced a mounting debt crisis, Ceauşescu resolved to pay off Romania's creditors by the end of the decade. To achieve this he ordered the mass exportation of the country's agricultural produce and industrial manufactures. The result was a collapse in the standard of living, and the deaths of thousands as a result of poor nutrition and lack of modern medical care. Ceauşescu responded by introducing austerity measures such as the 'Rational Eating Programme', which set per capita limits on consumption. The long-suffering people of Romania were finally released from the tyrant's grip when the popular revolutions of 1989 brought the totalitarian regimes of Eastern Europe crashing down. The fall of the the 'Genius of the Carpathians' proved to be bloody: after a summary trial, on Christmas Day 1989 he and his wife Elena were executed by firing squad as he sang the 'Internationale' and she shouted 'You motherf–rs!'

The Romanian communist dictator Nicolae Ceauşescu and his wife Elena, c. 1989.

The Macbeths

The Ceaușescus were, like Serbia's Milošević couple, a modern version of Shakespeare's infamous partnership of murder and ambition – the Macbeths, the ultimate ruthless couple. Their bloody lust for power leads them to murder and betrayal that return to haunt and finally undo them. Each proves as vicious and culpable as the other, the scheming Lady Macbeth initially the most heartless – inciting her vacillating husband to kill the sleeping Duncan ('screw your courage to the sticking place, and we'll not fail') – while he later proves equally calculating, secretly ordering the murder of Banquo ('Be innocent of the knowledge, dearest chuck, till thou applaud the deed').

Shakespeare had been a drinking companion of some of the conspirators in the Gunpowder Plot, and wrote *Macbeth* – predicated on the heinous crime of killing a king – as a way of distancing himself from them. His characters were loosely based on Macbeth, king of Scotland (1040–57) – who claimed the throne after killing the ineffectual king Duncan in battle in 1040 – and his wife, Queen Gruoch. Far though from being a scheming murderer, Macbeth won respect for his wise leadership, and though Duncan's son Malcolm did indeed defeat him at the Battle of Dunsinane Hill (1054), he retained his crown for another three years until killed by Malcolm at the Battle of Lumphanan.

The Ceaușescus – as inseparable a partnership as the Macbeths – have more in common with the fictional than the historical characters: Nicolae in his obsessive thirst for power and denial of reality, and his wife Elena in her malevolent influence behind the scenes. Living in luxury while the poor starved, she was loathed by her people, yet unlike Lady Macbeth – who finally dies consumed by guilt – she seemed incapable of remorse. Compared with these two, Shakespeare's Macbeths seem almost benign.

Thomas Hampson as Macbeth and Violeta Urmana as Lady Macbeth in a 2006 production of Verdi's opera.

Francisco Macías Nguema, who officially called himself 'The Unique Miracle', was the corrupt, demented, homicidal, skull-collecting first president of Equatorial Guinea in West Africa. Under his rule, the country descended into barbarism, culminating in the slaughter of his people. In a continent that has endured governance by a legion of bloodthirsty madmen, Macías Nguema stands out as one of the worst.

Francisco Macías Nguema 1924–79

For the first 44 years of Macías Nguema's life, Equatorial Guinea was a Spanish colony. Three times in succession Nguema failed the civil-service entrance exams, only passing on the fourth occasion because the bar was purposely lowered by the Spanish to enable him to do so. Thereafter he occupied increasingly influential positions, eventually gaining a seat in the national assembly.

In 1968 Spain granted the country independence, and in the subsequent presidential elections Macías stood on a left-leaning, populist platform. He won. Initially, Nguema appeared to promote a free and liberal society, but the honeymoon period lasted a mere 145 days. Nguema had developed an intense hatred of the Spanish (perhaps as a reaction to his earlier dependence on them) and, indeed, foreigners in general. Spanish residents became the target of state-sanctioned terror, and by March 1969 over 7000 of them had abandoned the country – many of them skilled workers. In their wake, the economy collapsed.

Initially, some within the government, such as the foreign minister Ndongo Miyone, attempted to rein in the excesses. But they paid a high price for doing so. In the case of Miyone, he was summoned to Nguema's presidential palace and beaten, then hauled off to prison and murdered. Similar treatment was meted out to others who dared to oppose Nguema: ten of the twelve ministers who formed the country's first post-independence government were killed. In their place, Nguema appointed relatives or members of his clan, the Esangui. Thus one nephew was made commander of the national guard, whilst another was simultaneously minister of finance, minister of trade, minister of information and minister for security. The dreaded security services were manned entirely with his placemen and he ordered them to bludgeon his victims to death in a stadium as a band played 'Those Were The Days, My Friend'.

As Nguema tightened his grip on power (he made himself president for life in 1972), the killing became ever more capricious. On two occasions he had all former lovers of his then mistresses put to death. More broadly, two-thirds of the members of the national assembly and all the country's senior civil servants were arrested and executed. The more fortunate fled into exile. In 1976, 114 senior civil servants – all of whom had been appointed by Nguema to replace those he had previously got rid of – petitioned him for a relaxation of the persecution. Every single one of them was subsequently arrested, tortured and murdered.

The same year also saw the closure of Equatorial Guinea's central bank and the execution of its director, as all meaningful economic activity – other than that directed towards the benefit of Nguema – was brought to a standstill. From then on, all foreign currency that entered the country was delivered directly to the president and hoarded. When Nguema ran short of funds, his forces oversaw the kidnapping and ransoming of foreign nationals. In his determination to control all aspects of life, Nguema ordered that all libraries and all forms of media be shut down. Already, in 1974, the country's education system had effectively collapsed after the expulsion of the Catholic mission. During late 1974 and early 1975, all religious meetings, funerals and sermons were banned; churches were closed down and the use of Christian names was forbidden. The only form of worship permitted was of Nguema himself, with people required to acknowledge that 'There is no God other than Macías' and 'God created Equatorial Guinea thanks to Papa Macías'.

Over time it became clear that Nguema was clinically insane, talking to himself and alternating between mania and depression. Drugged up on stimulants, he ordered the building of a vast new presidential palace in Bata, but then decided to retreat instead to his home town in the Mongomo region of the country. There, he kept the entire national treasury in bags, alongside a range of human skulls, fuelling terrifying rumours of his supposed magical powers.

Nguema finally fell in August 1979 in a military coup led by his nephew, Teodoro Obiang Nguema Mbasogo – who continues to rule to this day – although not before setting fire to much of the country's wealth. He tried to flee, but was locked in a cage suspended in a cinema where he was tried for 80,000 murders and sentenced to death. The new regime had to get Moroccan mercenaries to carry out the execution – fear of his magical powers prevented local troops from doing it themselves.

During his decade-long reign of terror, Nguema had brought Equatorial Guinea to its knees. Out of it's population of over 300,000, some 100,000 had been killed and 125,000 had fled into exile as Nguema transformed his country into a hell on earth. After a reign of almost 30 years, his nephew's tyranny remains one of the most corrupt and repressive in Africa. Torture is endemic, and local radio hails him as a 'god' while he grooms his son to succeed him.

Francisco Macías Nguema, the brutal ruler of Equatorial Guinea, who destroyed his country's economy and drove out or killed two-thirds of the Equatoguinean population in the 1960s and 1970s.

THE DOGS OF WAR

Fact, as they say, is often stranger than fiction. Frederick Forsyth's classic thriller *The Dogs of War* (1974) tells the story of the dastardly British mining entrepreneur Sir James Manson and his efforts to overthrow the government of 'Zangaro' – a made-up African country where vast platinum deposits have been discovered. Manson employs a band of hard-nosed mercenaries to assist him in the endeavour, and the Soviet-aligned President Kimba is eventually deposed and executed by the novel's anti-hero, 'Cat' Shannon'.

Since Forsyth published his book in the early 1970s, there has been some speculation that he himself was involved in planning a coup to remove Macías Nguema in Equatorial Guinea – though nothing has ever been proved. Even more strange, the scenario he outlined found echoes in an alleged plot against the same country in 2004, when 69 supposed mercenaries were arrested at Harare airport and their Boeing 727 – set to be loaded with £100,000 worth of weapons and military hardware – seized by security forces. The men were later accused of planning the overthrow of Equatorial

Guinea's dreaded dictator Teodoro Nguema. Their leader, Simon Mann, a former British SAS officer who had helped found the private military company Sandline International, was found guilty of attempting to buy arms for the alleged coup and sentenced to seven years imprisonment. Another of those involved in the plot was Sir Mark Thatcher, son of the former British prime minister, who was charged in 2004 with 'funding and logistical assistance in relation to [an] attempted coup in Equatorial Guinea'. After a time under house arrest, he was found guilty in 2005, after successful plea bargaining, of purchasing an aircraft 'without taking proper investigations into what it would be used for' for which he received a four-year suspended sentence and hefty fine.

In 2007, however, Mann was extradited to Equatorial Guinea where he was sentenced to more than 34 years in prison.

Old Etonian and former British Army officer Simon Mann is arrested in Harare, Zimbabwe, 7 March 2004.

Pol Pot, the communist Khmer Rouge leader who created the democidal hell known as Democratic Kampuchea, only ruled Cambodia for four years, but in that short time he murdered millions of innocent people – half the population – impoverished the country, killed all intellectuals, or even people who wore spectacles, and tried to restart time at a diabolic Year Zero.

Pol Pot   1925–98

'Pol Pot does not believe in God, but he thinks that heaven, destiny, wants him to guide Cambodia the way he thinks it the best for Cambodia . . . Pol Pot is mad . . . like Hitler.'

PRINCE NORODOM SIHANOUK, FORMER RULER OF CAMBODIA

Born as Saloth Sar, Pol Pot (a revolutionary name he adopted in 1963) was the son of a wealthy farmer. His family were courtiers to the Cambodian royal family and in 1931, as a child of six, he moved to the capital city, Phnom Penh, to live with his brother, an official at the royal palace, and was educated at Catholic and French schools. In 1949 he went to Paris on a scholarship to study electronics, and became involved with the French Communist Party and with other left-wing Cambodian students studying in Paris. Pol Pot was never academically inclined and was forced to return home after failing his exams.

After a spell as a teacher, in 1963 Pol Pot began to devote all his energy to revolutionary activities. That same year he was appointed head of the Workers' Party of Kampuchea – effectively the Cambodian Communist Party, also referred to as the Khmer Rouge, which strongly opposed the existing government of Prince Norodom Sihanouk. The Prince – and sometime King – had led the

Khmer Rouge leader Pol Pot ruled Cambodia for just four years from 1975 to 1979, but in that time wiped out half of his country's population. Pictured here at a press conference in 1979 shortly after he was deposed by a Vietnamese-sponsored invasion, Pol Pot boasted to Japanese journalists that invading Vietnamese troops had been unable to wipe out Khmer Rouge guerrilla forces.

country with irresponsible self-indulgence since independence from France in 1953. Pol Pot forged links with North Vietnam and China, which he visited in 1966. He was impressed with Chairman Mao's Cultural Revolution. Indeed Mao was to be his main patron and hero. The following year he spent time with a hill tribe in northeastern Cambodia, and was impressed by the simplicity of peasant life, uncorrupted by the city.

In 1968 the Khmer Rouge launched an insurrection, seizing the mountainous region on the border with Vietnam. The United States, embroiled in the Vietnam War and fearing that North Vietnamese troops were using Cambodia as a safe haven, began a bombing campaign, which radicalized Cambodia in Pol Pot's favour. In 1970, Prince Sihanouk was overthrown in a right-wing coup by former defence minister Lon Nol. The Khmer Rouge's shadowy army of guerrillas in black pyjamas soon controlled the countryside.

On 17 April 1975 the capital finally fell to the Khmer Rouge. Pol Pot – ruling with a tiny clique of comrades such as Ieng Sary and Khieu Samphan under the anonymous cover of 'The Organization' – declared that 1975 was 'Year Zero' and started to purge Cambodia of all non-communist influences. All foreigners were expelled, newspapers were outlawed and large numbers of people with the merest taint of association with the old regime – including all religious leaders, whether Buddhist, Christian or Muslim – were executed. There were even reports of people being killed because they wore spectacles – a sign of 'bourgeois intellectuals'.

Pol Pot – now known as 'Brother Number One' – then embarked on an insane and doomed attempt to turn Cambodia into an agrarian utopia. The cities were cleared of their inhabitants, who were forced to live in agricultural communes in the countryside. In terrible conditions, with food shortages and crippling hard

THE KILLING FIELDS

Under the Khmer Rouge, urban areas of Cambodia were emptied of their inhabitants. The capital, Phnom Penh, once a vibrant city of 2 million people, became a ghost town. Following Chairman Mao's dictum that the peasant was the true proletarian, Pol Pot believed that the city was a corrupting entity, a haven for the bourgeoisie, capitalists and foreign influences.

City-dwellers were marched at gunpoint to the countryside as part of the plans of the new regime to abolish cash payments and turn Cambodia into a self-sufficient communist society, where everyone worked the soil. The regime made a distinction between those with 'full rights' (who had originally lived off the land) and 'depositees' taken from the city, many of whom were massacred outright. Those depositees – capitalists, intellectuals and people who had regular contact with the outside world – who could not be 're-educated' in the ways of the revolution, were tortured and killed at a number of concentration camps, such the S-21 prison camp (also known as 'Strychnine Hill'), or taken straight to the 'Killing Fields', where their rations were so small that they could not survive. Thousands were

labour, these communes soon became known as the 'Killing Fields', where several million innocent Cambodians were executed. Despite a massive shortfall in the harvest of 1977 and rising famine, the regime arrogantly rejected the offer of outside aid.

The country was now riddled with spies and informers, and even children were encouraged to inform on their parents. Pol Pot went on to conduct purges within the Khmer Rouge itself, leading to the execution of more than 200,000 members.

External enemies proved more difficult to suppress, however. With only China maintaining support for the regime, Cambodia become embroiled in a conflict with Vietnam, whose forces invaded and captured Phnom Penh on 7 January 1979, forcing Pol Pot and the Khmer Rouge to flee to the western regions and over the border into Thailand. The new Vietnamese-controlled regime tried Pol Pot in absentia for genocide and sentenced him to death. Undeterred, Pol Pot directed an aggressive guerrilla war against the new regime, and kept an iron grip on the Khmer Rouge. As late as 1997 he ordered the execution of his colleague Song Sen, along with his family, on suspicion of collaborating with Cambodian forces. Shortly afterwards he himself was arrested by another senior Khmer Rouge figure, and sentenced to life imprisonment, dying in April 1998 of heart failure.

In his murderous, almost psychotic, schemes for a communist utopia, Pol Pot, Brother Number One, outran anything in George Orwell's imagination. During a reign of just under four years, he oversaw the deaths of between two and five million men, women and children – over a third of the entire population of Cambodia.

forced to dig their own graves before Khmer Rouge soldiers beat their weary bodies with iron bars, axes and hammers until they died. The soldiers had been instructed not to waste bullets.

Those who were spared immediate execution became slave labourers in the programme of agrarian collectivization. Hundreds of thousands of civilians – often uprooted and separated from their families – were worked to death, or starved because of a lack of rations. Many more were executed in the fields for the most minor indiscretions – such as engaging in sexual relations, complaining about conditions, stealing food or espousing religious beliefs.

Some of the Killing Fields containing mass graves have now been preserved as a testimony to the genocide perpetrated by Pol Pot and his followers. The most infamous of the them is Choeung Ek, where 8895 bodies were discovered after the fall of the regime.

Racks of human skulls and bones of slaughtered Cambodians, a grisly reminder of the atrocities perpetrated by Pol Pot.

Illiterate, garrulous and burly, as terrifying as he was ridiculous, Field-Marshal Idi Amin Dada was a buffoonish bully and sadistic mass-murderer who earned the soubriquet the 'Butcher of Uganda'. The *soi-disant* 'Last King of Scotland' impoverished Uganda, once the Jewel of Africa, a megalomaniacal cannibalistic loon who killed so many of his countrymen that the crocodiles of Lake Victoria could not consume them fast enough.

Idi Amin 1925–2003

'Hitler and all German people knew that the Israelis are not people who are working in the interest of the people of the world, and that is why they burnt the Israelis alive with gas.'

IDI AMIN, TELEGRAM TO KURT WALDHEIM, SECRETARY GENERAL OF THE UNITED NATIONS, 1972

As a boy, Amin was abandoned by his father, and received little in the way of formal education. In 1946 he enlisted in the King's African Rifles, and went on to distinguish himself for his marksmanship and sporting abilities – he was nine times heavyweight boxing champion of Uganda. In the 1950s he participated in the suppression of the anti-British Mau Mau insurgency in Kenya, serving with distinction but attracting suspicions for using excessive brutality. Nevertheless, he was promoted to warrant officer, and in 1961 became only the second native Ugandan to receive a commission.

After Uganda gained its independence from Britain in 1962, Amin emerged as a high-ranking military officer under Prime Minister Milton Obote, becoming deputy commander of the army in 1964. This was a period of economic boom and an era in which the new federal constitution balanced the desire for regional autonomy with the centralizing impulses of national government. Yet all of this was destroyed by Obote, who in 1966 arrested several government ministers and suspended parliament and the constitution. In their place Obote installed himself as executive president with vast powers; Amin was made overall commander of the army and

Idi Amin, pictured at the 1978 Organization of African Unity (OAU) Summit in Addis Ababa. President of Uganda between 1971 and 1979, he is thought to have tortured and murdered some 300,000 of his own people.

played a leading role in suppressing the opposition to Obote's coup, resulting in hundreds of deaths.

In January 1971, when the president was out of the country, Amin seized power, encouraged by his patron Britain. Initially he was welcomed by many who had grown resentful of Obote's growing tyranny. Such supporters were further encouraged by Amin's early acts of reconciliation: political prisoners were released, the emergency laws relaxed, the secret police disbanded. Amin also promised free elections.

However, the killing soon started. An abortive invasion from Tanzania by Obote supporters in 1972 prompted Amin to create 'Special Squads' to hunt down suspected opponents. He created an all-powerful secret police, the Public Safety Unit, dominated by Muslim Nubian and southern Sudanese tribesmen who delighted in killing. As he gradually killed more and more ministers, lawyers and anyone of any prominence, he created a further special murder corps called the State Research Unit under Major Farouk Minaura, a Nubian sadist. Massacres followed – targeted initially against Obote's Langi tribe and the neighbouring Acholi clan. But anyone suspected of harbouring dissent was deemed a legitimate target. Amin's victims included Chief Justice Benedicto Kiwanuka, Joseph Mubiru, the former governor of the Ugandan central bank, Anglican archbishop Janani Luwum and two of his own cabinet ministers. Rumours began to emerge that Amin practised blood rituals over the bodies of his victims, even indulging in cannibalism. Many of the bodies, dumped in the Nile or on the streets or found hooded and tied to trees, were sliced open with organs missing, clearly the victims of tribal rites. Amin himself often asked to be left alone with bodies in the morgues, which he visited frequently, and it was clear he tampered with the cadavers. 'I have eaten human flesh,' he boasted, 'It is saltier than leopard flesh.' The terror extended to his own wives: the beautiful Kay died during an abortion, but Amin had her body dismembered and then sewn together again. Lesser women suspected of disloyalty were simply murdered.

Increasingly, Amin ruled by autocratic whim. In addition, huge amounts of money were diverted to secure the support of the Ugandan military. As money ran short, Amin simply ordered the central bank to print more. Inflation soared, economic life entered on a downward spiral and consumer goods ran short.

With his popularity plummeting, Amin sought a scapegoat and settled on Uganda's wealthy Asian community, who controlled much of country's trade and industry. In August 1972 he ordered Asians with British nationality to leave the country within three months. As some 50,000 fled, including much of the country's skilled workforce, the economy began to collapse.

As his country suffered under his depredations, Amin began to lose touch with reality, possibly suffering the insanity of tertiary syphilis. He began awarding himself various medals, including the Victoria Cross, and such titles as 'Lord of All the Beasts of the Earth and the Fishes of the Sea and Conqueror of the British Empire in Africa in General and Uganda in Particular'. He also insisted on being carried on a wooden litter, with British expatriates (organized by Major Bob Astles, his chief British henchman) serving as bearers. Equally strange was the bizarre correspondence he engaged in with other world leaders. He thus offered Ted Heath, the former British prime minister and keen amateur conductor, a job as a bandmaster after his 1974 election defeat; on another occasion, he advised Israeli prime minister Golda Meir to 'tuck up her knickers' and run to the US. More sinister was his praise for the Palestinian terrorists who carried out the massacre of Israeli athletes at the 1972 Munich Olympics, and his admiration for Hitler's treatment of the Jews.

In 1979, with Uganda's economy and society having all but collapsed and Amin deeply unpopular at home, he sought to divert domestic attention by invading Tanzania. It proved to be a fateful decision. In response, Tanzania mounted a counter-invasion. Amin's army collapsed and he fled – eventually settling in Saudi Arabia. He would live on in exile until finally dying, peacefully in his bed, in 2003.

Idi Amin virtually destroyed Uganda, murdering 300,000 people; many more were forced to seek refuge abroad. And even with his removal from power, the agony did not end for the Ugandan people. Obote returned to power in flawed elections in 1980 and plunged the country into civil war; by the time he was overthrown in 1985, several hundred thousand more Ugandans had perished. Such was the legacy of Amin.

THE ENTEBBE RAID

In June 1976 Idi Amin invited an Air France plane hijacked by Palestinian and German terrorists to land at Uganda's Entebbe airport. Upon landing, the hijackers released all non-Jewish passengers and took the rest into the airport terminal, demanding the freedom of some 40 Palestinians imprisoned in Israel and a further 13 in Kenya, France, Switzerland and West Germany. Captain Michel Bacos – followed by the rest of the crew – refused to leave without the remaining passengers, while a French nun offered to take the place of one of the hostages but was forced to leave by Ugandan soldiers.

If their demands were not met by 1 July, said the hijackers, they would begin executing the 83 Jewish hostages and 20 others held. On the night of 3 July, after an extension to the deadline, the Israeli Prime Minister Yitzhak Rabin (later assassinated for making peace with the Palestinians) dispatched a commando unit which staged a stunning raid. The surprise was complete: no one could have expected faraway Israel to cross half of Africa to rescue its own. Despite Ugandan resistance, 'Operation Thunderbolt' rescued almost all of the passengers. Three hostages were killed, as was one Israeli soldier, Yonatan Netanyahu – the older brother of the future Israeli premier Binyamin Netanyahu – in whose memory the operation was retrospectively renamed 'Operation Yonatan'. All seven of the terrorists and 45 Ugandan soldiers were killed. The whole assault lasted just 30 minutes. The raid was an astonishing achievement that symbolized Israeli military power and daring.

One of the hostages, 75-year-old Dora Bloch, who had been admitted to hospital in Kampala before the Israeli raid, was not rescued. She was subsequently dragged from her bed on Idi Amin's orders and murdered by two Ugandan army officers.

A wounded hostage is stretchered away by Israeli soldiers, July 1976. Of the 103 mainly Jewish hostages held by Palestinian and German terrorists at Entebbe, the Israelis rescued all but three, caught in the cross-fire as Israeli troops stormed the airport building.

Joseph-Desiré Mobutu, the dictator of Zaïre for over three decades, preferred to be known as Mobutu Sese Seko Kuku Ngbendu Wa Za Banga – 'the warrior who knows no defeat because of his endurance and inflexible will and is all powerful, leaving fire in his wake as he goes from conquest to conquest'. His presidency became a murderous and inept kleptocracy, epitomizing the corruption in the heart of darkness that was the governance of Africa.

Mobutu Sese Seko

1930–97

> 'If you steal, do not steal too much at a time. You may be arrested . . . Steal cleverly, little by little.'
>
> MOBUTU SESE SEKO GIVES HIS PARTY MEMBERS ADVICE ON HOW TO BE CORRUPT

Mobutu's father died when he was just eight. He was educated in missionary schools, and in 1949 he joined the army of what was then the Belgian Congo. In 1958 he joined Patrice Lumumba's National Movement, and after the country was granted independence in 1960, Lumumba became prime minister and Joseph Kasa-Vubu president. Mobutu was appointed army chief-of-staff.

It was a time of deep uncertainty. Congolese troops had mutinied against their Belgian officers, there were attacks on foreigners, and the mineral-rich province of Katanga had seceded. In response, Lumumba appealed to the United Nations, and a peace-keeping force was dispatched to the region. After another revolt – this time in the diamond-rich Kasai province – Lumumba looked to support from the Soviet Union, with whose military aid he retook the province. Under pressure from Western governments, President Kasa-Vubu ordered the dismissal of the prime minister, but Lumumba refused to go. Each man called on Mobutu to arrest the other. Crucially, the Americans – who had become concerned over Lumumba's Soviet connections – sided with the president, as did

Mobutu Sese Seko, the extraordinarily corrupt president of Zaïre from 1965 to 1997, photographed in 1988.

Mobutu. In January 1961, on Mobutu's instigation and with CIA encouragement, Patrice Lumumba was arrested and executed by Katangese forces.

The country remained deeply divided. Katanga and Kasai remained beyond central control, and there was also an alternative government (set up by Lumumba's supporters) in Stanleyville. Katanga's revolt was finally ended in 1963, but a year later Lumumba's former power base in eastern Congo revolted. It was against this background that in 1965 Mobutu, backed by the CIA, seized power.

Mobutu re-established central authority across the entire country. Foreign investment was encouraged, the economy stabilized, output increased and work begun on various major construction projects. Mobutu continued to receive US patronage, with the Americans seeing him as a pro-Western bulwark in Africa. At the end of the 1960s the future of the Congo seemed bright.

Yet more troubling developments were under way. In reasserting power over the whole country Mobutu had massively increased the repressive apparatus of the state. All other political parties apart from his own – the Mouvement Populaire de la Révolution (MPR) – were banned. A personality cult centred on Mobutu began to emerge, and to legitimize his position he embarked on an 'Africanization' drive, which in 1971 saw the name of the country changed to Zaïre, while the capital, Léopoldville, became Kinshasa. He himself took on his own lengthy new title.

At the same time, Mobutu set about plundering his country's wealth. In 1973 he seized some 2000 foreign-owned businesses and properties, which he then either kept for himself or distributed to relatives or associates. Funds were funnelled abroad, and a range of luxury properties appeared across Zaïre and in various desirable locations in Europe. Wherever there was money to be made, Mobutu ensured he claimed a slice of the profits. In so doing, he made himself one of the world's richest men, with an estimated fortune by the 1980s of $5 billion. Meanwhile, Zaïre's economy crumbled as commodity prices fell, foreign investors stayed away and the grandiose projects in the 1960s turned out to be expensive follies. Corruption was endemic and massive: in 1977 even Mobutu admitted that 'Everything is for sale, anything can be bought in our country.' The state's infrastructure all but collapsed, and inflation and unemployment soared. Many starved, disease spread and any opposition was either ruthlessly repressed or simply bought off.

In the post-Cold War world, the West no longer needed Mobutu's undemocratic regime as a bastion against communism. Responding to international criticism, in 1990 Mobutu declared that he was prepared to end the dominance of his MPR party. Yet the ailing tyrant postponed planned presidential elections and, as a result, the country slid towards civil war. In the end, Mobutu's downfall was precipitated by external events. After the Rwandan genocide in 1994, Mobutu gave thousands of those responsible refuge in eastern Zaire, from where they mounted attacks back over the border into Rwanda. In response, the Rwandan government lent its support to Congolese opposition forces to Mobutu, led by Laurent Kabila. In 1997, as Kabila's army advanced from the east towards Kinshasa, Mobutu fled into exile.

Not long after his forced departure, Mobutu died in Morocco. Meanwhile, Zaïre literally ceased to exist, being renamed the Democratic Republic of Congo. Kabila became the new president, but proved to be little more than a petty tyrant himself, and in 1998 Congo plunged once more into civil war, this time involving the armies of Congo's neighbours, who all wanted a piece of the country's mineral wealth. In the four years until a peace deal was signed in 2002, some 3 million people died in the fighting, and the provinces are still being looted and terrorized by rampaging militias. Now ruled by Kabila's son, Congo remains a colossal tragedy of murder, war, rape and starvation, in a land plundered to extinction by Mobutu.

KLEPTOCRACIES

In 2004, Transparency International listed the ten worst kleptocratic rulers of recent times. Mobutu came in third, followed by Sani Abacha (Nigeria, 1993–98; stole US$2–5 billion); Slobodan Milošević (Serbia/Yugoslavia, 1989–2000, US$1 billion); Jean-Claude Duvalier (Haiti, 1971–86, US$300–800 million); Alberto Fujimori (Peru, 1990–2000, US$600 million); Pavlo Lazarenko, Ukraine (1996–7, US$114–200 million); Arnoldo Alemán (Nicaragua, 1997–2002, US$100 million); and Joseph Estrada (Philippines, 1998–2001, US$78–80 million).

Second was Ferdinand Marcos, Philippine president from 1965 to 1986, who with his wife Imelda – famed for her vast collection of shoes – plundered the Philippine economy through a system of 'crony capitalism', amassing a vast fortune while ordinary Filipinos went hungry. Opponents were arrested by the military – over 60,000 from 1972 to 1977 – and many tortured and murdered, including opposition leader Benigno Aquino. A popular rebellion in 1986 finally forced him from office and he fled with his wife to Hawaii. Transparency International put his stolen wealth at US$5–10 billion, others much higher. Marcos died in 1989 before he could stand trial.

The worst kleptocrat was Mohamed Suharto, Indonesian president from 1967 until 1998 but virtual military ruler from 1957. His brutal regime saw 2 million massacred following an attempted Communist coup in 1965, 250,000 killed in his 1975 invasion of East Timor and hundreds of thousands tortured and murdered during his dictatorship. Spectacular economic growth brought limited benefit to his people, far more to Suharto and his cronies, who fabulously enriched themselves, his wife's lucrative commission earning her the nickname 'Madam Ten Percent'. His klepocracy was laid bare after his forced resignation in 1998 following Asian financial meltdown: US$15–35 billion according to Transparency International. Disputed claims of ill health, however, allowed him to escape justice; he died in 2008.

Born in Yogyakarta, Suharto was the second president of independent Indonesia and stole an estimated $35 billion.

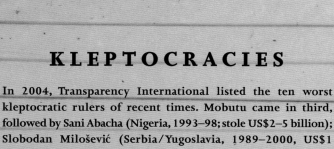

'The Beast', Salvatore 'Shorty' Riina brought decades of murder and mayhem to the streets of Sicily. He was a man for whom violence was second nature, ruthlessly eliminating any rivals – the brutality of his killings made all the more chilling by the cool detachment with which he carried them out. A long-time member of the island's Mafia, by the early 1980s he had risen through a series of multiple murders to become the most powerful man in the entire organization, his name a byword for bloodshed and corruption.

Salvatore Riina b.1930

> 'His philosophy was that if someone's finger hurt, it was better to cut off his whole arm just to make sure.'
>
> MAFIA INFORMANT ANTONINO CALDERONE ON SALVATORE RIINA

The son of Giacomo Riina, a local gangster arrested in 1942 for smuggling cigarettes, Salvatore (Totò) – was raised in Corleone and introduced there to the local Mafia by his uncle. After his first murder for them, he joined the 'Family' aged 18. The following year he killed a man in an argument and was sentenced to six years in prison for manslaughter. There he linked up with two other Mafiosi – Luciano Leggio and Bernardo 'the Tractor' Provenzano – and, on their release, the three men set up a rival faction, with Leggio as boss. They soon clashed with Michele Navarra, head of the Corleone 'Family', who sent hitmen to eliminate Leggio, but when they bungled the attempt, Riina and Provenzano – on Leggio's orders – gunned him down and Leggio took control of the Corleonesi. They were still a provincial concern, regarded by their Palermo counterparts – who referred to them contemptuously as 'the peasants' – as small fry, but that was soon to change.

Over the next ten years, Riina and Leggio systematically murdered Navarra's ex-supporters, until, in 1969, they were brought to trial, only to be acquitted after threats to jurors and witnesses. Riina, however, was indicted on another murder charge later that year, and went into hiding, remaining in the shadows for the next 23 years. That didn't stop him, however, from continuing with the Corleonesi, and when Luciano Leggio was finally imprisoned in 1974 for the murder of Michele Navarra, he became the new leader. In the same year, he married his wife, Ninetta, by whom he had four children, two of whom, Giovanni and Giuseppe, followed him into the Mafia and, ultimately, into prison.

The 1970s were a boom time for the Sicilian and the currency of that boom was heroin – 'white gold'. Mafiosi swiftly became 'trading posts' between the poppy fields of the East and lucrative cities of the North American continent, where generations of Italian immigration provided the perfect opportunity to develop their franchise. More than one real-life Tony Soprano emerged in this period along the US eastern seaboard, while back in Sicily the Mafia evolved into a genuinely transnational business – refining, shipping and distributing the drug and raking in hundreds of millions of pounds' worth of profits every year.

Unsurprisingly, such wealth created greed and rivalry, and Riina was determined his 'Family' should emerge as the dominant Mafioso faction. The result was brutal infighting in the late 1970s and early 1980s, which culminated in the 'Great Mafia War' – the Mattanza – that began in 1981. Riina's hitmen took out the leaders – and many subordinates – of all rival factions. The scale of the bloodletting was extraordinary. At least 200 people – among them Stefano Bontade, Salvatore Inzerillo, Gaetano Badalamenti, Filippo Marchese, Giuseppe Greco and Rosario Riccobono – are known to have perished in the years that followed. Many simply disappeared – victims of lupara bianca (the 'white shotgun' in Sicilian) – their bodies never found.

Riina also orchestrated the murder of many important dignitaries, including judges, lawyers and police, the most prominent being General Carlo Alberto Dalla Chiesa, appointed as prefect for Palermo to tackle Mafia feuding there.

Eventually, the carnage provoked a response. A growing anti-Mafia movement developed within the province, led by two magistrates – Giovanni Falcone and Paolo Borsellino – who were to become the greatest foes the Mafia ever faced. Together, they presided over the first 'maxi trial' of 1986–7, in which charges were brought against 474 men (many of whom, however, remained 'on the run' – including 'Shorty' Riina). Over a hundred were acquitted, but the rest were sentenced to some 2500 years in prison. A decisive blow had been struck against the Mafia, and further 'maxi- trials' followed.

Inevitably, Falcone and Borsellino had made themselves the Mafia's 'number one' enemies, and Riina was determined to have his revenge. In May 1992, Falcone, his wife and three bodyguards were killed by a roadside bomb near Palermo, and less than two months later, Borsellino was blown up by a car bomb, together with five bodyguards. The killing did not end there. Determined to protect his empire, Riina initiated a terrorist bombing campaign aimed at forcing the state to abandon its judicial assault on the Mafia. Ultimately, however, this served only to stiffen the resolve of those determined to break the Mafia, and in January 1993, following a tip-off from his chauffeur, Balduccio di Maggio (several of whose relatives were later murdered in reprisal), Riina was arrested as he waited in his car at some traffic lights.

In absentia, Riina had already been convicted and sentenced to two life sentences, but to these were now added further guilty verdicts relating to over a hundred other murders. 'The Beast' was sentenced to spend the rest of his life behind bars, where he remains to this day.

Salvatore 'Totò' Riina, arrested in Palermo on 15 January 1993, after a concerted effort by the Italian government to root out the Mafia.

THE SICILIAN MAFIA

La Cosa Nostra – 'our thing' – such is the term by which many refer to the Sicilian Mafia, yet for years some doubted its very existence, claiming that the 'Mafia' was a figment of over-active imaginations; the creation of those who had failed to understand the Sicilian mindset or were obsessed with Hollywood gangster movies. It was only in the last quarter of the 20th century, as the outrages perpetuated by 'Totò' Riina's Corleonesi made the Mafia impossible to ignore, that the reality became clear.

The Mafia of recent times is very different from what went before. It first emerged in the late 19th century in the context of burgeoning economic opportunity. Some in Sicily became rich – others grew jealous of those riches and decided to use violence to gain a share – either by murder and stealing, or by agreeing to protect people's wealth in return for a share of the fortune. It was into this gap that stepped the 'Mafiosi' – the 'men of honour' as they liked to call themselves. In the words of one late 19th-century observer, they made themselves captains of what might be called 'the violence industry'.

Until the rise of both the heroin trade and the Corleonesi, these Mafiosi operated almost entirely within geographically based 'Family' structures. Each 'Family' worked within their territory more or less independently of the rest. They extorted money from businesses, engaged in racketeering, and cut deals with the political authorities to provide cover for their actions – a malign, corrupting, yet at times scarcely noticeable reality just below the surface of Sicilian life. Totò Riina changed all that, making the Mafia more powerful and conspicuous than ever before. The irony is that, in so doing, he may also have paved the way for its destruction.

Italian military police stand guard outside the small Sicilian town of Corleone, 1992. The town is known as the birthplace of at least nine Mafia bosses, including members of the Corleonesi, Genovese and Morello families.

Jim Jones was a self-obsessed American cult leader who manipulated the poor and vulnerable, demanded their complete obedience, and ordered the murder of those who questioned his integrity. At the end he killed or convinced nearly a thousand people – including two hundred children – to take their own lives in a jungle settlement in South America called 'Jonestown', constructed around his own warped and paranoid fantasy.

Jim Jones 1931–78

'I am the Way, the Truth, and the Light. No one can come to the father but through me.'

JIM JONES

James Warren Jones was born in Indiana to a family that was struggling to cope with the effects of the Great Depression. From early in his life he developed an empathy with the plight of the poor, and as a teenager he became strongly involved with a Pentecostal church, preaching on street corners in deprived areas to both white-working-class and African-American communities. With his jet-black hair and olive skin, his shades and his fixed and confident grin, Jones was a handsome and charismatic figure. In the late 1940s he became interested in socialism and communalism as an answer to what he saw as the destructive force of capitalism. He also argued for integration and reconciliation between the races.

But even from an early age there were hints of a darker side. He clearly hated rejection, and once shot a friend who refused to concede to his demands. For many years his wife Marceline – who held traditional Methodist views – suffered his jealous tirades and manipulative behaviour. When Jones briefly rejected God early in their marriage, he threatened to kill himself if she continued to pray, and he forcefully and unsuccessfully tried to adopt the 12-year-old son of Marceline's cousin, against the boy's wishes. His behaviour was often hypocritical, demanding fidelity and clean living from those around him, while he himself relied on antidepressants and embarked on a series of extramarital affairs.

In 1952 Jones seems to have recovered his faith, partly thanks to the fact that he saw in Marceline's Methodism a religion that was interested in the plight of the poor. He even, for a short time, became a Methodist student pastor. But Jones's idiosyncratic personal views – an ill-defined mixture of Christianity and socialism, traditional family values and social liberalism – led him to establish his own church, the 'People's Temple', in which he would have a privileged position. The People's Temple set up a soup kitchen and offered support to the poor and social outcasts, such as former prisoners and drug addicts. There was also a strong streak of charlatanry, with Jones promising miraculous cures for all kinds of ills, including cancer, in an attempt to recruit more followers.

In 1965 Jones moved with his family and 140 followers to Ukiah in northern California, apparently because he believed it would be safe from nuclear attack. By 1968, as his following dwindled, he affiliated the People's Temple with the Disciples of Christ, a larger church group, which gave him renewed credibility and access to 1.5 million members.

As his cult grew again, so did the scrutiny from journalists and politicians, and accusations began to emerge that Jones was taking funds from cult members for his personal use. Eager to escape this scrutiny, in 1977 Jones and his followers moved to Guyana, where, in the rainforest, they set up an agricultural commune called 'Jonestown'. In the process, his followers handed to Jones control of all their possessions.

Away from the glare of the public eye, Jones began to tighten his grip on his followers. There were

reports of beatings and death threats, and each person was required to confess their sexual practices and fantasies, while women were encouraged to criticize their husbands' skills in bed. Jones told his congregation that he was the only true heterosexual among them, although in 1973 he had been arrested for lewd contact in a known meeting place for homosexuals.

On 17 November 1978 United States Representative for California Leo Ryan arrived in Guyana with a group of journalists and concerned family members to inspect the camp. After fourteen members of the cult agreed to defect, Jones – gripped by paranoia – believed that his fantasy was crumbling around him. On 18 November, as Ryan and the defectors made their way to the aeroplane that was due to fly them home to the United States, they were attacked by members of the People's Temple. Ryan was shot dead, along with three journalists and one defector. Back in the camp Jones ordered his followers – whom he had trained for mass suicide on many occasions – to come together and drink a punch laced with cyanide. The vast majority went through with it unthinkingly; babies had the lethal cocktail forced into their mouths with syringes, while anyone who objected was coerced or shot. Jones took an easier way out, shooting himself in the head. When Guyanese troops arrived at the scene to pursue those who had committed murder on the airstrip, they were greeted by the sight of nearly a thousand bodies – men, women and children – slumped together on the ground.

Jones began life as a pious man with a social conscience, who refused to judge people on grounds of wealth or race. But his vision of a socialist utopia was ultimately indistinguishable from his own manic desire for domination – and when that control was threatened, he was prepared to bring destruction down on all those around him.

Reverend Jim Jones in Jonestown, Guyana, where he induced 900 members of his cult to commit suicide.

SEERS AND CHARLATANS

Seers, charlatans and false prophets such as Jim Jones have been a feature of most societies for centuries, offering a popular alternative to conventional religion in the form of charismatic leadership, visions of the future and miracle cures.

In the ancient world, one of the most notorious charlatans was Alexander the Paphlagonian (2nd century AD), who prophesied the second coming of Apollo and claimed that Asclepius, the Greek god of healing, had been reborn as a snake. Alexander sat in the temple of Asclepius in Paphlagonia, offering sage advice while the tamed snake, with a fake human head attached, wound itself round his body.

More recent medical charlatans have included 'Dr' John Brinkley (1885–1942), who made a fortune in America by attaching goat glands and testicles onto more than 15,000 men, whom he had convinced would thereby experience an increase in virility. Another such was 'Dr' Albert Abrams (1863–1924), who invented something called 'the dynomizer', an electronic device that he claimed could diagnose disease from a single blood sample, which he asked his patients to send through the post. He even claimed that he could heal them over the telephone.

Of modern American cult leaders, the most infamous since Jim Jones was David Koresh (1959–93), whose Branch Davidian religious sect was based at a ranch called Mount Carmel in Waco, Texas. Koresh believed himself to be a modern-day Old Testament prophet, but in reality he was a womanizer who claimed that he was entitled to 140 wives, and who forced himself on girls as young as 12. A botched raid by the FBI on the ranch at Mount Carmel in February 1993 led to a 51-day siege, which ended with a gun battle and massive fire, in which 82 cult members – including 21 children – perished.

Fire and smoke consume the compound of David Koresh's Branch Dravidian cult at Waco, Texas, 19 April 1993, bringing the FBI's 51-day siege of the sect's headquarters to an apocalyptic end. The fire is believed to have been started by members of the cult itself after tear gas was used by the FBI in an effort to end the siege.

Charles Manson was a bloody aberration in a decade that preached peace and love. A perverted and pathological fantasist, he used his devious powers of manipulation to snare others into his depraved web of hatred and violence, attracting a small band of twisted devotees who were prepared to commit cold-blooded murder on his command.

Charles Manson b. 1934

'Used to be being crazy meant something. Nowadays, everybody's crazy.'
Charles Manson

Born in Cincinnatti to a teenage single mother who once tried to exchange him for a pitcher of beer, Manson spent much of his youth in teenage reformatories, sodomizing a fellow inmate at knifepoint when just 18 years old. By 1966, an accomplished armed robber and pimp, he had spent more than half of 32 years of life in custody. When he was released on probation in 1967, the year of the 'summer of love', he moved in with Mary Brunner, a 23-year-old librarian at the University of California, Berkeley, establishing himself as a hippie guru in the Haight-Ashbury district of San Francisco. He subsequently requisitioned an old school bus and began travelling around California with a group of devotees, mostly women, forming a quasi-religious sect centred around his domineering personality. At its peak, this sect – later named the 'Manson Family' by the media – contained more than one hundred people, who referred to Manson as both 'God' and 'Satan'.

Obsessed with The Beatles, and having learned to play the guitar in prison, Manson was eager to establish contacts in the music world. In the spring of 1968, Dennis Wilson of The Beach Boys picked up two hitchhiking females, who turned out to be members of the Manson Family. He returned to his home in Pacific Palisades, Los Angeles, to be greeted by Manson and more than twenty Family members, who for the next two months took over Wilson's home.

In November 1968, the Family moved on to establish a commune at the empty Barker Ranch, in Death Valley, California. By that stage, they had been joined by Charles 'Tex' Watson, a hitchhiking Texan who soon became Manson's chief lieutenant. They spent their time practising a set of religious doctrines that Manson had cobbled together from an eclectic mixture of contemporary music, science fiction writing, Scientology, the Book of Revelation and racist fantasy. Borrowing the title of a song by The Beatles, Manson prophesied 'Helter-Skelter', an apocalyptic race war between blacks and whites, at the end of which the Family would emerge from an underground city below Death Valley and assume a position of world leadership. They would control the black man and, in Manson's words, 'kick him in the butt and tell him to go pick cotton and go be a good nigger'.

In July 1969, Manson told his followers they would have to trigger Helter-Skelter themselves. On 8 August, he ordered 'Tex' Watson and three female members of the Family to go to the former home of an old acquaintance – a record producer called Terry Melcher – and 'totally destroy everyone . . . as gruesome as you can'. As Manson knew, Melcher had moved away and the house was now owned by Sharon Tate, actress and wife of the Hollywood film director Roman Polanski, who was working in Britain at the time.

A police mugshot from 1969 of the American cult leader and multiple murderer Charles Manson.

(LA5)LOS ANGELES, Dec.2--CULT
LEADER?--Charles Manson, above,
34, was described today by the
Los Angeles Times and attorney
Richard Caballero as the leader of a quasireligious cult of
hippies, three of whom have
been arrested on murder warrants
issued in the slayings of actress Sharon Tate and four others
at her home. Manson is in jail

As midnight approached, Watson cut the phone lines and broke into the house, assembling Tate and three friends (Wojciech Frykowski, Abigail Folger and Jay Sebring) who were staying with her. Briefly the four women managed to escape their captors, but they were hunted down, stabbed and shot repeatedly. Tate, who was eight and a half months pregnant, was stabbed 16 times, plaintively crying 'Mother' with her last breath. Before the assailants fled, they wrote 'PIG' on the front door with a towel dipped in Tate's blood.

The next evening, six Family members, this time including Manson himself, made their way to the home of Leno La Bianca, a supermarket executive, in Waverly Drive, Los Angeles. They broke into the house and tied up La Bianca and his wife, Rosemary. Then, at Manson's prompting, they stabbed the couple in a ferocious frenzy. La Bianca was left with a carving fork in his stomach and steak knife in his throat, while his wife was stabbed 41 times. 'HELTER SKELTER!' was daubed in blood on the walls and 'Tex' Watson carved the word 'WAR' onto La Bianca's stomach.

> 'totally destroy everyone . . .
> as gruesome as you can'
> CHARLES MANSON

The Dark Side of the
Summer of Love

The 'Summer of Love' of 1967 is now regarded as the high point of hippie culture in the United States, marked by free love, drugs, rock music and an awakening political consciousness, centred on the Civil Rights movement and the Vietnam War. Critics of the hippie movement focused on the debauchery and disorientating social anarchy that characterized this period, leading to disillusionment, excess and, in some cases, death. When Jim Morrison, lead singer of The Doors, died in Paris in July 1971, apparently of a drug overdose, it seemed to many that the innocence of the era had finally been lost.

Even during the heyday of the hippie movement the United States was experiencing a marked period of racial tension. Within a few months of the Summer of Love, on 4 April 1968, Martin Luther King – figurehead of peaceful protest – had been assassinated, and his death sparked days and nights of rioting and looting in deprived black urban areas across the United States. The

Vietnam War had not only poisoned politics but created an atmosphere of turmoil and antagonism. Robert Kennedy, running for president, had raised hope and faith – but was assassinated like his brother John F. Kennedy in June 1968.

The last year of the vibrant 1960s is sometimes seen as the moment when the hippie movement began to go seriously wrong. First there were the

Police soon traced the crimes back to Manson and the Family, who had been moving between Spahn Ranch – owned by an octogenarian dairy farmer, who let Manson stay there in return for sexual favours from his female followers – northwest of Los Angeles and the Barker Ranch in Death Valley. After a number of abortive raids, police finally located Manson at the latter on 12 October 1969, hiding in a bathroom cabinet. At his June 1970 trial for conspiracy to murder, he gloried in the media spotlight, shaving his head, trimming his beard into the shape of a fork and declaring 'I am the devil.' He was sentenced to death in June 1971 but spared execution after California abolished the death penalty. Today, he is prisoner B33920 at Corcoran State Prison.

In appearance a typical product of the 1960s hippie revolution, Manson's warped and sadistic mind was the complete antithesis of the ideals behind the so-called 'Summer of Love'. Tapping into the fears and prejudices of contemporary America, he harnessed savage bigotry and drug-fuelled decadence to play out his perverted fantasies.

Manson murders, then, on 6 December 1969, at the Altamont Free Concert, the hippie dream turned into nightmare. The concert – which was intended to mimic the success of the Woodstock Festival that had taken place four months earlier – was headlined by the Rolling Stones but poorly organized. The venue, the speedway track in Altamont, northern California, was chosen at the last minute, and security at the event – which attracted anything between 300,000 and 400,000 young people – was placed in the hands of the Hell's Angels, the notoriously violent biker gang, who, it was alleged, had asked to be paid in beer.

The sound system at the concert was faulty and the stage was only four foot high, surrounded by a ring of Hell's Angels, some of whom sat on their motorbikes. Over the course of the day, the Angels became increasingly intoxicated and unruly, controlling the crowds with sawed-off pool cues or driving directly at them on their motorbikes, causing a number of serious injuries. At one stage, the Angels even climbed on stage and knocked Marty Balin, the guitarist from Jefferson Airplane, unconscious.

Worse was yet to come. When Meredith Hunter, an 18-year-old black man possibly high on drugs, pulled a revolver on one of the Angels, he was stabbed five times and beaten to death in front of television cameras. It soon passed into folklore that the Stones, who were in the middle of their set, had been playing 'Sympathy for the Devil' when Hunter had been killed, although this was not in fact the case. The Grateful Dead, one of the bands present on the day, later wrote a number of songs about the event – one of them ominously entitled 'Manson's Children'.

Mick Jagger sings at the ill-fated Altamont Free Concert on Saturday, 6 December 1969.

Colonel Mengistu Haile Mariam helped overthrow Emperor Haile Selassie, seized power in Ethiopia, murdered his own ministers with a machine-gun, imposed a brutal Leninist tyranny and repressive police-state, ordered the murder of millions of his countrymen and created, by policy and blunder, a famine that killed millions more. He ranks as one of Africa's most disastrous monsters.

Mengistu Haile Mariam

b. 1937

As a young man the dwarfish Mengistu joined the Ethiopian army, and, after graduating from the country's military academy, he was sent to the United States for further training. It was there, in the tense racial atmosphere of the late 1960s, that Mengistu became interested in Josef Stalin and attached to the Marxism of the USSR. He returned home to Ethiopia in 1971, having developed radical ideas about how his country should be governed.

In 1974, the long-serving and ageing Emperor Haile Selassie started to lose control of his inept and corrupt if picturesque regime; he proved incapable of aiding the people in a terrible

Mengistu Haile Mariam led a bloody coup against the Ethiopian Emperor Haile Selassie in 1974, setting up in his place a military junta known as the 'Dergue', which ushered in a 17-year period of bloody repression, genocide and terror before Mengistu lost power in 1991.

famine. Opposition intensified. A junta of around a hundred military officers came together, calling themselves the 'Dergue', or committee, and overthrew the emperor in a bloody coup. From the moment it seized control, the Dergue took a systematic approach to the purging of its enemies. Sixty of the key officials under the emperor were rounded up and put before firing squads without trial, setting the tone for the new regime. Within months, the patriarch of the Ethiopian Orthodox Church was murdered. In 1976 Mengistu addressed a huge crowd in the capital, Addis Ababa, holding up large bottles that he claimed were filled with the blood of his enemies.

Until its overthrow in 1991, Mengistu and the Dergue was responsible for the deaths of millions of Ethiopians. In an echo of Pol Pot's brief regime in Cambodia in the later 1970s, hundreds of intellectuals, particularly those with any association with the old regime, were rounded up and shot in order to purify the country in the name of revolution. The rival Ethiopian People's Revolutionary Party suffered particularly over the following years – membership was enough to secure abduction and near certain death.

The Dergue governed by cultivating an atmosphere of fear and paranoia. Local committees, called 'Kebeles', were set up across Ethiopia, with the power to monitor and name potential 'enemies of the revolution'. The names of suspects were then filed by the central administration and soon rounded up by militiamen in the pay of the regime. Many bodies turned up the following day, or weeks later; others were never found. In the event that the bodies were returned for burial, the Kebeles demanded that the victim's family pay for the cost of the bullets used to kill their loved one.

By 1977 Mengistu, with ruthless efficiency, had established himself as the leading force in the army, and in the Dergue. As Ethiopia adopted an aggressive approach to neighbouring Eritrea, Mengistu shot a fellow Dergue member who had argued for a more cautious foreign policy. He personally purged the Dergue by executing rivals and opponents with a machine-gun. He also ordered the assassination of any other former comrades who stood in his way, and in 1987 declared himself president for life.

As president, the first changes that Mengistu implemented made some progress in dismantling Ethiopia's archaic, almost feudal land system. But the mass forced relocations of people to new collective agricultural settlements proved disastrous, and caused further tragedy. Mengistu not only killed his own people but fought a long and bloody war with his rival leftist dictator Mohamed Siad Barre of Somalia. Hundreds of thousands died.

The suffering of the Ethiopian people was to some extent ameliorated by support from the Soviet Union, to whom Mengistu had offered up his country as a satellite state, although much of the Soviet aid was spent on military expenditure. When the Soviet Union began to flounder in the mid-1980s, the withdrawal of aid meant that Mengistu's response to the devastating famine of 1984–5 was entirely ineffectual. When news of the famine first broke, the regime condemned it as enemy propaganda; but it was only international aid that prevented the death toll rising beyond the already shocking figure of 1 million. In 1991 Mengistu was finally deposed by the Ethiopian Revolutionary Democratic Front, a military coalition of opposition groups, as well as Eritreans and Tigrayans. Mengistu fled to Zimbabwe.

In December 2006, after a 12-year trial, an Ethiopian court convicted Mengistu in absentia of genocide – the death of untold millions – and sentenced him to life imprisonment. Meanwhile, the former dictator continues to live in comfort in Zimbabwe, on a large ranch.

ROBERT MUGABE

Seeking refuge in Robert Mugabe's Zimbabwe, Mengistu Haile Mariam found a man after his own heart. For Mugabe is responsible for the murder of thousands in the Matabeleland massacres, and for plunging his country into a state of economic and political despair.

Mugabe had all the credentials to be a hero for Zimbabwe's black majority. From the 1960s he became a key figure in the opposition to the minority white rulers of the country, then known as Rhodesia, and was imprisoned for ten years for subversion. In 1975 he emerged as the leader of the Zimbabwe African National Union (ZANU), which launched a guerrilla war against the white regime. When in 1980 peace was restored and black-majority rule instituted, Mugabe was elected prime minister. Initially he proceeded cautiously, seeking a broad base of support among both whites and blacks, but before long he moved against his black rival, Joshua Nkomo, who spoke for the Ndebele people, while Mugabe derived his support from the majority Shona tribe. As tribal tensions increased, clashes in Ndebele areas such as Matabeleland were dealt with bloodily by Mugabe's troops.

In 1984 Mugabe effectively established a one-party tyranny. He became the country's first executive president in 1987, and subsequent elections have been characterized by widespread intimidation and violence. Mugabe has also encouraged his paramilitaries and thuggish war veterans to seize the remaining land still held by whites, and the resulting chaos has led to a catastrophic decline in agricultural output. In recent years, the black community has also suffered displacement following large-scale schemes to destroy shanty towns in areas where the opposition is strongest.

Despite the opposition of the Movement for Democratic Change, corruption and intimidation ensured that Mugabe's party managed to hold onto to its grip on power in the elections of 2000 and 2002. Meanwhile, any sign of dissent was mercilessly suppressed by his secret police, the Central Intelligence Organization.

Mugabe has presided over the destruction of a nation. The country boasts great natural resources and rich farming land that once made it one of the most prosperous countries in Africa – but now there are frequent food shortages, and raging inflation. In 2008, Mugabe lost an election but he consolidated his tyranny and defied the world, using widespread murder, torture, arrests, violence and election fraud.

Zimbabwe's President Robert Mugabe who was re-elected in uncontested elections in 2008.

Saddam Hussein, the dictator of Iraq, aspired to be an Arab hero and conqueror, but his long reign of ruthless oppression, sadistic cruelty, gangsterish corruption, unnecessary wars, mass murder and a ludicrous personality cult led to a series of political miscalculations that brought about the destruction of his regime and his own death on the scaffold.

Saddam Hussein

1937–2006

'*What has befallen us of defeat, shame and humiliation, Saddam, is the result of your follies, your miscalculations and your irresponsible actions.*'

SHIA IRAQI ARMY COMMANDER IN 1991, INAUGURATING THE UPRISING AGAINST SADDAM'S RULE THAT WAS SUBSEQUENTLY CRUSHED BY THE DICTATOR'S FORCES

Saddam was born in a small Sunni village close to the town of Tikrit. His father died before he was born so he was brought up in his stepfather's house – repeatedly beaten and spending much of his youth as a 'street kid'. In 1947 he went to live with his mother's brother, with whom, at the age of ten, he received his first schooling.

In the early 1950s Saddam moved with his uncle to Baghdad and tried to get into military college but failed the exams. Meanwhile, he imbibed from his uncle a hatred of British influence in the Kingdom of Iraq, became a regular participant in anti-government demonstrations, and formed his own street gang to attack political opponents. In time he became drawn towards the Ba'ath Party, which combined socialism with anti-Western, pan-Arab nationalism, and in 1958 he participated in the army coup led by Brigadier Abdel Karim Kassem that overthrew and murdered King Faisal II. Many, especially the Ba'athists, were disappointed that Kassem failed to lead Iraq into a union with neighbouring Arab countries, and in 1959 Saddam was involved in a failed attempt to assassinate Kassem, after which he went into exile in Syria and Egypt.

A Ba'athist-dominated coup in 1963 induced Saddam to return, but the new ruler of Iraq, Abdul Salam Arif, soon fell out with his Ba'athist allies, and Saddam was imprisoned for several years before escaping in 1967. He went on to become the right-hand man of the Ba'ath Party leader, Ahmad Hassan al-Bakr, and after the party seized power in 1968, he emerged as the strong man of the regime, becoming vice-president, as well as head of Iraq's security apparatus and general secretary of the Ba'ath Party. He deliberately fashioned his regime on that of Stalin, whom he studied.

From his new position Saddam oversaw the nationalization of the Western-owned Iraqi Petroleum Company, using the funds accrued to develop the country's welfare state (especially its health system). He also initiated a major drive against illiteracy, made improvements to Iraqi infrastructure and generally sought to encourage modernization and industrialization. At the same time, however, he also worked assiduously to accumulate power to himself, moving loyal lieutenants into key positions, building up a brutal secret police and strengthening his grip on levers of state.

In mid-1979 Saddam pressured the ailing al-Bakr to resign, and assumed the presidency himself. He immediately summoned the Revolutionary Council, comprising the senior Ba'ath Party leadership, and announced that 'Zionism and the forces of darkness' were engaged in a conspiracy against Iraq. Then, to the horror of his audience, he announced that those involved were present in the room. While Saddam sat smoking a huge cigar, a series of names were read out, and, one by one, 66 people were led away. Subsequently 22 of these men were found guilty, and Saddam personally supervised their killing, requiring senior figures in the Iraqi leadership to carry out the death sentences.

Saddam set about transforming Iraq into what one dissident labelled the 'Republic of Fear'. His notorious secret police, the Mukhabarat, together with the state internal security department (the Amn), established a fierce grip over the entire country. Regular massacres were carried out of Jews, Freemasons, communists, economic saboteurs or merely people who crossed Saddam or his greedy, pitiless family, all of whom served in his government. Purge followed upon purge, attended by show trials and televised confessions. Over the subsequent two decades Saddam Hussein killed at least 400,000 Iraqis – many of whom endured all manner of torture. His psychopathic sons, particularly the sadistic, demented heir apparent Uday, conducted their own struggles for power and brutal reigns of terror, personally torturing their enemies. At one point, Saddam's two sons-in-law, fearing murder by Uday, fled to Jordan but were tricked into returning and then slaughtered by Uday.

Not content with dominating Iraq, Saddam was also determined to assert regional hegemony. He invaded Iran in 1980, using Iran's Islamic revolution of 1979 as a pretext to seize Iran's oilfields, and thus sparked a disastrous eight-year war that ended in stalemate and cost over a million lives. Adept at playing off the great powers against one another, he was significantly aided by the West, which regarded Iran as the greater of two evils.

During the war, Iran had encouraged the Iraqi Kurds to mount an uprising against Ba'athist rule. Saddam responded in merciless fashion, deploying mustard and nerve gas against the civilian population –

THE IRAN–IRAQ WAR

In September 1980, Iraq went to war with Iran. Saddam's ostensible aim was to capture the Shatt al-Arab waterway that separates the two countries, but in reality he wanted to secure the Iranian oilfields and strike a blow against Iran's Islamic revolution which threatened to seduce his own Shia minority.

After some initial successes, the Iraqi army was pushed back. Saddam's forces seemed on the verge of collapse until the US provided Iraq with satellite intelligence on Iranian troop manoeuvres, allowing Saddam to deploy his aircraft with greater effect.

Certain aspects of the Iran–Iraq conflict – including trench warfare, barbed-wire fences and soldiers attacking machine-gun emplacements across open ground – echoed the fighting of the First World War. But there were some sinister innovations, such as Iran's sending of human waves of young boys – who were told that they would become 'martyrs' if they were killed – across minefields. No less horrific was Saddam's profligate use of chemical weapons against the advancing Iranian troops.

The conflict settled into a war of attrition. By the time a ceasefire was agreed, in July 1988, both sides were effectively back where they had begun – with over a million lives lost.

An Iranian soldier equipped with a gas mask during the Iran-Iraq war.

most notoriously at the town of Halabja, where some 5000 Kurds died in a single attack in March 1988. Four thousand villages were destroyed and 100,000 Kurds slaughtered.

The end of the Iranian war left Iraq exhausted despite huge oil revenues. In August 1990 Saddam invaded and occupied Kuwait. It proved to be a catastrophic miscalculation. The United Nations authorized a massive US-led military coalition to drive the Iraqis out of Kuwait, which they swiftly achieved in 1991. Iraqi Kurds and Shiites – encouraged by the coalition – rebelled against Saddam, but without Western military support they were brutally put down.

By the ceasefire agreement, Iraq had agreed to abandon nuclear, chemical and biological weapons. Yet Saddam failed to cooperate with UN weapons inspectors, barred them entirely from 1998, and engaged in constant military brinksmanship and diplomatic chicanery.

Saddam's situation was transformed by the al-Qaeda terrorist attacks on America on 11 September 2001. President George W. Bush – confident after overthrowing Al-Qaeda's backers, the Taliban, in Afghanistan – advocated 'regime change' in Iraq and the creation of Iraqi democracy to encourage freedom in the Arab world, citing as justification Saddam's dictatorship, continued pursuit of weapons of mass destruction and support for terrorist groups. Ironically, there were no weapons of mass destruction but fearing that the truth might expose his regime's weakness to Iran, Saddam miscalculated (for the second time) that America would not dare invade. In March 2003, US-led coalition forces invaded and overthrew Saddam, who was finally captured, tried and sentenced to death. His execution, embarrassingly bungled, symbolized the incompetence and lack of preparation of the well-intentioned US/UK invasion and the subsequent military quagmire. Nonetheless the sentence was richly deserved.

A ruthless, militaristic autocrat who invaded Kuwait in 1990 and killed thousands of his own people, Saddam Hussein ruled Iraq from 1968 until he was deposed by invading American forces in 2003.

'Turkmenbashi' – the 'Father of the Turkmen' – was one of history's most absurd monsters. President of Turkmenistan from 1990 until his death in 2006, he led one of the newly independent republics that emerged from the old Soviet Union and modelled it around the one thing he loved best: himself. Vulgar, vain, greedy and deluded, this surreal post-modernist dictator not only took state-sponsored narcissism to new levels of insane egotism, creating a cult around his own personality and his own holy book, but also terrorized his people with his secret police and impoverished them by building preposterous palaces and monuments of literally gold-plated grandiosity.

Turkmenbashi

1940–2006

'I had read about beatings and electric shock therapy which I experienced in prison but it was the unexpected techniques that really damaged me. I was fitted with a gas mask and the air vent was closed. They played tapes of my relatives being beaten after they were arrested. Their suffering was mine.'

BORIS SHIKMURADOV, TURKMENISTAN'S FORMER FOREIGN MINISTER, ON HIS TREATMENT BY TURKMENBASHI

The young Turkmenbashi – born Saparmurat Atayevich Niyazov – barely knew his parents. His father died fighting for the Soviets during the Second World War, while his mother (and the rest of his immediate family) were killed during a massive earthquake in 1948. At 8 years old, Niyazov was forced to live in a state-run orphanage and then later with distant relatives.

Niyazov found an opportunity to escape the misfortunes of his childhood by training to be an engineer and joining the Communist Party, to which he was admitted in 1962. Rapidly gaining a reputation for his enthusiastic and rigid defence of communist doctrine, he became first secretary of the Communist Party of the Turkmen Soviet Socialist Republic in 1985 – somewhat surprisingly as an appointee of Mikhail Gorbachev, the man who was about to attempt the reform of the USSR. Five years later, as the USSR was beginning to unravel, Niyazov became chairman of the Supreme Soviet of the Turkmen SSR – president in all but name.

In August 1991, when hard-line members of the Soviet establishment attempted to oust Gorbachev in a coup, Niyazov supported them, understandably anxious to support the system to which he owed so much. However, when the coup collapsed – and along with it, the Soviet state – Niyazov moved quickly to reinvent himself. Niyazov the ardent communist became Niyazov the Turkmen nationalist, saviour of his people.

In October 1991, Niyazov oversaw the creation of an independent Turkmenistan and became its first president. A few months later, in June 1992, he became the country's first 'elected' leader when he won a presidential election (hardly surprising, given that he was the only candidate). A year later, he began to use the title 'Turkmenbashi' – 'Father of the Turkmen'. In 1994, a referendum approved an extension of his presidential term to 2002. Then, in 1999, his handpicked parliament declared him president for life.

To discourage any challenge to his rule, Turkmenbashi's government revoked all internet licences in 2000, except for those owned by the state-owned Turkmen Telecom company, and a year later all internet cafes were closed down. According to their leader, the World Wide Web and the hi-tech revolution of the late 20th century were not for the Turkmen people. Neither were the benefits of Turkmenistan's huge natural-gas resources. Despite boasting the second largest reserves in the former Soviet Union, the population at large endured abject poverty, earning barely enough to survive. As the scale of repression within the country grew, so too did discontent, but this was vigorously suppressed, a failed assassination attempt on the president in 2002 providing the pretext for a crackdown on growing domestic and foreign opposition. The secret police were omnipresent, arrest and torture endemic.

Entrenched in power, Turkmenbashi set about building one of the most weird personality cults of the 20th century. He renamed the days of the week and months of the year after various Turkmen heroes – including, of course, the president himself and members of his family. January became 'Turkmenbashi', and April Gurbansoltanedzhe – named after the president's mother. Among the curious decrees Turkmenbashi issued was the 2004 order banning men from having long hair and beards. Another ruling the same year insisted that all licensed drivers must pass a morality test, while in 2005 all video games were banned within Turkmenistan. He once suggested building a giant ice palace in the blisteringly hot Karakum desert.

Alongside these strange, but arguably relatively harmless diktats, were other, darker commands. In early 2006, a third of Turkmenistan's elderly people had their pensions stopped; many others had the amount they received reduced. Further policies seemed designed to ensure that as few members of the population as possible made it to pensionable age. In 2004, for example, the president suddenly sacked some 15,000 members of his country's health service – including nurses, midwives and orderlies – replacing them with poorly trained army conscripts. The consequences for the standard of health provision in the country were devastating. Similar in effect was the 2005 decree that closed all hospitals outside Turkmenistan's capital, Ashgabat – a decision taken on the grounds that the people should come to the city for treatment, no matter where they lived. Rural libraries were also shut down as part of the same law – the reasoning being that normal Turkmen did not read books. Those unable to stifle their literary inclinations altogether were furnished with one volume of essential reading: the *Ruhnama* – a would-be national 'epic' that Turkmenbashi himself had written.

Nothing encapsulates this ridiculous dictator's egotism and megalomania more eloquently than the giant gold-plated statue he had erected of himself opposite his equally extravagant presidential palace in the heart of Ashgabat. Towering 120 feet above the city, it rotates full circle each day: a reminder to all citizens – should the countless presidential photographs that adorn each street fail to do the job – of their all-controlling ruler's watchful eye.

Turkmenbashi died in December 2006 and he was succeeded by one of his henchmen. His dictatorship remains in place – not unlike the tyrannies with appalling human rights that continue to rule the other former Soviet republics in Central Asia.

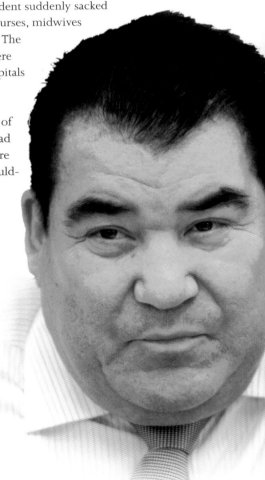

Saparmurat Niyazov, generally called Turkmenbashi, who ruled the gas-rich Central Asian republic of Turkmenistan for 21 years. This photograph was taken on 2 November 2006, shortly before the president's death.

THE FOLLIES OF TYRANNY

I met a traveller from an antique land
Who said: Two vast and trunkless legs of stone
Stand in the desert. Near them on the sand,
Half sunk, a shatter'd visage lies, whose frown
And wrinkled lip and sneer of cold command
Tell that its sculptor well those passions read
Which yet survive, stamp'd on these lifeless things,
The hand that mock'd them and the heart that fed.
And on the pedestal these words appear:
'My name is Ozymandias, King of Kings:
Look on my works, ye Mighty, and despair!'
Nothing beside remains. Round the decay
Of that colossal wreck, boundless and bare,
The lone and level sands stretch far away.

Percy Bysshe Shelley's poem 'Ozymandias', written in 1817, was inspired by the huge ruined statues of Pharaoh Rameses II that litter the deserts of Egypt. Rameses, who extended Egypt's empire into the Near East in the 13th century BC, was among the earliest of a long line of kings, emperors and dictators who have indulged their vanity by erecting massive monuments to their own glory – whether they be statues, gaudy palaces, triumphal arches or monstrous mausoleums.

Vast and lavishly appointed imperial palaces have always been a particular favourite, from Nero's Golden House, its marble inlaid with gems, seashells and precious metals, via the gilded city-within-a-palace at Versailles, symbol and power base of the absolute monarchy of Louis XIV, down to Turkmenbashi's gold-domed presidential residence in Ashgabat. Turkmenbashi was not the only dictator of the modern era to have lavished untold resources on his domestic arrangements. Among the more egregious manifestations are Saddam Hussein's many palaces across Iraq, in which even the lavatory seats are made from solid gold, and Nicolae Ceauşescu's ironically named 'Palace of the People', the third largest building in the world, built on the backs of 20,000 labourers and unsurpassed for its architectural bombast and hideously ill-proportioned dystopian aesthetic. Similarly bloated is the Basilica of Our Lady of Peace of Yamoussoukro built by President Félix Houphouët-Boigny of the Ivory Coast at at a cost of $300 million.

Mausoleums – sometimes displaying the embalmed corpse of the dear dead leader – have always been a favourite with tyrants. Pharaoh Khufu's Great Pyramid at Giza, Emperor Shi Huangdi's burial mound with its underground army of life-size terracotta warriors, the Mausoleum of Halicarnassus, built for a Persian satrap in the 4th century BC, and the extravagant tombs of the communist dictators Mao Zedong and Lenin all embody the occupants' aspirations towards immortality. The generations that come after can only gaze in wonder at such folly.

The Basilica of Our Lady of Peace of Yamoussoukro, constructed at lavish expense between 1985 and 1989 by President Félix Houphouët-Boigny. It is currently listed as the largest church in the world, bigger even than St Peter's in Rome. The government of Ivory Coast was declared bankrupt in 1997, shortly after Houphouët-Boigny's death.

The 'Butcher of the Balkans', Slobodan Milošević brought genocide and slaughter back to Europe for the first time since the Nazi death camps. Unleashing a vicious regular army and bands of his personally coordinated militias onto a bemused civilian population, he started a series of wars aimed at eradicating un-Serbian nations from what he regarded as Serbian soil, often ordering wholesale massacre and rape. It was as if the murderous warlordism of the 17th-century Thirty Years' War had returned to the civilized continent of Europe.

Slobodan Milošević
1941—2006

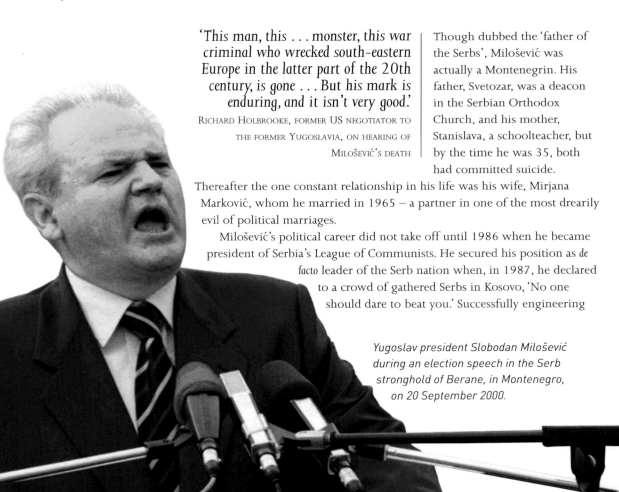

'This man, this . . . monster, this war criminal who wrecked south-eastern Europe in the latter part of the 20th century, is gone . . . But his mark is enduring, and it isn't very good.'
RICHARD HOLBROOKE, FORMER US NEGOTIATOR TO THE FORMER YUGOSLAVIA, ON HEARING OF MILOŠEVIĆ'S DEATH

Though dubbed the 'father of the Serbs', Milošević was actually a Montenegrin. His father, Svetozar, was a deacon in the Serbian Orthodox Church, and his mother, Stanislava, a schoolteacher, but by the time he was 35, both had committed suicide. Thereafter the one constant relationship in his life was his wife, Mirjana Marković, whom he married in 1965 – a partner in one of the most drearily evil of political marriages.

Milošević's political career did not take off until 1986 when he became president of Serbia's League of Communists. He secured his position as *de facto* leader of the Serb nation when, in 1987, he declared to a crowd of gathered Serbs in Kosovo, 'No one should dare to beat you.' Successfully engineering

Yugoslav president Slobodan Milošević during an election speech in the Serb stronghold of Berane, in Montenegro, on 20 September 2000.

the dismissal of Ivan Stambolić – his mentor and early patron – as president of Serbia, he himself took on that role in early 1988. (Milošević was later charged with ordering Stambolic's kidnap and murder in 2000.)

Yugoslavia was itself the flawed creation of the ruin of empires in 1918, dominated until the Second World War by the Serbian monarchy yet comprising Muslim Bosnians and Kosovan Albanians, Orthodox Montenegrins and Serbs, and Catholic Croats. Out of the brutal ethnic slaughters of the two world wars, the long-serving dictator Marshal Josip Tito, whose Partisans had liberated Yugoslavia from Nazi occupation, had created a strong regime, using his own charismatic personality and, less well-known, terror, secret police and concentration camps. Yet Tito controlled the deadly ethnic feuds of the Balkans and gave his peoples almost 30 years of peace and order. But the revolving presidency implemented after his death in 1980 left a stewing ethnic cauldron lacking a strong hand to control it. Milošević filled this vacuum with his death squads, condottiere and psychopathic warlords, coordinated and financed at his personal command.

Setting his goal as the creation of a 'Greater Serbia', Milošević deployed the Yugoslav National Army (JNA) – then the fourth largest army in Europe – against would-be secessionist republics. Meanwhile, Serb separatist forces within such republics were encouraged to rise up. Lacking a large Serb population, Slovenia was allowed by Milošević, after a 'ten-day war', to go its own way after declaring independence in June 1991. Not so with Croatia and Bosnia-Herzegovina: he was determined that their sizeable Serb minority populations would remain within Yugoslavia. Milošević loyalists helped carve out Serb autonomous enclaves in each: first Milan Babić in the Serb-dominated Krajina region of Croatia, and then General Ratko Mladić and the psychiatrist-turned-demagogue Radovan Karadžić, within Bosnia. Paramilitary gangs bearing outlandish names – Arkan's Tigers, the White Eagles, the Chetniks – rampaged through Serb-run Croatia and Bosnia, bringing death and destruction wherever they went. In the process they endowed the lexicon of conflict with a new term, *ethnicko cis cenje terena* – literally the 'ethnic cleansing of the earth', or simply ethnic cleansing.

The conflict revealed to the world images it thought it had left behind: emaciated men and women trapped behind barbed wire in concentration camps in the heart of Europe; mass rape; the deliberate shelling of cities such as Vukovar, Sarajevo, Dubrovnik and Mostar; and the indiscriminate killing of innocent civilians. Finally, genocide returned to the continent when 8000 Bosnian Muslims were slaughtered by Serb forces under General Mladić in the town of Srebrenica in July 1995.

The conflict finally ended in 1995, after NATO and Croatian offensives turned the tide decisively against Milošević's forces. Milošević negotiated the Dayton Peace Accords and was allowed to remain in power – even to claim credit as the man who brought peace to the Balkans. It did not last. Having secured the position of president of Yugoslavia (reduced to just Serbia and Montenegro) when his tenure as president of Serbia ended in 1997, he soon embroiled his forces in a new war, this time over the province of Kosovo. An armed uprising there for independence in 1999 met with vicious Serbian repression, and ethnic cleansing once more returned to Europe. This time, though, it prompted a 74-day NATO bombing campaign, ordered by US President Clinton and UK Prime Minister Tony Blair, which forced Milošević to back down.

With Serbia's economy already on the brink of collapse after the imposition of sanctions in the wake of the Bosnian conflict, fresh international penalties spelt the end for Milošević, and after federal presidential elections the next year he was forced by mass demonstrations, reinforced by the country's military, to concede defeat to the opposition candidate, Vojislav Koštunica. In 2001, he was arrested by Serb authorities and later that same year sent to The Hague to be tried by the International Criminal Tribunal for the Former Yugoslavia for war crimes and crimes against humanity. That trial was still ongoing when Milošević died of heart trouble in March 2006. Benefiting at first from the appeasing tendencies and naive shock of Western ministers, all Milošević achieved was the slaughter of many thousands, the impoverishment of his nation and his own destruction. Serbia is now a flourishing democracy.

HUNTING WAR CRIMINALS

After the Nuremberg Trials of Germany's surviving Nazi leaders in 1945–6, there was a growing determination that those responsible for the worst crimes should never be allowed to escape justice. The London Charter of August 1945 had established the nature of 'war crimes', 'crimes against the peace' and 'crimes against humanity'; the aim was to create a new, universally applicable concept of international law, centred on human rights.

In the years that followed there were major efforts to track down the remnants of the Nazi hierarchy – many of whom had fled as the Second World War drew to a close. One of the most dramatic hunts culminated in 1960 when agents of Mossad, the Israeli intelligence service, kidnapped Adolf Eichmann in Argentina. Since Eichmann, the effort to locate and prosecute other Nazi war criminals has continued. In 1987, in another high-profile case, Klaus Barbie, the SS 'Butcher of Lyon', was sentenced to life imprisonment by a French court for his role in organizing the deportation of Jews from Lyon to Nazi concentration camps.

War crimes have also been perpetrated in other, more recent, conflicts. This realization led to the founding of the International Criminal Court (ICC) at The Hague in the Netherlands in 2002. Though not endorsed by all states, the ICC has achieved some notable successes in its pursuit of war criminals. June 2007 thus saw the beginning of the trial of Charles Taylor, president of Liberia from 1997 to 2003, who stands accused of war crimes and crimes against humanity as a result of actions committed by his forces in Liberia and Sierra Leone during the early 1990s. Taylor, a brutal warlord, led an army of children and teenage thugs, grew rich on blood diamonds and almost destroyed Liberia: another of Africa's true monsters. More recently still, the ICC has brought indictments against those believed to be involved in the Darfur genocide in Sudan.

In addition to the ICC, various other bodies have been involved in the hunt for and prosecution of war criminals. The best-known of these is the International Criminal Tribunal for the Former Yugoslavia, established in 1993 to bring to justice those responsible for crimes during the Balkan Wars of the early 1990s. In 1996 a Bosnian Serb, Dusan Tadić, became the first man to be convicted by the tribunal when he was found guilty of murder and torture. Other prosecutions have followed, most notably that of Slobodan Milošević – the first ever sitting head of state to be indicted for war crimes (see main text). Having evaded capture for more than a decade – despite an international warrant for his arrest – Milošević's Bosnian Serb proxy Radovan Karadžić was

'End of the Road', an American cartoon from 1946.

finally run to earth in July 2008 in Belgrade, where he had been working under a new identity as a New Age healer. Ratko Mladić, who with Karadžić was responsible for events on the ground in Bosnia, remains at large at the time of writing. The fate of Milošević stands as a clear message to them and others like them: for the perpetrators of the most terrible crimes, there is no escape from justice.

The most powerful, wealthy and murderous criminal of the 20th century, Pablo Escobar was the paramount Colombian drug lord, who became the mastermind and kingpin of the international cocaine trade. He accrued billions of dollars, and in the process was responsible for hundreds of kidnappings and murders. A godfather figure of unrivalled magnitude, and a law unto himself, Escobar threatened the very integrity of the state of Colombia.

Pablo Escobar 1949–93

'The ingeniousness of my brother was extraordinary.'
Roberto Escobar

Escobar was the son of a peasant and a school teacher, and grew up in a suburb of Medellín. He became involved in criminal activities from an early age, stealing cars and even, it was said, gravestones, which he sandblasted before selling them as new. He graduated to minor fraud, selling contraband cigarettes and forged lottery tickets, and then in the late 1960s, as demand for cannabis and cocaine multiplied, he saw an opening in the drug trade.

During the first half of the 1970s Escobar became increasingly prominent in the 'Medellín Cartel', in which a number of crime syndicates cooperated to control much of Colombia's drug-trafficking industry. In 1975, a leading Medellín crime lord, Fabio Restrepo, was assassinated, and Escobar soon took over his operation.

In May of the following year, Escobar was charged with organizing a drug run to Ecuador. He tried to bribe the judges who were presiding over his case, but when that failed he murdered two officers who had arrested him and the chief witnesses, thereby ending the proceedings. This became part of an established pattern, a strategy called *plata o plomo* ('silver plate or lead bullet' – i.e. accept a bribe or face assassination). He killed many thousands, on his orders or personally, often with astonishing savagery.

Escobar was also a savvy political operator, aware of the need to grease the palms of local politicians. In Medellín he was also a Robin Hood populist, contributing small but significant portions of his personal fortune to local building projects or struggling football clubs, gaining him some popularity among the people of the city. He briefly ran his own newspaper, and in 1982 he became a deputy for the Liberal Party in the Colombian Congress.

By the early 1980s Escobar's cartel monopolized the South American drug trade, and was responsible for an estimated 80 per cent of cocaine and cannabis shipped to the United States, Mexico, Puerto Rico and the Dominican Republic. His operation involved purchasing coca paste in Bolivia and Peru, processing it in drug factories dotted across Colombia, and then smuggling thousands of tonnes every week out of the country and into the United States, by sea, air and road.

In 1989 *Forbes* magazine listed Escobar as the seventh richest man in the world, with an estimated fortune of $24 billion. He owned many beautiful homes, a private zoo, numerous yachts and helicopters, a fleet of private aeroplanes and even two submarines; he also kept a private army of bodyguards and assassins on the payroll. He was utterly unforgiving to those who threatened his position, even in the smallest possible way: after catching a servant stealing silver from one of his palatial homes, he had the unfortunate man tied up and thrown into the swimming pool, leaving him to drown.

It was not long before Escobar began to be targeted by the United States authorities. In 1979 the USA and Colombia had signed an extradition treaty, as part of a tougher approach to the drug trade. Escobar hated this treaty and began a campaign of assassination against anyone who supported it or who called for stronger policies against the drug cartels. He was widely believed to have been behind the storming in 1985 of the Colombian Supreme Court by leftwing guerrillas, which left eleven judges dead. Four years later Escobar ordered the murder of three presidential candidates, as well as the downing of an airliner, which killed 107 people, and the bombing of the national-security building in Bogotá, killing 52. The same year two of his henchmen were arrested in Miami, trying to buy missiles.

In 1991, as the net seemed to be closing in around him, Escobar offered a deal to the Colombian authorities: in order to avoid extradition he would accept five years' imprisonment. As part of the deal, Escobar was allowed to build his own 'prison', which naturally turned out to be another luxurious palace, from where he could direct his drugs empire by telephone. He was allowed to leave to attend the occasional football match or party, and was also permitted to receive visitors, including prostitutes (the younger the better) and business associates, two of whom were murdered on his premises – he liked to torture his victims personally.

On 22 July 1992, as he was being transferred to a tougher prison, Escobar managed to escape. The Colombian authorities launched a massive manhunt, with help from the USA, and also from Escobar's enemies, including Los Pepes (People Persecuted by Pablo Escobar), a paramilitary group composed of his victims, and members of the rival Cali Cartel. During the 16-month search, hundreds of people – both policemen and Escobar's henchmen – were killed. Escobar was eventually tracked down to a safe house in Medellín and shot in the leg, torso and head as he attempted a daring rooftop escape; he died instantly. It was 2 December 1993, the day after his 44th birthday.

Escobar's supporters regarded him as a dashing hero and a champion of the poor, but in reality he was an outlaw of unrivalled greed and sadism. His token gestures of philanthropy did not disguise his scant regard for human life, and at the height of its influence his cartel was responsible for an average of 20 murders every month.

Pablo Escobar was leader of the Medellín drug cartel from 1975 to 1993, becoming one of the richest and most powerful criminals of the 20th century.

THE CALI CARTEL

After the violent demise of Pablo Escobar on the rooftops of Medellín in December 1993, the Cali Cartel – which had expended its own foot soldiers and funds in joining the effort to track down Escobar – was left in a position of prominence, taking control of the trafficking networks of the fractured and disorientated Medellín Cartel.

Like its rival, the Cali Cartel had been formed in the early 1970s, initially concentrating on fraud, kidnapping and extortion, and only later becoming involved in the drugs trade. Whereas the Medellín Cartel was known for its wild gangsterism and the extravagant lifestyles of its members, Cali had more of a white-collar, 'gentlemanly' ethos.

It was founded in the city of Cali in southern Colombia by Miguel and Gilberto Rodríguez Orejuela, two brothers from 'respectable' families. As Cali began to engage in the cocaine trade in the late 1970s, they established cells in American cities such as New York, which ensured them a steady line of distribution. Unlike Escobar, the Rodríguez Orejuela brothers preferred to avoid high-profile confrontation with the state. But they were equally ruthless, telling their operatives that should they betray the cartel, their families would be killed.

The Cali also became associated with a sinister form of vigilantism, in which they would remove from the streets those they considered 'undesirable' – for example, petty thieves, sex offenders and, somewhat ironically, drug addicts. Those thus 'cleansed' would then be murdered.

The most elusive of the Cali Cartel was Francisco Hélmer Herrera Buitrago. Escobar ordered his assassination, but when gunmen opened fire at a sporting event, Herrera escaped, although 11 people around him were killed. Seemingly in direct retaliation, the Cali Cartel abducted and murdered Gustavo Gaviria, Escobar's cousin. In 1996 Herrera turned himself into police, the last of the seven leaders of the Cali Cartel to be detained in a massive counter-trafficking operation, run jointly by the Colombian and US governments.

Colombian drug lord Gilberto Rodríguez Orejuela, a founder of the Cali Cartel and one of Pablo Escobar's deadliest rivals, is escorted by police at Bogotá's army airport of Catam on 12 March 2003. Orejuela was later extradited to the Unites States where he faced charges of drug trafficking and money laundering.

Osama bin Laden is the fanatical mastermind of the murderously spectacular 9/11 plane-bomb attacks against the Twin Towers and Pentagon that killed thousands of innocent people in the name of an intolerant and dogmatic distortion of the Islamic faith. Promoting a 'Jihadi' ideology that glories in killing and endorses a nihilistic cult of suicide, he aims to eliminate American and Western power, wipe out Israel and restore a caliphate over any part of the world ever ruled by Islam. But his only real practical policy is terrorizing innocent people and destroying tolerant democratic societies, using impressionable youths as living bombs against victims chosen solely because they are citizens of the free, democratic West.

Osama bin Laden b. 1957

'The pieces of the bodies of infidels were flying like dust particles. If you would have seen it with your own eyes, you would have been very pleased, and your heart would have been filled with joy.'

OSAMA BIN LADEN, AT THE WEDDING OF HIS SON FOLLOWING THE MURDER OF 17 US SOLDIERS IN THE SUICIDE BOMBING OF THE USS COLE, 12 OCTOBER 2000

Bin Laden was born in Riyadh in 1957, the son of Muhammed Awad bin Laden – who acquired huge wealth after his construction company secured exclusive rights from the Saudi royal family to religious building projects within the country – and his tenth wife, Hamida al-Attas, subsequently divorced. The only son of that marriage, though with numerous siblings on his father's side, Osama – after his mother's remarriage to Muhammad al-Attas – was raised as a Sunni Muslim, displaying uncompromising piety from an early age. He studied at an elite school and then King Abdulaziz University, marrying his first wife, Najwa Ghanem, in 1974. He has had another four wives, divorcing two, and has fathered between 12 and 24 children.

In 1979, bin Laden, together with thousands of other devout jihadists – known collectively as the mujahedeen – travelled to Afghanistan to repel the Soviet Union's invasion of the country. He joined fellow militant Abdullah Azzam and established Maktab al-Khadamat, a paramilitary organization devoted to help fight what he saw as jihad (holy war). The war was also backed and funded by the United States, ever fearful of Soviet expansion, and when bin Laden returned to Saudi Arabia in 1990, he was widely feted for having resisted the forces of communism. Already, though, he was making plans for a new organization to further his goal of driving America ('the Great Satan') out of the Muslim world. It would become known as Al-Qaeda ('the Base').

Following the Gulf War of 1991, bin Laden denounced the Saudi

Osama bin Laden during an interview with Pakistani journalist Hamid Mir on 10 November 2001. In the article, bin Laden said he had nuclear and chemical weapons and might use them in response to US attacks. Mir told Reuters that he held the two-hour interview with bin Laden in Arabic at a secret location.

royal family for allowing US troops to be stationed in the country, upon which, in 1992, they expelled him. He moved to Sudan, from where, working with the Egyptian Islamic Jihad (EIJ), he masterminded the 29 December 1992 attack on Aden in which two people were killed. Following an unsuccessful assassination attempt, however, on President Mubarak of Egypt in 1995, the EIJ were expelled from Sudan, prompting bin Laden to return to Afghanistan, where he allied himself with the Taliban, bankrolling training camps for thousands of jihadists.

In 1997, he sponsored the infamous Luxor massacre of 17 November, which killed 62 civilians, and the following year Al-Qaeda bombed US embassies in Nairobi, Kenya, and Tanzania, killing nearly 300 people. A more sinister trend emerged in October 2000 when, once more in Aden, a suicide bomber attacked the US navy ship *USS Cole*, killing 17. Such bombing swiftly became Al-Qaeda's 'weapon' of choice, militant young Muslims being indoctrinated to seek martyrdom. Later the same year, bin Laden, with his lieutenant Dr Ayman al-Zawahiri – whom he had first met during the Afghan war – co-signed a *fatwa* declaring that Muslims had a duty to kill Americans and their allies.

Bin Laden and al-Zawahiri subsequently concocted their most ambitious plan yet. Early on the morning of 11 September 2001, two teams of jihadis boarded four passenger jets at airports in Washington D.C. Boston and Newark. Authorities learned shortly afterwards that the planes had been hijacked by 19 Middle Eastern men. At 8.46 a.m. local time, American Airlines Flight 11 flew into the north of the Twin Towers in New York, the biggest buildings in Manhattan. Then, as television cameras were trained on the unfolding disaster, United Airlines Flight 175 slammed at 9.02 a.m. into the south tower. Thirty-five minutes later, news filtered through that American Airlines Flight 77 had crashed into the Pentagon in Virginia, and at 10.03 a.m. United Airlines Flight 93, destined for the White House, was brought down over Pennsylvania by heroic passengers, who heard the fate of the other planes as they frantically called their relatives on onboard telephones.

Apocalyptic scenes followed in New York. The Twin Towers, both of which had been fatally weakened by the impact of the jets and ensuing fires, collapsed to the ground – the south at 9.59 a.m. and the north at 10.28 a.m. – killing thousands of victims still trapped inside, and sending out a cloud of dust that engulfed the south side of Manhattan. Excluding the hijackers, nearly 3000 people died that day – 246 on the jets, 125 in the Pentagon and 2603 in the Twin Towers (including 341 heroic firefighters and 2 paramedics).

The World Trade Center south tower bursts into flames after being struck by hijacked United Airlines Flight 175, while the north tower burns following an earlier attack by a hijacked airliner in New York City on 11 September 2001. The stunning aerial assaults on the huge commercial complex where more than 40,000 people worked on an average day were part of a coordinated attack aimed at the nation's financial heart. They destroyed one of America's most dramatic symbols of power and financial strength and left New York reeling.

Committing itself to a war on terror, America vowed to hunt down bin Laden, who already topped the FBI's most wanted list. Allied forces soon toppled the Taliban regime in Afghanistan, where Al-Qaeda had been allowed to operate for years, but bin Laden fled to the mountains bordering Afghanistan and Pakistan. A chance to capture him there was missed in late 2001 when advancing troops failed to search the Tora Bora caves where he was almost certainly hiding. When the caves were subsequently raided in August 2007, he was gone.

Since 9/11, radicalized Muslims, led by bin Laden's twisted message of hate and violence, have relentlessly continued Al-Qaeda's murderous campaign. On 12 October 2002, three bombs exploded in Bali, killing 202 people, and injuring a further 209. Then, in 2004, a series of bombs exploded on the Madrid rail network, killing 191 people and wounding 1755. The following year, on 7 July, London was the target, three bombs exploding within a minute of each other during the morning rush hour on the London Underground system and another on a bus in Tavistock Square less than an hour later. Besides the four suicide bombers, 52 commuters were killed and 700 injured. Further carnage was only avoided a fortnight later when the bombs of four would-be suicide bombers failed to explode. October of the same year saw a second attack on Bali, 20 people being killed and 129 injured. In Iraq, through a ruthless campaign of bombing, Al-Qaeda has focused on fomenting sectarian slaughter between Sunni and Shia Muslims to foil American plans for Iraqi democracy. Meanwhile, bin Laden, planning new outrages, is still at large.

SUICIDE BOMBING

The use of suicide attacks is not new. During the last stages of the Second World War, as Japan faced almost certain defeat, Japanese kamikaze ('divine wind') pilots crashed their planes into Allied warships, continuing a long tradition of sacrifice and suicide. The idea was first mooted in October 1944 by Vice-Admiral Takijirō Ōnishi of the Japanese navy who, sent to attack a US fleet off the Philippines with a hugely inadequate squadron, realized that the only way to inflict significant damage was to use his planes as guided missiles. There was no shortage of volunteers, each taking as their motto 'One man – one ship'.

Attacks peaked during the 82-day Battle of Okinawa when, on 6 April 1945, nearly 1500 Japanese planes managed to sink more than 30 US warships, as part of Operation Kikusi ('floating chrysanthemums'). One kamikaze pilot, Lieutenant Yukio Sekio, summed up the perverted ideology of his fellows: 'It is better to die', he said, 'rather than to live a coward.' In total, the war saw around 5000 kamikaze attacks resulting in 36 US craft sunk and 368 damaged. The Japanese also used suicide speedboats; suicide torpedoes fitted with a tiny cockpit and periscope; suicide midget submarines carrying explosives instead of torpedoes; suicide divers carrying explosives; and suicide infantry-men carrying anti-tank mines.

The USS St Louis *explodes after being hit by a Japanese kamikaze pilot off Leyte Gulf, the Philippine Islands, in 1944.*

METRO BOOKS
New York

An Imprint of Sterling Publishing
387 Park Avenue South
New York, NY 10016

The publishers would like to thank the following for permission to reproduce photographs and images in this book:

AKG Images 1, 11, 12, 15, 19, 37, 44, 57, 60, 61, 64, 67, 77, 87, 97, 104, 105, 113, 123, 133, 139, 153, 187, 193, 194, 219, 220, 235, 243, 245, 246, 253, 254;

The Bridgeman Art Library Palazzo Barberini, Rome 2, 129, National Gallery, London 12, Louvre, Paris 23, Bibliothèque Nationale, Paris, Giraudon 25, Brooklyn Museum of Art, New York 27, Whitford Fine Art, London 33, British Library, London 36; 75, 82, Walters Art Museum, Baltimore 38–39, Private Collection, © DACS /Archives Charmet 47, Collection of the New-York Historical Society 49, San Vitale, Ravenna, Giraudon 51, Museo Archeologico Nazionale, Naples 52, Palazzo Ducale, Venice 58, Bibliothèque Nationale, Paris 66, Westminster Abbey, London 96, Private Collection 108, 122, 131, 201, 251, 309, Museo de Bellas Artes, Zaragoza 126, Biblioteca Medicea-Laurenziana, Florence 127, Prado, Madrid, Giraudon 135, Lambeth Palace Library, London 137, Private Collection, Archives Charmet 149, Musée Condé, Chantilly, Lauros, Giraudon 152, Phoenix Art Museum, Arizona 157, Victoria & Albert Museum, London, The Stapleton Collection 163, Bibliothèque Nationale, Paris Archives Charmet 165, Art Gallery of New South Wales, Sydney 170;
Art Archive 8, 43, 63, 68, 103, 111, 115, 118, 134, 141, 155;
Ancient Art & Architecture Collection 17, 91;
Getty Images 18, 84, 92, 110, 173, 176, 182, 197, 203, 207, 209, 211, 212, 213, 215, 224, 231, 248, 278, 280–281, 284, 285, 293, 295, 298, 300, 306;
Ackland Art Museum, North Carolina 21;
Kobal Collection 24, 31, 41, 86, 107, 119, 175;
BBC 29;
Private Collection 30, 46, 71, 149, 190;
Corbis 159, 316, Bettmann 34, 177, 183, 195, 229, 241, 242, 279, 292, Adam Woolfitt 70, Charles & Josette Lenars 73, Hamid Sardar 79, Church of St. Peter, Avignon, Giraudon 93, Ralf-Finn Hestoft 101, Christie's Images 121, Yann Arthus-Bertrand 146, Reuters 179, Leonard de Selva 185, Dave G. Houser 188, Hulton-Deutsch Collection 199, 206, 222–223, EFE 225, Ira Nowinski 249, Peter Turnley 263, Cezaro de Luca/epa 266, Horacio Villalobos 271, Bernard Bisson Sygma 274, Robbie Jack 275, Alain Nogues Sygma 282, Kapoor Baldev Sygma 287, Origlia Franco Sygma 289, Tony Gentile Reuters 290, Peer Grimm/epa 305, Milos Bicanski/epa 307, Jose Miguel Gomez Reuters 312, Reuters 313, Sean Adair Reuters 314–315;
British Library 53;
Alamy Jupiter Images, Agence Images 76, Alberto Paredes 89; Ivan Vdovin 277;
Worcester Cathedral Photograph by Mr Christopher Guy, Archaeologist. Reproduced by permission of the Chapter of Worcester Cathedral (UK) 81;
Collection International Institute of Social History, Amsterdam 55;
Topfoto 95, 140, 164, 169, 191, 200, 227, 230, 237, 239, 272;
Mary Evans Picture Library 99, 116, 145, 147, 158, 161, 171, 181;
PA Photos AP 91, 259, 296, 297, Lai Seng Sin AP 236, Hans-Peter Baker AP 256, Reporters Press Agency 257, George Osodi AP 260, ABACA 302;
Peter Higginbotham 125;
National Gallery of Ireland 143;
Lebrecht Collection 151, 205;
National Archives of Russia unknown photographer, 1921 217;
RIA Novosti 233;
Rex Features 261, 267, 269, 302;
United States Holocaust Memorial Museum 265;
Camera Press Eric Vandeville Gamma 311.